6-21-54

For Ellen —
with love — and
much appreciation
for everything — and
for the memories —
I wish Sam could
read it —

Sincerely

Ken

The CHOW DIPPER

As a POW & in Politics He Was Always . . .

The CHOW DIPPER

A Personal
and
Political
Odyssey

Introduction
by
William F.
BUCKLEY

PULITIZER PRIZE WINNER
KEN TOWERY

EAKIN PRESS Austin, Texas

FIRST EDITION

Copyright © 1994
By Ken Towery

Published in the United States of America
By Eakin Press
A Division of Sunbelt Media, Inc.

ISBN 0-89015-965-3

10   9   8   7   6   5   4   3   2

Library of Congress Cataloging-in-Publication Data

Towery, Ken
    The chow dipper : a personal and political odyssey
        p.   cm.
    Includes index
    Summary: A chronicle of the author's experiences and views on journalism,
politics, and government.
    ISBN 0-89015-965-3 : $22.95
    1. World War II, siege of Corregidor.   2. Prison camps.   3. Politics — 1960s–
1980s.   4. Journalism.   5. Government.   I. Title.
E83.866.M33P37   1994
355'.0092 — dc20
[B]   94-21952
                                                                                        CIP
                                                                                         AC

Contents

Preface

"Where shall I begin?" asked the White Rabbit.

"Begin in the beginning," said the King. "And go to the end and stop."

But where does one begin when the beginning cannot be remembered, and where does one end when the end is not yet?

Then there is the larger question. To what end should one begin at all, and to what end should the tale be told?

There was a time, many years ago, and when we were much younger, that the answers were much clearer. Then, fresh from years in Japanese prison camps, it was obvious that the story simply had to be written. For if it were written all sorts of lessons would be revealed; the world would take note and undoubtedly become a better place because of it. Surely the world would no longer tolerate, much less reward, stupidity and duplicity in its political leaders. Surely self-serving politicians would be driven from their temples, not worshiped and glorified. The world would be made safe for those leaders who merely sought to serve the public interest. Such is the hope, and the blessing, of youth.

For various reasons it was not written. That is probably for the better. Time and tide has had its say, its own lessons. The sharp edges of earlier experiences have been dulled, if not lost. War is not the only teacher. It may not even be the best teacher.

Other wars have come and gone. Self-serving, duplicitous politicians continue to hold occasional sway in various bailiwicks of public life, some in low places and some in high. They, too, earlier than most, have learned the lessons of time and tide. And of human nature.

So the question recurs. To what end?

The answer, to me, is not easy. Or even totally clear. To be honest, portions of this book have been most difficult to write. It is not easy to go back and live again those years and events one has spent a lifetime trying to blot from memory. I doubt I would have undertaken the task were it not for continuing encouragement from friends and family. Beyond that, there is the matter of hope. The hope that my own children's children will perhaps better understand one of their forebears and the age in which he lived. And the further hope that somewhere, sometime, some reader will find something written herein useful in his or her own life. If that happens, the effort will not have been in vain.

It is not intended that this be a "kiss and tell" book, designed to reveal the "whole truth" about personalities or events dealt with. Nor is it intended that this be a chronological historical account, complete with names and dates of events covered. There may well be things written here that have not been written by others, particularly in the political years, but those instances are incidental to the story, not its driving force, not its reason for being. In that sense certain things written here may prove of some interest to those who write history, or those involved in contemporary politics and government. But in the final analysis this will be merely one man's view, one man's thoughts, of events, people, and policies with which he has been associated over many years.

Concerning the King's admonition to the White Rabbit, we merely picked a day that stood out in memory as the beginning. It could have been any one of any number of days. The end we are not sure about.

Concerning the title: It seemed to fit the story we tried to tell. All of us are chow dippers. All of us, if we have a conscience, must wrestle with the problem of being fair, of trying to treat others as we would like to be treated. Too, it seems many of us, perhaps most of us, are prisoners of something that happened in our past or an accumulation of somethings. The passage of time has shown me, at least, that this is not always totally bad.

While the words and thoughts are my own they belong, in a very real sense, to many others. They belong to those who have shared and shaped my life and thoughts over many years. Most will not be named, out of a sense of gratitude (lest they be blamed). Others, also out of a sense of gratitude, will be.

My thanks go first and foremost to my family. To my wife, Louise, who somehow tolerated this whole affair and who helped in ways too numerous to mention. To our daughter, Alice, who not only encouraged the effort, but in her own inimitable way insisted on it. And to her husband, Lennie, whose support, particularly during the early, more difficult stages, made the effort much easier. To my sisters Irene Wood of Carlsbad, New Mexico, and Elgene Allen of Rockport, Texas, along with myself the only remaining members of our once large family, and to our son, Roland, all of whom have waited long and patiently, and probably quite nervously, on the outcome.

And to Jon Ford, a friend who read the completed draft with an editor's eye and was kind enough to say all of it wasn't bad. To Niki Papanicolas in Virginia, Carolyn Bacon in Dallas, Ray and Judy Macha in Floyd County, Robert McLellan in Washington, John Knaggs and Jimmy Banks in Austin, and Joe and Linda Boerner of Lubbock, all of whom helped with advice and encouragement.

To all these I say thanks. And to my own God I give thanks. Thanks for giving me as mother the gentle and patient Lonie Bell Cowart (1884–1974) and a reasonably tolerant father, Wiley Azof Towery (1875–1943), of whom I can be proud. Kerosene may have been very dear in our household, but I do not recall either telling us to blow out the light when we were in the process of learning, or trying to learn.

Foreword

Very early on in the Nixon administration I had a visit from Frank Shakespeare. He had been a friend for a good many years, had graduated from Holy Cross College, and still a young man, had had an illustrious career in broadcasting. Specifically, when I first knew him he was "president of CBS" (CBS-New York). What this meant was that he was the chief operating officer of Station 2, the CBS outlet in New York City.

Above all men, he admired Frank Stanton, who was president of CBS, period. President of the entire company, the network, the stations owned by the network, sundry properties of various kinds here and there. Stanton was not the king of CBS. That was Bill Paley. But Stanton was the great craftsman. In his memoirs, James Michener wrote of Stanton that he was the most "efficient" man Michener ever knew, by which he meant that there was practically no disparity between Stanton's talent and Stanton's output. Michener put them both at the 98 level.

The plot thickens, you will be glad to know. Because what happened was that two years before Nixon became president, Shakespeare approached me with one simple question. It was this: Did I believe that Nixon was tall enough in the political world to warrant Shakespeare's going to work for him as a dollar-a-year man?

What Frank Shakespeare cared most about was the durability of our stand against expansionist communism, and in the declining days of President Johnson, Shakespeare wished to associate himself with a Republican figure who would revive the doctrine of containment, and perhaps probe the possibilities of liberation.

I have no reason to suppose that my judgment in the matter was conclusive, but I did in fact tell Shakespeare that I thought

a) Nixon had a good chance to be nominated and elected, and that b) he was probably the preeminent viable candidate whose commitment to the anti-Communist struggle was unimpeachable. Shakespeare signed up, and shortly after his election, Nixon called him in: Would he consent to serve as the director of the United States Information Service?

The post was made for Shakespeare. He believed that the primary non-nuclear weapon of the United States was — is — the ideals we live for. The suggestion that he head up the agency charged with communicating these aspects of America to the rest of the world was the consummation of the dream of a successful broadcaster.

But Frank is a careful man, and undertook a few explorations designed to satisfy himself that he would have the freedom of movement he wished for. It was then that he discovered that although he would be in charge of an agency of some 11,000 employees, he had, under the law and civil service regulations, the power to appoint exactly four men to his staff. Years later he would tell me that, intelligently and resourcefully guided, four men can change the orientation of an agency.

All of this was made immediately familiar to me because he approached me shortly after his own appointment to ask if I would agree to serve a three-year term as a member of the United States Commission on Information. This was a five-member board, at least two members of which must be of a different political party from the remaining three. He wished to take a board, whose life during its existence had been pretty sleepy, shoot it a great dose of adrenaline, and elevate it to prominence in the affairs of the USIA and, derivatively, in the enunciation throughout the world of American policies. He approached me with two pieces of information he considered to be vital. The first was that the great Frank Stanton had consented to serve as chairman of the commission. The second, that he had got an agreement to serve as his policy manager, Ken Towery. As one might expect, my next question was: Who is Ken Towery?

The basic facts were easily and quickly revealed. Towery was a Texan from modest background. He was captured in the Philippines by the Japanese soon after Pearl Harbor and served three and a half years in prison camps in China. After his release he returned to Texas and went into journalism. His dogged and resourceful journalism had got him a Pulitzer Prize. He served with Senator John Tower as press chief in Tower's first term. Above all: Towery was an utterly committed anti-Communist and anti-socialist. Shakespeare was telling me that with Towery at his right hand, the USIA could make important strides in a cause with which both of us were associated.

And so in due course I was introduced to this quiet, angular, retiring gentleman, with the soft voice and manners. I would see him frequently in the few years ahead, and I would come upon traces of his work. Ken is the man who disturbs the local scene only by his extreme abnegation. Sometimes the person in the office who never complains about anything at all, or who never asks for any favor of any kind, causes a bizarre irritation. Because the day inevitably comes when you find yourself wondering: Why hasn't Jasper complained about anything? Asked for anything? In the case of Ken Towery, one discovers in the first half of this book, this is in part a stoicism that is genetic and was probably enhanced by his experience in the terrible Japanese camps. In part because he tended to associate himself, in his long and active professional life, with persons and enterprises with which he was in essential harmony. As the right-hand man to Director Frank Shakespeare, Ken Towery was happy and productive. He felt the satisfaction of the person who feels the spiritual harvest of his own work, rather like a doctor administering medicine to his own children.

What Ken Towery has done in his autobiography is tell us what happened to him. He is not much given to emotive detail. A paragraph in *One Day in the Life of Ivan Denisovich* can inflame the reader with the horror of Gulag more effectively than the half dozen chapters Ken Towery has given us. It is something of a relief when, along the line, he confesses that he really felt good about it when he learned that the commandant of one of his camps was actually hanged.

He spends practically no time at all describing his domestic life, taking us instead to the newspaper that hired him, and then on to John Tower's first campaign. It is only when he gets to Tower that he attempts anything on the order of portraiture. His relations with the late Senator Tower were unusual in that manifestly the senator needed the professional help of Towery, but a kinship did not really develop. This was an aspect of the unusual character of Senator Tower. A crisis came when Mrs. John Tower II attempted to take over the Senate campaign Towery was supposed to be running. The senator won reelection to a third term, and, to the satisfaction of Ken Towery, simultaneously disposed of wife #2.

But the senator was headed for the ultimate humiliation, his rejection as secretary of defense by the Senate body in which he had served three terms. On the simple questions whether John Tower suffered from personal weaknesses that honorable men might have thought disqualifying, Ken Towery is simply discreet. It is a part of the character of Ken Towery that he tells the reader what he thinks it right for the reader to know.

After the political campaigns and desultory service to Bush and John Connally, the author spends time with the Corporation for Public Broadcasting, but little by little the accumulation of bureaucratic overhead and political cross-purposes gets to him. And — he returns to Texas, buys two local newspapers. And looks back on a life in which so very much happened. A world war, during which he was the prisoner of barbarians. A lifelong cold war, during which he occupied an important post in the ramparts. Service to critical men exercising public office, and seeking public office. Through it all he maintains a steadfastness of character and a commitment to his ideals, which energize his book, even as they have energized his life.

Frank Shakespeare was correct in his assessment of Ken Towery. And he would prove again and again how distinctive were his services, how valuable his loyalty. All those who were ever associated with him (can there be an exception to this, other than from Mrs. J. Tower II?) were elevated by the experience; and like so many others, will enjoy and profit from reading his political odyssey.

— WILLIAM F. BUCKLEY
June 1994

PART I

The War

ONE

Fortress Corregidor

It was a day of hope. It was a day of foreboding. We were fewer than we once were. We were more than we would be.

The long journey from Cabanatuan prison camp was over, and another camp awaited. Surely it would be better than the last.

The day was clear and cold, but no colder, we would learn, than usual for November 11 in that Manchurian city the Japanese called Mukden and the Chinese called Shenyang. The prisoners were lined up in rows, standing as close to attention as their condition allowed. An aging Japanese colonel in full military regalia, and with attendants of all ranks standing behind, prepared to speak.

Around us rose the smokestacks of an industrial city. To the west the plains of Manchuria faded from view, blending into uplands that ultimately opened onto that great Mongolian desert called Gobi. To the north, some few hundred miles, was a place we knew only as Siberia. To the east, a thousand miles as the crow flies, the emperor sat upon his throne. And to the south lay the past.

It was the past we hoped we would be escaping. The Philippines had fallen. The promised planes and tanks had never come. Bataan had finally been overrun. Corregidor had finally been pounded into utter destruction and submission. The Japanese reigned supreme throughout Asia. Prison was our lot.

Prisoners from throughout the Philippines had been gathered in various camps, most of those from Bataan and Corregidor, near a place called Cabanatuan in central Luzon. Prisoners from Bataan, after an ordeal that became known as the "Death March," went first to a camp called O'Donnell and finally to Cabanatuan. Those from

Corregidor, after being kept on the island for a time to burn the dead and load Japanese ships with war booty, were transported to Manila, where they were marched down what was then known as Dewey Boulevard on their way to Bilibid Prison. Ultimately, they were crammed into windowless boxcars for the journey to Cabanatuan and marched to the camp some twenty miles distant.

Four months later, some of the healthiest were selected for work details throughout Asia. We were among the first to leave Cabanatuan, and the first to be sent to China. A month-long voyage on the prison ship *Tottori Maru*, a train ride from Pusan, Korea, up across the Yalu River into the home of the ancient Manchus, had brought us here.

The commander's interpreter took his place and called for the attention of the prisoners. The colonel, he said, would speak to us.

The colonel spoke of many things. He spoke of religion, and of ethics. He spoke of the spirit of Bushido, and how it was more ancient than the teaching of Confucius, more sacred than the teaching of Christ, more honorable than the teaching of Buddha. He spoke of the emperor and his eternity, reminding us that the emperor was a sun god and the direct descendant of sun gods. He spoke to us concerning the position of all Japanese in the grand scheme of things. And he spoke to us concerning our own place in the scheme of things.

He spoke to us of yellow men and white men. The yellow man and the white man were eternal enemies, he said. And as long as there was a white man in Asia there would be no peace in Asia. In the hierarchy of men, he told us, the lowest of yellow men were higher than the highest of white men, and that we, as prisoners of war, were the lowest of the low.

As prisoners we had no rights, he said. We had betrayed the true spirit of soldiers by surrendering, rather than fighting to the death. He recognized, however, that we had been betrayed by our officers, that they had surrendered us and we were following orders, that this was something in our favor. Nevertheless, that did nothing to change our present circumstance.

Would this never end?

This was not really what I had in mind when, on my eighteenth birthday, I volunteered to enter the army and go slay dragons. It all seemed so simple then. Hitler was on the rampage and surely we would be in the war soon. But it wouldn't take long. Besides, times were hard. For those of us on the bottom end of the economic totem pole, the depression was still with us. Our family had lost its farm and we had left my beloved Rio Grande Valley in search of better things, things which then were not at hand.

Who knows for sure what triggers a youngster's decision in matters such as this? It just seemed the thing to do. It would mean one less mouth to feed during difficult times. It would mean an opportunity to be part of a great undertaking that was sure to come. It might mean the satisfying of a wanderlust that had plagued my heart for years. And it might mean the fulfilling of another dream I had had for years, the dream of someday writing.

I had always been fascinated with the written word, and admired beyond measure those who could cause others to think, as, to me, only the written word could do. Too, in my more irrational moments, I dreamed of going around the world and then writing about the stirring adventures that would surely ensue. Never mind how. Those details should never trouble a South Texas farm boy. If others could do it, so could I, given time.

When the recruiting sergeant said there was an opening on Corregidor and that Corregidor was "overseas," I was immediately interested. I asked where Corregidor was. He said it was an island in Manila Bay, some 7,500 miles distant, and that on that island there was an artillery regiment where replacements were needed. This was entirely too good to be true. I would go to Corregidor, serve my three years, fight a war should it engulf that region, earn $21 per month, take my discharge there, and proceed around the world. Then I would return home the envy of six brothers and two sisters. They would be as proud of me as I was of them. It would be very simple.

Fortunately, the recruiting sergeant was an understanding fellow. He quickly provided the necessary papers. There was a swearing-in ceremony, and, with eleven dollars in the pocket of a new uniform of which I was very proud, the journey began. That, as of this writing, was fifty years ago.

I arrived on the island in the latter part of March or early April of 1941, after a twenty-two-day voyage on the USS *Republic*, a troop ship out of San Francisco. The time between enlistment and embarkation was spent on Angel Island, in San Francisco Bay, awaiting transportation. The trip itself was mostly uneventful. Other than a horrible sea sickness that afflicted many of us when we encountered the swells out of San Francisco, a fake finding of scarlet fever on board just as we entered the harbor at Honolulu (which naturally resulted in a quarantine for the duration of our stay there), and a beautiful few moments as we entered the San Bernardino Straits, the voyage has mostly retreated in memory. But those beautiful few moments have stayed with me, off and on, all these years.

We had been at sea for some twenty days when the Republic slipped into the straits just as dawn was breaking. For some reason, possibly sleeplessness, anxiousness, or the oppressive heat below, I was on deck when the skies began to lighten, signaling the coming dawn. There then began a changing kaleidoscope of colors, the likes of which I had never seen before, or have seen since. At that point appeared myriad small, palm-covered islands, through which the ship threaded its way ever so slowly. The sea was not merely calm, but still and smooth as glass. A number of island fishermen in their *bankos*, small, outrigger canoes, were casting nets in the morning light. Tinges of color began to appear in the sky and were reflected on the water. The tinges turned to hues of pink, orange and red, and grew bolder until the entire sky took on an unreal shade of redness, and the water itself reflected its color. Suddenly, it appeared we were sailing atop a huge bucket of crimson paint, from which emerged scores of palm-studded islands.

Almost as quickly as it began, it ended. The colors faded, the sun showed its face, and the islands took on bolder relief. The ship gradually increased its speed, and soon we cleared the straits and entered the China Sea.

Some two days later we sailed past Corregidor, docked at Manila, and transferred to harbor boats that took us back to the island we had just passed.

Corregidor proved an idyllic place in peacetime. The island lay athwart the entrance to Manila Bay, only three miles from the southern shores of Bataan Peninsula, and some seven or eight miles from Batangas Province to the south. Shaped somewhat like a tadpole, the deeply ravined island rose abruptly from the sea to a point some 500 feet above sea level, where it flattened out into what was called Topside. It was here that most of the troops were garrisoned, and it was on the seaward perimeter of Topside that most of the giant coastal defense guns were located. Their function, should war ever come, was to keep an enemy navy from entering Manila Harbor, where, at a place called Cavite, a portion of America's Asiatic Fleet was berthed.

Just off the eastern end of Corregidor, a few hundred yards from what would be the tail of the tadpole, rose another mountainous island called Caballo, the home of Fort Hughes. South of Fort Hughes, between Caballo and Batangas Province, lay Fort Drum, which was essentially a concrete battleship, built on a much smaller island. Still farther south, just off the northern shore of Batangas Province, lay Fort Frank, on an island called Carabao. Between the four islands, and the fortifications and men on them, the harbor would be secure — as long as they held.

The 59th Regiment of Coast Artillery manned the huge coastal defense guns. The task of defending the big guns themselves fell to the 60th Coast Artillery, a regiment of anti-aircraft cannon with supporting units. It was to this regiment I was assigned, and within the regiment, to Battery C, captained by a West Pointer named Ames but run by a first sergeant named Beeman. Ames was a well-educated New Yorker; Beeman, a child of Southern bayous. My own impression was that not much love was lost between them.

At various places around the island, tunnels had been dug. These housed ammunition and other supplies in peacetime, and in war would be home for Command Headquarters, plus hospitals and non-combatants, such as the quartermaster, finance offices, and other operations usually found far to the rear of combat.

Life on the island was surely a reflection, however dim, of Kipling's India. The forts were garrisoned by some 6,000 white men, surrounded in the distance by a sea of brown people going about their own business in their own way. The transformation of Asia had not yet occurred. Asia was still Asia. The East was still East. And the Philippines, while not quite the Orient, was Asia. Parts of northeastern Luzon were still marked "unexplored" on *National Geographic* maps, meaning, I suppose, they had not yet been mapped.

Moros still occasionally ran amuck, binding themselves with cord so blood from any anticipated wounds would not run so readily. Then, taking up the bolo, they would dispatch as many Christians as possible before entering their own heaven. Populations had not yet exploded in the islands, in obedience to the church's teachings and advances in medical technology.

Word from the old soldiers had it that heads were still taken in the remotest jungles, and the blowgun was still used for hunting by a few tribes.

All in all, looking back, it was a soldier's paradise. It was a time when a soldier's life revolved around the bugled sounds of reveille and taps, of order and certainty. Years of planning and work by the engineers had essentially eradicated the scourge of malaria from Corregidor. With the work of the engineers on the terrain of the island, the exceedingly heavy rainfall during monsoon seasons was quickly channeled to the sea.

In short, it was a fortress with a purpose, however ill-fated that might ultimately turn out to be. Of the troops it was expected, indeed demanded, that they look to their training, their weapons, and their personal hygiene. In at least part of this we had the help of a Filipino called Jawbone and his cadre of aides.

Jawbone, so called because of his proclivity for arguing interminably over the price of anything he was about to buy, or about to sell, had been with the battery longer than any but the oldest could remember. He had come "from the provinces," where, as a youngster, he saw his father killed by a giant python. The reptile, according to Jawbone's version, was in a tree above a jungle trail and fell upon his father, crushing him lifeless before he could be rescued by villagers, and creating a fear of the jungle in the youngster that never left him. He had come to Corregidor and taken up life in a small Filipino barrio near the docks at a place called, in navy terms, "Bottomside," and worked himself into the system of service personnel that had become a way of life in foreign duty posts. Ultimately, he worked his way up the ladder, until he became master of his own cadre of helpers, and had his own home away from home in the battery.

For about one-tenth of each man's paycheck, Jawbone saw to it that our clothes and sheets were laundered, our shoes were cleaned of the monsoon mud, and that we knew something about the community beyond our own. He had become, and remained, a much loved and respected member of our battery.

Training was constant and rigorous. Our primary training was in artillery, but the understanding was that we might also have to fight as infantry, so we trained in both. The thinking was, among those who did such things, that war was probable, if not inevitable.

As months passed the thinking changed. Months before war came, our leaders told us that war was not only inevitable but imminent. Planes were forbidden to fly over or near the island. Even the fabled *China Clipper* was rerouted to prevent approaching the island's defense perimeter. Batteries were put on rotational alert, and at least one battery in the regiment was stationed at their guns, where they lived for weeks on a twenty-four-hour basis with live ammunition at the ready. Thus did we train and wait.

But even under those circumstances life had to go on. Except for those on alert, the routine of garrison life continued pretty much as usual. In our own battery Sergeant Beeman, never a bundle of joy, became ever more irritable. Perhaps the thought of impending war had something to do with his attitude, but the troops attributed it to other things. He had never thought highly of green "replacements" from the United States in the first place. They were a pain that must be tolerated, but not necessarily appreciated. They had not yet learned to appreciate his way of life.

Beeman was not a large man, as I remember him, but he had a countenance that loomed large for those of us fresh from the States. His face was like an old, wrinkled road map made of shoe leather, reflecting both his time in the tropics and his years in service. At that time, he had some twenty-seven years in the army, just three years short of retirement. His service spanned the Boxer Rebellion in China, guard duty on the Trans-Siberian railway following the Bolshevik Revolution in Russia, and a tour in the Philippines. After that duty he had returned to his native Louisiana, only to find such changes, and so few opportunities, that he reenlisted and went back to the Philippines, where he had stayed, without leaving, for twenty years. He was home. Late arrivals were merely intruders.

Beeman's frustrations grew to the boiling point. Garrison routine called for a certain ritual each morning. There was reveille, the wake-up call, followed immediately by formation and calisthenics, then breakfast, then duty formation before troops went to stations. At that point there was "sick call," wherein those who thought they had health problems could fall out of line and report to the hospital. Quite often these health problems cropped up a few weeks after a trip to Manila.

There were always a few who had to go for syphilis shots, and some for gonorrhea treatments. Usually it was no big deal. The men with syphilis would probably die, given time. In the meantime, they would forfeit their pay, or as much of it as it took to pay for their treatments. Western thought had not reached the stage where a man's indiscretion, not to mention his sins, could be blamed on society, and society made to pay for it. The men with gonorrhea would probably live, if they were lucky. But the list had been growing of late, and on this particular morning the sergeant exploded.

It all began innocently enough. Men were required to attend the morning formation in undershirts, in order that a quick inspection could tell who was, or was not, properly attending to personal hygiene. It was expected, nay, demanded, that all be in place when the morning roll call began. On this morning one man overslept and slipped into the last rank, hoping he would not be noticed. A futile hope. Beeman spotted him and ordered him front and center to take his tongue lashing. Only then did the sergeant notice that the man, in his hurry, had slipped on a pair of "skivvies," leather-soled house slippers, rather than his regulation army shoes.

So angry that he sputtered, Beeman shouted that this was "what the new, streamlined, modern, 1941 soldier looks like." He exhorted us to take a good look at the man, and see what the army was coming to, and he wasn't going to have it. Lecturing the men at length on the evil of their ways, he finally ended his tirade with "and not only that, you are going over there to Manila and contaminating our women." Thereby making evident the true source of his worries.

He was a good old soldier. He would fight one more war, complete his thirty years of service to America in a Japanese prison camp, and die there.

It came time for our battery to again move to alert status, so in October we took leave of Topside barracks and pitched squad tents in the jungles surrounding our guns.

The anti-aircraft batteries were stationed on the island's highest points, and our own was on top of what was called Morrison Hill, on the north side of the island nearest the North Channel, and nearest Bataan, some three miles distant. Below us, in a position carved from the side of the steep hill, was Battery Morrison, a field artillery outfit equipped with 155mm howitzers, manned by Philippine Scouts. Slightly to the west of Battery Morrison, and below us some 400 feet, was heavily forested James Ravine, where remnants of the 4th Regiment of U.S. Marines, driven from their duty post in Shanghai by the Japanese invasion of China, would take up residence shortly before our own war began.

Actually, Corregidor was an extremely well-fortified fortress, as were the other islands that made up the defenses of Manila Bay. The seacoast defenses alone numbered fifty-six guns in twenty-three batteries, ranging in calibre from twelve-inch, long range guns and twelve-inch mortars down to 155mm's and three-inchers. The twelve-inch guns of Batteries Smith and Hearn had ranges of 29,000 yards (about seventeen miles), which was sufficient to keep enemy ships well out of range. Then there were the anti-aircraft guns, twenty-eight in all. To this was added the six fourteen-inch guns of Fort Hughes, Fort Drum, and Fort Frank on nearby islands, plus an assortment of twelve-inch mortars and lesser guns.

Our own battery consisted of four guns, three-inch cannon capable of firing, at that time, up to some 27,000 feet, or about five miles high at extreme range. Each gun had a crew of five men on the platform, plus a number of ammunition handlers whose job it was to see that the platform had enough ammunition at all times during action.

Around the gun a barricade, of sorts, had been built. This consisted, in our case, of fifty-five-gallon oil drums filled with soil and reinforced, outside the parapet, with layers of sandbags to a height of about six feet. At various distances within the parapet, barrels were turned on their side with the open end pointing inward. These were filled with live ammunition, so that the ammunition crew would have cannon shells within ready reach as the gun revolved around the platform.

The guns were connected by an electrical cable to an optical range finder, through which approaching planes were tracked as they entered the island's defense perimeter. Results of the range finder's work was fed into still another device, something of an early day computer, which, given what it received, was supposed to relay to those of us on the guns, through another electrical cable, where the planes would be at any given second while within our range. On the guns our job was to see to it that we had an exploding shell at that point and at that time. My own job was to take care of the vertical aiming of the gun. On the other side of our gun a private named Underwood handled the horizontal aiming. Between the two we were supposed to keep the gun on target, or where the target would be when the shell exploded some five miles high. In the pecking order of privates, ours were prestigious positions.

Around the battery perimeter machine guns were stationed on towers, to guard against low flying attacks. Among the machine gunners were Johnny P. Turner and "Little George" Williams, so called because there was, within the battery, a much larger man, physically, also named George Williams and known as "Big George." Both Turner and "Little George" Williams were from ranches in West Texas.

Our gunner, the man who rammed the shell home in the breechblock and pulled the lanyard, was a corporal from California named Southwell. The relay man, who removed the shell from the fuse-cutting device and placed it in the breechblock, was Francis Tuerman, a Pfc from Decatur, Texas, and a most honorable man. During that last fateful week of Corregidor he would die where he had fought, within the parapet of number-two gun.

Among the ammunition handlers I now remember only a man named H.C. Griffith and a man named Wise. Other faces are there, but the names are not.

All four guns were crewed in the same fashion, and across the island, in other exposed places, were a number of other batteries of the 60th Regiment. If all went well, each gun could fire a round every eight to ten seconds. Each battery could put up about twenty rounds a minute and for the regiment as a whole we could put up better than a hundred rounds each minute.

Our position atop Morrison Hill occupied a space some 100 yards in diameter. There, for six months, some 120 men fought the first stage of their own little war. For some, it would be a lifetime. Within that circle there would be much living, and much dying.

TWO

"Go to your guns, and God bless you"

News of Pearl Harbor was delivered to me by an excited hospital orderly in the early morning hours of December 8, Philippine time.

The navy had been hit hard, he said, and the Japanese were expected to hit the Philippines at any moment. The hospital, because of its location and exposure on Corregidor, would probably be a target, and all patients were being moved immediately to space in Malinta Tunnel. I should make ready for the move.

Our battery was on alert, standing by their guns on Morrison Hill. After some discussion, I was given the choice of going back to the battery or going to the tunnel. I chose to return to the battery.

I was in the hospital for two reasons. One, a persistent low-grade fever that would not go away, but primarily because of a condition known among the soldiers as "blue balls," brought on by a rupture of blood vessels in or around the scrotum, which in this instance was brought on by lifting crates of ammunition from an awkward stance.

In the center of our guns was an ammunition storage room, deep underground and accessible by a circular stairwell designed to prevent entry by bombs. We had received a new shipment of ammunition and I had been assigned the task of moving the cases, each weighing about seventy-five pounds, down the stairway and into the storage area, where they could be retrieved for restocking the gun pits. It was during this exercise that the accident occurred. I did not have both feet planted firmly when lifting, the doctors said, and that caused the problem.

Since our battery was on alert status, I took to the hospital my full field pack, including a gas mask which was hung by the bed. After two weeks there the swelling was subsiding, but the fever had persisted. It was the fever, I was told, that caused them to think I should go to the tunnel, rather than back to the battery. But the thought of resting comfortably and safely under 300 feet of rock while my comrades fought a war did not, somehow, seem the thing to do. So daylight found me once again on Morrison Hill.

A certain indefinable strangeness of mood ran through the battery as daylight came that morning. The true devastation of Pearl Harbor was not yet known to us. All that was known, in the ranks at least, was that a surprise attack had wreaked considerable damage to a few ships at anchor and that we could expect the Japanese to hit the Philippines in due course. We did not know that even then they were on their way, and that if fog had not rolled in over the island of Formosa during the night, they would have already been there.

A somberness born of apprehension enveloped the battery as it was assembled by Beeman. He gave us the barest essentials, all he knew. Then Beeman ceased being Beeman, or the Beeman we had known.

With a quietness we had never known in him, he told us we were at war, that we must gird our loins and do our duty. He told us it would not be an easy war; that we would not have an easy time of it.

Then, as the men stood in stunned silence, he wiped tears from his eyes and said, "A lot of you are not going to make it through. I don't know who they will be, but some of us won't make it. I just want all of you to know I respect you as much or more than anyone I've ever soldiered with. I love you all. Go to your guns, and God bless you."

He walked away into the jungle.

Tears? Love? Strange, very strange. Much discussion followed the old man's comments as we went to battle stations. What brought on this unusual behavior? Had his courage left him? Had his nerves broken? Would he be up to it? Did he know something we didn't know and would not be told?

It remained for our gunnery sergeant, a man named Ingram, to put it in focus. A veteran of some fifteen years in the army, Ingram summed it up with "Don't worry about it. He's just been through all this before." Which may, or may not, have helped.

I do not remember Captain Ames being at that early morning gathering of the troops. It is possible he was, but if so his presence made no lasting impression on me. Most likely he was at a gathering of officers at Command Headquarters in Malinta Tunnel, getting the word on what happened at Pearl Harbor, and what to expect in due course as far as we were concerned.

He, and we, did not have long to wait or to wonder. Even as we went to our guns, and as the emotional impact of Pearl Harbor began to sink in, Japanese heavy bombers were on their way to the Philippines from Formosa. Before the day was done, the U.S. Army Air Force in the Philippines would lay in ruins. And, completely unknown to us, an invasion fleet, also headed for the Philippines, had left Formosa the day before Pearl Harbor was attacked. It would arrive two days later.

War did not come to Corregidor at once. The Japanese bombers ranged across Luzon that first day, laying waste to Clark Field and its B-17 bombers all lined up neatly in rows, and the fighter base at Iba. But they avoided Corregidor, as they would do until they had completed their primary objective of destroying American air and sea power in the Philippines. The next day they were back, and the next day. They turned their attention to the area around Manila, the air fields, and the navy's facilities at Cavite, inside Manila Harbor.

We sat on our gun parapets, in fascination and awe, as events unfolded around us. The bombers came in waves, always staying outside range of our guns, as they pounded Cavite, small ships in the harbor, and the bases around Manila. It was an unreal experience to witness war from the top of an island 500 feet above sea level, as if we were sitting in a giant amphitheater safe and sound while bombers came in waves above and smoke and flames billowed up from below and all around. We, or some of us, flattered ourselves by thinking they were careful to avoid our guns because they knew how heavily fortified we were, and that perhaps that was a good omen. It later became obvious to even the rank and file that they were merely taking first things first. Destroy our air and sea power and we would be left to shift for ourselves. Our time would come. Still, when we looked around, and looked at ourselves, we felt we were up to the task.

Not much news is given to the ranks under circumstances such as ours, or at least that was the case then. It was much later that the true nature of the defeat at Pearl Harbor was relayed to us with any clarity, and only then did it become apparent that no help was on the way or would ever be on the way. But still there was enough information floating around for us to know that the Japanese had devastated our air fields and the airplanes along with them, that the major ships of our Asiatic Fleet had left for southern waters, that heavy troop landings were being made on Luzon, and that all was not going well.

After those first few days, the bombers disappeared from our scene for some two weeks. We were told later that they were giving their attention to the invasion effort, paving the way for landing and advancing troops in northern and western Luzon while the ill-equipped and ill-trained Philippine Army rushed to meet them, aided by the 31st American Infantry Regiment and such other units as could be mustered. History, of course, records it as a losing effort, and within days the defending forces had fallen back, and had been driven back, into the Bataan Peninsula. Here, north of Mariveles Mountain, on a line running from Manila Bay in the east to the China Sea in the west, the stage was set for the Battle of Bataan.

Almost exactly one month after the main enemy landings in northern and western Luzon, those of us on Corregidor could see the flash of artillery fill the night as the opposing armies set about their tasks, the Japanese determined to continue their lightning attacks aimed at subjugating all the Philippines and the Americans and Filipinos equally determined to stop them.

When they did return, however, it was with a vengeance. On December 29 they were back in force. Corregidor is not a large island. At the widest point it measures only about two and a half miles and is only about three miles long, with half that length being a thin strip that curls east and south toward Fort Hughes. Over that small patch of ground the Japanese kept nearly 100 bombers for some two and a half hours. There were heavy bombers, medium bombers, dive bombers, as well as those planes called fighter escorts.

It is perhaps strange that while this was my own baptism under fire, it is not among those events, before or afterward, that stand out most clearly in my memory. I do remember the constant rain of bombs, the incessant roar of our own artillery, the blasts that shook the island, the strange rustling, whistling sounds of descending bombs that we would become used to. So accustomed to, in fact so attuned to, that we could soon tell, while going about our assigned tasks on the guns, if the bombs were to fall within a few yards or a few hundred yards.

And I do remember that when the bombers finally left and quietness again descended upon the island, Corregidor was never again the same, nor were those who manned the guns. In a somewhat dazed and detached condition we surveyed the devastation wrought by the

THE CHOW DIPPER

bombers. The hospital, where I had so recently lain, was in ruins, being among the first things hit. Topside barracks, where we had lived before moving to the guns, was in ruins. Across the island the same condition prevailed. Power and communications facilities were hit, as was the small, winding rail line designed, in the beginning, to bring ammunition from Malinta Tunnel to those of us on the guns.

While physical damage to the island was considerable, the loss of life and limb was not so great. At the end of the day Corregidor counted some 100 men dead and wounded, and nearly all our guns were still intact. Those who kept track of such things reported that our regiment brought down eighteen medium bombers, and our captain claimed, rightly I hope, that our battery of four guns brought down three of those. Wherever truth might lay, I know only that they did not again visit us with low-level or medium bombers until near the end of the siege of Corregidor. When they came again, as they did the next day, and the next day for more than a week, it was with high-level bombers, pounding the fortress from heights of five miles.

Thus did the siege of Corregidor, as seen by those of us on the guns, begin.

We settled into a routine. Every day the bombers came, usually varying their bombing runs from east to west, and from west to east. Every day those of us in the 60th Regiment returned the fire as best we could. Others, if they were wise, sought cover. Before long our guns became our security blanket, providing us a cover for our fears and allowing an interlude wherein time at once stood still, yet dragged on to eternity. While we were firing we could not look up from our assigned tasks. We watched them come in, watched them form themselves into bombing runs and make their approach to the island, but from then until they left our range it was a matter of doing our job. And, when the two and a half hours were over, we had to survey the damage and count.

Sometimes, when relative peace returned to the island, I thought of the incongruity of our situation. Because of the smallness of the island, because of the height at which the planes were flying, the bombers would release their bombs well before coming physically over Corregidor. And because of the range of our guns we would begin firing at about the same time they released their bombs. Thus their bombs on the way down passed our shells on the way up. It was entirely possible that the bombers would kill the men on the guns and in turn be killed by the men on the guns, who were perhaps already dead. And the souls of the departed would mingle, somewhere, awaiting final judgment by an almighty God of all men and of all the universe. Then there was no question on what that judgment would be. Now, in retrospect, who knows? I am not quite so certain.

I know not how, or if, that question troubled others, but for me it caused more inner turmoil than any other aspect of my existence at that time. It was one thing to give up one's life for his country, for his family, for his friends. Was it not Christ who taught that "greater love hath no man . . ."? It is quite another thing to knowingly consign one's soul to an eternity in hell for the same purpose. I had been brought up in a quiet home, a Christian home with few outward manifestations of religion, but where it was taught we should live by the "Good Book," in all our dealings, in all our associations with fellow humans. We were taught to pray — in private but not in public, because the prayers of others were no substitute for our own. We were taught, essentially, to live by the Ten Commandments and Christ's teaching of "do unto others." And we were taught that there was a heaven and a hell.

One of those commandments, of course, was "Thou shalt not kill." It did not say, according to the way I read it, "Thou shalt not kill except in time of war." The only consolation I could find, as I tried to sort the matter in my own mind, was that the same God who, according to Moses, handed down the commandments to the ancient Hebrews also told them that since they were the chosen of God they could go forth and slay their enemies without mercy. But even that offered no real solace for my mind. It offered only contradiction and confusion, causing more turmoil. And, as all soldiers know, the battlefield is no place for confusion. Nor is it a place where one can, for long, contemplate the mysteries and contradictions of war or life. Eventually one comes to grips with reality, and the reality of the moment was that the enemy was before us and it was either them or us, or both them and us.

For the most part the siege of Corregidor is a blur in my memory, a thousand memories rolled into one. The bombers came again and again. The men mounted the gun platform again and again. The fortress shook incessantly. The living and the dead were counted frequently. Official historians eventually would note that by January 7, 1942, some two weeks after the first bombs hit Corregidor, "bomb craters were uniformly scattered over the island, and one could hardly walk more than twenty-five yards in any direction without stumbling into one."

On January 25 I completed nineteen years on earth and began my twentieth. At the time it seemed most of those years had been spent atop Morrison Hill, on the platform of number-two gun. And that was only the beginning. By the time the siege ended in May, the scene that had been presented in January would be a comparative paradise.

We had moved our bunks and personal belongings from squad tents in the jungle to the area immediately surrounding our guns, where the men tried to fashion some sort of living quarters. There we would not have to make the increasingly long trek up the hill each time the air raid siren sounded. After the bombers had gone, there was a time of communion when thoughts turned to other things — of home, of family, of what we would do when this was all over. Friendships that formed during months prior to the war — friendships generally founded on like backgrounds, experiences, and interests — grew stronger as men sat in the quietness of the jungle night, revealing things about themselves they would never say under other circumstances. In some ways this was most pleasant; in some ways it made it all much more difficult when one or the other of them did not make it through the next day.

Life during those times was made a little more tolerable by a man named Chambers, from a place called Potlatch, Idaho. Chambers was the ultimate scrounger. He often used any temporary lull in activity to scour the island for just about anything that would make his life, or the life of his friends, more comfortable. Among his findings was an old, abandoned, vehicle formerly used by a searchlight battery, which he parked in the jungle near our gun. It later was pressed into service as a temporary ambulance when we had to transport our own wounded to the hospital. He also found, or otherwise acquired, a guitar with which he entertained himself and anyone else who would listen during those evenings when the daytime bombers had left and the night bombers had yet to come. Chambers would usually respond to requests from listeners, but left to his own devices would call up his favorite, a barracks room ballad he called "Lulu." The verses of the song consisted of an endless recounting of his version of what went on during the day.

A problem eventually developed, not over the verses but the

chorus. After every verse he would pick up the chorus, "Bang me Lulu, bang me. Bang me good and strong. You'll miss this good old banging when I am dead and gone." All of which proved too much for a young lieutenant named Pace, fresh out of West Point. His position, as an "observer," or aircraft spotter, was some four or five feet to the east of our gun pit, which placed him well within earshot of Lulu's problems. He was a good man, well respected by the troops despite the feeling, in some quarters, that he took himself a little too seriously, or that he probably could have passed himself off as a clergyman for the Church of England in a different setting. He finally tired of Lulu and ordered that her joys, or proclivities, no longer be recounted for all to hear. Whether the problem was the chorus or the decibels was unclear. Chambers, taking the position that if he could not sing what he wanted then he would sing nothing, did just that.

A few weeks later an artillery shell hit the canopy over Pace's head. I would read in a newspaper a few years later that he had been given the Silver Star, posthumously.

Another unforgettable person was Francis Tuerman. There was a bond between us not shared by others. Eight or nine years older than I, he was a ranch hand in West Texas before the war. His father had been killed by the kick of an unruly horse, and Francis was left to care for his mother. Economic circumstances finally forced him into the army, where a guaranteed $21 per month sounded pretty good. He was a tall man, with a quietness and dignity about him that somehow seemed out of place in the old regular army.

Once, during peacetime, he saw me writing a letter home. He waited until no one was around and asked if I would write his mother for him. Somewhat perplexed, I noted that she would no doubt recognize it was not his handwriting, and this might cause concern. He assured me that would be no problem, saying that my writing was just better than his. When the letter was finished, I gave it to him for signing. He hesitated, looked around, and asked if I would sign his name, saying again simply that my handwriting was better than his. Only then did I realize his situation. From then on I wrote his letters, saying what he wished to say and signing his name.

When the war came and the siege dragged on, a string of bombs, one of many, dropped across our position. One bomb fell within some twenty feet of our gun, burrowing into the ground but not exploding. Had it done so the gun and gun crew would have been no more. The bomb men came and examined the situation, concluding that under the circumstances we would have to live with it. It would be too risky to try to disarm. We lived with it. Later, as we watched another group of bombers form into a bombing run, someone on the platform said something like, "I hope to hell they don't explode that damn bomb," meaning he hoped the shock and vibration from the anticipated bombs did not cause the buried bomb to go. Tuerman's response was, "It doesn't matter." Challenged by others on the platform who thought it did indeed matter, Tuerman said, and I remember it to this day, "Look, I have made my peace with my God. If it weren't for the rest of you here, I wouldn't care if a bomb hit this breechblock right now. I am ready to go." He said it with a calm conviction that left no room for further discussion. We turned to our task.

Somewhere in his family archives there may be a picture of Francis Tuerman of Decatur, Texas, in uniform, with the inscription, in my handwriting, "To mother, with love. Francis." And somewhere in the American cemetery in Manila is a marker for Francis. But there is no body there. It was turned to ashes by the blast of a Japanese artillery shell inside Battery C number-two gun pit. There was nothing to bury. His ashes are now a part of Corregidor.

After the first few weeks of bombardment the pace slackened drastically. The Japanese mounted their first major offensive against the lines in Bataan, and the bombers were needed there. Not that they ignored the island. There was seldom a day in which they were not present in some numbers, but the severity of the attacks diminished.

It was a time for trying to repair damages and working on a tunnel started earlier to house our kitchen, after our original field kitchen had been blown away. Not that the kitchen was much needed. We had long since been placed on half rations, and hunger was added to our unfortunate condition. When we were not on the guns, or not working in the tunnel, the men, or at least some of us, scrounged the island for something to eat. Little was to be found. Occasionally a few of us would drive down into James Ravine to try our luck with the marines, who had their own mess and were much better fed, at that point, than we. Not only that, the ravine, being on the north side of the island, was reasonably safe from shelling from Batangas Province in the south, where the Japanese had recently mounted field pieces. At the time the shelling posed no real military threat, but it did cause concern when we were away from the security blanket of our own guns. The shells fell at a rate of about one each minute, which was not much, unless one happened to be nearby.

It was also a time in which men were afforded the opportunity of some reflection. While we had not yet come to understand that President Roosevelt's promise of help in the way of "hundreds of planes and thousands of men" was merely political rhetoric, we had come to realize that the battle was ours to win or lose, and that the forces arrayed against us were far greater than our own. No doubt there were those who did despair, but I know of none. There was rather a feeling that somehow, someday, we would prevail. The Malay Peninsula was overrun, Singapore fell. The Dutch East Indies fell. Eventually, as we saw it, everything was swept away except for Bataan and Corregidor. And eventually the military bastions were not the only things swept away. Also swept away was a good bit of the faith, among the rank and file, in those who were in charge.

How could this happen? How could Pearl Harbor be caught napping, when we on Corregidor were on alert, waiting? How could Clark Field in the Philippines be caught with its planes on the ground, when we all knew Pearl Harbor had already been hit? How could the mighty (we assumed) fortress of Singapore go under with only something like a three-day fight, delivering some 90,000 Englishmen, Australians, and New Zealanders into captivity? How could the Dutch, whom we had always thought of as a serious fighting force, give up the fight so quickly in the Indies, taking down with them a band of unfortunate Americans who became known as the "Lost Battalion" and would be forced to build railroads for the Japanese in places like Burma? How could all this happen unless someone up there screwed up royally?

There must, of course, be a vast gulf between the way a private sees a war and the way that same war is seen by generals or politicians. And years after the war, by reading the "official" documents regarding the siege of Corregidor, one could see just how little we knew of what was going on. Or, for that matter, how little we should have known. We knew nothing of the cables going back and forth between MacArthur and Washington, the apparent hopelessness of our situation, the debates over position and who thought what was important. We were not told of the finite food supply, how much or how little there was of it, or how long it was supposed to last.

To us the things that were important were close at hand. When we looked out over the China Sea, searching for the anticipated arrival of American ships, we saw only Japanese cruisers, well beyond the range of our coastal guns. When we looked up, the planes were tiny specks, emitting a drone that became, after weeks and months, terrifying in its own right. When we looked toward Bataan the artillery flashes grew steadily more intense.

And when we went for food, there seemed to be less and less of it. The morning meal, served at break of day, eventually became a piece of toast and a cup of coffee, weak coffee. The noon meal eventually became nothing. The evening meal, served in darkness, became whatever the cooks happened to have or could scrounge, rice with raisins, rice with canned salmon, or sometimes chipped beef. And very little of it. Perhaps it was our imagination. Perhaps it was because our dwindling body weight and body strength was demanding more, and more was not possible. But for whatever reason there developed a situation on Corregidor that a diplomat might say was "not conducive to good morale." Rumors abounded that others ate better than we on the guns. Inhabitants of Malinta Tunnel, derisively called "tunnel rats" by men on the guns, were, according to the rumors, faring exceedingly well. That, combined with the fact that they were not sharing the daily strains of battle with us, soon created an atmosphere where they were actually despised, and in a way hated more than we hated the Japanese. Malinta was full of frightened, cowering personnel whom we could see served no useful purpose. They did not contribute to the effort, as we saw it, but ate the rations—rations that otherwise could have, and would have, gone to the men on the guns.

Malinta Tunnel was an engineering masterpiece. The hill through which it ran rose abruptly at the beginning of the tadpole tail of Corregidor. At some time in the past engineers had bored, blasted, or otherwise hacked a tunnel through the base of the hill, connecting the main portion of the island to its curling tail. Off the main tunnel were numerous laterals, all dedicated to various uses. In peacetime it was a quiet place, entered only by a few persons on official business and small, trolley-type electric rail cars that plied the rail line between topside and bottomside. When war came the scene changed rapidly and drastically. Probably one of the earliest to move into the tunnel was the hospital, into predesignated laterals. It was a happy move, for the regular hospital was among the first things hit. Also moving there were Gen. Douglas MacArthur's Command Headquarters, the ordnance people, the quartermaster (or supply) units, the finance people, those people not needed on the guns.

By the time I made a trip to the tunnel in wartime, in company with others from the battery to obtain a load of ammunition, it seemed that fully half the island's population must have been crowded into the tunnel and its laterals. In a way it was a frightening experience to enter the tunnel, but it gave us some sort of inner satisfaction, for the inhabitants seemed to regard us in awe, as if we were from another planet. One would have thought that with 300 feet of solid rock overhead, with no danger of having to face the bombs, and later the shelling and the bombs, they would have felt perfectly safe. But such was not the case. Their eyes held more terror than those who daily faced that threat. It is possible that a psychologist could explain all this, but then, a psychologist would not have been on the guns.

Perhaps a glimpse of the two worlds of Corregidor can be found in the diary of a hospital assistant, published in the official army history of the siege of Corregidor nearly fifty years after the event. She wrote:

> Under the deepening shadow of death life on Corregidor took on a faster, more intense tempo. The smallest and most simple pleasures became sought after and treasured as they became increasingly rare and dangerous — an uninterrupted cigarette, a cold shower, a stolen biscuit, a good night's sleep in the open air.
>
> There was a heightened feeling that life was to be lived from day to day, without illusions of an ultimate victory. Many sought forgetfulness in gambling. There was no other way to spend the accumulated pay that bulged in their pockets and they rattled the dice or played endless bridge, rummy and poker.
>
> Jam sessions attracted great crowds which gathered in the dark and hummed softly or tapped feet to the nostalgic swing of the organ, a haunting guitar, or a low moaning trombone. Sometimes a nurse and her boy friend of the evening would melt into a dance . . . The eyes of the onlookers would grow soft and thoughtful, while other couples would steal out into the perilous night . . .
>
> Still others sought the consolations of religion and the symbols of another world, a better world of sweet and eternal peace. The Catholics gathered at dawn in the officers mess of Malinta Tunnel where one of the tables was converted into a simple altar, and kneeling on the bare cement under the high white washed vault they listened devoutly and a little desperately to the same hushed phrases that had been whispered in the Catacombs.

This was obviously a world we on the guns knew not. Nurses and their boyfriends melting "into a dance"? Other couples stealing "out into the perilous night"? Eyes growing "soft and thoughtful"? The "officers' mess"? Ours was a different world.

In theory the supply units in the tunnel were supposed to deliver our rations, bring us our replacement ammunition when supplies got low, come and pick up our dead and wounded after the daily bombing runs were over. At first it worked that way, but as the siege wore on and as the battle intensified, it did not. On many occasions we had to make the winding trip down the bombed out trails to deliver our own wounded to the hospital, or to replenish our ammunition supply.

One such trip stands out in my memory, reminding me then and now it is dangerous to categorize men. We received word that a submarine had eluded the blockade and had delivered a supply of newer ammunition with thirty-second mechanical fuses, which would allow us to reach higher altitudes. The problem was that if we wanted it, we had to come get it. The ammunition had been delivered into Malinta Tunnel, but from there the responsibility was evidently ours, so we went. It was dusk and if the bombers stuck to their routine we had a while before the sirens sounded again. Weary and exhausted, we loaded our ammunition while the tunnel's cowering inhabitants watched. As we left the tunnel's west entrance we passed a group of men gathered there for a breath of fresh air. Among them was a tall, dignified individual wearing the eagle of a colonel's rank. There was a sadness about his eyes as he greeted us. Somewhat startled at being addressed by an officer of such rank, I stopped. He asked how things were going "up there."

"It's pretty rough," I answered.

"It sounds like it," he said. "It sounds awful." Then he added, "God bless you. You're all we have left."

There was something about him, something about the way he spoke, that said more than what he said. It said, to me at least, "If I could help, I would." I believed what he said, and what he didn't say.

We returned to the guns, but I felt there was at least one in the tunnel who would have helped us, if he could.

I do not know why that one small incident has remained in my memory all these years. Perhaps because it challenged thoughts that were rapidly crystallizing in my mind, thoughts which said all men on the guns were doing their duty and were therefore worthwhile, and all men in the tunnel were not doing their duty and were therefore not worthwhile. Could it be that those of us on the guns were not quite as brave as we thought, or forced ourselves to believe, and that not all men in the tunnel were quite the cowards they seemed? That the principal difference between us was circumstance — that most men will rise to the occasion if circumstance dictates, no matter the hardships? That only some men, given the opportunity by circumstance, will seek the path of safety and security, no matter the humiliation involved?

At least some of the bitterness engendered by these conditions rubbed off on our officers, and would dog the trails of both officers and men in the months and years to follow. Among soldiers trained to follow orders of those in higher rank, conditioned to think the reasons for their own lowly status is that others are better trained, more experienced, and somehow smarter, the blame tends to go up the ladder, whether justified or not. Who was allowing these conditions to exist? Certainly not the troops, according to the way the troops saw it. Who could make things better? Again, certainly not the troops, as the troops saw it.

At least some of the officers did little to counter the feeling that was developing. In our own battery the captain insisted, for instance, that officers have their own latrine, even under conditions that existed. Such officers had obviously been indoctrinated into the belief that "familiarity breeds contempt," and were determined not to bare their rear in the presence of enlisted men doing the same. It was a small thing, a silly thing, but it did nothing to elevate them in the eyes of the men. Not when men were fighting and dying along-side. It is true, of course, that familiarity may indeed breed contempt when that familiarity reveals weaknesses in character previously obscured by rank, position, or circumstance. But it also proved true in the terrible years to follow that familiarity fosters respect and admiration when it reveals strengths that would otherwise be obscured by rank, position, or circumstance.

I saw none of this spill over into the way men went about their duty. They never slackened, never spoke of it openly. The attitudes just seemed to contribute to the war becoming intensely personal, with each man knowing that there was someone out there on the other side with whom he was in mortal combat, and over whom he had to prevail. Eventually we came to realize that those who were left would have to meet the enemy on the beaches and in the fox-holes. In the meantime, we, or at least I, developed a little cocoon in which life went on. When the bombers came there were things to do, and when they left one went about other things, preparing for the next wave. Part of me seemed always back among my family. There was peace, no matter what was going on around me.

I do not know the thoughts of men on a winning drive, where the tanks roll forward, where planes in the sky may well be your own, where this or that hill is taken, where this or that town is taken and it is on to the next, minus, of course, those friends left along the way. I only know that on Corregidor it must have been different. True, some things were similar. People died. But here there was no advancing, no retreat. The ground we contested today was the same ground we contested yesterday, last week, last month. It was the same ground where this friend or that friend had fallen during that time. And we knew also it would be the same ground we would contest, and where more men would fall, tomorrow and tomorrow and tomorrow.

Under those circumstances, and despite the closeness of the men who inhabited it, our little plot of land atop Morrison Hill became a somewhat lonely place, visited only on a more or less regular basis by people from the quartermaster corps, who would drop our meager supplies of food just off the roadway by our gun and speed away, lest they get caught away from the tunnel while bombs were falling. Occasionally our battalion commander would come, but never, to my knowledge, our regimental commander. Once we even had a visit from The General himself.

It had been a particularly devastating attack. The bombers had concentrated on the northern side of the island, and particularly on and around Morrison Hill. The battery had suffered heavy damage, and when the attack was over men were called to begin the repair work. For some reason I was the only one in our gun pit when suddenly, walking through the zig-zag entrance to our gun, there appeared Gen. Douglas MacArthur, followed by a retinue of officers. I had never before seen the general in person, certainly not standing within three feet. The dust and smoke of battle was still in the air, as was that acrid smell that goes with exploded bombs. Perhaps the attack had addled my brain, but for whatever reason I remember thinking, "What are these crazy nuts doing out in this?" As quickly as I could recover my senses I drew to attention and saluted. He returned it, asking in the next breath if the captain was around. I replied that I thought he was taking care of some problems at the range finder position or at number-three gun, and that I would go find him. I do not remember where in fact I did locate Ames, but I did, and relayed the message that MacArthur was in number-two gun pit, waiting for him. Needless to say, he hastened.

The next scene would have been somewhat comical, had it occurred anywhere else under other circumstances. MacArthur was in khakis, with his ever present head gear. Ames was in khaki, sweaty and dirty. He drew to attention and saluted just as MacArthur thrust out his hand to shake hands. Ames then lowered his salute and stuck out his hand, just as the general pulled his hand back and returned the captain's salute. The general smiled, even laughed. They finally got their act together, saluted, and then shook hands.

MacArthur asked Ames how things were going. Ames' response was that the battery had been pretty badly hit, but that everything would be in order soon. MacArthur told Ames, "You and your men are doing a fine job. We're proud of you." He went on to say something to the effect that he merely wanted the troops to know they were not forgotten, to keep up the good work and so on. It was clearly a "show the flags" visit. Then they left.

The whole meeting lasted no more than fifteen minutes. But still, he didn't have to come at all.

A few nights later we heard the roar of PT boats as they curved around the northern shore of Corregidor, below our position, and headed south. At the time we thought perhaps they were on their way to engage an enemy vessel. Rather, they were taking the general on the first leg of his voyage to Australia.

Gen. Jonathan Wainwright, until then commander of the troops in Bataan, took over command of the Philippine defense and soon another chapter would unfold.

Soon after Wainwright took over, the Japanese mounted their heaviest and final assault against the lines in Bataan. Previously beaten back by Bataan defenders, the Japanese threw heavily reinforced divisions against the lines, by then manned by half-starved, ill, exhausted troops. The lines bent, then broke. The Japanese troops overran the peninsula, and on the night of April 9, 1942, the Battle of Bataan was over.

Those of us on the guns had no way of knowing this at the time. The southern slopes of Mariveles Mountain were clearly visible to us, of course, but the northern slopes were not, and that is where the lines were. We could know the terrible intensity of the battle only by the sight and sound of artillery blasts as the last battle went forth. But suddenly that stopped, and in its place there was the visible, and to us terrible, spectacle of ammunition dumps being blown up on the southern slopes. It was a clue that could have only one meaning. Soon the word spread that it was over.

History would record that the Japanese quickly herded the prisoners into long lines headed north to a place called Camp O'Donnell. The march itself, which came to be known as the "Death March," would indeed live in infamy, but it was also a precursor of what was ahead.

A few managed to get across the narrow North Channel to Corregidor, floating on rafts, logs, small boats, anything that would aid in the crossing. It turned out they were leaving the frying pan for the fire. Then, sometime during the night, as chaos engulfed the area, a massive earthquake struck. To the men from Montana, Idaho, and California it was probably no big deal, but for myself, having grown up where the earth never moved, it was a terrifying experience. The earth heaved and shook with a sound I had never heard—a strange, rumbling roar that seemed to come from everywhere. My first thought was that the ammunition dumps on Corregidor were being deliberately blown up, as they were across the channel in Bataan. Nor did it help much when someone shouted "Earthquake!" We had been told that eons of tidal flow in and out of Manila Bay had eroded the island's base, so much so that it was not unlike a giant ice cream cone, wider at the top than where it joined the ocean floor. The thought flashed through my mind that the island was simply going to break off and go under. Ludicrous thoughts, I know. But the times did not give rise to clear thinking.

The Japanese lost no time in mounting the final attack against Corregidor. Even as the southern shore of Bataan Peninsula was being cleared of military and civilian personnel, they established their artillery positions and began firing on the island. The North Channel, running between Corregidor and Bataan, was only some two and a half miles wide, easily within range of even their smallest artillery. And our position, being the highest point on the north side of the island, was among the first to come under attack. Not that it mattered. Within a few days they had completed installing an overwhelming array of artillery pieces that brought the entire island under incessant bombardment, night and day.

We were essentially powerless to do anything about it. The guns of our own regiment were for use as anti-aircraft fire and could not be lowered into position for counterfire against ground targets in

Bataan, even if they could have been of any use. The big guns of the 59th Regiment were designed and built for defense against distant targets at sea. Only a very few could be brought to bear on targets in Bataan to the north or Batangas to the south. Between the two regiments we were supposed to hold Manila Harbor until the Pacific Fleet, stationed at Pearl Harbor, could fight its way across the Pacific, clear the path, bring reinforcements, all that sort of thing. But there was no more Pacific Fleet, certainly not one that could tackle the Japanese at that stage. Even our giant twelve-inch mortars, which could theoretically have been brought to bear on Bataan, had no ammunition designed for use against land-based personnel. About all we had in the way of effective counterfire were a few 155 howitzers manned by the Philippine Scouts, part of the well-trained, disciplined Philippine Division under the command of American officers. But even they were, for the most part, quickly silenced by the overwhelming superiority of the Japanese assault.

We soon learned it is one thing to be under concentrated aerial bombardment; it is quite another to be under bombardment by both air and artillery. Even under the worst of battles, the bombers eventually had to return to their bases for more fuel, more bombs, offering us at least a little respite. The artillery had no such limitations. It was constant, unrelenting, everywhere. The Japanese raised tethered observation balloons on the southern slopes of Mariveles Mountains so that any movement on Corregidor could be seen and pinpointed for artillery. Giant, sensitive sound detectors augmented the balloons, so that any nighttime activity involving vehicles could likewise be pinpointed.

A trip down the hill to replenish our drinking water was a harrowing experience, undertaken only under extreme circumstances. We dug trenches from gun to gun, during the night, in order that communications be maintained. We dug holes around our guns in which to sleep, or try to sleep, when duty did not call us to the guns. In my case the hole was some six feet long and four or five feet deep, about ten or fifteen feet from the gun. It was covered by sheet metal, which was covered by soil, with an opening at one end into which I would crawl. Lying there at night, with exploding artillery shells shaking the earth around me, and with an occasional giant black tropical ant being shaken down upon me, I could not escape the feeling that I was in a grave, from which I would emerge if all went well. And if it didn't, well . . .

The bombers did not neglect us, but my most vivid memories of that last month on Corregidor, until the invasion itself, involve not the bombers but the artillery. Perhaps it is because until that time we on the anti-aircraft guns gave tit for tat. If the bombers were there, we were in action. Now, suddenly, we were being fired upon incessantly and could do nothing about it. Neither, apparently, could anyone else.

Thus, from an ant's eye view of the war, did the siege of Corregidor wind its way to ultimate conclusion. The island was reduced to rubble. The beach defenses were destroyed. In our own battery, one gun and part of its crew, along with parts of the crews from other guns, were blown away by artillery fire. Then we had the partial makings of four gun crews and only three guns to worry about. Accordingly, we were told that every fourth day one crew would have the day off, and we would rotate which guns the remaining crews would operate. It didn't really matter to the bombers overhead, or to the sweep of history. There were not that many days left.

And what does one do with a "day off" under those conditions? Scrounge for food.

On one such occasion, I and two other members of the battery, Leroy Wyse and Richard Urling, left our position to seek our fortune in anything edible. The word from others was that nothing was out there, but there was always the chance that something had been overlooked, that a cache of food could be found somewhere on the eastern part of the island where it was anticipated the invasion would ultimately come. We made our way down the southern slope of our hill, through what was left of the forest, unseen by enemy observers on Bataan, through Malinta Tunnel with its cowering inhabitants, and onto the area around what was then called Infantry Point. Suddenly we found what we were looking for, we thought. We came upon a small hill, around which a road had been cut, and in the face of which a small tunnel, or dugout, had been carved. The tunnel was only about six or eight feet high and some twenty feet long. In it were cases of canned food.

Two problems quickly developed. The first was that the cache was guarded by a marine gunnery sergeant, and he was in no mood to give up anything. This was to be used, he said, in the event of the invasion. His duty was to see that it was there when needed. The second problem was that enemy observers, probably in one of the balloons tethered on Bataan, had seen us enter the hole in the face of the hill. Until then it had apparently gone unnoticed.

As we wheedled and argued with the marine, trying to convince him that a few cans of food would never be missed, artillery began pounding the area. It did not take them long to find the range, and their fire became exceedingly accurate. The marine, needless to say, was furious. We had given his position away. The argument quickly dissolved into an exercise of self-survival. We began trying to seal the entrance with cases of canned food. As the sergeant passed the cases from the back of the tunnel, we stacked them in the entrance while shells exploded on the face of the hill near the entrance. Actually, it was probably a useless endeavor. Had a shell hit the entrance it is unlikely that a few cases of canned goods would have made any difference. But fortunately, that didn't happen, and the barrier at least kept out the shrapnel.

The dust and smoke raised by the bombardment must have convinced the gunners they had achieved their objective, and they moved elsewhere in the area, now joined by a number of additional guns. When shelling around the entrance subsided, we quickly moved enough cases to make an escape, leaving the sergeant to his cache and his duty. His store was still intact, and so were we.

As we began our trek back to our own position on Morrison Hill we passed the entrance to the medical lateral of Malinta. There, under a sheer rock cliff that protected them from enemy fire from Bataan, a table had been set for the evening meal. Pie was on the table. It was the officers' mess. A nurse called out to us, asking if anyone had been hurt "out there." It was a perfectly logical question, reflecting her own concerns and compassion. To us it was a silly question. Nearly the whole eastern end of the island had taken a pounding. Fires were everywhere. Surely people had been hurt. She would see them shortly.

We returned as hungry as we had been when we left. Next day we were back on the guns.

The end was near. From our position atop the hill we could see various types of small vessels and barges congregating behind Cabcaben, a small spit of land extending out into Manila Bay from the southern tip of Bataan. Rumors spread that they were preparing for the invasion, but surely they would not use that as a point of departure. It was too visible, too obvious. Perhaps it was merely a ruse to divert attention from more significant activity elsewhere. It turned out to be no ruse. But before then, in the last few days, the bombers and the artillery had more work to do. So intense did the artillery become that it resembled the fire of machine guns. Each day it seemed to become more intense, more concentrated. Early in the bombardment of Corregidor the Japanese had mounted more than 100 guns against the island, ranging in size from 75mm howitzers to giant 240mm howitzers. A couple of days before the invasion, General Moore, the garrison commander, estimated that the island was hit by 1.8 million pounds of artillery fire. That was for one day, and it did not include the bombs. As mentioned earlier, it was a very small island.

Finally, they made their move. The invasion was mounted along the north shore of the eastern end of the island, in the area where we had had our unfortunate, or fortunate, experience at the food cache, little over a mile from our position on the hill. The word came to disable any artillery pieces that could still operate, to pick up rifles, to take our positions in the jungle, or what used to be the jungle, on the slopes below our guns, overlooking Bottomside and Manila Bay. There we would await the advance of the Japanese.

In the semidarkness of a full moon, on the morning of May 6, it all came to a head. A sergeant, I believe his name was Perry, guided us to the area we were to defend and told us to get situated. I was armed with a Browning automatic rifle, a clip-fed weapon capable of disposing of twenty rounds in an instant, theoretically up to several hundred rounds per minute. Because of that I was given first choice of where to locate, and chose a spot near a huge bomb crater. The bomb had cleared a swath of trees, giving me what I thought would be a fairly good field of fire. If they came from the direction I thought they would, I could at least see them before they saw me. To my right was a man named Leath, whom I did not know well. To my left was a man named Shook, from a place called El Dorado, Kansas. Both were armed with bolt-action Springfield rifles. And, of course, bayonets.

Shook was one of the youngest men in the battery. I never heard him admit his age, but the word around the battery was that he had lied about his age and entered the army at sixteen. He had been there little over a year, and was then seventeen, if the rumors were right. He was a friend, a good soldier, a good man. He had always been a happy youngster, but in that last month his face had grown older and had about it a haunted, somber look. It was as if he knew.

By this time fighting had been raging for hours on the beaches between North Point and Cavalry Point. The first landing attempt, shortly before midnight on May 5, had been repulsed with heavy casualties, but others followed and by midmorning were well established, along with tanks. Enemy airplanes of all types were overhead, moving about at will, selecting targets as they wished. On our part of the island the Japanese had begun "walking" their artillery up from the shoreline, a customary procedure to destroy any defenses in front of advancing troops. At that point we got word of attempted landings at Bottomside, on our part of the island. Evidently at least a few enemy troops got ashore on the slopes below us, for before the artillery got to our position we came under small-arms fire. I figured it was machine-gun fire, from a distance, merely spraying the area since it seemed to have no specific target. At first it seemed so harmless, given the power of bombs and artillery to which we had become so accustomed. And since the island was then shaking from bomb and artillery blasts, there was no real indication of where the fire was coming from. Nevertheless when it began clipping limbs and branches from the trees around us, we did take notice.

I had already thought through a course of action, as far as the artillery was concerned. I could hear, then see, its withering advance up the slope. I thought I had figured out how far it was advancing with each volley. My thought was that a barrage would be laid down directly in front of us, about where the bomb crater was, and that the next would hit where we were hunkered in our foxholes. The solution, I thought, was that as soon as the volley hit in front of us, I would have time to run quickly to the bomb crater, get down in it, wait for the next rounds to hit where our foxholes were, and then return to that position as the barrage moved up the hill, there to await the advancing troops.

But, as the poet reminds us, the best laid plans of mice and men often go astray, and this was one of those occasions. Rather than hitting in the bomb crater in front of me, the next volley hit in the trees, or what was left of the trees, above our heads, showering down on us the blast and shrapnel that goes with that sort of thing. When I regained my senses I called out to Leath, asking if he was all right. He was. I called Shook. There was no answer.

The artillery blasts moved on up the slope.

My right leg seemed asleep, numb and tingling. The right knee and right elbow were bleeding from several small pieces of embedded shrapnel. The wounds were of no consequence and the shrapnel would be removed later that morning by a Filipino medical corpsman. The leg gradually regained its feeling but was still not up to par when another sergeant made the rounds, telling us to pick up our gear and report back to our battery position at the top of the hill. There we were told that it was all over, that a cease fire was to go into effect at noon. The Japanese had taken possession of the eastern end of the island, everything east of Malinta Tunnel. Obviously, under those conditions Malinta was theirs for the taking, with its hundreds of wounded in the hospital laterals, the General Command Headquarters, its inhabitants, and what was left of the meager food supply for the island.

Thus, with a bang, a little blood, much trembling and trepidation did my own small part in the defense of Corregidor come to an end.

Historians have long debated the wisdom or folly of certain decisions and actions made by those in charge, beginning with Pearl Harbor and ending with Corregidor. For those of us on the guns and in the foxholes the arguments afford small solace. We had failed. Now it would be up to someone else. About the only solace we would have in the years ahead would be the feeling, more truthfully the hope, that our efforts were not entirely useless. We could always tell ourselves that we disrupted the Japanese timetable, that we gave America some time to come to grips with reality, to rally together for the job ahead. Something to fight for.

To a soldier, where the only real alternatives are victory or defeat, it may be a self-serving hope. But without hope, what is left?

THREE

The Surrender

I returned to our position on top of Morrison Hill in a somewhat dazed condition, helped along by someone I cannot remember. The right leg was still not operating properly, but with activity it regained its normal usefulness. A Filipino medical corpsman probed around and removed the small pieces of shrapnel from the knee and elbow, put some iodine on the punctures, and moved to the next soldier. It was the least of my worries.

Something akin to chaos prevailed. Obviously the old order was passing, though it had not yet passed completely. Some of the men were straggling in, congregating in the area of our mess tunnel, where the cooks were trying to supply what little food they had to men who hadn't eaten since the previous day, where the wounded were being cared for, where sergeants were trying to get a head count of who was where, trying to find out what was expected of us next.

We had been told that a cease fire was to go into effect at noon, but that was still a couple of hours away. In the meantime we were to destroy our weapons and take whatever cover was available. No need to suffer still more casualties in a cause already lost. Overhead a few bombers were still ranging the island, and from Bataan a few artillery units were still doing their thing. Whether they had simply not gotten the word, or were merely determined to get in a few last licks, we had no way of knowing. It didn't matter. The effects were the same.

Scores of Philippine Army soldiers, many of whom had gotten across the North Channel after the fall of Bataan, were quickly shucking their uniforms, changing into civilian clothes under the hope they would be mistaken for civilians and be allowed to go free.

Jawbone was made a rich man, at least temporarily, as men in the battery loaded him down with money from their pockets, knowing they could never use it and hoping he could make it through. If so he would be thus rewarded for long years of faithful service. I do not know what happened to him, but even if he did make it through, I doubt that his dowry made it with him.

Word came that we were to move to the Middleside area, to be there before dark, and there to await our new masters. We were there, and so were they.

I can still remember the terrible psychological impact of those hours. It is one thing to be defeated, no matter how valiant the struggle. In normal life there is always time to lick one's wounds and prepare for another contest, another day. We were not only defeated in battle, we had to go forth and meet an armed enemy as unarmed, essentially naked, supplicants, not knowing what to expect, but knowing there would never be another day. We had not only failed utterly, the future was not ours to control, or even question. I do not know how others remember the moments, but for myself about all I had left was a feeling of complete tiredness, of utter exhaustion, of fear and hope. I tried, as best I could, to keep it all under control.

The Japanese troops quickly spread over the island. New landings were made on the main part of the island, and by nighttime little campfires began to show up as small groups went about the task of preparing their evening meal. By and large they appeared to be a highly disciplined army as far as their own organization was concerned, but obviously given leave to confiscate whatever they wished from their prisoners, seemingly a time-honored practice among conquering armies. Most of them were not in a pleasant mood, having taken part in an invasion in which they lost an estimated fifty percent of the landing force. Many of them were much larger, much taller, than I had expected. Those in our own ranks who had spent time in China or other parts of the Orient identified them as Imperial troops from Mongolia and Manchuria. Our own bayonets were, or rather had been, dull olive drab in color. Theirs were polished steel, longer, more fierce looking, glistening in the moonlight. Subsequent events would prove they had no qualms about using them, even against helpless, unarmed prisoners.

While those of us in the ranks did not know it, we were not even then considered prisoners of war. Negotiations were still going on between Wainwright and Gen. Masaharu Homma, commander of the Japanese forces in the Philippines, over Homma's demands that all American forces in the Philippine southern islands be included in the surrender, not just those on Corregidor. Until that was accomplished, we would be considered mere hostages, with the implied threat that our lives could be forfeited.

During the afternoon and night, many of us from Battery C, along with many others, congregated in the vicinity of a tunnel that had been dug into the side of a hill at Middleside during the battle. Mostly it served as an ammunition depot and supply center, but for now it provided cover from sporadic artillery fire that was still going on. Not all of it was from the Japanese. A battery of Philippine Scouts, manning 155mm howitzers, simply refused to quit. Their regiment had suffered mightily during the battle. One battery, just below our guns on Morrison Hill, had come under such intense attack from Japanese 240mm howitzers during the battle that the entire side of the hill above them had collapsed over them, killing more than seventy men in one fell swoop. Finally someone convinced them they must quit, that they were endangering the lives of others who had already destroyed their weapons and were powerless to defend themselves.

We spent a restless, sleepless part of a night. Long before daylight a group of us were rounded up and marched to the beaches where the landings had taken place. Our mission: to transport wounded Japanese soldiers across the island, around Malinta Hill, and onto waiting ships.

We moved in darkness and arrived in darkness, save for a full, or nearly full, moon. Ours was not a large detachment. Others probably went to other places along the beach. I doubt that our detachment numbered more than a hundred men, but the only one I remember is me.

The aftermath of a battle can never present anything but a gruesome sight, but in the tropics there is a certain smell, a certain stench, that pervades the air and that one does not easily forget. Swollen, bloated bodies lay on the beach, washed by gently lapping waves. Bodies bobbed in the tide flowing out to the China Sea. Blood-soaked bodies of the still living lay on the ground or on stretchers. They had been there for at least twenty-four hours, perhaps more. It was they whom we were to take to the ships.

We were lined up and a Japanese who spoke a smattering of English gave us our instructions. He went away. But first things must come first. The soldiers began their systematic search of all prisoners in the detachment. Most in the group had already gone through the exercise and had nothing left—no watches, no billfold, nothing but their clothes. Up until then I had escaped, and had on me a billfold with ten or twelve Filipino pesos in it, along with some family pictures that I prized highly. I also had a pocket-sized copy of the New Testament, which also contained some family pictures. Both the billfold and the New Testament had been in my field pack, in the gun pit, when shrapnel tore through the bag and left its mark on both. I wanted very much to bring it home someday.

It came my turn. He could not speak English and I could not speak Japanese, but I got the message. I delivered up my billfold, thinking he would rifle it for the money and return the empty wallet. When he started to put the entire wallet in his pocket, I, unthinking, reached for it, protesting that he could keep the money, but that I wanted my pictures back. Furious, he grabbed his rifle, with bayonet attached, thrust the bayonet under my chin, against my throat, and began screaming a tirade. I froze, suddenly realizing this was no time and no place to press the issue. The moon glistened on his bayonet, and he was clearly an unhappy man. Quite honestly, I thought this might be the end. It was stupid of me, given the circumstances around us, with bodies bobbing in the water, with his comrades lying at our feet, to argue a point of principle, to be anything but the model prisoner. I had not yet learned, but I was learning.

I said nothing and tried not to move a muscle. Then a nearby Japanese said something to him and he backed off. I later figured he was told something like "Look, we brought these people here to carry the wounded. It won't help if we have one less for the job." At any rate he put the billfold in his pocket and began examining the Testament. He said something to me, and I guessed he was asking what it was. I answered it was a Bible. He asked the nearby soldier something, got a reply, and handed it back. I kept it all through the prison years. What he didn't know, and what I didn't tell him, was that I had a five-peso bill in my watch pocket. Months later it would pay for a few ounces of salt.

Daylight had not come when we finally began the trek from the beach, over the hump of the tadpole's tail, around and along the sheer cliff of Malinta Hill's southside, down to Bottomside, and onto the docks where a ship was waiting. Each stretcher had two carriers. It was not pleasant duty, but when it was over they did give us something to eat. I don't remember what, but I do remember that they fed us before sending us back to the area from whence we had been dragooned. And I don't remember whether it was that afternoon or the next day that we were all assembled at Bottomside to discard our helmets, as the ultimate act of submission, and, against the backdrop of Malinta Hill, to raise our hands in surrender while cameras ground away. It had been a hard won victory for Homma, and he was determined to milk it for all it was worth.

Years later he would be hanged. A charge that weighed heavily against him was his treatment of American prisoners of war on Bataan. I suspect one of the reasons he was hanged was that MacArthur wanted him dead, which was fine with me.

We were then moved to an area on the southern shore of the island's tadpole tail known as the 92nd garage motor pool. Before the war the garrison had a personnel strength of some 5,000, all of whom had a military reason for being there. But with the fall of Manila, the movement of MacArthur's headquarters, along with relocation of the Philippine government, the evacuation of Cavite Naval Station, and the remnants of Bataan defenders who could get across the channel, that number had grown to some 11,000, all of whom were now congregated on and around the asphalt lot of the motor pool, an area that had previously housed a few hundred men at most. There were no sanitary facilities, no mess facilities, no housing of any kind. Men sat and slept shoulder to shoulder, beginning on the rocky beach and extending across the parking area and up the surrounding slopes. Sanitary pits were dug and some sort of cooking facilities were assembled as men tried to bring a little order to the chaos around us. And it was here that the transformation from the old order to the new order was made complete.

The conquerors wasted no time in establishing their supremacy. The island still had to be cleaned up; war booty still had to be loaded on Japanese ships. They did not pass word to our officers when they required this many men, or that many men, for this purpose or that. They came directly into the gathering, lined up as many as they wished and marched them away for their assigned tasks. Some were detailed to bury and burn the dead, which still lay where they fell. Others, including myself, found ourselves in long lines, like so many ants, carrying food from the navy's tunnel to waiting ships. Sack upon sack of sugar, case upon case of canned food — food that we on the guns never knew existed — were transported to the ships. The trip from the tunnel to the dock was approximately one-quarter of a mile, each sack of sugar weighed 112 pounds, which was only slightly less than I weighed at the time. The men had been on half rations or less for five months, and here we were loading Japanese ships with food we felt we should have already consumed. It is true, of course, that even at half rations the food would have lasted only another twenty days or so, but that is a fact that escaped us at the moment. Somebody was to blame, and we did not put too fine a point upon who that somebody was. It was anybody and everybody who was in position to see that we were treated fairly, which, given the evidence around us, we did not feel was the case.

It would have been different, no doubt, had we been well-fed, strong, soldiers. But we were not. We were half-starved, totally exhausted, in many cases ill, but the line had to keep going. Guards armed with bayonets lined both sides of the march, and men who staggered or tried to rest drew their immediate attention. And, when the day was done, we made the trek back, along the road that had been cut halfway up the precipitous face of Malinta Hill's south side, out along the tail of the island, to drop exhausted on the asphalt pavement of 92nd garage.

Along the way, going and coming, we had to detour a few feet around the bodies of six American soldiers lying on stretchers in the roadway. Those details assigned the task of burning and burying had not yet gotten that far. I supposed they had been wounded (otherwise why the stretchers?) but had lain there and died. Now maggots crawled from their eyes, their nose, from where they had been wounded. So tired was I that I began to resent the few extra steps it took to go around the bodies, and when they were finally burned I walked ankle-deep through their ashes with a feeling of relief, and hated myself for the feeling.

Not all men drew the details of loading supplies or of burning and burying. Some were assigned other tasks, and still others managed to luck out, sometimes escaping the work details and spending their time scrounging the island for food of whatever kind. Under those conditions friends quickly formed themselves into small cadres, in which each tried to look after the welfare of the others. Our own cadre, or cell, consisted of a man named Roy Creecy, from a place called Willow Creek, Montana, Johnny P. Turner and George Williams, both from West Texas, and myself. Creecy, at twenty-seven the eldest, went by the nickname of "Sheepherder" because of his origins in the Montana ranch country, and Turner was generally called "Tombstone" because he once slept through a practice air raid drill. We were all of rural, hardscrabble backgrounds and had become friends during the days of peacetime in C Battery. Williams was born in a small place called Wolf City and entered the army from Mertzen. Turner was from farther west, out around Ozona. Now we banded together, not out of a conscious determination to do so, but because it seemed the natural thing to do. And we did undertake the conscious decision of trying to help each other survive. We had no idea of what might lie ahead, but we knew what the present entailed.

Of the four, Turner was the most resourceful, rivaling Chambers in his ability to scrounge. Once, at the end of the day, he came in with some sweetened chocolate and a few other items with which he made a sort of gravy that was out of this world, certainly out of that world. There was not much of it, split four ways, but the memory lingers. We were destined to travel many of the same paths during the next three and a half years. Occasionally we were split up, one going to this or that camp, but we began together and ended together, and, for the most part, remained together throughout. And we all survived, in one condition or another.

Thus did three weeks pass. It was three weeks in which rank and position were essentially swept aside, where, for all practical purposes, officers simply became irrelevant, where the natural order of men became established, not unlike that of horses in a corral or in a pasture. The central leader in any cadre was just as likely to be a private or a corporal as was anyone else. How men had performed in battle, and how they performed now, was of much more influence than any rank or position they might have held previously. Men who had "gotten religion" during the battle, promising their Maker anything He might require if only He would see them through, and who now sought to survive by less than honorable means, were shunned by others. They found themselves floating around the fringes, seeking to attach themselves to anyone who would provide succor.

And it was during this period that much of the resentment built up over the preceding months welled to the surface. Those officers who had performed well during the siege of Corregidor, and whom the men knew had performed bravely and well, maintained the respect and indeed the devotion of those who knew them. But even they, in many cases, had to endure the humiliation that came from others who did not know. It sometimes took strange form.

The area of the 92nd garage butted up against the somewhat rocky beach not far from what was known as Monkey Point. In a way it probably proved a life saver, for the waters afforded an opportunity to cleanse and cool off from the oppressive tropical heat at the end of a day. I had completed a day on the line, moving supplies, returned and rested a while on the asphalt, then entered the water to cool off. The waters were crowded, so I waded out some distance to a point where the water was chin deep, and was standing there when I recognized a man who, until a few days before, had commanded a regiment. He was a full colonel. I had never heard anything bad about him. As far as I knew, and as far as I was concerned, he had done his duty. We did not speak, for we had not yet adjusted to the point where a private soldier could engage a full colonel in conversation. As we stood there he submerged his head underwater and came up, only to find a long string of human feces floating inches away from his face. Someone, perhaps someone too ill to make it out of the water in time, had violated all the rules and simply defecated in the water, where hundreds of others were crowded. The colonel exploded, naturally enough, complaining of the undisciplined chaos that had emerged in the setting around him. But, unfortunately, in his tirade he blamed it on undisciplined "men." It was a poor choice of words. In the army of that day there was a clear distinction between "officers" and "men," not only in rank or position, but in matters of speech as well.

A nearby enlisted man jumped at the chance. He cursed the colonel unmercifully, with words like "You son of a bitch. What makes you think an enlisted man did it? It could just as easily have come from one of you guys." Others gathered around, sharing the man's thoughts and words.

I was stunned. I waded out of the water and returned to my little plot of ground next to Creecy, to whom I relayed the incident. He asked who the colonel was, and when I told him he merely laughed, and then laughed again. "It served the bastard right," Creecy said. "They've put crap in our face for a long time. Maybe now they'll know what it's all about." Creecy used strong language as a matter of course, so that part of his response was not particularly shocking. But the implications of his response were obvious. The old order had indeed gone and a new, though not necessarily better, order for the years ahead was evolving in its place. Creecy had always been a good soldier, doing his duty, earning a Silver Star, dreaming of his everlasting hills of Montana, respecting authority, never complaining. Now things were different.

Finally, it came to an end. The booty was loaded, the dead buried or burned. We were told to prepare to leave — for where we did not know. We were marched to Bottomside docks. On the way I tried to fix the scene in my mind, which was not a difficult task for it would have stayed with me anyway. The island fortress that had once been so green and beautiful was now a barren, desolate, denuded, pock-marked wasteland, simmering under a tropical sun. Back there on Morrison Hill, and elsewhere over the island, lay Pace, Tuerman, Strauss, "Alabama" Freeman, Standifer, Shook, and many, many more.

We boarded small ships and left for Manila.

Corregidor gradually receded and finally faded from sight, a small dot that became smaller and smaller and then went away.

FOUR

The Emperor's Guests

We landed on the southern fringes of Manila, where one more humiliation awaited us before entering prison camp. We were assembled on a broad avenue known as Dewey Boulevard, and, with Japanese infantry and cavalry alongside, marched through the streets with loud speakers blaring, impressing upon the Filipinos the invincibility of the Japanese army and the vulnerability of their protectors, the Americans.

Perhaps their tactic made its point, but I am not altogether sure. Filipinos by the thousands, encouraged to turn out for the show of Japanese force, responded with a show of sympathy and affection for the straggling, struggling prisoners, many of whom were by this time so ill they could barely walk. Many Filipinos tried to break through the lines set up by Japanese soldiers and press water and food upon the prisoners. A few succeeded before being beaten back. The entire route was marked by shouts of encouragement, of "Good luck, Joe," "See you soon, Joe," or "We're with you, Joe."

The words may not have filled our stomachs, but they did our souls. Under the circumstances, it was probably more important.

At the end of the march we entered Bilibid Prison, a way station on our road to Cabanatuan Prison Camp #3.

The Cabanatuan prison complex consisted of two camps some twenty miles east of the town of Cabanatuan, approximately one mile apart. The march from Cabanatuan to the camp itself followed a ride in boxcars from Manila, some eighty miles to the south. It was a hot, miserable trip under a blistering tropical sun, jammed standing into boxcars so tightly there was no room for movement, and little room to breathe the air that was available to breathe. In my own case I was lucky. As each car was filled with the prescribed number of prisoners, filling of the next car began. Those at the head of the line were forced back into the corners; those on the end of that particular group, where I happened to be, ended up near the open door. There, when the train started moving, air was available. Those in the back had no such luxury, and many passed out from heat and suffocation. They would be lifted by those around them, passed over the heads of others to the area around the door where they were revived by the presence of air from the outside.

In this fashion we moved from Bilibid to Cabanatuan. There we were given a ball of rice, roughly the size of a grapefruit, and the trek to camp began.

Under normal conditions the march would not have been difficult. A twenty-mile march, even under full field conditions, and even under a tropical sun, would not ordinarily be a problem for soldiers trained under those conditions. But by now the men were not up to it, or would not have been up to it save for the encouragement of accompanying Japanese guards with fixed bayonets. With their help we made the march before nightfall, passing the incompleted Camp #1 along the way. That camp would soon be the home of those from Bataan, then imprisoned in a place called Camp O'Donnell many miles to the west.

Camp #3 lay upon the banks of a great curve in the Pampanga River, which proved a most fortuitous circumstance. Further to the east, rolling hills turned somewhat abruptly into towering mountains. Taken together the terrain provided reasonably good drainage for the camp, a blessing not shared by those who would inhabit Camp #1, and perhaps a blessing not appreciated by others who have not shared space with 7,000 others under such conditions.

The unpaved road over which we had come bisected the camp. On one side, between the road and the river, lay quarters for the prisoners. On the other side was quarters for the captors. The road continued in a northeasterly direction toward the mountains, and, as we would see, would be used frequently by trucks filled with Japanese soldiers sent there to contest with guerrillas holed up in the fastness of the jungles.

The quarters consisted of long, barrack-type structures with thatched roofs and split bamboo flooring on which perhaps 200 prisoners slept. The structure was elevated some four feet above ground, with an entrance at each end. Between each split bamboo was a small space, providing a means for air to circulate from underneath the structure. That, combined with circulation from windows along the sides and the two doors, afforded a reasonably cool sleeping place for the hot tropical nights. Approximately eighteen inches separated the sleeping space of one prisoner from another. It was not comfortable, just as any corrugated surface cannot be comfortable for sleeping, particularly for men grown so thin. But rainy season was upon us, and it was the best we had encountered to that point in our new incarnation.

It was not the space or the quarters, however, that occupied the minds of the prisoners. It was the food. The food consisted of a small amount of rice three times each day, sometimes helped along with a few bamboo sprouts. The rice rarely amounted to more than one-half of a canteen cup each meal. In short, it was starvation rations and would not be long in taking its toll.

Before the prisoners had time to adjust to the new rations, they had to adjust to the new order. Within the first few days three prisoners escaped. They were not gone long. Within a matter of days they were back, turned in by Filipinos who were too terrified to do otherwise. The men were brought back into camp and staked out in full view of others to undergo their punishment. Three poles were set up, one for each prisoner. Each was forced into a half-standing, half-kneeling position with his hands tied behind the pole and his feet bound to the base. They could neither sit nor stand. Thus they remained bareheaded under a blazing sun for two days, while Japanese guards taunted, kicked, and beat them. Other prisoners were forbidden to approach, or bring water or food. They could only watch and listen to the screams. Early on the morning of the third day, perhaps symbolically, they were paraded through the camp and then, at sunrise, and standing before their own graves, shot.

One, from a small town in West Texas, cried out just before the rifles cracked for someone to tell his mother, and to tell her of his love.

Within a matter of days the word passed that we were all to be placed in ten-man squads, and that if one from the group escaped the other nine would be shot. Many in camp reasoned it was all a bluff, that surely there could be no moral justification for shooting nine innocent men for the transgression of one. Before our stay in Cabanatuan ended, we would know it was no bluff.

As the lesson soaked in we began to realize, if not understand, the manner of men who were now masters of all East Asia, and our own fate as well. If one wishes to be charitable, I suppose it could be reasoned that the Japanese were just not prepared to provide food and shelter for some 20,000 American prisoners of war, plus many thousand more Filipinos. The thinking then, however, was somewhat different. The picture that emerged was one of unspeakable cruelty. It was not at all unusual for the Japanese to bring captured Filipino resistance fighters into the camp and use them for bayonet practice, screaming in their own inimitable way as the poor bound prisoners gave up the ghost.

Our own food situation grew no better, and soon illness and near starvation became the order of the day. At first it was only two or three, laid low by malnutrition and finished off by dysentery, diarrhea, or some other ailment. But daily the count grew. The line of bodies being carried to the burying fields along the banks of the Pampanga lengthened.

Bad as it was, in other places it was worse, much worse. A chaplain was transferred to our camp from Camp O'Donnell, where prisoners from Bataan, Americans and Filipinos, were being kept. I do not know why he came. Perhaps someone had persuaded the Japanese it should be done. Nevertheless, he brought tales of men dying at the rate of fifty and sixty each day, then nearly five times our own rate. I do not remember it making us feel better, only that it was perhaps a portend of the future. They had, after all, nearly thirty days on us. Would another thirty days bring our dying rate up to theirs?

No matter. Life, as we had already learned and as we would be reminded many times, must go on as long as there is life. While a good bit of confusion did prevail during those first few weeks, and while the natural order of men had not yet been established, a sort of routine did set in. Men would arise in the morning and line up for the day's first serving of rice. Work details, selected from among the able-bodied, would commence their tasks. Usually it was a trip to the nearby hills for wood with which to cook the rice. Some would dig latrines, some would dig graves. Those who escaped work details would usually take refuge on the shady side of their barrack, trying as best they could to conserve what little energy they had left.

The matter of food became an obsession, and the pangs of hunger dominated not only the thinking but the actions and reactions of life within the camp. Long before the noon rice was to be served, men would line up in the hot sun, waiting. That same situation prevailed with the evening meal. The effort was to be as near to the front of the line as possible, lest the food run out before the end of the line was reached. Fights and near fights were not uncommon as men scuffled for a place in line, or when charges of favoritism were hurled at the "chow dipper" for perhaps giving his friends a little extra, or what was thought to be extra.

The role of the chow dipper was a precarious one at best under those conditions. The system was that the Japanese would give the prisoners a certain amount of rice for the day. This was cooked in a number of large iron pots, by American cooks, and allocated to the various barracks in accordance with the number of mouths to feed. Each barrack selected one of its own to distribute that food among its members. The task not only required a man strong enough to carry the buckets of rice; it required near sainthood as well. And sainthood, under the conditions prevailing, proved to be an impossibility.

I would have to confess that during those first few weeks in camp I was mostly an observer, and probably not a very good one at that. By the time we entered Cabanatuan my condition could probably be described only as extremely poor. Within a few days I came down with dengue fever, called "break-bone" fever, a viral disease transmitted by infected mosquitoes. It was a terribly debilitating ailment, bringing high fever and a terrible aching of the bones. No treatment was available, of course. One either died or survived on his own. Gradually, in my case, the fever subsided, only to be followed by an infection of the liver and a condition called "yellow jaundice." This became coupled with either diarrhea or dysentery, I knew not which, but I did know it was not a good sign. Either had the potential of draining whatever reserves might be left, and a severe case of either was generally the precursor of death.

At that time we had open pit latrines, some four feet wide, perhaps eight feet long and five or six feet deep. A cluster of them lay about 100 yards from our barrack, across a small ravine or depression, and alongside the path of the daily procession to the graves. On this particular day I had made the trek several times, each time with increasing difficulty. Toward evening my strength gave out and I collapsed on the slope about fifty feet from the latrine. I knew, or thought I knew, what it meant.

I tried to arise but was unable. I imagined that someone would see me and offer help. What seemed like an eternity passed and no one came.

The mind does strange things under such circumstances. I leave to better brains than my own the official explanation for all this. But I am not at all persuaded it is not simply a matter where the mind, not being able to influence the present, not being able to command the body any longer, retreats into the more peaceful and ordered world of the past, all the while being tugged back into the reality of its present.

Knowing that I was lying on the ground 7,000 miles from home, I somehow began to believe I was lying in the farm fields of my beloved valley. It was something I had done as a child many times, lying on my back, gazing at drifting clouds, dreaming of what might be, and reveling in the distant call of white-winged doves. The valley had not yet been converted into groves of citrus. It was mostly brushland and new farms. Wildlife was still in abundance. The buzzard still sailed the skies looking for dead and dying creatures.

In that state I reasoned that if I were dying there must be buzzards high in the sky, watching and waiting. I rolled over onto my back, searching. All I saw was the open sky and a swarm of flies from the nearby latrine. I remember thinking what an ignoble way this was for it all to end. Could it be that not even the buzzards cared? Better to have fallen on Corregidor. And who, if anyone, would tell my mother? How could I ever finally tell my father how sorry I was for being such a disobedient son?

Suddenly, through the swarm of flies, loomed the bearded face of Roy Creecy. The present was back. He ordered me to get up and walk. I told him I couldn't. He said I must, and pulled me up. With one arm around his shoulders I made it back to the barrack. He had seen me fall, he said, and came as quickly as he could. It had seemed much longer.

At that time there was a practice among the prisoners of taking bits of charcoal, pounding the bits into a powder, mixing it with water, and drinking it as a remedy for diarrhea. I don't know that it ever did any good, but some said it did and that was enough. Also, there was a tree growing not far from the barracks, and from it prisoners would strip the leaves and boil them into a kind of tea which was supposed to be helpful. It was terrible tasting stuff, but possibly it helped, for the diarrhea did slack off and quit. And, as luck would have it, the Japanese brought in a few food supplies captured somewhere and turned them over to the American doctors for use by those who were most ill. In terms of medication, it was about all the doctors had to pass out.

Among the supplies were a few cans of condensed milk. Our barrack was determined to have ten who would probably not make it unless help could be given quickly. A doctor named Brown made the selection. He looked at my eyes, the color of my skin, asked about the color of my urine, took my temperature, and made his decision. I and the other nine selected would receive one can each meal to share. That allowed about three teaspoons for each man to add to his allowance of rice. As one would die, or become better, the remaining milk would be divided between the others. It reached the point where one other man and I shared one can. There were only a few days of that comparative luxury before the supply was gone, but by then our condition was much improved and the future less bleak. The fever never left entirely, seeming to go up during the day and down during the night. But now I was mobile and began to take my turn on work details into the hills for wood.

By then prisoners from Camp O'Donnell, those captured on Bataan, had been transferred to the completed Camp #1 nearby. Filipino prisoners had been freed, or paroled, not out of any humanitarian instincts, but simply because it was much cheaper to scatter them to their homes and let them feed themselves. Besides, they were in no physical shape to pose a threat.

Those transferred to Camp #1 were in even worse condition than those of us in Camp #3, according to all we heard, and the pressure to attempt escape that much greater. When they entered the new camp they came under the general rules and regulations that governed us in Camp #3 including the rule that nine would be shot if one escaped. Evidently at least one man was not yet a believer, and nine were shot.

The news spread like wildfire and had its intended effect. At that time there was little, if any, structured communication between the two camps despite their closeness. The Japanese did all they could to prevent contact and communications, in line with their general rule of keeping the enlisted prisoners separated from their senior officers and divided psychologically among themselves. Nevertheless, "grapevines" were established and word passed. The net result of the executions was to cause prisoners to constantly try to keep track of the other nine men in one's own group, lest one be missing at roll call. It also had the effect of allowing two or three guards to take 150 or more men into the hills on work detail without worrying about anyone disappearing into the forest.

Seen in retrospect, the Japanese did everything possible to reduce what was once a proud fighting force to utter submission, powerlessness, humiliation, and dependency. We were told we were not even to be considered as prisoners of war, that we were "guests of the emperor," and that our fate depended on his benevolence. The ultimate insult was added to injury as armed guards paraded through camp with folded American flags, which they would unfold with great delight, lay upon the ground, and use as a tablecloth for their evening meal while sullen prisoners stared helplessly. We were, no doubt, being conditioned for the years ahead. They had won the battle and believed they would ultimately win the war. At that point they had no reason to think otherwise.

I'm not at all sure that every cloud has a silver lining, but some do. In this case the "guest of the emperor" bit did inject a note of humor into a situation sorely lacking in humor. It gave the men something to joke about, a way to find a degree of humor in their own condition. And since humor is good at relieving tensions, it was called upon in all sorts of situations. The scarcity of food was attributed to the emperor's concern that his guests not become overweight and slothful, the rigid security measures to the emperor's concern that his guests not wander unknowingly into the forests, where they might run afoul of unfriendly natives. It was for our own good that we learned how to be humble before the Japanese. This would be important in the future. Truly he must be our friend and benefactor. For, after all, not everyone could someday boast that he had been a guest of the emperor of Japan. We were most fortunate to have such a host. So it went.

The human mind has, or seems to have, its own way of comporting to the reality of its surrounding. Many years later I would be amused, then perplexed, then disgusted, at the pronouncements of any number of "social scientists," securely tenured in some university somewhere, as they sought to explain human behavior on the basis of observations of rodents, dogs, cats, chimpanzees, or assorted members of their own grouping. Here, in the confines of barbed wire and guard towers, thousands of men lived under controlled conditions. They had practically no communication with the outside world. They had no radio, no newspapers, no television. They went to bed at the same hour. They arose at the same hour. They ate the same food. They lived under the same rules and regulations. Not only were individuals punished, but groups were punished for the infractions of individuals. Every effort was made on the part of the captors to destroy individuality and instill uniformity. Yet individuality persisted. It not only persisted, but in its own way it blossomed as men sought, perhaps unknowingly, to maintain both their existence and their identity.

Every day "Good Deal" Brill made his rounds, hawking his wares. I know nothing of his background, other than that he was from one of the burroughs of New York City and that he was Jewish, information which for some reason he felt necessary to make known to his prospective customers. His wares consisted of spoons, canteen cups, perhaps the lid of a canteen, a fork or two, just about anything he had traded for. Money, in addition to being practically nonexistent, was of little use within the camp. But the utensils of everyday prison life did have some utility, and Brill became the recognized vehicle for exchange. Personal possessions of prisoners were meager at best, but as they died their belongings would be taken over by friends who would distribute them to other friends in need. Sometimes men would end up with more of some items than needed. This was where Brill came in.

The first time I saw Brill he showed up at our barrack with only a few items, looking for trades. He set his own value on the items — a good spoon might be worth two forks, a canteen might be worth two canteen cups. Nevertheless, any item he offered for trade was always a "very good deal" for the other. He repeated the phrase so often it became his trademark.

Within a few months Brill had become a walking magpie. The last time I remember seeing him, he had items of every description penned, sewn, or otherwise attached to his clothing, making his rounds, drumming up trades, clanging as he walked. I still had the five-peso bill that I had gotten by with on Corregidor, and on that occasion traded it to Brill for a few ounces of salt. I have no idea where he got the salt, nor do I know to what use the money was put, but the salt served me well for many weeks.

I do not know whether Good Deal Brill survived the camps, or if he, like so many others, gave up the ghost in that camp or some other, or on some prison ship headed for still another camp. But I do believe that when his time came, if it came, he was still Good Deal Brill, looking for a trade.

The question arises: Why did he act as he did? Why seek to accumulate items for which he had no use? He could, after all, use only one spoon. He could go nowhere. He could not trade for food, for at that time men would fight over food, certainly not trade it away. Nothing he had would make life easier for him. So why?

Perhaps it was his way of trying to preserve his individuality, his identity. I doubt that it was a conscious effort. More likely it was the outgrowth of a deep desire to excel in something he knew he could be good at, and, in the process, to gain a certain amount of respect from others despite the ludicrous appearance he exhibited on occasions. In the end he benefited, as did others.

In this fashion the camp took on its own life. In the morning the dead were buried. Work details were assembled and sent to the hills. Others were assigned duty in camp. Still others merely struggled for existence and waited. The wait wouldn't be long, surely. Within a matter of a few months it would all be over, the tanks and planes would come. All we had to do was hold on a little longer. Someday soon there would be plenty to eat, a bed to sleep in, a chair to sit on. Someday soon it would not be imperative that we stand at rigid attention and bow low when a Japanese came within view.

It was the evenings that made life bearable. Then, after the last meal and before the day was done, men would gather in small groups and discuss matters of great moment, of days gone by and days to come, of dreams and hopes. And to contemplate what strange quirks of fate had brought us where we were.

Little "ifs" seem to loom large in our lives, though they often go unrecognized at the time. In my own mind I reasoned that if things had gone differently on a certain day at Thomas Jefferson High School in San Antonio, I would not be where I was . . .

The so-called Great Depression was upon the land. After struggling for years with its effects, my father had finally lost the farm and we had moved to San Antonio, where he found some acreage south of town on the Medina River, in the process making the humiliating transition from farm owner to sharecropper. A comparably well-educated man himself, he put great stock in learning and therefore found a home in the city, near schools. He daily made the trip back and forth to the new farm, trying to get it organized. The plan was that we would ultimately move to the farm, once things settled down.

Obviously, it was a traumatic experience for everyone. The school year had begun, so it meant not only leaving friends and familiar surroundings, but entering a world we had never known. I enrolled in Thomas Jefferson High School at age fourteen, in a school that was entirely different from that in Raymondville. The kids were well dressed, the floors were polished tile. I was addressed as "Mr. Towery" by the teachers. The curriculum involved subjects we had not troubled with in the valley, including a course in botany. It was the closest thing they could offer, they said, to courses in agriculture-related subjects I had studied at Raymondville. I took it, and took a seat in the back of the class in an effort to go unnoticed.

At the end of the first week, on Friday, the teacher called on me to describe some particular microbe. I did not know the answer, and said so. She reminded me the answer was in the assigned reading for that day, and finally, when she had completed her lecture, pointedly said, "Mr. Towery, we study here at Thomas Jefferson."

I had always tried to be a somewhat studious pupil, reading nearly anything I could get my hands on, other than Shakespeare (whom I had not yet learned to appreciate). The teacher's remarks humiliated me beyond measure. Never mind that I could perhaps blame my own ignorance at the time on the turmoil of our move, trying to get settled into a new home, adjusting to conditions I had never known. She knew only two things: She had made an assignment that was not carried out, and she was going to make an example for the rest of the class. I could feel the gaze from other students as the new kid, fresh from the brush country of the Texas–Mexico border, exposed his dumbness. It was a humiliation I was not going to go through again. By day's end I had decided I would never go back to that class.

By the time I got home that evening, my plans were formed. When darkness came I took an apple and a change of clothes, stole out of the house, walked across town to the railroad yards, and waited for a freight train headed south. I knew nothing of which train went where, but inquiry among others also waiting indicated that a Missouri–Pacific, or "Mo-Pac" as they called it, would be the best bet. One came by, I caught it, climbed up the ladder into an empty refrigerator compartment, and the next day found myself in familiar surroundings. I walked to the golf course in Raymondville and asked the manager for permission to sleep there at nights. I had caddied there quite often when duties on the farm were slack. Indeed, at one time we had farmed the acreage before it was turned into a golf course. The area now encompassed by fairways one, two, and three were our horse pastures, the rest devoted to crops of various kinds.

According to my own immature and tortured reasoning, I would make enough money by caddying after school to pay for food and whatever else I might need. The lodging would be free.

Monday morning found me back in my old class, much to the surprise, and probable consternation, of classmates and teachers I had left a week before. My explanation was that I had just decided to come back because I liked it better.

The ensuing weeks were not easy. I did manage to keep up my studies, but the business of trying to eat off the proceeds of caddying at a country golf course was not a financially rewarding experience. There were hungry days and lonesome nights.

Two older brothers had remained in the valley, and no doubt the word passed quickly where I was. But to his credit my father did not come running. He reasoned, I suppose, that it would be better to let me sweat awhile, to allow time for me to see the error of my ways.

My father was a believer in the "spare the rod, spoil the child" school of thought, or at least that was the impression gained over the years by six brothers and two sisters. But when he did show up, a few weeks later, it was not to harangue. He merely asked how I was getting along, and said that my mother missed me and wanted me to know that she hoped I would come home. I told him I didn't want to go back to Thomas Jefferson, and in fact wasn't going to go back to it. He did not insist, repeating that my mother wanted me home. There was, in truth, a terrible longing to be home. Back with my parents, my brothers. It was merely the thought of that school, that teacher, that humiliation, that had stood in the way. We returned together, my mother kissed me, told me she was happy, and nothing more was said. It was nice to be home.

Within a matter of weeks I "hired out" on a stock farm in DeWitt County, near the small town of Yorktown, and passed the winter there. The farm was owned and operated by two German brothers named Toerck and their wives, who were sisters. They were hardworking, wonderful people, but different. They poured syrup on their sausage. And where we had always preserved our meat by salting or canning, they preferred the smokehouse — that and sausage. They wasted nothing. When time came to kill hogs, everything but the

THE CHOW DIPPER

squeal found its way into something that would later be consumed, from pickled pigs' feet to smoked ham to a sort of sausage made from all manner of leftovers. Since my pay consisted of room and board, and a dollar or two now and then, I saw to it that I ate well and slept well, except for the infernal ticks and chimes of ancient German clocks that seemed to be everywhere.

A man named Hitler had come to power in Germany, and the two brothers, Rudolph and Henry Toerck, would frequently gather around a shortwave radio and listen as he addressed crowds of cheering Germans. Shaking heads and worried looks usually followed. I once asked what it was all about. Trouble, I was told, nothing but trouble. They regarded Hitler as a demagogue, a "national socialist" who spelled trouble for the German people, and probably the world. They had no use for socialism, either the nationalist kind or the international kind. The idea of a national socialist workers party was worrisome, even if it might be helping the German nation stand on its own feet. At fourteen years of age I did not understand, and could hardly have cared less. What happened a world away was of no concern to me, and I couldn't understand why it concerned them.

By early spring the farm on the Medina was ready. I took my leave of the Toercks and rejoined the family there. It was a wonderful life for a youngster. Two hundred acres of fields to work in, 500 acres of pasture to hunt in, and a clear, flowing river to swim in. The farmhouse was small, old, and unpainted. Household water came from rainwater, collected in a cistern that caught runoff from the roof. There was no electricity. All in all it was not unlike the home we had left in the valley, except there we had to haul our household water.

A new high school, called Luther Burbank, opened in town on what had been a seventy-five-acre vegetable farm run by Belgians, and I enrolled there. No bus route extended to our farm, so my father daily took my younger brother James and me to school, dropping him off at Harlandale and myself at Burbank. It was a good school, much more to my liking, in a working-class neighborhood. And while it had the usual high school curricula, it also had a heavy emphasis on vocational and industrial education. I did well and the world looked good.

It did not last long. We managed to get in one crop and were preparing for another when word came that the farm had been sold and we must leave. My father, with the help of a sympathetic banker, bought a small house in town for $2,000, on a street then called Dittmar, just off South Flores Street, within walking distance of school. We moved there, along with a few chickens, a milk cow, and, of all things, a young horse we had raised from a colt in the valley. He was part of the family. The cow was led daily down to the banks of the San Pedro River, where she passed the time grazing and doing what cows do. My mother began selling eggs, milk, and butter to the neighbors. My father, finally reaching the depths of those years, was forced to begin working for the government. A skilled carpenter and builder, he found employment on a public works project, building barracks at a nearby army air force base.

It was then, finally, that I began to comprehend the silent suffering of my parents. My father, according to family lore, had been a person of some substance in his native Monroe County, Mississippi, where his father and grandfather were buried. He was a surveyor, a county supervisor, an owner of sawmills, and an employer of many hill country folk. Since he had a better education than most in that vicinity, he also took his turn at teaching school. Then a great storm, probably what is known today as a hurricane, swept through the area, spawning tornadoes, killing many, laying waste to the countryside, and destroying vast tracts of timber on which the sawmills depended. It would be years before the trees grew. The only thing to do, if his children were to have a future, was go somewhere else.

He looked at Florida and didn't like what he saw. He had heard great things of Texas, where many in the extended family had gone long before. The Rio Grande Valley was being opened up. Land was available. There one could grow three crops each year. It must have sounded very promising. He sawed enough lumber for two houses, ordered it shipped, loaded his family on Model-T Ford trucks, and set out. Then, within a matter of ten years, the economy essentially collapsed. Now he was reduced to this. For the first time I could see some of his own humiliation. Perhaps I was getting older.

The desire to go back to the farm, to be his own man, evidently never left him, however, for he kept searching for another place, which he finally found some fifteen miles down the Medina from the farm we had left. It would be available "sometime soon." In the meantime, I was preparing for my senior year.

It became obvious, even to a teenager, that the family was struggling. I decided to enter the Civilian Conservation Corps, generally known as the CCC. It would afford the family another $22 each month, and give me $8 a month. With a great deal of reluctance, and some argument, my parents agreed. They thought I should continue in school, no matter how hard things were. My argument was that it would help out, and I could always get an education later.

It was a good experience. The work was hard, the food was good, the discipline strict. The camp, located in a national forest fifteen or so miles east of Crockett, Texas, was run by one retired army captain and a few helpers, mostly from the Forest Service. We built roads through the forest, fought fires, planted trees. For those of us who wished, there were classes at night. To duplicate the effort today would require a host of government bureaucrats, social workers, counselors. Congressmen might even get involved. Highly paid network TV types would be in abundance, complaining that we were being forced to work too hard, that not enough attention was being paid to the finer things of life, that black people were in one camp and white people in another, that actually the whole thing was a scheme by Roosevelt to condition us for war. But for us things went well. With the monthly $8 that came to us we paid for our laundry, our haircuts, and whatever other incidentals we might require. The rest we could save, or squander on frivolities. I saved.

Christmas approached. I asked for leave to go home. It was granted. I went to Crockett, thinking I could catch a freight train from there. There were no trains. The nearest rail line went through a town called Jewett, some sixty miles north. I hitchhiked there and waited for a train. It was bitterly cold, snow was on the ground, I was running fever with a case of flu or something, but I was determined to be home for Christmas. The rail ran parallel to the highway. The train never came but a truck did, and I caught a ride to Austin, where I boarded a freight train on the north bank of the Colorado River headed for San Antonio. Many years later, while dining in the Governor's Mansion in Austin, I would silently reflect upon that incident. I had boarded the freight no more than twelve blocks away. I said nothing about it to the governor and his friends.

But now is not then. The train lumbered into San Antonio with a boxcar half full of fellow travelers. As we approached the city a Mexican man, anxious to be the first off, stood in the doorway, with his arms spread-eagled, one hand holding each side of the opening. Others crowded close behind. The train slowed, but not slow enough to satisfy the first in line. Shouts arose for him to jump, lest the train enter the freight yards and the domain of the "yard bulls," the railroad security force. He held on, fearful of making the jump. Someone planted a foot in his back and kicked him out. He tumbled down the rocky embankment and the rest followed. We walked away, and I presume he did also.

I walked across town to home. It was a wonderful Christmas. In another month I would be seventeen years old.

In the spring my enlistment was up and I returned home. By then the family had taken over the new farm. I could be of some help. At best, though, it was a shoestring operation. Working capital was scarce. A few cows, a few sows, a few scattered rains do not add up to much on a dry land farm. Fortunately my father had kept his job in town, for in time it became apparent the venture was not going to be successful. The price of cattle and hogs was hardly enough to pay for the food they consumed, much less provide food for others. I began looking elsewhere for work.

It was a time of much wandering, of many freight trains and much hitchhiking. On one such trip to South Texas, during the fall, I caught a ride with a Californian, in Texas on vacation. He was somewhat crippled in his left leg and wanted someone to help with the driving. He was to tour the valley and return to California, where he was a union electrician with the Holly Sugar Beet company. As he would tell me, on the way to the valley, he was a committed socialist. He did not call himself a Communist, but he spoke highly of the society the Communists had built in the Soviet Union. There was justice. There the workers ran things. And socialism was coming to America too, he said, but not without much turmoil. Roosevelt's policies, he said, were merely designed to protect capitalism. But it would only slow, not prevent, the coming struggle. The best place for me to be during that time of upheaval, according to him, would be in the army. That would be the safest place. In the meantime I might find work in California. He had heard that some of the aircraft factories might be hiring. Perhaps I should check it out.

By the time we got to Edinburg, we had made a deal. If I found nothing in the area I would join him, at a predesignated place. I would do the driving to California.

He seemed a good man, a decent man, but one obsessed with politics. For five days I heard little but predictions of the glorious day when socialism would eradicate the world's ills.

It was at least different. Politics was never discussed in our family. I occasionally heard my father talk politics with his peers, but it was not a subject of household conversation. He was a Jeffersonian

THE CHOW DIPPER

Democrat, a "states rights" Democrat who, being a Democrat, voted for Roosevelt twice but was troubled by his seeming lust for personal power. I did hear him say that neither Roosevelt nor anyone else ought to have three terms. I don't know what he did when faced with that prospect, for the feeling of party loyalty was exceedingly strong at the time. Indeed, while local politics was discussed in terms of personalities, national politics was discussed in terms of party identification. It was very important, according to those running for office, that white people remain in office. And the only way to be sure that white people remained in power, and the "niggers" kept in their proper place, was to vote Democratic.

We parted company in a town called Santa Anna. He returned to his job and I scouted for work. The aircraft factories were indeed hiring a few helpers, but first there was a small hitch. One had to belong to the union, and that would cost $165. I did not have the money. No problem, I could pay it out over a period of time, along with my dues. I do not remember the pay but it sounded very good, considering that my last job was driving a tractor at fifteen cents an hour. But somehow, at the time, I could not see the propriety, or the morality, of having to pay one group of people for the privilege of working for another group of people.

I caught a freight to Yuma, Arizona, and there found a railroad tank car loaded with 9,000 gallons of wine consigned to a distributor in San Antonio. I figured if I stayed with that car I would make it fine. The Arizona desert is a beautiful sight under a full moon, as are the slopes of the mountains in New Mexico. Contemplation, under the circumstances then prevailing, came easily. This was not a way to spend one's time and ever hope to get anywhere. Perhaps the electrician was right. Perhaps the army would be a good place to spend some time, not for the reasons he advanced but for any number of other reasons. It at least deserved some thought.

By the time I arrived home, the idea had pretty well jelled. I discussed it with my parents, who were not terribly impressed with the thought. My father thought war was probably coming, despite Roosevelt's solemn campaign promise that he would never, no never, send an American boy to fight and die on foreign battlefields. But his reasoning was that it would be far better to enlist in the National Guard, rather than the army. That way I could at least stay around home until there was some sort of general mobilization. My mother, of course, wanted her son close. In the end they acquiesced, and on my eighteenth birthday I visited Fort Sam Houston to inquire about the formalities. The army was even more anxious than I, and a few days later I arrived at Angel Island in San Francisco Bay en route to the Philippines.

So, little "ifs," little quirks of fate do indeed have a bearing on our lives, particularly when they are helped along with stubbornness and stupidity. There I sat, in a prison camp near Cabanatuan in central Luzon, wondering if things were to get better or worse.

In October word passed that the Japanese were to select a group to go to another camp. No one knew where, or when, or who would go. Rumor soon had it that the group would go to Japan, then the southern islands, then here, then there. One prisoner even had it on the highest authority, a prison guard, that we would go where the weather was cold and the people ate black bread. Surely that could not be true, for where in the Orient was there such a place, where the Japanese held sway? A degree of excitement fueled mostly by apprehension permeated the camp. Some feared to go; others feared to stay. Within a matter of days it all came to a head. A group of 1,500 of the healthiest were to be selected. This meant, or seemed to mean, that physical labor was to be involved. That meant, or it might mean, that the food would be better. Surely they could not expect any sustained labor out of starving men.

There was a desire among the various cadres to stick together if at all possible. Turner, Creecy, Williams, and I were all on the list to go, provided that the doctor would clear us as being physically fit for the venture. In my own case I was running a fever of 101 when checked the day before we were to leave. The doctor, an American named Brown, told me I would not have to go, unless I wanted to. The fever would be sufficient grounds for rejection, and someone else could take my place. I asked for guidance. He could give none.

He knew what we all knew. The mathematics of prison life stared us in the face. The daily death rate was not improving. The food supply was not improving. We were essentially powerless to change any part of the equation. The next camp might be worse, but it might be better. We chose the hope.

The march from camp to Cabanatuan was made in darkness. It was what was known as a "forced march," fast with no rest. Again the boxcars, this time back to Manila. Evening found us on the docks of Pier Seven, hungry and completely exhausted, alongside a ship called the *Tottori Maru*. There we were given a ration of what I regarded as the worst to that time, dried, salty fish boiled into a mush of bones and rotten odor. For those of us already in the early stages of scurvy, it was sheer torture. Small sores had begun to appear inside my mouth and around my lips. Every bite was an excursion into misery. Finally, I merely put the bones in my mouth and sucked the juices.

We spent a night or two on the docks, waiting for the arrival of other prisoners who were supposed to join us from the southern islands, and finally boarded the ship. Officially, we were 31 officers and 1,962 enlisted men. A few hundred Japanese soldiers boarded as well. They took the aft part of the ship. The prisoners were forward. I don't remember exactly what day it was. My own notes say we left camp on October 6, 1942. That would have us leaving the Philippines on the seventh. But the official version, compiled by the War Department after the war, had us leaving on the tenth day of October.

The date bore little relevance then and bears little now. Then, every day was just another day through which we hoped to live, and from which we hoped to escape.

FIVE

Voyage to Uncertainty

The *Tottori Maru* was not much of a ship. In fact, there were those aboard, knowledgeable in such matters, who called it a thin-hulled tub. In its previous life it had been a British cargo vessel, probably plying the waters between Malaya and the various ports of England, carrying whatever the trade demanded. The Japanese took control of it, so the story went, when they captured Singapore. It was converted into a troop transport, of sorts, whether for the movement of prisoners or short-haul movement of their own troops, I do not know. The forward "hold," that portion of the ship where bulk cargo had been carried, was used for the prisoners. Within it were multi-tiered "bays," which allowed room for prisoners to sit but not stand. Approximately four feet separated the floor of one bay from the floor of the bay just above. Each prisoner was allowed about twelve inches between himself and the next. Needless to say, it was an extremely crowded situation.

The ship left Manila Bay through the North Channel, between Corregidor and Bataan. The island still bore evidence of its recent past, but one thing was apparent. The green was coming back, the jungle was taking over. That, at least, made me happy. My own private hopes were that the island could forever rest in its memories, and, in the doing, hold fast the memories of those resting with it. I would not see the island again, or set foot on it, for a quarter century.

We cleared the channel, entered the South China Sea, and turned north. Good. Perhaps it would be cooler where we were going.

The men normally lay with their feet to the bulkhead and their head toward the central hold area. This allowed a bit of air in the oppressive heat and stifling air conditions. Within a few days the heat would be no problem, but for the moment it was.

Men were allowed access to the deck, but little room was there. The deck was also where latrines had been placed, and it soon became necessary for the port side of the deck to be reserved for the lines of men taking turns at the latrines. As the number of those suffering from dysentery and diarrhea grew, some would simply leave the latrine and go to the end of the line, knowing that by the time they had worked their way back to the front of the line, it would be that time again. Within a short time the whole area became a slippery, filthy mess, as some managed to make it and others didn't. It was an area to be avoided, unless one had business there.

I remember the day but not the date the first man died and was buried at sea. The thought of spending eternity among the sharks, squid, and plankton of the sea seemed so alien to mankind's makeup. And I remember that it seemed too soon. I never thought we would make the trip, which rumor had it would take some ten days, without some deaths. By then days without deaths were rare indeed. I just never thought they would start so soon. I was wrong, as I have quite often been.

Our rations for the trip were not memorable, but I do recall that we were daily given some dry, salt-free crackers. They were small, round, on the order of soup crackers. That, and water, was our sustenance. I would take the crackers, soak them in a canteen cup of water, add a few grains of my precious salt, and that would be the meal. It is possible we occasionally got some rice. A note found in my files years after the event says we were given a meal of rice on October 15 in the port of Takao, Formosa, but if so the memory would not last for me. All I can remember are crackers, water, and the blessed salt.

The ship plowed northward, along the coast of Luzon and into the Straits of Formosa. The weather cooled considerably and the seas roughened.

Suddenly, perhaps the second or third day, there was a scream of "Torpedo!" from prisoners on the deck. Those prisoners below, hundreds of them, immediately rushed to a few narrow passageways leading from the holds to the deck. In an instant the way was blocked. Pandemonium broke out as men sought ways to get out of the hold. I don't know why, but we thought we would fare better on the deck than in the hold.

In the center of the hold was an opening or hatchway, some

twenty feet square, through which cargo had been lowered and removed during the ship's previous incarnation. Across this opening ran a large steel beam extending to the bulkhead on either side of the ship. I presume its purpose was to reinforce the hold area and strengthen that part of the ship. On the floor of the hold, around which the prisoners' sleeping quarters were built, lay a small pile of life jackets. There were only forty or fifty, and would have made scant difference to the hundreds assigned to that hold, but for the moment they were terribly important.

Like everyone else my first reaction was to rush for the ladders leading up to the deck. Seeing there was no hope there, I turned to the central cargo area, thinking I could perhaps reach the beam crossing the hatchway. Even by standing on top of the life preservers, there was no way.

And by then there were prisoners ringing the hatchway, screaming for life preservers. Without thinking much beyond the moment, I began tossing up life jackets. Perhaps I could help a few. Then the thought hit me: What am I doing here? I had better look to my own safety.

Straddling the beam immediately above me was a young, blond prisoner with a terrified look about his countenance, leaning down with arms outstretched, screaming for a jacket. He had missed one of those already thrown up, as another prisoner grabbed it and disappeared toward the side.

I grabbed two jackets, one for me and one for him. Holding the end of one jacket, I tossed him the other end of the same jacket. If he wanted it he would have to pull me up. He pulled me far enough to grab the beam. I let go his jacket and climbed up and out.

I hurriedly cleared the hatchway before looking to sea, in the direction other prisoners were pointing amidst the general shouting. There, heading for the ship's port side from about a 45-degree angle to the stern, two torpedoes were making their run. One was slightly in front of the other and appeared aimed at the ship's midsection. The other, perhaps 50 yards behind, appeared to be headed for the ship's stern. At that point they had almost completed their journey and were about 200 yards away.

The sea was rough and the old ship lumbered in the heavy swells. The lead torpedo was casting heavy spray, making it all the more terrifying to those like myself who had never seen one in action. The other must have been running slightly deeper, for its spray was only seen occasionally. I awaited what appeared to be the inevitable, praying, I am sure, that a joking remark by a prisoner as we boarded the ship would come true. He had quipped that "the hull of this tub is so thin a torpedo would probably go all the way through without exploding." A wish is often the father of thought.

Then, for reasons no one knew at the time, the lead torpedo stopped casting its spray. Whether it was continuing its course slightly deeper or had simply quit is unknown, at least to me.

The other kept coming. I do not remember any great commotion among the prisoners. There was just this terrible silence as men braced for the expected. Then, at the top of one of the huge swells, the captain swung the lumbering old tub hard to starboard. The stern swung to port side in the bottom of the swell, and the torpedo passed harmlessly behind. I cannot remember, but I suppose there was cheering. One thing I do remember, however, is that I was terrified. It is one thing to view danger with means at hand to perhaps counter that danger. It is quite another to toss helplessly in a vast ocean while imminent destruction bears down.

We were accompanied, at a distance, by small subchasers. They immediately headed for the area the torpedoes apparently came from and began making their circles and dropping depth charges, replete with erupting geysers.

It was with mixed emotions that we witnessed the scene. No one wished them to succeed in their task, but I suppose most shared my own thoughts. I hoped the sub would survive, but I also hoped we would be left alone. There was no thought of placing blame. The submarine and its crew were merely doing their duty. Our prison ship, contrary to all the international rules of warfare at the time, was unmarked. For all appearances it was a cargo ship heading for Japan. In the rules of warfare it was fair game.

We continued the journey in rough seas. The next day we stopped and lay at anchor off an island near the southern coast of Formosa. The weather turned cold, or at least it seemed cold to those of us still in light tropical clothing. The wind was from the northwest, coming, according to those who knew the geography of the area better than I, from mainland China.

The ship lay at anchor for days, tossing and straining at the end of its tether. Word passed that the reason for the delay was the presence of submarines in the area. We were in a heavy Japanese shipping lane, where a multitude of ships plied the waters between the conquered territory to the south and their homeports to the north. The captain had orders to lay at anchor and wait until conditions were better.

Finally, we resumed the journey, putting in at the port of Takao in Formosa. It was a beautiful harbor. In fact, at the time I could not imagine a more beautiful place on earth, except, perhaps, the brush country of South Texas. The weather had warmed considerably and we were taken off the ship for unexplained reasons. Probably it was to take on supplies, since the original plan called for some ten days at sea and we had already consumed those.

Some of us, perhaps all of us, were doused with water and given various examinations. There were those who thought our captors were trying to determine if we were fit to continue the journey. It was probably a bunch of medical interns being exposed to diseases and conditions they had never seen. I don't remember anything ever coming from it, although a small group of fourteen were taken to a hospital, having been classified as unfit to continue the journey.

While in port someone picked up a rumor that another prison ship had gone down in the same waters. The date was uncertain. One account had it a few days before our own narrow escape. Another a day or two later. At any rate, most thought it was merely a rumor spread by our captors to further the intimidation process, to keep the prisoners terrified and therefore more manageable. In future years we would find that it was in fact true — 1,773 prisoners had gone down. Seven prisoners survived the sinking. They, too, were traveling in an unmarked ship.

We boarded ship and continued the journey, but not for long. Apparently the subs were still waiting. Either that or they couldn't make up their minds where we were to go. After about a day we returned to port. Another day there and it was again to sea. After more delays and seemingly aimless wandering in the waters around Formosa, the ship headed north, toward the home waters of Japan. By then most assumed that Japan was our destination, and for some it was. In cold and stormy weather the ship put in at Kobe, Japan, and 16 officers and 569 enlisted men were "transferred to a Fusan Hospital," physically unfit to continue the journey (according to the War Department's Liaison and Research Branch of the American Prisoner of War Information Bureau, compiled by Capt. James I. Norwood and Capt. Emily L. Shek and issued in July 1946).

Again to sea. The weather grew colder and eventually, almost one month to the day after we left Manila, landfall was made at Pusan,

---

Korea. We left ship and assembled for another of those marches through the city, accompanied by a show of force on the part of the Japanese army and much blaring from truck-mounted loudspeakers, reminding the populous again of the invincibility of their own troops and the vulnerability of the Americans. The world was their oyster.

When that was over, things began looking up. We were issued warmer clothing, put on a train with real passenger cars, and given strange tasting food that all seemed to come out of a pickle jar. The blinds were drawn so we could not see the country we were going through. We left on the final leg of our destination at nightfall, still not knowing where that would be.

By then another group of men, around sixty according to my memory, were too ill to continue the journey, even by our captors' standards. We were told they would remain in Korea until they recovered, if they recovered. They were to join us in our new camp. By November 11, 1942, we had traversed the length of Korea, crossed the Yalu, entered upon the plains of Manchuria, and arrived at Mukden's Hoten Prison Camp #1.

Of the 1,993 who began the voyage, we were now 1,188 enlisted men and 14 officers.

SIX

Chow Dipper Among Starving Men

The commander droned on and on. There was much he had to tell us. This may well be a war that lasted a thousand years, he said, but in the end Japan would be victorious, no matter what.

Occasionally he would pause for his interpreter, Corporal Noda. We marveled at the man's fluency in our own native tongue. Indeed, he handled the English language better than most of his listeners. He would paraphrase the colonel with phrases like, "The commander says you must be aware . . ."

We would soon find out why his diction was so good, why he was so knowledgeable in the language, why he used colloquialisms so frequently and in the right places. He was born in America, went to the finest California schools, and was a graduate of the University of California at Berkeley. He had concluded he was more Japanese than American and returned to the land of his fathers, where he joined the army to contribute his bit to the glory of the emperor. In time we would also learn that he was one of our worst enemies. He understood how we thought, how we would react. Too, it would become apparent he had to prove he had no love for the Americans just because he was born there and went to school there. Indeed, just the opposite.

Suddenly, the commander stopped in midsentence. For an instant he craned his neck and peered over the standing prisoners. Then he began pointing toward the rear ranks, screaming as he did so. A bevy of armed guards hastened to the area of his concern.

A prisoner, stricken with dysentery and too ill to stand longer, had fallen from ranks and was relieving himself at the base of a nearby tree.

The prisoner was hustled away by guards. The commander was still screaming as they disappeared toward the barracks we would soon occupy.

Corporal Noda then informed us that it was impermissible for a prisoner to relieve himself when the commander was speaking. Such acts were insulting to the dignity of the commander. Furthermore, when the commander was speaking we must all pay strict attention. Failure to do so, he said, would result in the severest of punishments.

The incident seemed to break the old man's train of thought and finally we were told to break ranks, that we would now receive our numbers. We had been numbered before, in Cabanatuan, but these were to be our permanent numbers.

Creecy, Turner, Williams, and I huddled to assess the situation. Perhaps it would be important somewhere along the line that we have numbers close together. We understood this was to be our permanent camp, but who could tell? By this time there were few things we could be sure of, other than our position in the world that awaited. The commander had made that plain enough.

We stuck together like fleas during the numbering process and ended up with Williams numbered 856, Turner 857, I got 858, and Creecy 860. Another prisoner, named Cook, somehow got between Creecy and myself and ended up with 859. No matter, we were happy with our luck. For a few months it would be important.

We were then divided into groups of about ninety and marched to our quarters. I ended up in Barracks #11, along with Creecy, Turner, Williams, and Cook. We entered the barracks by number, taking space in order. Our cell was still intact.

The camp gave every indication of having been used before, probably by the Japanese army or its puppet Manchu army. The barracks were long, low, and doubled walled, with the space between the walls filled with dirt. The roof was likewise covered with dirt. An entrance was near the center of the building, and near either end were "storm" entrances, with the outside door opening into a small room, off of which one door opened into a room probably occupied in a previous era by noncommissioned officers. Another door opened into the quarters we would occupy. Some of our own senior noncoms would occupy the small room; the larger area was for the rest of us.

Down the center of the building ran a walkway, perhaps five feet wide. On either side of the walkway a floor had been constructed, approximately two feet above the walkway. Against the wall was a shelf running the length of the building. Each prisoner had enough space on the floor for his straw mattress and enough space on the shelf for his personal belongings. About twelve to eighteen inches separated the space allotted to each prisoner.

In the center of the walkway stood a stove, or what passed for a stove. It was constructed of bricks, some three feet high and perhaps four feet long. The rules said that when the temperature dropped to 14 degrees on the Centigrade scale, coal would be issued. It was a rule honored occasionally, and with limited coal. The bricks never, in my memory, got hot. But they did get warm enough that one could lean against them for a period and absorb a few degrees of heat. Part of the top of the stove was made of cast iron, and this portion did sometimes get hot, a fact that was made use of on many occasions as time went on.

The winters of Manchuria and the winters of Siberia are separated only by the Amur River. It was November and the ground was already frozen at the surface. Within a matter of days, winter had begun in earnest.

To our captors' credit it would have to be said we were provided with enough woolen blankets to survive the winter, had the food been adequate. Whether by accident, snafu, or design, we were given six good quality woolen blankets, meaning we had something to sleep on as well as sleep under. We were issued one change of woolen underwear, a pair of hob-nailed leather shoes, and woolen socks.

The food was a different matter. The first meal was terrible, and following months afforded little change. The one staple in the diet was a tasteless grain called kaioliang, not unlike a grain grown in other parts of the world, called hygeria in South Texas and commonly used for feeding chickens or farm animals. The grain was boiled, sometimes with a little cabbage, sometimes a few carrots, into a sort of soup which was ladled out to the prisoners, about one-half canteen cup per meal. It was a diet almost completely devoid of protein, animal or vegetable. It would not be too much of an exaggeration to say it was also devoid of calories. It was certainly devoid of sufficient calories. In short, it was a diet that through either ignorance or design on the part of the Japanese would shortly begin the process of reducing the prison population.

Prisoners first affected were those who came out of Bataan and off Corregidor. In deplorable condition when they entered prison, their health had deteriorated further in Cabanatuan and on the *Tottori Maru*. They were simply in no shape to last long in sub-zero temperatures with inadequate calories. Signs of malnutrition, scurvy, and beri-beri began showing up quickly. The illness called beri-beri is essentially divided into two categories, dry and wet. In dry beri-beri the illness is manifested by a destruction of nerve endings in the feet and legs caused by prolonged malnutrition. It is a terribly painful condition. In my own case the feet and legs seemed on fire, with thousands of tingling pin pricks taking place over the affected area. There was no relief from it. Prisoners would pack their feet in snow, trying to relieve the burning.

The really tragic cases, however, were among those affected by what is called wet beri-beri. I do not remember prisoners dying from dry beri-beri, where that was the only cause of illness. Usually there were other contributing causes as well. But with wet beri-beri it was different. For some reason, among some people, the disease caused a retention of water in the body. The condition was evidently not as painful as the dry, but it was nearly always fatal. Swelling would begin at the feet and gradually progress up the legs. By the time it reached the body's midsection, it was all over. One of my more painful memories is the daily sight of a close friend hobbling slowly on hugely swollen legs, his hands cupped under, and holding up, testicles swollen to the size of large grapefruits, and insisting "I'm gonna make it."

He didn't.

My own condition continued to weaken. The fever that had plagued me for months was still with me and now a persistent cough added to my problems. My weight loss also continued. Finally, when I was unable to stand, I was taken on a stretcher to another barrack that had been converted into what was called the hospital. I would spend the next six weeks there.

Actually, the hospital served more as a gathering place than anything else. It was here the early morning death squads could come to gather the bodies, rather than having to make the rounds of the other barracks. Two American doctors, one named Herbst from some place in Ohio and the other named Schabert, were in attendance but there was little they could do. Both were witness to conditions and illnesses they had never encountered and never anticipated. A Japanese doctor, of sorts, was in charge of the operation. We were given a little more food than that given to other prisoners. For breakfast we were fed boiled cornmeal, occasionally with sugar in it. To help overcome the lack of vitamins we were occasionally given the husks of rice, a by-product of the rice polishing process. We never got the rice, only the husks. It helped.

The allocation of space within the hospital was the same as that in the barracks. Men were crowded together, lying on thin straw mattresses. By then the entire camp had become infested with body lice, which found a haven in our woolen undergarments, adding their bit to our misery.

I remember nothing of the first days in the hospital. For all practical purposes I was out of it. My first memory was to awaken to the sounds of ward attendants discussing the fact that it was December 8, one year from the time the Japanese hit Pearl Harbor and the Philippines. I figured I was getting better. I could at least comprehend time. If my luck held, I would see my twentieth birthday.

My space happened to be about four or five feet from the stove in the center of the walkway that separated the two sides. We were probably allocated a little more coal than those in the barracks, but it seemed to make little difference. When morning came, our canteen of water was frozen solid and the stovepipe was encased in a sheath of solid ice.

To my left lay a black-bearded man from some place in Maine. Both he and I would finally make it through, but the space to my right would be occupied, in the few weeks I lay there, by four who didn't. One would be brought in, stay a few days, and die. His place would be taken by another and the process repeated. Those of us who rapidly became "old timers" learned to hope the dead would be moved quickly, for when the blood quit circulating and the body became cold, the lice lost little time in departing the scene to search for a new home, which was always the closest living body. In this case it was me.

I developed a horror of those lice. I lay there, helpless, watching hundreds of the little creatures crawling this way and that, looking for a warm body where blood circulated, and I knew that before morning came many would join those already comfortably at home in the comparative warmth of my own small space on earth.

We were attended by a few enlisted men who had been medical corpsmen back when things were more normal. One was an American named Brown, and another an Englishmen known to the ward's inhabitants simply as "Ginger." Ginger was a fair-skinned, red-headed veteran of many years in the British army. Brown was much his junior.

He wanted someday to become a full-fledged doctor. They did the best they could. They worried over us. They sometimes shouted at us. They encouraged us. They removed the dead as quickly as they could. There was little more they could do. Thus did the weeks pass.

A tall Indian from Wisconsin was brought in and laid directly across the aisle from me. He appeared to be in fairly good physical condition, but he was terribly ill. In addition to a few other problems he had a severe case of malaria, a hangover from his days on Bataan. The word was he did not have long to live. The malarial seizures would hit him and he would shake like a leaf in the wind from head to toe, trying to stifle moans and groans as he did so.

He had something else as well. A pair of fur-lined shoes, something we had not seen before.

The Japanese had selected a group of the healthiest prisoners for work at a factory on the outskirts of Mukden, a few miles from camp. That, after all, was why we had been brought here, and factory officials were anxious for the labor. It was a long walk in bitter cold, and those selected were issued fur-lined shoes for the trek. Despite the hardships entailed, the prisoners preferred work to staying in camp. While there the factory furnished the noon meal, which, from what we heard, was much better than that provided prisoners in camp. The army wanted it that way, too, since the factory paid the army for prisoner labor. In some ways it helped everyone. A little more food could be divided between those still in camp, and the army received extra money to do with as they wished. Therefore, those who worked in the factory were afforded a little extra attention. Hence the shoes.

Upon entering the hospital ward I had been propped up by a board, with head and shoulders elevated somewhat to keep me from choking on the effluent coughed from my lungs. From that position I daily watched the soldier's shakings, and admired, then coveted, that pair of shoes. Someday, if all went well, I would be back out there in that bitter cold. It would be nice to have a pair of shoes like that.

On about the fourth day the shaking ceased and he lay still. It was over. I tried to rise, determined to crawl to where he was and possess the shoes. It was all in the mind. Too weak to rise, too weak to even crawl, I lay there and watched others try to do the same. I had not been the only one with the thought.

Within a few minutes Ginger had heard. He showed up to take charge of the body and personal effects. One of the first things he did was remove the shoes. Cries of outrage arose as Ginger gathered the shoes and a few belongings and started to leave. He got the message quickly. Others wanted the shoes.

"Why do you want them?" he asked no one in particular. "You can't use them, you don't need them. I'll see that they go to someone who needs them and can use them."

With that he left.

Next morning Ginger showed up for duty wearing a pair of fur-lined shoes.

Who could argue? Certainly not I.

The dead man was taken away, to a warehouse, where his body would be stacked with scores of other frozen bodies to await the spring thaw.

Creecy was brought in. He had always been the strongest of our foursome and I was surprised to see him. He had pneumonia, they said, but a couple of weeks later he was strong enough to return to the barracks. He wasn't well, by any means, but that wasn't the criteria.

Late in February the doctors decided I was going to make it. The coughing had subsided somewhat. The blood coming from my lungs was no longer apparent. The fever had become what they called low grade, rising in the afternoon and going down at night. It was time to return to the barracks. I still had one small problem. I was too weak to stand for more than a few minutes, and even then could not stand erect. But someone would help and in time things would be better. I was weighed and told my weight, in kilos. When I asked how that translated in pounds, the answer was eighty-seven. I was five feet, nine inches tall.

I returned to my old spot in Barracks #11, back with Williams, Turner, and Creecy. It was good to be back. If one must die, it is better to die among friends. If one may live, it is better to live among friends.

During my absence from the barrack certain changes had been made in camp. The old commander, Colonel Matsuyama, who had greeted us on the first day, had been relieved and a new commander, Colonel Matsuda, was in his place. Some thought it a good omen. Perhaps, the reasoning went, the army or factory or somebody else had decided that if the men all died, or were too weak to work, the factory would be short-handed. Perhaps it was merely a practical move, but it was welcomed. Things could hardly get worse. A new second in command, a short, barrel-shaped captain named Ishikawa, who would become known as "The Bull," was also installed. In time he would become part of camp lore.

More men had been chosen for work in the factory. They left camp early in the morning and returned about dark. They were always full of tales about what went on during the day. It seemed like an exciting world out there, or at least a world none of us had encountered to that point.

Not all of it was pleasant. The Japanese had firmly entrenched themselves in Manchuria many years before, exploiting the area's rich natural resources and turning it into an industrial heartland for war making. A puppet Manchu emperor, who as a child had sat on the throne in Pieping and would become known as the Last Emperor of China, now sat on a throne created for him by the Japanese. Southeast of us the Japanese still battled the armies of Chiang Kai-shek. Far to the west, Mao's Communist armies were holed up in the hills of Yenan Province, waiting for the right time to strike. In short, most of China was in turmoil. Even in Manchuria, where the Japanese army had imposed its own brand of order, starvation and privation were no strangers. The sight of freezing and frozen beggars lying by the roadside elicited much comment from the prisoners when they returned to camp.

As did the large dogs who fed upon the frozen corpses.

The dogs were actually rather fearsome creatures, large, wild with heavy coats of fur. They roamed the area, finding food where they could. Occasionally they wandered through the barbed wire into camp, perhaps in the off chance they might fare as well there as by the roadside. It did not take the prisoners long to decide they might provide a ready source of protein themselves. The battle was on.

But to begin with, the prisoners were forced to realize, early on, that the dogs were stronger than all but a few of the camp's inhabitants. This called for teamwork. It called for strategy and tactics. Long ropes were fashioned from the short ropes used to tie supplies brought in from the outside. Snares were constructed, and when a dog inadvertently stuck his head through one, the snare was tightened and he was set upon by a group of prisoners, some holding him as best they could while others beat him to death with whatever was available. Then he was eaten.

The English prisoners, together with the Australians and New Zealanders, had joined us in Korea. They were generally in much better physical condition than the Americans, which led to somewhat better success on their part when it came to doing battle with the dogs. On one occasion it also provided a little humor.

A team of Britishers had succeeded once again. They took the carcass, and, thinking they were unobserved, stashed it in a snow bank, where they figured it would freeze solid and afford them some protein, a little at a time over a period of time.

Fortunately, or unfortunately, they were not unobserved. Someone from our barracks saw where they hid the animal. He gathered some friends and, in the dead of night, liberated the carcass and gave it a new, more decent resting place in a different snow bank.

In due time the men from Barracks #13, the English barracks, discovered who did the deed, or who they thought did the deed. Perhaps it was tracks in the snow. Perhaps a friendly tip. Nevertheless, they determined to retrieve their prize or obtain retribution. Their honor was at stake.

They sent word that if their dog was not returned, they were coming to get it. It was not returned, so they came.

Then it became a matter where the inhabitants of Barracks #11 felt they should defend their own fellows, even if they didn't know exactly what it was all about. So they streamed out. The sides lined up.

For a while both sides stood and glowered, shouting at each other. Finally, with the temperature hovering around 30 degrees below zero on the Centigrade scale, and seeing no satisfactory solution to the matter, the Britishers returned to their barrack.

It was at that point that I finally got the full story. I had heard that someone in Barracks #11 had come by a dog, but for some reason it was all a big secret. When I said something about how nice it would be to have a piece of the dog, I was told by Cook to just be patient. Sure enough, when everything calmed down, the dog's liver was divided between Cook, Creecy, Williams, Turner, and myself. Cook had seen the scoundrels remove the dog from its hiding place, and he threatened to tell the Britishers if he didn't get a share. He got it, and divided it with those in our cadre.

Up until then we had never really treated Cook as part of our group. He wasn't from our battery on Corregidor. He wasn't part of our cell at Cabanatuan. We had not shared our hopes and fears with him. But on that occasion he earned his place. Turner did the cooking. Looking back, it probably wasn't much — just a few slivers of a dog's liver. But then it was a sumptuous treat, long to be savored in the palate and in memory.

When the episode was over, there was much laughter and satisfaction in the barrack. We had finally won a battle. Turner even reduced the event to poetry, a lengthy poem no doubt long lost to what might have been appreciative audiences. I remember only the beginning: "It happened one night . . . and it wasn't Halloween, when Barracks Eleven stole a dog from Barracks Thirteen."

I took no real part in the affair of the dog, other than to share the glory and the liver.

I was still too weak to do much more than walk a few feet, but the strength was gradually returning. In time I was put on a detail to fetch water and fill the canteens of men working in the factory. It involved a trip of only about 300 feet, with a small bucket. But it seemed a very long distance with a very big load. I would fill a bucket with hot water, cover it with a lid, and begin the trek. After a few feet I would sit down on the bucket, regain some energy, then begin again. In the barrack I would then go from place to place, filling canteens left by those who had gone to the factory before daylight. In this way a certain amount of strength began to come back.

Our food ration also improved a little. Our captors began issuing a little cornmeal, which became our morning meal in the form of mush, and for some reason we were given copious quantities of garlic. We ate garlic roasted, like popcorn. We ate garlic raw. We ate garlic in our soup. We also began receiving soybeans in our soup every third day. Then they provided the soybeans in a smaller, but daily, ration which came with the evening soup. It helped. Everything, that is, except the barrack room odor, to which we ultimately became immune.

So immune were we that on one occasion, when Corporal Noda and his guards entered our barrack for the nightly head count, we were puzzled when he seemed taken aback. Upon walking through the door he stopped, as if he had run into a brick wall, and suddenly began shouting "My God, air it out. Air it out. You smell like a bunch of guineas."

It was later explained to me, by someone knowledgeable in such matters, that Noda was not talking about the kind of guinea I was familiar with. In South Texas a guinea was one thing. In some other areas of the country, as it was explained to me, a guinea was evidently something else. Noda, being a child of Berkeley, understood this. I didn't.

The winter wore on. Even so, it eventually began to lose its grip. As it did so, another worry surfaced. Soon the ground would be thawed enough for graves to be dug—graves that would receive those who had died during the winter and were now stacked, frozen, in warehouses. The problem would be that the bodies could thaw before the ground did.

All able-bodied men, other than those working in the factory, were put to work digging graves. Since that did not include myself, and since I had been assigned the duty of keeping others supplied with drinking water, I could only listen to the travails of the grave diggers at the end of the day, one of whom was Creecy. By then he had recovered enough that he could swing a pick, even if slowly. It was slow going as men chipped away at the frozen earth. Each day it was a matter of inches, but eventually the job was done.

On a cold day in March 1943, the frozen bodies of 176 men, nearly all of whom had died within 90 days of our arrival, were laid to rest in the homeland of the ancient Manchus. By the time winter ended, the number had risen to 205, more than 17 percent of all American enlisted men in camp. It was from that contingent that practically all the dead were counted.

Winter gave way slowly and grudgingly. The dogs, finally realizing there were others as hungry as they, had long since learned to keep a respectful distance. My own strength gradually improved and I was given additional camp duties, primarily working in the barracks laundry room. It was not what would normally pass for a laundry room, but there were facilities for boiling water, hence clothes, which made it possible to finally get a handle on the lice situation.

Too, I was chosen, one way or the other, to be the "chow dipper" for our barrack. I never knew why I was chosen. Perhaps it was because I was hardly in any physical condition to take advantage of the position. There were certainly few in the barrack I could have argued with. Or perhaps the other men appreciated the job I had tried to do in keeping their canteens filled. Whatever the reason, the job was mine and I did not relish the prospect. Experience had taught that the role of chow dipper was usually short-lived and carried with it the likelihood of some controversy. It could hardly be otherwise when men are starving.

The mechanical part of the job simply involved arising early, going to the kitchen, picking up the ration allocated to one's barrack for that meal, taking it back to the barrack, and dispensing the food.

For breakfast and supper this usually consisted of two buckets of whatever was available. For lunch, when some prisoners were away at work in the factory, it was usually one bucket, or part of a bucket. So far, no problem.

But how does one look at a bucket of thin soup, then look at a roster of starving men, and devise a system fair to all, or as fair as one can make it?

The answer proved relatively simple. I would take my own ration first, sit the canteen cup down beside the bucket, and let every man measure his own ration against mine as he came through the line. Anyone who was dissatisfied with his own ration could exchange his for mine. His cup would be placed where mine had been, and all others could do the same. A roster was kept, by prison number. If I misjudged, and one or two rations were left, one or two men would get an extra ration.

Obviously, it became very important that I quickly learn how to judge the amount that would be available for each man. Seldom did we receive exactly the same amount of food. But I did learn, and in all that time only one complaint arose. A tall, thin youngster from Alabama, who went simply by the name Bama, returned with his cup, in a huff. He had returned to his pallet, glanced at his neighbor's ration, and determined that he had been shorted. He then returned with his complaint.

I told him to take mine and leave his. He measured his against mine and said, "I'll keep mine. You got less than I did."

Bama was a good man. He was just hungry. Perhaps he spread the word, for from that day forward I never had a complaint, and from that day forward, regardless of whatever "reorganizations" the camp went through, I was the chow dipper for whatever group I happened to be in.

While it was then remote from even my imagination, there would be times later when I would dine with governors, sit in council with secretaries of state, be received in the White House by presidents, influence the careers of people who would be ambassadors, advise and argue with senators and congressmen, sit in the highest councils of government, and be given professional honors beyond my wildest dreams. But nothing in the secular world, the world apart from my family, has approached the honor of being chosen as chow dipper for starving men.

I suppose it could be argued that all honors carry both a blessing and a curse. I believe that to be the case in my own experience. The blessing was that the experience reinforced and solidified the teaching of my parents, that we "do unto others." The curse was that it has caused me to judge others, to form opinions about them on the basis of how I think they would have acted in a similar situation. And this judgment has not seemed a conscious effort on my part. It seems only to have grown out of the experience.

I cannot imagine Lyndon Johnson, for instance, ever having been chosen as chow dipper in the first place. And certainly, given his proclivities, it was a job he would not have kept for more than a few days in any event. He pandered to, was chosen by, and was bankrolled by people who wanted and expected something extra, even if it had to be taken from others. In the process he became very rich and very powerful. The same could be said about any number of elected officials, con men in public robes, who grace our offices today. It could also be said of those who cling to them like leeches, in the hope that they, too, will share in the riches and the power.

We are taught that we should not make judgment of others, only of ourselves. In our hearts we know that to be the right course. But how can we love what is good and remain indifferent to what is bad? How can we love truth unless we hate lies? How can we fight for principle unless we fight against that which is unprincipled? And how can we separate evil from the evildoer? We are told it is possible, but I have not yet reached that state of perfection. The curse of the chow dipper, I suppose, is still with me.

The weather warmed. Three men, thinking they could possibly get to Siberia and there be received warmly by the Soviets, departed camp in the dead of night. North of Shenyang was a city called Harbin. Those who knew China said it had a large population of White Russians who had fled there when the Bolsheviks won their revolution and established their own brand of paradise. The hope of the three was that they could get that far, perhaps blend in with the population, find some sympathetic souls, and get enough supplies to make it the rest of the way. Then, they thought, it would be a safe trip home. It was a forlorn hope.

They were gone about a week. I was at work in the laundry room when they were brought back. The three were made to retrace their escape route, which brought them by the laundry room, then across the prison compound to a drainage ditch, where they had managed to crawl under the barbed wire entanglement. All hands were ordered inside, but I peered out a window as they passed, perhaps ten feet away, beaten, bloody, and surrounded by a retinue of chattering Japanese. The infamous Corporal Noda, the graduate of Berkeley, was interpreting. One clearly bore wounds from a bayonet, or knife of some kind. Dried, caked blood colored his shoulder and chest area. The men could barely walk.

It was said they were given a military trial. At any rate, they were shot.

Months later, I would be on a grave-digging detail in a field on the outskirts of Shenyang when our new interpreter, a Hawaiian-born Japanese named Kashima, told us that this was where the three were shot. He was a witness. We pressed for details. He said merely that they were wrapped in white strips of cloth, "like . . . what you call it?"

"Like mummies?" I asked.

"Yeah, like mummies," he said. "They were wrapped like mummies and shot."

Why like mummies?

He didn't know.

"They just wrapped them and shot them and then went up there," pointing to where the bodies lay, "and got stethoscopes and listened to their heart. Then they buried them."

SEVEN

A Web of Stability . . . and Permanence

In July we moved to a new camp, some four miles away and perhaps one-half mile from the factory.

We had heard rumors, picked up by prisoners who worked at the factory, that a new camp was being built. But rumors were a dime a dozen. This one happened to be right.

The new camp was a great improvement over the old. It was no less a prison; indeed, in some ways it was much more so. The buildings, including the barracks, were of brick. A brick wall, some eight or ten feet high, topped with an electric fence and with guard towers at the corners, formed the enclosure. The inevitable barbed wire fence was some thirty feet inside the wall, providing space for guards to patrol the area and make their presence constantly known.

Clearly, the prison was built with security in mind, as all prisons are, but it was new, clean, and had certain creature comforts unknown in previous camps. It had running water. Cold, but running. Inside the wall the camp was divided roughly in half — one side for the prisoners and the other for general camp administration, quarters for guards and their officers, supplies, the usual paraphernalia that would necessarily go with such an operation. Prisoners were allowed a few more inches of sleeping space. A bathhouse was provided. Every other evening the baths were open to enlisted men, who now numbered considerably less than the original band who had entered the old camp in November. On alternate evenings the baths were reserved for the eleven American and two or three British officers. In due course the battle against the lice would be won.

By the time we moved to the new camp, our food ration had

been increased to the point where dying had largely stopped. Hunger was still with us, but not starvation. The factory wanted more workers, and they obviously didn't want prisoners who couldn't produce. The struggle now would be against time, a struggle all lose in the long run, but which in the short run is more preferable than a struggle against imminent disaster. A new sense of hope seemed to emerge, perhaps slowly, almost imperceptibly. Laughter began to be heard more frequently. More than a year had passed since Corregidor went under. Surely it wouldn't be long now. A year later, two years later, we would still feel that way.

Somehow the lives of captives and captors became woven into a web of stability, order, and permanence. The peculiarities, foibles, eccentricities of each guard became known and anticipated by the prisoners. In time they even acquired names, names that meant nothing to them but did to the prisoners. There was Eleanor, a slow-witted individual with a face not at all unlike his American namesake. Eleanor was not a camp favorite, nor was his namesake, or his namesake's husband. There was Abe, a short, thin guard who was suspected, by the prisoners, of having a traveling Middle East rug merchant for a father. And there was the Kiyotski Kid, so named for his propensity for standing men at attention and forcing them to bow to him, repeatedly and almost endlessly. He had a thing about being properly recognized and respected. His usual target was some poor prisoner who had failed to quickly notice his arrival on the prison side of the compound, but he was not above inflicting the same punishment on Chinese coolies guilty of the same infraction when he prowled outside the walls. When it was all over he would be found with a small bullet hole through his head. Whether it was put there by a prisoner or a Chinese, I do not know.

There was Banana Nose, who had a proboscis entirely out of place on a Japanese face. And the one called Goonya, or Girl. He was fair-skinned, generally smiling, seldom troublesome. But he had one problem. During the daily body search of those returning from the factory, he seemed to linger entirely too long while examining the crotch area, sometimes lapsing into a semitrance while making a strange whistling sound as he sucked in his breath. I never understood him.

Aside from the regular prison guards there was the army. It was army troops that manned the guard towers, walked the perimeter, and generally made their presence known both at camp and at the

---

A Web of Stability . . . and Permanence

factory. They were usually troops on rotation, assigned to their duties after a long stint on the battlefields somewhere in Asia. They were fully aware of their position and made others aware as well. After all, we were their prisoners. The regular prison guards were merely their agents to see that we were constantly reminded of that.

It was also the army that provided the officers to oversee all aspects of the camp's operation. By and large they were a mixed lot. There was Captain Ishikawa, "The Bull," a short, fat, dedicated servant of the emperor and all things Japanese. He considered himself the ultimate Samurai warrior, unfortunately stuck here among prisoners where he could achieve no great glories for the race and the empire. Still, he was a man of duty and of honor, as he saw it. He was not guilty, as far as I know, of willfully torturing prisoners. He did not seem to wish to inflict punishment if there was no just cause to do so. As long as everything went well, as long as he received no reports of prisoners being caught smoking at the factory, or failing to properly salute soldiers or guards, or reports of shirking at our labors, he could be almost benign. But a report on any infraction, particularly when he was officer of the day, would send him into a rage where anything could happen. One of his favorite punishments was to stand the offender at attention, walk off some fifty or sixty feet, remove his sword and scabbard from his belt, aim the sheathed sword at the prisoner, then rush full tilt, bowling the prisoner over like a pinball. All this was accomplished with much shouting, and always in view of assembled prisoners.

As the camp's "adjutant," he had great influence over the actions, if not attitudes, of other officers who seemed to share his penchant for punishment but not necessarily any sense of restraint brought on by the "spirit" of Bushido. One of those was the camp's doctor, whose name has long since escaped me. He could be the smiling, obeisant Oriental, full of compassion for his patients, or he could be as sadistic as any warped barbarian. Once, after I had gone to work at the factory, we returned to camp to find the doctor installed as the officer of the day, which meant that for a twenty-four-hour period he was virtually an extension of the emperor's will. It was in December of 1943. The ground was already frozen. During the walk to the factory in the early morning hours, ice would form on eyebrows, beards, any hair touched by breath. Still, winter clothes and winter shoes had not been issued. The temperature on this day was hanging around zero, with approximately six inches of snow on the ground.

We walked through the front gates of the prison to find the doctor, complete with his sash of office, standing on the platform ready to oversee the count and the search. But first he wanted to ask some questions, before we were turned over to the searchers.

Did anyone have any problems?

No one moved from ranks. No one spoke. He repeated his request. Did anyone have any complaints? Did anyone have any health problems? He was in charge of things today, and if anyone had any complaints, now was the time to bring them forth. He would look into them.

Finally, someone spoke from the ranks. We needed some winter shoes and winter clothes, he said. Prisoners were getting frostbite. The doctor wanted to know if this was an isolated complaint, or if others also felt that way.

Emboldened by the courage of the one who had spoken out, others did the same. The good doctor then asked all those who had spoken to step forward, out of ranks. They did so, maybe fifteen men in all.

He flew into a fit of rage. When the Japanese army conquered Manchuria, he screamed, the Japanese army eradicated frostbite in Manchuria. There could be no more frostbite in Manchuria, so the complaints could not be true. They were groundless.

To prove his point he ordered them to remove their shoes and walk around in the snow, barefoot, in front of the other men, as punishment for making slanderous charges against the Japanese army.

It is said that the gods grind exceedingly slow, but exceedingly fine. After the war was over the doctor would be tried, fortunately by the Chinese government of Chiang Kai-shek, and hanged by his neck until dead.

The charge? They said he did not show proper respect to a prisoner, Gen. Jonathan Wainwright. They said he even slapped the general on one occasion. And they said it happened on Chinese soil, so they claimed the right to conduct the trial. The Associated Press reported the verdict in three or four lines. I would read the report while lying in a Veterans Administration hospital in Kerrville, Texas. It did not make me unhappy.

And then there was a small cadre of Chinese who served as our work supervisors at the factory. They seemed to fit, in the scheme of prison life, somewhere below the Japanese but above the prisoners. A few had uniforms, after a fashion, but carried no arms and had no disciplinary authority. It was merely their way of staying alive and making a living in a world not of their making. As time wore on, it would become apparent they were as much prisoner as we. Perhaps the principal difference was that they would return to their own families after the day's work was done, while we went behind the walls. Another difference was that they did not have to undergo the obligatory body search when leaving the factory.

In time that would be important. Between a few of us, at least, there would evolve a sort of subcultural relationship, wherein they lived their lives and we lived ours. But at critical points we helped each other.

Guh Ching-yu was a youngster of about my own age whose family roots were somewhere in the farming country south of Manchuria. He was small in stature, much lighter in complexion than the generally larger and darker Manchus, and, as it would develop, not only intelligent but wise beyond his years.

He began showing up in camp during the fall of our first year in the new camp, when, in the early morning hours, prisoners headed for factory work were lined up, counted, and turned over to those who would escort them to their destination. He was one of the escorts. Once there, he became a sort of combination work supervisor-guard. He manned one of the guard shacks occasionally, but generally roamed the factory compound doing whatever was required of him.

At that time it was customary for factory workers to leave camp first. After that ritual was completed, those designated for work in the camp or the farm fields, of which I was one, would depart for their own chores. Ching-yu quickly earned a reputation of being able to scream almost as loudly as our regular guards, or the army troops for that matter, when it came to shaping up the lines and hurrying the process. But the prisoners saw that he did so with a smile, perhaps even a twinkle. He soon became a sort of favorite among the prisoners, who nicknamed him *"Show-hi,"* or "Little Boy" in Chinese.

My first summer and early fall in the new camp were spent mostly in field work. Soon after we arrived in Shenyang the Japanese interrogated us as to our past work experience, along with all sorts of questions about our family, our education. We were "evaluated" by teams of people posing as psychologists. The size and shape of our skull was measured. The length of our breastbone was measured.

The distance between our chin and the beginning and end of our sternum was measured. Almost every dimension of our body was measured. They said it would be important. That was enough to raise suspicions that some of us might be assigned to work useful to them, so most of us responded with answers that did not prove helpful to them, and, in some ways, did not prove helpful to us as well.

My own response, truthfully, was that I was a farm worker, that I was principally a farmer who raised cattle. I neglected to say that in America that involved handling tractors, trucks, and other machinery. I was worried that if they knew that, I might well end up doing just that. So until the factory got to the point where they wanted more manual labor on the construction gangs, my principal duties were working in the farm fields.

It was not unpleasant work. Hard, but not unpleasant. It got us out beyond the walls, where we could see something of how the Chinese lived, and threw us in contact with those who made their living wresting food from the earth. I came to appreciate them, even love them as a people.

They were a poor people, terribly poor. But there was among them a sense of humor entirely lacking among the Japanese we had known. They could, and did, laugh at us and with us, and they seemed to enjoy it when we did the same with them. They called us the *"Tabeezers,"* or "Big Noses." It was an appellation generally reserved for "barbarians" from the north, but, like the word *gringo* of the Texas–Mexican border country where I grew up, it could be used with or without a smile. There was a sense of fatalism among them, perhaps born of their ethic or religion, or perhaps born out of centuries of oppression by this or that warlord or this or that government. Whoever was running the government at the time seemed somehow irrelevant to them. The Japanese were merely the latest rulers they must obey, if not please. Their real struggle was with the earth and the weather. And many, many spirits. If the time came when the spirits were sufficiently displeased with the rulers, whoever they might be, that displeasure would be communicated to the people, and the time would be ripe to take action. In the meantime, one must bear one's burden — and wait.

The earth people of China were good at waiting.

Once, on a grave-digging detail on the outskirts of Shenyang, the terrible thought crossed my mind that I might be looking at my own country 200 years hence. It was a small detail. We had to dig graves for only ten people who had not yet died. It was merely done in case; in order, I suppose, that we might stay ahead of the curve.

We were going through a small village, one of the many that ringed Shenyang, on our way to the field where we would dig. It was a beautiful day, late summer, clear sky, and we were beyond the walls. As we went through the village, I was struck with the seeming poverty and outright dirtiness of the place and its inhabitants. Really, they appeared to be little better off than we were. We at least had a clean place to sleep, however crowded, and a slit trench into which we could defecate. We had running water to wash our face and hands, and a bath to which we could occasionally repair. From where we were, as we traversed the village, I could see little evidence of that among those who stood and stared at the strange white men in their midst.

I suppose at first I was merely trying to make conversation, since one of our guards for the day was Kashima, our Hawaiian-born interpreter. He, of all our guards, seemed to have a degree of understanding for our plight. He really didn't seem to belong where he was. His story was that he had returned to Japan before the war to visit an aged and ill grandparent, that his stay was somehow prolonged because of that, and that he was subsequently drafted into the Japanese army. He ended up in our camp, where he finally replaced the infamous Corporal Noda, who had left to pursue his career in the Imperial Army. At any rate, he was one guard we could talk to when we were beyond the walls.

I made some comment about the squalor of the area we were going through. Kashima readily agreed. Yes, conditions were terrible. Then, somewhat stupidly, I wondered aloud why conditions were as they were. It was an opportunity, I thought, to safely gig the Japanese for those conditions that existed, since they had been in charge of things here since 1931.

Kashima was silent, but clearly troubled. My thought was that it would be better to drop the subject as gracefully as possible. I said something like, "Well, things would probably be a lot better if they would just clean up around here."

His answer was quick. "How can they clean up if they have no water? How can they bathe if they have no soap?"

What was this? A trace of compassion in the soul of a Japanese?

I said no more, nor did he. I remember feeling quite small. But I did reflect on the event, and have done so many times. True, I was taught as a youngster that no matter if one has only an apple crate to sit on, he can get up off the crate once in a while and sweep out from around it. I still think it is good advice. But the people who taught me that had never come face to face with the teeming millions of people who made up China. Nor have any of us come face to face with the teeming billions who will someday inherit the earth.

By this time I had begun to pick up a smattering of the language, largely at the prodding of another prisoner named J. D. "Ozzie" Osborne. He was a naval enlisted man, a petty officer and former signal man, as I remember it, on a small ship stationed in Manila Bay during the battle. He, too, was from Texas, from the coastal country around Corpus Christi. That, plus what appeared to be a determination on his part to help see me through the ordeal, had caused us to become acquainted back at the old camp. Different work assignments and different living quarters at the new camp did not allow much contact there, but he was determined to teach me certain things he thought might possibly be of some benefit later.

He thought it would be well for us both to learn Chinese, for instance, and for me to learn how to signal by semaphore in case we should ever need it. One could never tell what the future might hold. Too, it may have simply been that he was older than I, and he wanted to teach somebody something. At any rate, we became close friends over the years in prison. I was never an apt pupil at the semaphore business, but he did spark my interest in learning Chinese. He was not a master of the language at the time, but he worked hard at learning. He worked at the factory, where he came in contact with Chinese on a more regular basis than those of us who worked the fields, where that happened only occasionally.

The result was that by the time I got word in the fall of 1943 that I was to begin work at the factory, I had a smattering of Chinese. It proved highly beneficial.

Our captors had made it known that our only contact with the Chinese was to be work related, that we were not to engage in conversation with them. That was not difficult, since hardly anyone knew any Chinese anyway. But the message was plain. The same could be said of the Japanese. We were not encouraged to learn the language, but we were expected to know what they said. We were expected to understand the basic army commands, to count off in Japanese, to understand the words for "attention" and "salute," and to be able to interpret *"Shogoto, Shogoto"* or "work, work." We were also to know their words for "no rest, no rest," "water closet," and "Good morning, honored one."

Perhaps it was because stolen melons somehow seem sweeter, or perhaps because I had become fascinated with China itself, but for whatever reason I determined I would do all I could to learn the language. I never really succeeded, but the factory at least provided the opportunity to learn more.

My own diary, begun in September of 1943, and with only occasional entries throughout the remaining years, records that I began work at the factory on the first day of December. An entry made on December 9 makes note of that fact and goes on to say: "The work isn't terribly hard but it's terribly cold. Ice forms on the eyebrows, eyelashes, and mustache while we walk to and from work. We haven't been issued any winter caps or shoes yet, so there is quite a bit of discomfort among the men. Several rumors have come into camp lately. Among them are: Formosa is heavily raided, Burma is in Allied hands. Like most of the rumors, these are apparently groundless . . ."

My first job at the factory was that of a "hod-carrier." A new building was to be built and labor was needed to haul the bricks up to where Chinese bricklayers were working on the walls. In America the task would have been accomplished, I was told, by machinery. By cranes, hoists, whatever. Here it was accomplished on the backs of people, in this instance by the prisoners. The sides of the building were surrounded by scaffolding, on which there were steps. Prisoners loaded with bricks made the trek up the scaffolding, on the order of ants, one behind the other. A determination had been made to complete the building before the worst of winter descended upon us, so fires kept the mortar from freezing and the bricklayers worked at breakneck speed. This, of course, made it necessary for the lines up the wall to move quickly. It was tiring work, exceedingly tiring, but there was a certain reward involved. At the top of the work area, after we had unloaded our bricks, we walked a few steps along a runway and began the descent down another series of stair-like steps. During that brief period one could look out over the countryside, westward across the plains of Manchuria and onward toward the home of the ancient Mongols. Out there people roamed free on the steppes. Out there people mounted ponies and rode where they wished. Out there was freedom, and someday, God willing, we would have it. It all sounds silly now. But then it was important—a few brief moments of dreaming and back to reality.

When the building was finished I was assigned to new work inside the factory. It was a small detail, consisting of only five or six men. Our job was to disassemble machinery and lay it all out, piece by piece, in order that the Japanese technicians could make blueprints and ultimately, of course, duplicate it for their own purposes.

The factory had started life, we were told, as an operation by the Ford Motor Company. They had decided to open operations in China, and had completed one or two buildings before the Japanese moved in, conquering Manchuria as the first step in their plan for a "Greater East Asia Co-Prosperity Sphere." A few of the original machines were still there, as were many other machines the Japanese had brought in from Liverpool, England, and various places in the United States. Some of the prisoners who worked regularly in the factory, mostly those with backgrounds in working for industrial concerns before they came into the army, said the Japanese had evidently scoured the world for a few of the very best machines available. It was these machines they were interested in copying.

It was slow, tedious work. When the final blueprints had been made, the task of putting the machine back together began. It was at this point where opportunity came knocking.

By that time Guh Ching-yu and I had become friends. Perhaps not yet real friends, but at least acquaintances. The friendship would ripen and last through prison. I don't remember exactly what triggered the friendship. Perhaps it was the fact that during his rounds at the factory I tried to speak to him in his own tongue. Perhaps it was because he was intrigued by America and Americans and was happy that one wanted to learn of his own people. Or perhaps ulterior motives on his part had something to do with it, in the beginning.

Guh Ching-yu knew that a few Chinese workers were smuggling items out of the factory and disposing of them on the black market. I don't know how he knew, but he did. Among those items most sought after were roller bearings. He brought up the subject one day in a most casual way. I asked why roller bearings were wanted by the Chinese. I could see no way anything like a roller bearing could be useful to people who moved goods on horse carts with wooden axles.

Ah, but there was. By making certain modifications the bearings would fit nicely on the axle. Wheels ran smoothly. The carts could move with less effort, could carry more, all that. It required no great genius to determine that perhaps we could make certain arrangements, which we did.

When we put the disassembled machines back together, it was sometimes possible, indeed sometimes probable, that a roller bearing would be sidetracked. This would be left someplace where he could find it, or later, after sufficient trust had been built up, in his guard shack. In return he would smuggle items of food into the factory on certain mornings, usually burying them in a pile of sawdust on the factory grounds. For one who is hungry, an egg in a sawdust pile is highly recommended.

This did not happen daily, only occasionally. There were just not that many roller bearings available. And it was dangerous business. I have no doubt that he would have paid with his life had the Japanese ever become aware of the operation. For me it would have been punishment of some kind, but nothing like the price he would have paid. And I did not feel in much danger. It was not likely the machines would ever be put back on line, and if they were, and if they did not work properly, it could be months before the problem was found and traced. Maybe by then the war would be over.

Only once do I remember the situation ever becoming imminently threatening. I happened to be in his guard shack, an area completely off limits to prisoners, when a Japanese guard burst in. I do not remember exactly why I was there. It could have been one of three reasons, any one of which could have caused manifold problems. I could have been dropping off a roller bearing, I could have been picking up some food, or we could have been going over some phrases from a Chinese–English dictionary.

A little background on the dictionary might be helpful here. Guh Ching-yu had brought it to me, at my request. The Chinese characters meant nothing to me. I had to search the dictionary for the English words and phrases I wanted to learn, show them to him, and he would make the translation, slowly and repeatedly. In time I was able to carry on a halfway decent conversation with him, but only him. He knew what he had taught me. He knew the limits of my knowledge. Any attempted conversation with others was limited at best.

He had searched for weeks to find the dictionary. And when he delivered it, he apologized profusely. It was the only one he could find, he said, and it was put out by the "Reds." It was full of phrases like "running dogs of capitalism" and "workers, peasants, soldiers unite." Guh Ching-yu was an admirer of Chiang Kai-shek, and the "Reds" or "Red Soldiers" stood with the Japanese as people to be hated. The Reds were, he said, people with "rotten hearts." They sought to destroy family values, to destroy ancient traditions, to destroy the Chinese culture. Nevertheless, from my standpoint, the dictionary served a very useful purpose. I kept it hidden at the factory and when time and circumstances permitted would bring it out of hiding for another round of learning. It is possible that I was doing exactly that when the guard burst in.

The guard was clearly startled to find me in the shack. He was a regular army soldier, one of many who normally walked the factory perimeter with fixed bayonets to see that we stayed inside the fence, and to be on hand should trouble erupt. He immediately began shouting at Ching-yu, with an occasional glance at me. I stood frozen at attention, and silent. I became lost in the welter of words, but I got the message. It was the first time I had seen Ching-yu clearly frightened, but he rose to the occasion, lying like any of us would in a similar situation. He grabbed a shovel, which fortunately stood in the corner of the shack. Displaying the shovel, he said the prisoner had been digging a trench, or something on that order, had completed the task, and had entered the shack to see what he should do next. He was in the process of giving the prisoner those instructions, he said, when the guard came in.

It was a convincing display. The guard finally relaxed, and left with the admonition that prisoners were not allowed there, and it should never happen again. It didn't.

The process continued, but other arrangements were made.

I often wondered why Guh Ching-yu would take such chances. But he was newly married, he needed the money, and besides that he did not like the Japanese. They, too, he said, were people of "a rotten heart." He had to do their bidding, but he didn't have to like them.

I suppose it was that shared danger, and the trust that evolved from it, that led to our lasting friendship. I suppose also that the information that flowed from that friendship was every bit as valuable as the occasional bits of food. Ching-yu, while a long-term optimist, was a short-term pessimist, in keeping, it seemed, with most members of his race at that time. He believed that America would win the war, that the Japanese would ultimately be gone. But it would be a long time, he said, before that happened.

The camp was periodically swept with rumors, which were fed by the insatiable hunger for information on the way the war was going. Ching-yu would become the one reliable source I could check.

Someone would pick up a rumor at the factory that Hitler was dead, that the war would be over within a matter of weeks or months. No, no, he would say. Not yet. Not yet. He would let me know when the time approached.

In time other sources of information would open to other prisoners, some in unlikely places. A Californian, a member of my own regiment and battery on Corregidor, and who will be nameless in this account lest he now be happily married, somehow came into the good graces of an attractive Chinese woman who worked with him in the factory office. In fact, such good graces that within hours after the war ended she would appear outside the prison gate, complete with horse and carriage, and send word inside camp that she desired the company of her acquaintance, whom she identified by number. He did not keep her waiting long.

Then there was an Englishman, who, for purposes of this narrative, will be known only as "Robbie." He was one of those captured when Singapore went under. He was twenty-eight years old and had served half his life in the British army in India. As he explained it, he entered service when he was fourteen, under a provision that allowed youngsters to enter the army as a sort of "serving boy." On reaching the age of eighteen they could make a choice: to go into the regular army or to take their discharge. It was a provision, he said, that allowed youngsters in dire straits to enter upon new and useful lives. All in all, a beneficial policy, at least one that had been good for him.

At the factory Robbie labored alongside other prisoners and Chinese workers on various construction gangs. It was here that the foundation was laid for development of still another reliable source of information concerning what was going on in the world outside.

In prison there were few secrets, if any, among those required to work closely together. During work on the construction gangs, for instance, it was customary for a man, feeling the call of nature, to simply walk away from the group and relieve himself. On one such occasion Robbie was spotted by one of the Chinese workers, who immediately set up a howl, pointing, laughing, and calling the matter to the attention of other Chinese. One shouted that Robbie had "the penis of a horse." Others picked up the phrase, and, much to the irritation of Robbie, the phrase stuck. He became known among many of the Chinese simply as *"Maw-jeeber,"* or Horse Penis. It was not much of an exaggeration.

There must be pipelines in this world unknown to most of us.

Within a few months a Japanese guard showed up at a small laundry where Robbie, another Englishman called "Daisy" by American prisoners, myself, and two other American prisoners had been recently assigned. It was actually no laundry, but a place where we cleaned, in boiling water laced with caustic soda, oil-soaked rags from the machine shops. It was hot, dirty work, a place seldom visited by others.

The guard, a regular army soldier with fixed bayonet, wanted to see a certain prisoner, and he called Robbie's number. Robbie identified himself. What infraction had he committed? Never mind, he must accompany the guard. They walked away, to a secure warehouse.

In due time he returned to worried companions. Not to worry, he said, and he told us why. Further, he intended to exact his own price, should the individual ever return, which he had every reason to believe would occur.

Thereafter, when the guard showed up he carried, neatly tucked under one arm, a copy of the latest Japanese language newspaper. The two would retire to the secure warehouse, where, Robbie assured us with a grin, they spent their time reading and translating the paper. From that source we learned the Japanese continued to score great victories, but we noted those victories were constantly moving north, toward home waters. From that source we also got an occasional glimpse into the mood of his fellow soldiers as those victories moved closer and closer to home.

Two years had passed. My twenty-first birthday had come and gone, the second birthday in China. It varied from the sameness of all other prison days only by the fact that a mini-riot broke out at the factory when a prisoner rebelled at a beating being administered by Banana Nose. The prisoner, a red-bearded member of the construction gang, finally cracked and turned on his tormentor, who fled screaming for help from other guards. Within moments regular army troops showed up, replete with machine guns, bayonets, the works. We were hustled to camp, stripped of clothing, and forced to stand in the bitter cold as punishment. They were great believers in punishing the group for the infractions of individuals within the group. Those of us who lived long enough would see that same attitude spill over into policies of our own government, dressed up in different clothes and buttressed by seemingly rational political argument.

The camp commander finally began issuing, piecemeal, portions of Red Cross packages and letters from home. On January 10 parts of fourteen packages were distributed among the nearly 1,000 men in camp. The next day a few letters were distributed. I got a letter from my oldest brother, Raymond, and one from a Marcelle Johnson of Houston, whom I did not know and for which I was most grateful. The letters had been written a year earlier, after we had arrived in China and were finally officially reported as prisoners of war. They had lain in a warehouse for months. The commander said if he gave them out, we would have nothing to look forward to. So, given his concern, his compassion for those in his care, he had kept them safely locked away.

Prison life had settled into the dreary, monotonous routine of working, waiting, and trying not to offend our captors. The summer of 1944 arrived and prison life had become so normal, in fact, that even Major Hankins, contemptuously called "the Ground Hog" by other prisoners, and the highest ranking American officer in camp, was occasionally seen outside his quarters, exercising in the prison compound.

Officers were not required to work under camp rules, but they could accompany the men on work details if they chose. Only two did. Our daily treks to and from the factory were always led by a New Zealander, Captain Horner, and a young American second lieutenant named Matthews from someplace in East Texas. Horner, in company with many New Zealanders of that day, and unlike most Australians of that day, was even more British than the English. He was second in command of the British contingent that consisted of sixty Englishmen and forty Anzacs who had joined us at the old camp. He insisted, as best he could, that he be recognized by the Japanese as an officer of the British army, and that he be recognized as an arbiter at the factory in cases involving infraction of the rules by prisoners. His success was limited, yet he was there and the men appreciated it.

But it was Matthews that most men came, in time, to respect and love. Tall, thin, young and very blond, he was another who insisted on conducting himself in the manner befitting the uniform he once wore. He even wore his officer's cap, devoid of insignia under prison rules. His mission, he seemed to think, was to uphold a certain amount of dignity and look after the American prisoners especially.

At first Matthews was largely dismissed as irrelevant, as an exercise in vanity. The prisoners knew where the power lay, what the rules were, and who could mete out punishment. And experience had taught there was little officers could do, whether British or American, to alter that situation.

But Matthews persisted. Rain or shine, in bitter winter or hot summer, well or ill, Matthews was there, with his upright bearing, his officer's cap, marching at the head of the column alongside Horner, and quite often with a strutting Guh Ching-yu leading the way. At the factory he was not reluctant to intercede in squabbles between prisoners and guards, most often squabbles arising out of misunderstood commands, issued in Japanese to people who did not understand the language. Sometimes it helped. Sometimes it made matters worse. But in time the men came to believe he at least cared.

His reputation was helped when he got roughed up himself as a result of interceding for a prisoner. And his standing improved more when it was learned he was sometimes derisively referred to as "MacArthur" by his fellow officers. MacArthur may not have been looked upon as any sort of savior by the men, but they at least understood the reasoning behind the epithet, and, by and large, didn't appreciate it.

I do not mean to overdraw the picture. Matthews was not looked upon as any sort of Galahad. He was just a second lieutenant, a "shave-tail" who rose to the occasion and did, in the eyes of most men, what he was supposed to do. And acted the way he was supposed to act. That small act, wherever it occurs, deserves honorable mention. Even if it involves someone, rumor had it, who graduated from Texas A&M.

Among men so isolated for so long, so completely unaware of the march of events, so wrapped up with the daily struggle for existence, any real news of the outside world comes with shocking suddenness. Thus, in the fall of 1944 the rumor that a place called Fushun had been heavily hit by bombers came as an unbelievable fabrication. Fushun was said to be a large coal mining and steel producing center some sixty miles or so southeast of us. How could this be possible? Where could the planes have come from? Surely if planes could hit Fushun they had to be based somewhere quite close, and we had heard nothing to indicate anything like that was possible. But a check with Ching-yu indicated it did indeed happen. There were, he said, many planes and much damage. The planes came from "a long way away." They hit factories and rail lines.

Within a few days he told me of raids at Dairen, on the coast near Port Arthur, and around Lioyang and Anshan, all names that meant nothing to me at the time, but which he described as being quite close.

Even coming from Guh Ching-yu it was hard to believe. At that time we knew nothing of the B-29, nothing of its range and power. We did not have long to wait to see that range and power firsthand.

By December they were pounding Shenyang. The first visit was a joyous occasion. For reasons we did not understand at the moment those of us at the factory were hurriedly rounded up and quickly rushed back to camp, in the middle of the day. Something was afoot. But what?

EIGHT

Surreal Liberation

We were herded into the prison compound, but still nothing had been said concerning the reasons.

Soon they appeared, like something out of Buck Rogers. Even flying at an altitude we were unfamiliar with, they appeared massive. Each of the planes trailed a long contrail in the clear, cold, winter sky. It was, to us, an awesome sight. Men lay on their backs on the frozen prison compound, cheering as the spectacle above them unfolded, and as the ground beneath them rocked and shook. And cheered still more at the apparent ineffectiveness of fighter planes sent up to challenge the bombers.

Vengeance was ours, at last. Deliverance was soon to be ours, at last.

For the men in the sky it was probably just one more mission. For the men on the ground their world had changed completely. We were still in prison and would still be in prison, but things were different now.

A certain amount of worry did accompany the situation. Our prison camp was completely unmarked, and obvious military targets were exceedingly close. But surely, the men reasoned, we had been properly pinpointed on the appropriate maps. We couldn't be in all that much danger.

Targets for that first raid were mostly west of us. The bombers left our own work place intact, as they did an aircraft factory a few hundred yards east of us.

On December 7, in Asia three years to the day, minus one, from the day it all started, they came after that factory, and others.

Osborne and I were lying on the ground near the southwest corner of the compound, not far from the barbed wire fence and the wall. Those bombers making the run on the aircraft factory were spread out, in a sort of "company front" formation. That itself was worrisome. We did not know how wide a swath they would take. Otherwise it was a beautiful sight.

Before we heard the rustle of the bombs we saw another worrisome sight. The planes were bombing on a long, slow curve, and, for some reason, two planes on the edge of the formation departed course slightly. That meant, unless their bombs had already been dropped, they were either after something else or they were wounded.

Within a matter of seconds we heard the old, familiar sound. Bombs on the way. But this time there was a discordant note. One or two, or more, were clearly off key, away from the avalanche headed for the factory. Within another second it was clear they would fall extremely close, indeed within our midst. There was no protection. We were lying face down on ground frozen hard as concrete. Osborne reached out instinctively and clutched my wrist. I suppose he figured that if we went we would go together.

The first bomb hit thirty or thirty-five feet away. At first, stunned by the blast, I did not try to move my body, fearing it would not respond, indeed not knowing if it was all there. As feeling returned I sat up and looked at the scene around me, strewn as it was with bodies and parts of bodies. The blast had wrecked the guard tower, blown a hole in the wall, and rolled up the barbed wire fence on which now hung arms, legs, torsos, bits and pieces of bodies—steaming, steaming, giving up their heat in the frigid air.

Still sitting, and still trying to collect my wits, I watched as Stuckey, a giant, red-bearded airman from Mississippi, tried to help "Bum" Baumgardner from the area. Baumgardner's left arm was torn from the shoulder, dangling useless on a shred of skin. A piece of shrapnel had gone through his skull, entering over his left eye and out over his right. A portion of the skull hung down, covering his right eye. His black beard was covered with blood.

Stuckey's midsection was stained with blood, but I could not tell if it was his or Bum's. Before the night was out, Stuckey would be dead. A piece of shrapnel had torn through his liver. Baumgardner, seemingly against all odds, would eventually recover, minus one arm and with two sunken places in his skull. In time he again became his cranky, stubborn self.

Osborne stood first and helped me to my feet. We were both unscathed. Why, I don't know. How, I don't know. But I do know I offered up a prayer of thanks. Nineteen men were dead and more than thirty wounded, many of whom were farther from the blast than we.

A second bomb hit the latrine area of our barracks. No one was hurt there. All the men were out in the compound. It did structural damage, but not much. Fortunately it fell, of all places, smack in the middle of the straddle-type latrine. It was a phosphorous bomb, designed to cause fires rather than demolition. The result caused a small amount of humor to be injected into the occasion. Feces mixed with phosphorous, and plastered here and there, resulted in a peculiar condition, and odor, we had not encountered. And yes, it does burn when mixed with phosphorous.

I do not remember anything in the way of criticism for the errant bombs, or the errant bombers. There was discussion as to how or why it occurred. Some thought a couple of bombs had probably become stuck and the planes veered from the formation to try to shake them loose. Others advanced different theories. But other than the sense of profound loss for those killed and wounded, it was a subject the men did not dwell upon. It was simply one more price we had to pay.

That marked the end, if memory serves, of bombing raids against targets in Shenyang. Certainly there were not many more. Mostly it was a matter of a lone B-29 flying over on reconnaissance missions, trying to determine if anything worthwhile was left. The factory where we worked was evidently determined to be militarily harmless, for it was left intact. As was our work schedule.

The episode did, however, produce a marked change in the attitude and behavior of our captors. Some became more sullen, bitter, ready to punish for the slightest provocation. Others seemed to lighten up a bit, to treat the prisoners with a little more respect. And, in my own view, the prisoners themselves seemed to recover a large measure of the self-respect that had been all but beaten from them in the previous years. There would still be many months to go, and the uncertainty of the moment weighed exceedingly heavy on the men, but things were different. The end, while not in sight, was bound to be much closer than it was three years earlier.

Thereafter, events moved rather swiftly. In April another 250 or so prisoners, American and British, were moved to our camp from Japan and Korea, including a group of some 45 survivors from what began on December 13 as the transfer of 1,619 prisoners from the Philippines to Japan aboard the *Ory Oku Maru*. When what was left of the group finally reached Japan some six weeks later, aboard the *Brazil Maru*, it numbered about 450. Of that number there would be, two years later, less than 200 alive.

Among those who finally made it to our camp was a young Georgian named Shifflett from our own Battery C on Corregidor. Shifflett brought tales of incredible horror during the journey, of suffocation, of dehydration, of men drinking their own urine, of decapitations, and of other events unspeakable. He still carried, in an inflamed right leg, a .50-caliber machine gun slug received during a strafing attack on the ship in Manila Bay. It was removed and he survived with little apparent ill effects.

Then, in May, a group of some 316 senior officers, orderlies, and four civilians (primarily American, British, and Dutch generals and colonels) were moved to our camp from camp Cheng Chia Tun in Formosa. They, too, were being moved out ahead of the advancing American troops. Until then the Japanese had been very careful about keeping senior officers separated from the men, perhaps thinking better control could be exercised over both. Or perhaps it was the result of their own appreciation of rank and standing. Whatever the reason, the arrival of our senior officers was a welcome, indeed joyous, event. Not only did their arrival portend the closing stages of the war, it also relegated Major Hankins to the role of just another prisoner, not an unwelcome development in the eyes of many in camp.

The highest ranking American officer now became Maj. Gen. George M. Parker, Jr., once the commander of two Philippine divisions. General Wainwright was also in the group moved from Formosa, but he and a few close aides and officers were held a few miles distant. We supposed it was for reasons of safety, to prevent possible collusion between the men, the officers, and their much-loved former commanding general.

Parker himself appeared a kindly man, but the years in prison had not been kind to him. At times he appeared psychologically broken, incapable of decision. Not that it really mattered, for there were few, if any, decisions he could make that would have any effect upon our circumstances.

Still, I do remember a sad story about Parker and a decision he thought he had to make.

The war had ended. We were still in prison. The Japanese, many months before, had provided a couple of piglets to the prisoner side of the compound. Their promise was that if the prisoners would feed the piglets, with food the Japanese provided, the piglets, upon becoming grown, fat hogs, would become food for the prisoners. They would be slaughtered and the meat distributed to the prisoners.

Each day, as we went to and from work at the factory, prisoners would anticipate that great day when fresh pork would be added to our rations.

Suddenly, when the pigs became hogs, they disappeared. There was much grumbling and cursing. But what could be done?

In time one or two more pigs were provided. This time our captors really meant it. This time they would really give the meat over to the prisoners. It had all been a misunderstanding.

In prison hope springs eternal, as it does elsewhere. Prisoners on camp detail cared for the pigs, looking forward to that day when we would all share the bounty. The rest of us, passing to and from work in the factory and in the fields, also looked forward to that great day. The pigs grew fat. Even though two pigs divided among more than a thousand men would not be much, it was far more than we had.

But something happened. The war ended. The guard changed. A number of prisoners crowded around the pig pen, a small enclosure some twelve feet by twelve feet, to decide the fate of the pigs. General Parker, then the senior officer in camp, had to make the decision. He was undecided. They were really not our pigs. The pigs actually belonged, he reasoned, to the Japanese. There was a question, in his mind, how all this would comport with the Geneva Convention on Land Warfare. Were we entitled to take something that was not ours, even in this circumstance?

As he debated the issue aloud with himself, Col. K. L. Berry, who was standing less that three feet from me, turned to a Colonel Browne and asked, almost under his breath, "My God, Brownie, what are we going to do with a man like this?"

But, Parker aside, within the group there were others who took up the slack. There was Berry, the hero of the "Battle of the Pockets" on Bataan, a man who seemed to think he still had a mission in life. Tall, rugged in appearance, a handlebar mustache adorning his face, he would have looked perfectly at home leading a company of Texas

Rangers against the Comanches. When he learned that I had an information pipeline through Guh Ching-yu, he insisted on daily briefings of all we had heard, along with anything anyone else had heard.

How many trains had we seen ply the rails that day? Which direction were they going? Did the trains carry tanks or other armor? How many tanks? How much armor? How many troops?

Obviously, all this was of no consequence as far as the war was concerned. But it had consequence in the psyche of the prisoners. It made us feel, perhaps in a small way, that we were again part of the action.

Through it all Berry and I became close friends, or as close as a colonel and a private can become. And many years later, when I was working on a story that would result in my receiving the Pulitzer Prize, our trails would cross again.

Spring turned to summer, and work at the factory seemed to take on a sort of aimless reason, or lack of reason. They even brought in a new leader for those of us on the construction gangs. He took it upon himself to make us happy. He named our group "the sunshine group" and exhorted us to radiate sunshine, to smile, to be "happy with our work."

He was a complete nut. He could speak fairly good English, having spent much time, he said, "In Ohio, Cleveland." He became, quite naturally, "The Sunshine Kid." It pained him greatly that the prisoners could not, or would not, constantly smile and be happy with their work. And it pained him still more when one of his charges ran into trouble with the rules. On occasion, rather than turn them over to others for punishment, he would call us all together, make a speech, accept the blame himself, then take a switch and thrash himself about the arms and shoulders.

That made us happy. Then he was happy.

One day in early August, Guh Ching-yu came by the work site. He was still recovering from a bout he had had a few days earlier with a small, half-wild Mongolian pony. A guard was making his rounds on horseback, and Ching-yu decided he wanted to take a turn aboard the animal. He fancied himself something of a cavalryman and perhaps wanted to demonstrate his skill to anyone watching. The guard dismounted, Ching-yu climbed aboard, and was immediately thrown to the winds. His left foot caught in the stirrup and he was dragged hither and yon before a number of prisoners managed to bring the situation under control. I fussed at him considerably. Why did he take such foolish chances? He had a wife and newborn son. What would happen to them if he were killed?

His dazed response was simple. *"Sulla, mei-faz."* The *"mei-faz"* bit was typical Chinese. Translated it meant something like "whatever will be, will be." With the *"Sulla"* tacked on it essentially meant, "One has to die sometime, so what difference does it make." He shrugged, and I said no more. One can't argue with logic like that.

But now he wished to talk. It was not unusual that we talk. But it was unusual for him to be so open about our meeting. We went to a place not far from his guard shack. He was in a somber mood.

The war, he said, would soon be over.

Rumors had swept the camp for weeks about new developments in the war, each carrying with it the promise that within days it would all be over. But Ching-yu had always said no, not yet. Now he was saying soon. But why?

Russia had entered the war that day, he said, and Russia would not have entered the war unless Japan was beaten and the end was near. Otherwise they would have waited.

That was great news. I was elated. Finally, at long last, it would all be over. I could not understand why he did not seem to share my own joy.

Oh, it was very good news, he said. He was happy it would be over. But this did not mean the world would be free of trouble. Someday, he said, America and Russia would go to war.

I was astounded. Where did he get ideas like that? Russia was our friend and ally, I told him. There was no chance, no reason for us to go to war.

Yes, he said, they were now friends and allies. But they did not think alike. They were not "the same."

"The world is not big enough," he said with no uncertainty, "for the two to live without problems."

I told him I thought he was wrong, that I certainly hoped he was wrong, for I had had all the war I wanted for one life.

I should not worry too much about it, he said, nor should he. Here he raised his hands to either side of his mouth, and, rubbing thumbs and forefingers together, said, "When the time comes you and I will be old men, twirling our mustaches."

I went back to the group, relaying the message about Russia. That night, back in camp, we found that others had picked up the same information. Apparently it was true. The Soviet Union was in the war. But what next?

What was next was that on August 17, during the middle of the day, we were assembled at the factory and moved quickly to camp, without the usual search at either place. The prison was a bedlam, rife with rumors. Some even speculated the war might be over. Before the day was out there were reports that someone had seen two well-fed white men in American uniforms over on the Japanese side of the camp. Preposterous. Finally, the truth came out: The war was indeed over. The men who had been spotted were part of a four-man parachute team, two white men, one Chinese-American, and one Japanese-American. They had come to take control of the camp and make sure, if possible, there would be no slaughter of prisoners in the wake of the long war's passions.

At first they, too, had been taken into custody by Japanese soldiers who were unaware of what had happened. After much discussion with higher authority they were allowed in camp, but the Japanese retained their arms, and their control, for reasons that would soon unfold.

The next day, in the midst of all the excitement these events caused, a low-flying plane scattered leaflets over camp and the surrounding area. The message was both welcome and puzzling.

The war was over. Japan had surrendered.

But we were not free to go. We must remain in camp for now. We were not authorized to accept the surrender of any Japanese. That was to be the responsibility of the Soviet Union's Red Army.

Why? It was not explained. But it seemed strange. There was no Red Army in sight.

And in the general euphoria of the moment more planes began arriving, flying low over the camp and an adjoining field, dropping tons of supplies, clothing, food.

It was a makeshift operation, but who cared? We got our first up close look at the, to us, huge B-29 bomber. For this operation they came in low, and as slow as they could fly and stay aloft, dumping racks of supplies that were supposed to descend on parachutes. Most of the time the parachutes tore away and the supplies came plummeting down.

Never mind, there was plenty for all. Hundreds of Chinese ringed the field, behind a loosely drawn line of former prisoners, cheering and shouting at the spectacle, and sometimes sharing in the bounty. Indeed, so anxious were they, or so starved, that at first some broke through the field's guarded perimeter only to be killed by falling food and clothing. At the moment, in China, food and clothing were cheaper than lives. Who knew what tomorrow would bring?

The Soviets came. On August 20 the advance tank columns arrived and we got our first glimpse of the Red Army and the problems that would plague the world for the next forty years.

The Soviet commander gathered us for a speech. Several times he bragged on the magnificent feats of the Red Army, motivated as it was by the thoughts and principles of the Communist Party. The many successes of the Red Army proved the validity of that thought and those principles. Then, in a phrase that still rings in my ears, he shouted: "America has fought the Japanese for four long years without success. Only ten days ago we entered this war, and already we are victorious."

I did not cheer. I do not remember any who did.

But he could not "tarry" with us, he said through his interpreter, for he was under orders to have his tanks "at the 38th Parallel" by midnight two days hence. The advance columns were already well on their way.

We had no idea where the 38th Parallel was, or what significance it had in the grand scheme of those things decided while we waited. We were yet to hear of Yalta or the division of the world into Communist and non-Communist spheres of influence. It was not then a worry to us. It was merely puzzling, but only temporarily so. There were other concerns more immediate.

During the twilight hours in the evening of that day or the following, I am not now sure which, we were assembled in the compound. The Japanese were also assembled, and their arms were stacked. With much pomp and ceremony, a Soviet officer formally accepted their surrender. Then he told us, in so many words, we could have their arms and could do with them as we wished.

The occasion seemed to have about it an element of surrealism. As if it were unreal, but real. The thing of which dreams are made. As if one knows that he is living through a dream from which he will soon awake to find that what was may still be.

There was much cheering, but no bloodshed. There was no rush to pick up the arms and settle old scores. The Japanese were returned to their side of the camp, probably with great trepidation. The former prisoners, now under command of their own senior officers, took

---

over control of the camp, manned the guard post at the front gate, and generally went about the task of getting things organized differently.

The lock on the warehouse containing our undelivered mail was broken and the mail distributed. Many things had changed at home during the past three and one-half years. My mother was now living in Cuero, Texas, with an older brother. But why? Another letter explained. My father had died two years before.

It was terrible, saddening news, coming as it did in the happiness of the moment. I had dreamed, so often during the long years, of the day I would return. Then we would go fishing and I would try to make up for all the unhappiness I had no doubt caused him. I even had the place picked out, on the clear running waters of the Devil's River, upstream from where it joins the Rio Grande. It would be a happy time.

It was not to be.

The days following were wondrous indeed. Wondrous, though strange and chaotic. A team of American servicemen came into camp to bring us up to date on what had happened while we waited. We were told of a powerful bomb that had been dropped, a bomb they really didn't understand but which changed the face of war. A tall, thin sergeant named Fred Friendly explained to us the course and timing of battles leading to our liberation, and gave us an inkling of how things might have changed at home. I was merely one body in the crowd, listening awe-struck as Friendly's revelations came forth. Someday, many years hence, our trails would cross.

It was all very strange. But for the moment other things were at hand. The first units of the Red Army we had seen were merely racing to get to the 38th Parallel, to plant the flag and move on. They apparently gave little or no thought to establishing any sort of order in their wake. In fact, my own view was that they were deliberately creating chaos. They made certain the Japanese kept the factories intact, and left them, for the moment, with arms to carry out the task. Within days the bulk of the Red Army arrived, flowing like water over the countryside. Anything deemed worthy of "liberation" was liberated, including the melons of unfortunate street vendors, and including, for that matter, any Japanese woman who suited the fancy of the liberators. The factories were gutted, every machine that might have use was loaded on trains for transport back to the Soviet Union. In short, the entire region was being sacked.

And they began the process of rounding up hundreds of thousands of Japanese, both military and civilian, also for transport to the Soviet Union. This, to me, was one of the more tragic aspects of the Red Army's operation during those days. While I obviously had no love for the Japanese, I could see no reason for their being treated in such fashion, particularly the civilians. As far as I was concerned, the war was over. It soon became apparent they had a different war in mind, or the continuation of another type of war.

Under those conditions trouble was not long in coming. One of the first signs of trouble erupted at the airport. Efforts to quickly fly out the ill and elderly were hampered by a decision on the part of the Soviets that only one plane per day would be allowed to fly in and out. Further, that plane would have to bring enough fuel to make the return trip, since, they said, not enough fuel was available. This naturally led to a certain amount of squabbling, which was compounded when a Red Army soldier, armed with a machine gun, shot up the landing gear of the relief plane. The official version was, of course, that he was drunk and really didn't know what he was doing.

Shades of Guh Ching-yu.

Nor was the friction limited to the top level. What first began as a euphoric meeting between the Americans and the "Russians" soon turned sour in much of our personal relations. When our official status as prisoners ended, many headed for town, looking for those things men might look for after nearly four years of war and confinement. There they met armed soldiers who had swept down from Siberia almost unopposed, convinced they had single-handedly won the war and were kings of the walk. Given the differences in experience, it was probably quite natural that friction sometimes develop. It did. There were fights. A few Americans began wearing sidearms to town, which led to an order from General Parker that this be stopped. This was to be an area of Soviet influence. We were not to act as if it were not.

In retrospect, Parker was probably right. Given the trouble at the top, considering the fact that the Soviets still had given us no timetable for leaving Shenyang, and considering the emotions of the moment, I suppose he was doing the right thing. But then it seemed a chicken thing to do.

Nevertheless, we had adjusted to worse. All in all it caused hardly a blip on the screen. Men still roamed the town and did their thing, often followed by scores of Chinese, applauding and shouting, in

Chinese, "America is number one" and "America is good." The power of the hated Japanese had been demolished, and, in their mind, they knew who was responsible. Never mind that the Red Army of the Soviet Union was present, indeed everywhere. They were still the bad guys, the wrong kind of *"Tabeezer,"* the barbarians from the North. They would not be there forever.

Guh Ching-yu was almost a daily visitor to the camp. He took me to the outskirts of the city, where we viewed the tomb of Nurhachu, the man who consolidated Manchu power some 300 years before and went on to conquer China, destroy the Ming Dynasty, and found the Manchu Dynasty. We spent days roaming the old city, climbing the ancient walls that surround the inner city, and talking, talking.

He took me to his hovel of a home, where I visited with his wife and new baby son, and where I shared their food and listened as she scolded him mightily for spending so much time playing and not looking for work. His job at the factory was now over, of course, and she was concerned about what came next. Their world, too, had turned upside down.

For the moment, however, Ching-yu was apparently unworried. He had been loaded down with supplies. It was summer. The former prisoners would have no need, shortly, for blankets, shoes, and other supplies that had been dropped. They were certainly not going to pack all that stuff back to the United States, so some of it found its way to Ching-yu, whom many took to be their friend from days that were different. For the moment he was in good shape.

And besides, he seemed to want to learn all he could about America and Americans. On one occasion, after his wife had again prodded him to go out and bring home some groceries, he asked me, "Is it the same in America? Do husbands and wives quarrel in America the way they do in China?"

I told him I had no way of knowing, that I was not married. But I suspected that quarrels did occasionally erupt. He shook his head. Why? What would they have to argue about? I dropped the matter. My limited knowledge of the language didn't allow that much explanation.

But while he was not then overly concerned with matters of the moment, he was clearly worried about what would happen when we left. He understood, as I did not, that China's troubles were not yet over. Mao's "Red Soldiers" were still holed up in the West. Now their friends and benefactors, in the form of "Red Soldiers" from the Soviet Union, were in control of all Manchuria. In all probability the final struggle was yet to unfold.

And what part would America or America's friends play in that struggle? What would happen if the seeming chaos of the moment blossomed into even wider chaos? What would happen if it all happened before we left for home? Perhaps we would be separated. Things could get difficult.

He had an idea. We would exchange messages — messages that might be helpful if certain things happened.

For Guh Ching-yu I wrote a "To whom it may concern" letter, saying he had been a good friend and benefactor of American prisoners of war, that I hoped all friends of America would treat him accordingly. I do not know what his letter says. It is in Chinese, which I cannot read. I still have it, and it is highly treasured. I hope it says essentially the same. My hope also is that he destroyed my letter to him. The way things turned out in China, it could otherwise have served as his death warrant.

Finally, the commander of Soviet forces in Manchuria gave us permission to leave.

On the ninth day of September in 1945, if memory serves, we walked out of Hoten Prison Camp #1 for the last time, along the wall for the last time, past the MKK factory for the last time.

I remember looking back at what had been our prison for so long, and vowing that I would never again bow to an earthly creature.

And I remember being seized, somewhere along that march, with a great sense of trepidation. I know it doesn't make sense now, but then, for a few moments, it was very real. What was out there? What was waiting? How could I cope with a world outside the walls?

We walked a ways, boarded a train, and within a day or so arrived in Port Arthur, which the Chinese called Lushun, on the shores of the Yellow Sea.

It was dark. Flood lights played on a hospital ship. And upon our beloved flag. We went up a gangplank and saluted the flag. At the head of the gangplank, aboard the ship, a pretty young nurse sat behind a small table. She appeared small, delicate, even angelic.

She required of every man his name, rank and serial number.

My wits left me.

The voice. I had not heard the voice of a white female for nearly four years. It sounded so strange. So soft. So alien. I stood speechless.

Someone shouted, "Tell her your name."

I did. "Towery, R. K., Private, 18048698."

"Next."

Next was a Corporal Coley, from North Carolina, out of D Battery, 60th Coast Artillery on Corregidor.

Before she could say anything he said, "I've always said I would kiss the first white woman I saw when I got out of prison."

She looked at him, rose, opened her arms and said, "What's keeping you, soldier?"

To my own astonishment and the cheers of assembled ship's crewmen, nothing kept him.

The process of adjustment had begun.

I was shown a bunk. The long voyage home was here at last.

Wiley Azof Towery (1876–1943), the author's father.

Towery family — Left to right: mother, Lonie Belle Towery; brother, C. O. Towery; the author. Pictured in Mississippi just before moving to Texas.

Lonie Belle Cowart Towery (1884–1975), the author's mother.

Family home on Medina River south of San Antonio, off Palo Alto Road, ca. 1938.

Left: Ken and Louise Towery, wedding picture, 1947.
Below: Family portrait taken in Cuero to record the birth of daughter Alice Ann, 1955, as son, Roland, looks on.

Ken Towery in uniform, Philippine Islands, August 8, 1941.

Aerial view of Corregidor.

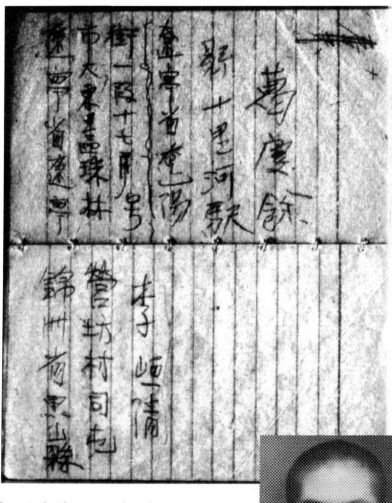

A message from Guh Ching-yu. When the Soviet Union's Red Army overran Manchuria in the final days of World War II, and seeming uncertainty marked the immediate future of the about-to-be liberated American prisoners of war in that region, as well as those Chinese who had opposed Mao, the author and his friend, Guh Ching-yu, exchanged messages designed to help the other should circumstances arise where they might prove useful. This is the message written in August, 1945, by Ching-yu, (in photo), a factory guard and work foreman who commited many acts of friendship toward American POWs during those years. Essentially, the message instructs other Chinese where they might direct the author to Ching-yu or his family survivors.

Former prisoners of Hoten Prison Camp #1 in Shenyang, Manchuria (which the Japanese called Mukden) preparing to leave camp and return home on September 9, 1945. Front row, left to right: Robbins of Washington; Gene Wooten of California; Shifflett of Georgia; George Williams of San Angelo, Texas; Galardi of Michigan. Back row, left to right: unidentified; Roy Creecy of Willow Creek, Montana; Johnny P. Turner of Ozona, Texas; the author; Alvin Winnikins of Green Bay, Wisconsin; unidentified. All are from C Battery, 60th Coast Artillery on Corregidor.

Towery family members on family farm south of Raymondville, Texas, in Rio Grande Valley, ca. 1928. Left to right: Dr. W. R. Towery, Mrs. W. R. Towery, Irene Towery (sister), Willis Ruble Towery, W. O. Towery, Ken Towery, Elgene Towery (sister), C. O. Towery, mother standing in front of the youngest, James, W. A. Towery (father), and David Towery. The farm is now a golf course.

Below: James Allen Towery, the author's brother, as an eighteen-year-old soldier on his way to the South Pacific. He served on many islands during the northward movement of American forces. He died at age thirty-seven from health problems arising from those conflicts. Right: The author in dress uniform after returning home.

Some of the ten giant 12-inch mortars of Battery Way. There were two such batteries on Corregidor. On Corregidor, the 59th Regiment had a total of 56 coastal guns and mortars, all of World War I vintage, ranging in calibre from 3 inches to 12 inches, with the longest range being 29,000 yards. It was the task of the 60th Regiment, armed with twenty-eight 3-inch anti-aircraft guns, to protect these guns, which in turn protected the southern flank of Bataan and kept the Japanese navy from entering Manila Harbor. By the time the Japanese invaded Corregidor only one gun, a 12-inch mortar from Battery Way, was still operational. It was manned on the final day in action by Battery "E," 60th CAC.

Thirty years after World War II, Ken Towery views the spot on the top floor of Topside Barracks where, during peacetime before the war, his C Battery, 60th Coast Artillery, was housed. Also viewing the destruction is Lloyd Wright, then head of the United States Information Service's publishing operation in Manila, and Marie Castillo, a reporter for the Manila Times.

The bombed-out remains of the post hospital, one of the first targets hit on Corregidor, with the North Channel and the southern slopes of Bataan in the background.

The twenty-fifth reunion of Bataan and Corregidor veterans in the Philippines.

Ken Towery at the Cuero Daily Record *editor's desk, October 1953.*

Where the story began: A typical small-town newspaper, the Cuero Daily Record *broke one of Texas' biggest stories — the veterans land scandal.*

Jack Howerton, publisher of the Cuero Daily Record, *seated at his "tidy desk."*

Land records checked: Inside colorful, old court buildings, the Cuero Daily Record followed the trail of the veterans land deals. Ironically, the white marble shaft in the foreground commemorates the county's World War I and II dead.

District Judge Howard P. Green reads the charge to the DeWitt County Grand Jury before it begins deliberations during its probe of what became known as the Texas veterans land scandals.

Jack Howerton (standing, publisher of the Cuero Dail Record *during the author's tim. at the newspaper, and the autho (kneeling) checking editions the beginning of a press run 1955.*

Cuero Record *publisher Jack Howerton and author outside the offices of the* Cuero Record, *after the author was awarded the Pulitzer Prize in 1955.*

The first of the trials in DeWitt County courthouse growing out of the veterans land scandals gets under way with District Judge Howard P. Green presiding. Lawyers for both sides are around the tables in the foreground, with jurors in background facing camera.

State's attorneys huddle prior to beginning of the first veterans land scandal trial in Cuero. At left is then DeWitt County attorney Wiley Cheatham (later the district attorney), at right is Attorney General John Ben Shepperd, and facing camera with arms folded is then district attorney Wayne Hartman. Other official is unidentified.

Ken Towery addressing the Texas legislature in 1955, following the breaking of the veterans land scandal stories in the fall of 1954.

Wiley Cheatham, former DeWitt County attorney, elevated to district attorney by former governor Allan Shivers during the prosecution phase of the veterans land scandals, looks over evidence with Deputy Sheriff Norman "Cutter" Dietz and State Highway Patrolman F. R. Byrnes, who assisted in the investigation. Dietz went on to become sheriff of DeWitt County, and Byrnes became sheriff of adjoining Goliad County.

Governor Price Daniel prepares to take his seat at the beginning of an impromptu press conference. Seated is Sam Wood, then chief of Newspapers Inc., Capitol Bureau, and Bo Byers with the Houston Chronicle. *Standing is John Ford (then an aide to Daniel) and the author.*

Left to right: Bill Oellermann, chairman of the Texas Public Broadcasting Association; Howard Gutin, CPB board chairman and San Antonio resident; and Ken Towery, CPB board member and Austin resident, met with Texas Governor William Clements November 5, 1987, when he signed a proclamation declaring Public Broadcasting Day in Texas.

Governor Price Daniel signs a proclamation as Bill Gardner, chief of the Houston Post *Capitol Bureau; Dawson Duncan, chief of the* Dallas Morning News *Capitol Bureau; and the author, then with the* Austin American-Statesman's *Capitol Bureau, look on.*

PART II

The Aftermath

NINE

Learning and Unlearning

When daylight next appeared, the hospital ship threaded its way out of the harbor, accompanied by a cruiser and several minesweeps darting here and there, blowing up floating mines that threatened our passage. We cleared the harbor and the ships headed south across the Yellow Sea en route to the island of Okinawa.

Offshore of that island we encountered heavy seas, and word came that a major typhoon was bearing down upon us. We turned again for the open sea and rode out the storm, strapped in our bunks as the ship tossed like a cork in the massive swells and waves. Eventually the storm passed, the waves calmed, and we returned to the island, going ashore in the midst of armaments we could never have imagined.

The war had ended. Terms of surrender had been signed aboard the USS *Missouri*, but peace had not yet come to all parts of the island. Still, enough of the island had been secured to provide a zone of relative tranquility, and it was here we remained while the new inhabitants picked up from the havoc of the storm. Within a few days that task was completed. Airstrips were repaired, planes returned to their base, and our journey continued, this time by air.

Back to the tropics. Back to the Philippines. Back to Manila Bay, whence the *Tottori Maru* had sailed some three years before.

It was a strange and different world. Manila displayed all the destructive earmarks of exceedingly heavy, and very recent, modern warfare. That was to be expected. But beyond that were differences I had never anticipated, indeed never dreamed of. Black people were present, and in uniform. Women were present, and in uniform. Youngsters not yet old enough to vote were wearing the stripes of master sergeants. Hundreds of thousands of men, gathered here to begin the final assault upon Japan, now milled about with no real mission save returning to their homeland.

We were ushered into the 29th Replacement Depot, a vast bivouac designed to provide a temporary home for soldiers in transit to and from duty assignments. Those with enough rank, or those who had physical problems requiring immediate attention, were afforded quick passage back to the States. The rest of us waited.

It all seemed so odd. A few short weeks before, we were in a world entirely different. There one knew that tomorrow would be the same as today. Here was mass confusion, or so it seemed. One could roam at will. There was food in plentiful supply, bunks to sleep on. And there were "recreation centers," where soldiers could while away the time with an occasional beer and a few kind words from pretty young women. It was very strange.

Under those conditions the former prisoners amounted to no more than a small drop in a large bucket. Around them were soldiers who had fought through the southern islands, taken part in the liberation of the Philippines, prepared themselves psychologically for the invasion of Japan, and now wished, no less than anyone else, to head for home. Together we waited.

During that wait, a telegram came. It said simply that "James is in the army in the Philippines."

James was the youngest of the family, three years younger than myself. I had no way of knowing where he was among the troops assembled in the Philippines, and initial inquiries with the army went unanswered. Someone suggested I try the Red Cross, which I did. Eureka. He was with a signal corps unit in central Luzon, near a place called Porac. In a gesture for which I will be forever grateful, the army provided a pass, jeep, and driver. In due course there he was, tall, blond, terribly yellow from the effects of an anti-malaria drug that all of us consumed as a matter of course in the tropics. He was standing by a dusty jungle roadway, waiting. It was a grand reunion.

His unit was responsible for establishing and maintaining the communications network needed by troops in forward battle zones. It was not the safest of battlefield jobs, but he had come through unscathed. At the moment there was not much to do. They were camped at the foot of a range of mountains, into which Japanese troops had been pushed and where they were holed up. The war was over, but the Japanese had not yet surrendered. A decision had been made to simply let them sit until wisdom prevailed. No need to shed more blood in a war already over.

Under those conditions we whiled away several wonderful days, comparing notes, swapping stories, remembering days together in the farm fields of South Texas. He brought me up to date on changes in the family, who was where and what they were doing. The war years had not been easy on the family.

Clearly, the future would require some getting used to. Even the terminology was different. The term "dogface" had disappeared, to be replaced with a new term, "GI." In our army, already the "old army," the term "GI" had been used to designate supplies, equipment. Now it was also applied to enlisted personnel. And a new term had crept into the language. Black troops were referred to as "Jiggs." I asked James where the term came from. He didn't know, but it seemed to have originated among white soldiers from the northeast, and just spread through the ranks.

In truth there was no love lost between the black and white troops at that particular place and time. So great was the animosity between them that the nearby communities of Porac, P.O. and Pampanga had been placed off limits during certain hours to both races. Evening hours in Porac, for instance, were limited to black troops and white troops on a rotational basis, never together. And both were forbidden to enter Pampanga during the evening hours.

Why the animosity? It all started, according to him, months before, on one of the southern islands. A black regiment was anchoring the flank for a white infantry regiment to which he was attached at the time. The white version had the Japanese attacking, causing the flank to fold and give way, with heavy losses among the white regiment. Now, suddenly, they found themselves in close proximity again, and there were scores to settle. It was not a pleasant situation. Japanese were in the hills, but the feuding, and sometimes the bloodshed, was among those encamped below. What, I wondered, did it portend?

All too soon it was over. A ship was scheduled to arrive in Manila to pick up troops bound for home, and my name was among those with a berth. I took leave of my brother. If all went well we would resume the reunion in South Texas, with sisters and brothers, and our sainted mother as the welcoming committee. Dreams of the jungle. But they did come true. Not exactly as we had thought, but who could complain?

I boarded the USS *Marine Shark* sometime in late October, headed, we thought, for her home port in Seattle, Washington. The ship, on her maiden voyage, had made passage from Seattle to Manila in the remarkable time of fourteen days, the captain said, and he was determined to equal or better that time on the return. The ship raced south out of Manila, negotiated the straits, and turned northeast across the Pacific toward home.

Suddenly, on a calm sea somewhere between the Marianas and Hawaii, in the vicinity of Wake Island, the ship's power ceased. We floated for days, moved only by the tide and a few gentle breezes, as crew members tried to repair the problems. A major bearing, we were told, had burned out.

Under those conditions there was not much to do, other than stay on deck, out of the stifling heat below, and gaze out across the endless, waveless ocean.

While thus engaged, I was approached by a fellow passenger. He was somewhat small, with a worried look about him.

Was I a former prisoner? he asked. He would like to visit, he said, if that was all right.

Sure. Why not? Visits were always welcome.

He wanted to know of conditions in prison camp. Were things as bad as he had heard? Had I seen many prisoners die? How did I feel about my former captors?

Clearly, the conversation was taking a turn I did not appreciate. I did not want to talk about it. Certainly not to a stranger.

It soon became apparent, however, that he was not so concerned about answers to his questions. He was more concerned with unburdening his conscience, hoping to find an understanding and appreciative ear.

He had been, he said, a cook for an infantry company throughout the long march from the southern islands. His company had suffered many casualties, but he had never fired a shot. He had never engaged the enemy, for which he had become an object of ridicule from his fellows. It stuck in his craw.

Finally, in the Philippines, his chance came to prove his mettle. His regiment had cut off and surrounded an enemy force, leaving them with no escape and no means of supply. The war was over, or nearly over, and the decision had been made to merely let them sweat it out, rather than risk more casualties. That would have been fine, but the starving enemy would occasionally steal down from the hills and make off with foodstuff. This infuriated him, and he complained to others in his company that they should "do something about it." His complaints fell on deaf ears. The reaction, he said, was always, "Look, if you want to go out there and kill them, go ahead. But don't bother us."

"They thought I wouldn't do it," he said.

So he took a rifle and trench knife, and in the evening went into a nearby field of sweet potatoes, where he found an unarmed Japanese soldier digging for something to eat. He approached the soldier and raised his rifle. The enemy soldier fell to his knees and raised his hands in supplication. All the ridicule, all the taunts came over the American soldier. He would show them.

He put down his rifle, pulled his trench knife, and killed the starving, unarmed enemy soldier. In fact, he said, he then "cut his heart out."

He seemed relieved, even a little proud. I was sickened, and went away, wondering then, as I do now, what it is in the human condition, or rather in the condition of some humans, that causes such thoughts and actions.

There are those who will argue, no doubt, that it is war itself that warps men's minds in such fashion. But millions of others have met the enemy in honorable combat and extended a helping hand when that combat ended. There is, in truth, a measure of respect for one's enemies that grows out of mortal combat. It is a respect sometimes lacking among those who have not tested their own courage against others, whether in battle or not. And courage is never proven, on the battlefield or off, against helpless adversaries.

The effort in ship's repair was only partially successful, and we limped into Honolulu days behind schedule. For the second time we were confined to quarters in that beautiful city. The captain wanted to depart as soon as needed repairs had been made. He felt, and he was probably right, that shore leave in Honolulu for men who had been so long among the battlefields of Asia might not be conducive to his plans.

The repairs were made. We left port with the hope, he announced, of trying to make up some of the time lost on the way. It was a futile hope. We were hit by massive storms somewhere west of the California coast. After two days of plowing into waves that washed the deck, the ship changed course for San Francisco. It was closer than Seattle.

Never could a coastline look more welcoming. The hills came into view, bathed in a declining sun, seeming to hang there above the horizon in a hazy mist. Gradually the outline took form, and finally, after nearly five years, I again looked up at the Golden Gate Bridge.

We sailed under the bridge on November 11, 1945. I had last seen it in March of 1941. Much had happened.

In some ways it was a strange, almost terrifying experience. There was, quite naturally, the euphoria of returning to my homeland. But suddenly I was swept with anguish, feeling so terribly, terribly alone. Would that Tuerman were beside me. And Shook. And Alabama Freeman. And a host of others. I had made it. They had not. For a brief instant my guilt knew no bounds. What was one to do? What could one do?

Once under the bridge we were met by a harbor boat, of sorts, which pulled alongside and escorted us to dock. Aboard, on deck, were women in uniform, perhaps members of service organizations formed for that purpose. They were shouting and waving, welcoming us home. Also on deck was a band, playing all the latest hits, with a loudspeaker blaring things like "Marezeedoats and dozeedoats and little lams zeedivey." And there was one about some fish trying to swim up a river in Sweden. Thankfully, there was one that could be understood: "Sentimental Journey."

In due course the ship docked and people went their own way, obeying their own orders. The former prisoners of war, or at least some of us, were hustled off to Letterman General Hospital, where we were to stay until transportation could be arranged to move us to a base closer to our own home. Some of us were allowed leave to visit the city; some were not. A preliminary medical examination revealed dark shadows in both of my lungs. I was confined.

Those who were allowed to visit the city returned with a strange story. To leave the hospital grounds, one was required to present his authorization to guards at one of several gates. The guards in this instance turned out to be Italian prisoners of war. Understandably, some of the returning Americans found that interesting, if not humiliating.

Clearly, this new world would take some adjusting to. Marezeedoats? Italian POWs guarding the gates, granting permission, or denying permission, for former American POWs to take leave in their own land? In time it probably would make more sense. Then it made none.

All that was as nothing, however, to what would follow. In a few days we were placed aboard a train, several hundred of us, for movement to Fort Sam Houston in San Antonio, Texas. It was an exciting, joyous moment. We were finally going home.

But then the cars were locked, sealed. There would be no exit until our destination. In town after town, city after city, crowds would wave and, when the train stopped, press forward against the glass of the windows, shouting, smiling, waving, throwing kisses to those inside. And those inside returned the gestures.

But there was no touching. It was heart-rending, traumatic. One wanted so much to be among them.

To this day I have never understood the logic of the sealed cars.

Eventually, we arrived in San Antonio. We went to a guarded staging area, then, in single file and under orders not to break rank for any reason, to barrack quarters prepared for us. The line was guarded by soldiers spaced at intervals. Their job was to prevent gathered family members from disrupting the proceedings. They were not entirely successful.

From there, in my case, it was directly to a bed in Brooke Army Hospital, under quarantine. I was given a mask, which was to be worn when anyone entered my room. The fear, of course, was tuberculosis. Initial tests came up negative, but the doctors were not satisfied. Something had caused the lung shadows and they were determined, I suppose, to find the cause. Nevertheless, the whole exercise resulted in a certain amount of testiness on my part. I wanted leave to go home. They said no. They were not impressed by, or seemingly concerned about, the emotions of the moment. We arrived at an understanding. They understood that if I were not permitted to go home, my continued presence would require a twenty-four-hour guard. My understanding was that they certainly had the means to provide it. In time it worked out. I was given a short leave.

I had a certain amount of sympathy and understanding for the authorities' position on the matter. At that time in our history, persons who had transmittable and potentially deadly diseases were not permitted to roam freely in society. Or at least the laws provided that they might be constrained. In the absence of positive proof of that condition, however, I felt they were acting somewhat arbitrarily.

The reunion took place in the lobby of the old Gunter Hotel in San Antonio. Family members had gathered there in company with many others bent upon the same mission, welcoming back those who had been away at war. It was a milling throng of anxious people, all searching for a familiar face. Occasionally a cry would go up as some family member recognized a returning son or brother. There would be shouts, embraces, tears.

I stood, searching. My memory is that the first face I recognized was that of my mother, and then, standing beside her, a brother, W. R., then his wife Velma, then others of the family. It was nice to be back. Even for a few days.

What followed were months of tests and treatment in various wards of Brooke Army Hospital. In addition to the lung shadows, for which they could find no definitive cause at the moment, my innards were evidently riddled with several kinds of parasites, some of which proved highly resistant to treatment. In time the army doctors had done all they felt they could do, and on a hot summer day in July of 1946 I took my discharge. There were no tears on my part, and I remember none on theirs.

Thus ended five and a half years of association with the army. In time I would reflect that, all things considered, I came out better than I went in. The health problems would plague me throughout most of my life, imposing their own brand of discipline and exerting their own influence on that life. But there were other, more helpful compensations. As a farm boy in South Texas I had felt that everyone else, especially those youngsters who lived in the towns and cities, were much more gifted than myself, much more intelligent, and probably much more courageous. I had always felt more at home among the animals and birds of the forest, and the crops of the fields, than among those who populated the towns and cities. But the years had taught me that I could at least adjust, that many others shared my apprehensions and fears, and that in the final analysis I could stand my ground in the face of danger and adversity, frightened though I was. That was probably the most important lesson of all.

Those lessons would be needed. The years that followed would require their own adjustment, their own lessons. James made it back safely, and together we roamed the old haunts, visiting family and friends, seldom speaking of the war years but worrying mightily about the future.

Many others were in the same boat. In one respect all doors were open. In other respects all doors were closed. Returning servicemen, in those years, were greeted everywhere with love and respect. It was a wonderful feeling. That was doubly true for those of us coming out of the prison camps. But none of us, or very few of us, heard the words, "Here take my job, I'll try to get another somewhere." Nor could we expect to hear it. The government recognized this problem, and, in an effort to provide some sort of transition cushion for returning servicemen, instituted something called the "52-20" program. It was designed to provide $20 per week for 52 weeks or $52 per week for 20 weeks, I can't remember which, to those who couldn't find jobs. At the urging of others I signed up. After collecting the money for two or three weeks, I never went back. It seemed so embarrassing and humiliating. Taking government money for performing no useful service was just not right.

But there was another government program that seemed to make sense. If we would agree to resume our education, the government would pick up the tab. That was something I always wanted to do, and one can usually justify doing what one wishes to do, even if it means adjusting one's thinking ever so slightly. The rationale in this instance was that we would become more useful citizens, that society would get back its investment in our education. It was a tenuous argument, granted, but it carried the day.

Problems immediately arose. Deadlines for enrollment in the fall semester for most colleges was upon us. Thousands of returning servicemen were enrolling. There quickly became no room in the inn. Too, I had not completed high school. It would be necessary to enter college under a probation schedule, which said, essentially, that one would be given a few months to prove he could make the grade. That was of no particular worry.

A small newspaper item reported that a new junior college was to get under way in Uvalde, Texas. The story quoted a Dr. Herschel LaForge, chairman of the trustees, as saying they hoped to begin operation in September. I called, and was impressed that he took the time to explain, to someone he didn't know, his plans and hopes for the new venture. He invited me to become part of it.

I took a bus from Cuero to Uvalde, only to find that the opening date had been delayed. A new, three-county junior college district had been voted into existence, but legal challenges were yet to be settled. The site for the new college was to be a former Army Air Force training installation, then sitting abandoned. I took up residence in one of the buildings, sleeping on a cot, and under blankets, furnished by a man named Landoldt, who, if memory serves, was superintendent of schools in Uvalde. With a truck borrowed from the National Guard, and help from a number of prospective students, we went about the task of assembling bunks and other furniture that might be needed to put the dream into reality.

In time it was done. Sometime in October an office was opened in the building where I slept. The registrar set up shop and I registered, becoming, I was told, the first student of Southwest Texas Junior College. There was no effort on my part to become the first student. I was simply there when the proper authorities showed up.

In many respects that first class was blessed indeed. It numbered less than a hundred or so students, most of whom were returning veterans who had hopes and plans, and were prepared to work hard to achieve their goals. There was, fortuitously, a faculty that was well prepared and that understood the problems of those it sought to instruct.

I had been out of school for some seven years, and the work was not easy. Had it not been for the personal involvement of teachers like Alvis Hannah, who ushered us through various courses in chemistry, and Maurice Litton, who counseled and cajoled us through courses in physics and mathematics, or Lillian Barklay, who sought to instill an appreciation of literature in all her charges, I would never have made it. It was not at all unusual for teachers to spend hours during the evening with questioning students. They, too, were caught up in the adventure.

In my own case the difficulty arose not simply from the nature of disciplined study. Prison camp and all its memories were not that far removed. The simple act of sitting in a comfortable chair, or lying in a comfortable bed, or roaming freely through the countryside would quite often transport me back to prison, where those things were not possible. The sound of a police or ambulance siren would awaken me from a dead sleep, disoriented, summoning me for another bout with incoming bombers. I'm sure many others shared those problems, or variations of them. They seemed to go with the territory, the process of adjusting.

During that first year I met and courted Louise Ida Cook, a

pretty young girl from the nearby farming community of Knippa. And, for reasons I have never fully understood, she agreed to become my wife. Perhaps it was a temporary loss of sanity on her part. At any rate we were married in Houston, Texas, in the early morning hours of May 4, 1947, in the presence of family members gathered for the occasion. Until then she had lived a relatively trouble-free life. Now she would be part of the struggle.

Eventually my studies at Uvalde were completed. After another year-long interruption for hospitalization and medical treatment in a veterans facility near Kerrville, I graduated and transferred to Texas A&M, where I hoped to finish my studies. Student enrollment in the little college at Uvalde had grown substantially, and it was with mixed emotions that we departed.

In fact, in a large way we felt responsible for helping it get started. In time the college would be peopled by those who, perhaps in a rare moment of wonder, would look back in embarrassment at those who began it all, who hung deer carcasses in the shower stalls, who staked alligators on the campus, who, in even more rare moments, sat and reminisced among themselves of battlefields hither and yon around the world. But who also did their best to master the art of learning. And who paid, or had paid, for the privilege of doing so.

The family had increased by one—a son, Roland, born in August of 1948. We moved into what had been an Army Air Force facility west of the Brazos River a few miles from Bryan. Running water and facilities for common bathing were only fifty or sixty feet away. It was somewhat rustic, but adequate. Young wives, or at least some of them, found the atmosphere somewhat intimidating. They found it embarrassing to go to the showers at 2:00 in the morning, after a friendly encounter with their husbands, and find a number of other wives there under similar circumstances.

After a few months we found housing on campus, in a collection of temporary plyboard buildings known locally as "Vet Village." They were located near Kyle Field, where the famed Aggie band would sometimes hold forth to the rousing cheers of just about everybody in hearing distance. Vet Village was home to a number of returning servicemen and their families. Each apartment, cramped though it was, had its own running water and bathroom. A brother in Houston, the one we called "Tuble," managed to find an electric fan at "wholesale" prices. I ordered a genuine wooden breakfast table from

Sears, which came unassembled and unpainted but with powdered glue that one mixed with water to stick it all together (and which, incidentally, we still have) and a genuine Bendix washing machine, which caused Louise to cry a great deal and made her the envy of the neighborhood (and which seemingly everyone else used as much as she, with her blessing). Finally, things were looking up.

I did reasonably well in my studies. I had chosen a course of studies which, for me, proved very difficult. But it was one in which I was terribly interested, involving the chemistry of soil and the physiology of plants growing in that soil. Perhaps my interest in the subject was a natural outgrowth of the farm years, but I thought it was more. On the farm we knew life on earth sprung from the soil. We knew how to care for that soil and its plants. We just didn't know, or at least I didn't know, exactly why. I hoped to find out.

Beyond that, however, lay something else. Somewhere deep in my psyche was a nagging doubt that I would ever be able to properly grapple with the society around me. What better course of action than to ultimately close myself off in some research laboratory somewhere, surrounded by the tools of the trade? Perhaps it would be one way to make some small contribution to society without having to come in close contact with that society and its problems. At the very least it would afford time to sort things out. In the meantime, society could go its way. I would go mine.

But why the seeming need for some sort of planned, self-imposed isolation? I was not completely certain then, nor am I certain today. Perhaps it was merely a result of the confusion and trauma of the moment, of having grown to manhood in the death and destruction of war and prison camps, and then being suddenly thrust into a different world, where the old landmarks were gone. Or, if not gone, were rapidly changing.

Locked in the time warp of prison camps, the sameness of prison camps, we had assumed all things would remain the same. That thought was the cocoon into which we had retreated, and which made existence possible. When we got back, if we got back, all things would be as they were. Life would be beautiful. God would still be on His throne. We would merely begin anew.

God was, in fact, still on His throne. But there seemed to be little agreement, among those who claimed to be His subjects, concerning just who He really belonged to. Or who belonged to Him. Or what He expected from His people. Or what His people expected from Him.

THE CHOW DIPPER

We had come out of the experience convinced that faith had played a dominant role in our survival, that without faith and hope all would have been lost. We made the round of churches, searching for some sort of spiritual home that recognized this, at least by inference. Instead, we were met by sermons exhorting us to ante up for the starving masses in Africa or some other place, in order that records somewhere reflect our collective goodness. We were met by prayers for peace in the future, but precious few prayers of thanksgiving, it seemed, for those who had given up their lives in order that the preachers and priests who prayed might do so in safety and security, or that the congregations might also meet in safety and security. And perhaps even fewer sermons dealing with what I thought was the fundamental message of Christianity, that we believe. Or the fundamental message of Christian ethics, that we be "merciful," one to another. I could not help reflecting, as I sat in various congregations, that had it not been for those who gave up their lives, and those who fought and came through safely, their pulpits could well be occupied by Shinto priests.

Now, upon reflection, it is probable that the fault, if there was fault, was my own. It is probable that I was simply not hearing, or I was being selective in my hearing. But then it was very important. I could see, or thought I could see, a certain smugness, a certain sense of self-righteousness, a missing of the point of it all. And I could see years of turmoil in trying to adjust into a society with which I could not yet come to grips. Better to seek a life that might afford a hiding place.

The stint at A&M did not last long — through the summer and into the fall. In those days I was required to report to the Veterans Administration every ninety days for chest x-rays. Shortly before Christmas in 1949 I reported to the veterans facility in Waco, underwent the routine x-ray examination, and sat down with the doctor for his response.

I could not return to school, he said. The dark areas in both lungs had begun to spread rapidly. I must enter the hospital. I asked if I could not go back and finish the semester. The answer was no. Very well, I would go back and check out. The answer was still no, I could not even go again upon the campus. They would notify the authorities to terminate my schooling immediately. They had reserved a bed, again in the Veterans Administration facility near Kerrville, in the hill country west of San Antonio, and I was to report there as soon as possible. If all went well I could perhaps expect to return to school in a few years.

Thus ended my formal education. All in all, it was a useful exercise. Much of that period has remained with me. Two things in particular.

Once, during a classroom lecture involving the aggregation of some particular molecules in the soil, I disputed, or rather questioned, the explanation of a Dr. Jones, generally respected as one of the nation's preeminent authorities on the subject, and head of the school's department of soil chemistry. He explained it again.

My response was "Well, that's not the way we learned it as sophomores."

He was very kind. Looking down with seemingly sorrowful eyes, he said, "Yes, Mr. Towery. As a junior you will have to quite often unlearn what you have learned as a sophomore. And as a senior you will have to unlearn many things you learned as a junior. And when you leave here and go out in the world you will have to unlearn many, many things you learn here. That is just the nature of learning."

That was one lesson learned that has remained learned.

Another. On one occasion, back at the Uvalde junior college, I broached the subject of religion with Alvis Hannah, head of the chemistry department. In a way he seemed to be something of a contradiction. He was, first and foremost, an exceedingly good teacher. In both classroom and laboratory, he was a patient taskmaster, but a taskmaster nonetheless. I suppose one could call him a scientist. He had the necessary degrees and the necessary turn of mind. Still, he was a regular churchgoer. He even conducted lay sermons on occasion. Away from the laboratory he was a kind and gentle man, a family man.

It was a time when "scientists" were feeling their oats. A few of the brainy ones had unlocked certain secrets concerning the atom. Others, the lesser lights, seized upon this as proof that if God were not dead, he was at least dying. Soon there would be no mysteries left. Science would know exactly how, when, and why the universe began, and what made it tick. There would be no need for "faith."

I asked Hannah about all this. If all went well, I would someday enter into that community of scientific truth seekers, but I did not believe it was necessary to give up one's belief in certain fundamental truths, or what one regarded as fundamental truths, in order to search for other truths. Did he have any guidance? How did he reconcile the matter in his own mind?

Yes, he was aware of the debate. He read all the literature. He attended the conferences. He realized that among his peers he was something of an outsider when it came to discussions concerning the topic, but it caused him no problem. He was a believer, but he could see no contradiction between believing in his God on the one hand, and trying as best he could to better understand the marvels and nature of his God's handiwork. He differed with many of his scientific brethren, and many of his religious brethren, in that he did not see his work as an attack upon God but rather as an attack upon the ignorance that kept men from better understanding God as he understood God.

He indicated, at least, that he did not regard God as being some white-haired old man with a long beard, but rather as a spirit, to be worshiped as such. Even if we were able to unravel the mysteries of creation all the way back to the first atom, or the first proton, or the first neutron, there would still be the question of how and why. As far as he was concerned, he was at peace. The Spirit was there. It would be there.

It was a comforting discussion. And while neither the lesson on learning from Dr. Jones nor the discussion on religion with Alvis Hannah made any vast or immediate changes in my life, both would be remembered and called upon throughout that life.

At any rate, the college days were over. I entered the hospital and began a regimen of complete bed rest, then the most often prescribed treatment for tuberculosis. Louise and the baby, then less than two years old, moved back to Cuero and took up residence for a while in my mother's small garage apartment. My mother probably provided a certain amount of comfort, helped in rearing the child, and no doubt imparted a certain amount of wisdom along the way. Louise, in turn, provided support and helped where she could. In time she found work in Kerrville and moved there, which allowed for occasional hospital visits. Those visits were, needless to say, about the only bright spots in an otherwise disheartening experience.

At that time the Kerrville facility was reserved almost completely for veterans suffering from tuberculosis. The disease had not yet been "conquered" by drug therapy, and about all the medical authorities could do was isolate patients away from the general stream of humanity, confine them to complete bed rest, feed them well, and hope for the best. In some cases surgery was employed, wherein a portion of the lung was removed, a number of ribs removed, and the chest wall collapsed. In some cases it was supposed to speed the process of recovery. In other cases it was regarded simply as a treatment of last resort. In my own case the doctors could see no benefit from surgery. The option turned out to be some eighteen months of bed rest and six months of "rehabilitation" before the two-year ordeal came to an end. All in all, I was very fortunate.

Hospital stays of that duration, and under those circumstances, required much in the way of what might be called mental adjustment. During the first few months it was merely a matter of lying in bed and staring at the ceiling, exerting as little energy as possible. Visits to the washroom or the laboratories were accomplished in wheelchairs, pushed by orderlies. Masks were worn at all times, save when we were alone in our own rooms. Visiting and visitors were not encouraged.

As the months went by, and as our condition improved, we were moved in a sort of orderly progression from one ward to the next, each time with a change in the color of our hospital attire, and a change in the color of the four walls that made up our rooms. Strangely enough, each move was accompanied by a certain amount of disorientation, perhaps indicating the extent to which the human psyche craves a degree of orderliness in all things. And the degree to which small things loom large in our everyday life.

Looking back it seems a valuable experience, though it did not appear so at the time. Then all we saw was a terrible interruption in our life plans. It brought into question the entire future that lay before us. We were told there would be no automatic reentry into college when and if the illness was finally controlled. We would have to undergo an unspecified period after hospitalization, building up a "work tolerance" before returning to campus. We would have to prove, by workplace experience, that we had the stamina to again undertake college studies. But who, pray tell, would be willing to hire an ex-tubercular with a history of repeated hospitalizations? How would that "work tolerance" ever be proven? How long would it take? What hope was there? Troubling thoughts for a young man with a family — probably even for a young man without a family.

Many other veterans at the hospital were in similar boats. Some were friends who had spent time in the same prison camps and were going through the same adjustment problems. Some were much worse off than I. In fact, some did not make it through. Still, the experience had its value. It afforded us time and a degree of mutual support. It drove home the realization that we all have a sack of rocks to carry in this life, and that no matter how much we think we are put upon, there are always others who would gladly trade places.

Eventually, the doctors gave me a reasonably clean bill of health. Louise packed our belongings, such as they were, and we returned to DeWitt County. For several months we lived with a brother in Yorktown, a small community some seventeen miles west of Cuero, where Louise found work in a government office concerned with regulating the production and sale of farm crops. In time we moved to Cuero, into quarters at an abandoned Army Air Force training camp known locally as Brayton Park. Luckily, I found part-time employment in a slaughterhouse, grading turkeys. The pay was forty cents per hour, the work was irregular and seasonal, the conditions somewhat less than ideal. In fact, if working conditions in turkey slaughterhouses have not improved in the past forty years I would have to recommend some other line of work. But it was a start.

My luck held. In a few months I heard there might be an opening for a reporter at the *Cuero Daily Record*. It would be a longshot, but what was there to lose? I had no formal training for the job, but perhaps I could learn. It would probably be better than what I had, if I could pass muster. At least at the *Daily Record* I wouldn't have to wade through blood, guts, and feathers to do my job. Surely not on a daily basis.

TEN

The Big Story

The *Cuero Daily Record* in those days was a dominant force in community life, largely by virtue of its long history and the presence and personality of its publisher, Jack Howerton. Howerton's father had founded the paper in 1894 as a one-sheet daily paper, printed front and back. In time the paper became the only survivor among several papers, some said because it insisted on concentrating on local news. The town was then a growing, roaring, frontier community, the terminus of the Gulf, Western Texas and Pacific railroad. In 1878 the old San Antonio-Aransas Pass railroad linking San Antonio and the Gulf Coast was completed through the county. Legend had it that the elder Howerton would ride his horse to the railroad station and make notes on who was traveling, where they were going, and what their business was. It made interesting reading.

In times past the community had been somewhat less than tranquil, situated as it was in the pathway of immigrants from Europe on the one hand, and cattle drives from the surrounding country to railheads in the north on the other. It had been home briefly to John Wesley Hardin, the most dangerous of Texas gunfighters who ultimately met his end in El Paso at the hands of a local constable. But that was only after he had dispatched some thirty of his fellow citizens, all of whom, according to him, deserved killing. It had also been the scene of the post-Civil War Sutton–Taylor feud, the bloodiest of all Texas feuds, which lasted for years and colored local politics and local sentiments long after it was over.

All that had faded into history. Local folks seldom, indeed almost never, spoke of those matters. There may have been some embarrassment over the fact that Hardin was part of the early history, and there may have been a certain amount of wisdom displayed in not mentioning the Sutton–Taylor affair, since one might bring up the subject in the wrong company. But for whatever reason the thrust of community life was now on building a future.

Howerton was absolutely convinced that the town of about 8,000 was poised for tremendous growth. The long war against Germany and Japan was over. A spirit of optimism prevailed. Oil had been found in the eastern part of the county, and that, combined with the rich farming and ranching areas to the west and north of town, was bound to have the desired results.

As a testament to his faith, Howerton had purchased and installed the *Temple Telegram*'s old printing press, preparing for the day when his *Record*'s circulation would expand far beyond its normal 3,600 daily. It proved to be a mistake, but one he probably never regretted.

I went down to see about the job, and was surprised. Howerton was a small man in his middle fifties, with wrinkles already spreading across his face. He was very quiet, almost apologetic in conversation, and an incessant smoker. There seemed to be a marked contrast between his personal manner and what I had come to expect by reading his occasional editorials, which, while well reasoned and thoughtful, left no doubt where he stood on public issues.

Yes, perhaps he could use an additional reporter. He felt he was pretty well covered on the city side of news, but the paper was weak in its coverage of the county's agricultural base. He would like to have better coverage in that area, primarily for the benefit of the Wednesday edition. That edition served as a sort of expanded weekly, picking up and rewriting stories of local interest that had appeared in the preceding daily editions, with the addition of news and feature articles of primary interest to readers in the rural communities. He had no one on staff who had a particular interest or understanding of that subject. While I would be expected to help out on the city side of news, the primary thrust of my reporting would have to be the agricultural community. If I was interested, he would give me a try. Certainly, I was interested. Indeed, I was elated at the prospect.

There was one small problem. I didn't know how to operate a typewriter. It would be necessary that I learn before coming on payroll.

Louise borrowed a typewriter from somewhere, and in the evening hours, after her work was done at the office, she instructed me in the ways of that remarkable machine. When we felt I had sufficiently mastered the process I again returned to the *Record* to take up my duties.

I was assigned a small typewriter stand, on which sat an ancient Woodstock, unused for who knows how long. Wrapping my legs around the stand, I began the "every good boy does fine" routine. When I came to the "f," it flew off and fell amidst the general clutter that marked the decor of the *Record*'s newsroom. A diligent search uncovered the item, it was glued back in its proper place, and, on that inauspicious note, my association with newspapers and newspaper people began.

I took up space between the paper's longtime managing editor, Harry Putman, and Nina Scarborough, an inquisitive and sometimes inquisitorial reporter who, with Putman, covered the usual goings-on throughout the city. Nina was a good reporter, usually a good, objective reporter. It was mostly when she felt someone was being unkind to a stray cat or dog that she came unglued. And woe betide the individual so inclined, whether he be city or county official. There were ways to get even.

Milton Binz sat nearby. He, with Putman, and with help from Howerton and his wife Polly, made up the advertising staff. Binz was a dedicated worker, but he was not noted for his ability to spell. I can still hear Putman shouting "Look it up in the dictionary," the reply to which was "How can I look it up if I don't know how to spell it?"

The news and advertising staffs took up a very small portion of the space used in the newspaper operation. We were sandwiched between an office supply operation in the front of the ground floor and the printing presses in the back. The second floor was entirely given over to commercial printing and to Linotypes, melting pots, composing areas, and printing machinery of various kinds.

The *Record* was then a "letterpress" operation, meaning the paper was assembled and printed by a process that required every line of type to be cast in hot metal, those lines of type to be assembled in page format, then reproduced by a process that ultimately resulted in the formatted pages again being cast in molten lead semi-cylinders which were then fitted onto the printing press. It was, needless to say, a labor-intensive operation, requiring the full-time services of some seventeen employees, in addition to certain part-timers and those required in circulation. Those familiar with the newspaper business know there are certain financial problems inherent in that sort of operation. For those not so blessed, it is still easy to see that the paper was constantly struggling to keep its head above water.

Financially the paper would have been far better as a strong weekly, but as far as Howerton was concerned it was begun by his father as a daily, that was the atmosphere in which he grew up, and as long as he was alive it would remain a daily, regardless of the difficulties that might be encountered. In short, Howerton was not the shrewdest of businessmen. He was simply a newspaperman of the old school. What that meant, I was yet to learn.

But for now I finally had a real job, paying ten whole dollars each day. At the end of each week there would be a check for $60. Sunday's were free, more or less. Louise was working for a local cotton merchant, making some $150 each month. Things were coming up roses, again.

A small frame home came up for sale on the edge of town, at the end of a narrow dirt road that later became Moss Lane. It had no running water, but there was a hand pump out back. We borrowed some money, paid $6,000 for the house and six acres, and with the help of brothers David and Raymond soon had ourselves a home with running water, indoor plumbing, electricity, butane gas, the works. One bedroom measured 12' x 12', the other 10' x 10'. There was space outdoors where the youngster and his dog could roam and grow. Who could ask for anything more?

I soon found that it is one thing to hold a reporter's job, and quite another to do justice to that job. I was at a complete loss. I felt I could write well enough to get by. At least I could write a simple declarative sentence, a facility I would find sorely lacking among many economists and "social scientists" with whom we would come in contact over the years. But while honest reporting may involve writing, writing does not necessarily involve honest reporting. I would have to learn how to be a reporter. That, I would find, is easier said than done, especially under circumstances then prevailing at the paper.

Howerton, as the paper's publisher and owner, had brought me on board with certain general observations of what he wanted done. Putman, on the other hand, as managing editor, had the responsibility of putting out a daily afternoon newspaper, and he wanted it as full as possible of local news, city news. Otherwise we would have to fill the paper with United Press wire service copy. He was not enthused over expanding the paper's agricultural coverage. A story concerning some recent agricultural development, or a feature story concerning some young farmer's success, would not be missed if it were never written. But it would be most embarrassing to miss some happening in a town of 8,000, which, within a matter of days, could become general knowledge and would raise the question: "Why didn't the paper have something on this?" And while Howerton signed the checks, Putman handled the day to day reporting assignments.

The net result was that my earliest days at the *Record* were not happy ones. I was a relative newcomer in town. I had no longtime friends in city or county government, both usual sources for news in communities big or small. I had no general body of knowledge concerning community life that could go beyond that which appeared in official records. My assigned rounds of places like the city hall, the county courthouse, the sheriff's office usually produced very little in the way of legitimate news. People who occupied those offices would normally call Harry if they felt they had anything interesting or newsworthy, from their standpoint. They had dealt with him for many years. Further, he wrote a daily column called "Town Talk," in which he was free to comment on matters around the city.

Usually, at the end of the day, Putman would bring forth the day's edition, with a number of news stories circled in red. He would point to each and say "I got that story. It should have been yours. Why didn't you get it?"

I had no answer. I had no answer because I simply did not know, nor did I know why things were working the way they were. Was this his way of teaching, or was it, as it seemed to be, merely his way of letting me know my absence would not hurt the paper? All I knew, or thought I knew, was that in time I would improve. I would probably never be a very good reporter, but perhaps there would come a time when I could carry my weight. Besides, someday I would return to school, to study and perhaps write about the peculiarities of molecules in the soil, rather than the peculiarities of human behavior.

As time went on I gradually became more productive. I spent more and more time in the countryside, even if it was after hours, attending community gatherings of one kind or another. The county at that time had two principal municipalities, Cuero and Yorktown, in which some 10,000 lived. But another 12,000 or so lived in small rural communities or on ranches and numerous small farms throughout the county. Most of the farms were owned by people of German descent, with a sprinkling of Poles in the western reaches of the county. They seemed appreciative of the attention and responsive to our efforts.

I would find that political and business leaders from the towns also attended those gatherings and followed our reports. After all, these were people on whom they depended for their respective livelihoods. Acquaintances were made, friendships were made, bonds of trust were established. In the world of newspaper reporting, those are valuable commodities.

Finally, things were coming together. I began to feel useful. Perhaps I was even doing a few things that would be remembered long after I was gone. It was a good feeling.

Then, one day, word came from the Veterans Administration. Every ninety days since leaving the hospital I had reported to their facility in San Antonio, where x-rays were made and reports pored over. Two years had passed. The doctors determined that I was ready to resume my studies. If I wished, I could return to school for the fall semester.

What to do? This was what we had been waiting for, hoping for. Prison and its aftermath, plus the long years of hospitalization, had already placed me well behind my peers, many of whom were now well established hither and yon. Perhaps now we could catch up. But there was the worry: Would another period of intense study merely result in another trip to the hospital? The doctors said that risk was there, but the decision was mine. For the moment, at least, I was fit.

The question filled my waking moments. Then, one day, a funny thing happened. It was one of those small, obscure moments that somehow have a bearing on our lives. I was on my way to the county courthouse for some forgotten reason, worrying about the decision that had to be made, when a small ground squirrel scurried from a clump of grass, heading for his nearby hole on the courthouse lawn. He stopped for a moment to complain about being disturbed, and I paused for a moment, mentally comparing his problems to my own.

How pleasant it would be, I thought, to return to school, continue the course I had set, and spend the rest of my time worrying about things in the natural world. But then another thought intruded. Surely the affairs of men were more important than the affairs of squirrels, even considering the joys afforded by the one and the heartaches afforded by the other. The decision was made. I would stay where I was, recording, as best I could, and in a small way, the affairs of men.

The squirrel went down his hole. I continued my journey.

While this was going on, another little drama was playing itself out within the staff. Howerton and Putman were longtime friends. They had gone to school together. Sometime after Jack took control of the paper Harry had come aboard. Most of his experience at the paper had been in advertising and news. He knew little of the mechanical side of the paper's operation. Howerton knew all aspects of the operation, and was involved in all aspects of it. Each had, or seemed to have, tremendous respect for the other. But they had some differences.

The two did not agree completely on the role of a small-town newspaper. When Howerton felt the need, he was not hesitant about involving the paper in a community disagreement. He would, on occasion, advise the community how it should vote concerning such matters as support for school bonds, or increased taxes for street maintenance, or whatever. Harry was reluctant to get into those matters, feeling the paper's job was to report the issues and let people fight it out among themselves. Besides, he said, he was the one who had to take the heat when he went forth to sell advertising. Nevertheless, that difference proved no great stumbling block in their relationship. Jack was, after all, the boss. It was his paper.

But there was another matter, one which would loom much larger as the years went by and play itself out tragically long after I left the paper. At the moment it was mostly an irritant.

Somewhere along the line Harry had acquired a taste for, indeed a fondness for, good bourbon whiskey. Jack was not so inclined. In fact, to my knowledge, he never took a drink. Indeed there were those who said the only real problem between the two men was that Jack never put bourbon in his water and Harry never put water in his bourbon.

I never saw Putman's drinking as being the problem that Jack saw. To me, it seemed Harry's drinking was mostly a crutch to get him over some temporary hill. I did not see it as any sort of permanent affliction. He normally wrote his column, for instance, in the afternoon of the day preceding publication. The day's paper was out. He had time to think. Occasionally he would sit at his typewriter and stare at a blank piece of paper, not an unusual situation for a writer to be in. If the muse didn't strike him soon enough, there was a bottle of Four Roses in the bottom desk drawer nearest his right hand. It seemed to help. Sometimes two or three trips to the drawer were required, but eventually the typewriter would begin to clatter and another column would spring forth.

Jack did not approve. He did not want any drinking during office hours, and certainly not on the job. What happened after hours was another matter, and none of his business. What happened at the office *was* his business. He made that known repeatedly. All to no avail.

The result was a sort of perpetual Mexican stand-off. It continued that way until one hot summer morning in 1954, within moments of when the staff assembled for work. Jack walked in and said he had an announcement to make. "Beginning immediately," he said, "Ken, you are the new managing editor. Harry, you will be in charge of all advertising. Everyone else will continue doing what you are doing."

He walked into his office and left us to sort things out. The process of sorting was not the smoothest of operations. Harry, naturally, was crushed. He simply could not believe his lifelong friend had done this to him.

He was not alone. I couldn't believe it either. Even more difficult to believe was that I suddenly found myself in the managing editor's chair. It was something I had not aspired to, something beyond my interests, something I did not need in terms of ego, and something for which I felt ill prepared.

My first move was to talk with Jack, to voice my own concerns, and ask if he might reconsider his decision. The answer was no, he had made his decision. He believed I could handle the job, that I could learn those things that needed to be learned, that I would have all the help needed. From his standpoint and the standpoint of the paper, the change was necessary.

What about Harry? How was this whole thing going to fit? He suggested Harry continue with his column, that he continue to contribute anything he wished to contribute, but that his principal duties be as head of the advertising section.

There was not much else I could say. The die was cast. If the job was mine to do, I would try to do it as best I could. During those first few weeks I probably made all the mistakes that could be made, but somehow, with the active help of the rest of the staff, we got by. Everyone, that is, but Harry. For days he suffered his humiliation as best he could, alternately fuming, getting red in the face, stomping out of the office. If he were still managing editor this story would have been placed there, that story would have been placed here, and this story didn't deserve that kind of treatment. At the moment, while I could sympathize with his feelings, I could fathom neither the depth nor reason for those feelings.

I suspect any trained, experienced newspaper editor would have agreed with him. Nevertheless, the responsibility was mine, I had to answer for it, so the paper's makeup would reflect my own thinking. In time the job became more comfortable. I tried to learn at least a smattering of nearly all aspects of the operation, from Linotypes, to composing, to the stereotyping process. I was never good at any of it, but at least learned something of the process in order that I might better understand the problems encountered by those doing the job. In truth, however, I never learned much about the advertising end of the business, other than its importance in the grand scheme of things. Nor could I have ever substituted for the lowest paid member of the press gang. And I did not learn much about the paper's finances. I did not ask, and was not told.

In time the rough edges caused by the abrupt change in jobs began to wear away. Putman and I developed a better understanding of our roles and of each other. We became friends, and, in fact, supporters.

Many years later, while I was working in Austin for a string of newspapers headquartered in Waco, Harry took his own life. A shaken Howerton traveled to Austin to explain the circumstances. Evidently, Harry's drinking problem had gradually worsened, until one day Jack was forced to tell him that it was either quit drinking or be fired. Harry chose to end it all.

Small-town daily newspapers were not all that unusual in those days. While they struggled financially, it was still possible to exist, perhaps even prosper, in certain markets. Giant media conglomerates were still in the offing, being confined, for the most part, to large metropolitan areas of the east and west coasts. The scourge of television was in its incipient stage, in the process of being discovered by politicians and other opinion molders. People still turned to the printed word for credible information. Under those circumstances it would perhaps be easy to glamorize, to a certain extent, the role of a small-town editor. It is true, of course, that he had much more influence over the totality of his own newspaper than would be the case if he were merely the editor of some corporate entity, with ultimate decisions over the paper's stance being made in some distant city or state. But far from being glamorous, the role of a small-town

THE CHOW DIPPER

editor was mostly just plain hard work. Long hours, many headaches, a few words of praise, much worry.

But then there was that feeling you got when you saw people come in and plunk down hard-earned money to see what you had wrought. And to indicate, by criticism or praise, that what we were doing had some bearing on community life. Somehow that made it all worthwhile. In time it would produce the feeling that you were the paper, and the paper was you. I began to see, in a small way, why Harry had been so terribly upset.

After the trauma of the changeover had subsided, and after the mechanics of the new position were partially mastered, the job became basically routine, or as routine as is ever possible in putting out a small daily paper with limited staff and resources. There was, of course, the task of providing and organizing the flow of copy to the men on the machines, providing the composing room with layout sheets indicating where specific stories were to appear, writing the heads for those stories, and doing it all within a four-hour time frame. The paper was supposed to be locked up at 12:15 P.M. It usually was. The work pace for all staff members during that time was little short of hectic.

Afternoons were given over to preparing "inside" copy for the following day's paper. This normally encompassed the usual goings-on of community life. Afternoons were also the time we could make our rounds, checking with the usual sources in an effort to stay abreast of stories or potential stories. Most of the time those visits, while pleasant, proved fruitless. But not always.

On a hot, sultry afternoon in late summer I stopped by the county judge's office. Nothing there. There seldom was. He was always reluctant to get involved with the press. He had a small ranching operation south of town, on which he had a small herd of fine cattle. There were those who thought the herd grew somewhat magically, all out of proportion to what could be expected from its normal reproductive capacity. But that was mere speculation. Perhaps his cows were prone to giving birth to twins. Such things do happen.

I went upstairs to District Clerk Pershing Hiller's office. Nothing there either. There seldom was. But then, the district clerk's office was not normally a news producing office. It was an office of record, and as a usual rule by the time anything important got there it was already known to everyone else. Still, it had to be checked. He was, after all, part of the courthouse establishment, and he did keep his eyes and ears open. And we was, in my opinion, a good, honest man.

As I passed his secretary's desk on the way out, she stopped me.

"Ken, what was that gathering about out at the country club last night?"

I didn't know. I hadn't heard about it. What did she know?

She knew nothing, other than it was a gathering of many black people and a few white people. She thought perhaps it was some kind of political gathering. That, naturally, would raise the antennae of people whose livelihood was politics, and would explain her concerns.

I wandered back to the office, not terribly concerned about what had transpired. Certainly I could see no story there for tomorrow's paper, and that was my concern at the moment. In time I would check it out, mostly as a favor to the lady who had brought it to my attention. Still, it was interesting. The country club seemed an unlikely place for a political gathering between blacks and whites.

Days passed. The paper had to be gotten out. Many more important things were on the plate. But the situation was still intriguing. Political gatherings were generally well publicized. Usually people involved in politics can't get enough publicity for their cause. Why had we heard nothing of this?

As time permitted, a few calls were made to people I thought might know what transpired. No one knew, or at least no one was committal. I turned in-house, which is what I probably should have done in the first place. At that time the *Record*'s Linotype crew was all white, the composing crew was all Hispanic, and the press crew, which also did the stereotyping, was all black. Chief of the press gang was Elvin Wright, in my opinion, then and now, a fine man in all respects. I asked him to see what he could find out in the black community. Days passed here also. In time he reported that the only thing he could find out was that "they were talking about land."

There was nothing wrong with that. Perhaps a little strange, but certainly nothing out of the ordinary, other than the locale and the participants, whoever they were. I asked Nina to try to find out who the white people were in attendance, more to satisfy our curiosity than anything else. She had pipelines throughout the city, and shortly word came back. More puzzles. The men she named had no experience, as far as we knew, in land transactions. One was a car dealer. Another was generally regarded as being involved with a Yoakum tomato shipper named C. O. "Booster" Hagan. Nina was suspicious that something shady was going on, but then Nina was suspicious about anything involving Hagan, or anyone connected with him. She was not the most trusting of souls, unless it involved her friends. Then she could be trusting to a fault. Within days another development occurred. Carl Weber, who ran the Lentz Feed and Seed store behind and across the railroad tracks from the *Record*, appeared in the newsroom with a curious document. He asked, "Ken, what do you make of this?"

One of his employees, he said, a black veteran named Elmo Battles, had come to him with a document he had received from the Veterans Land Board. He didn't understand the document and had brought it to him, seeking an explanation.

"I looked at it, and told him it looked to me like he had bought some land somewhere and this was a receipt for payment on the mortgage," he said.

"I've bought no land," was the reply. "How could I buy land?"

I looked at the piece of paper. I had to agree with Weber. It appeared that the veteran had purchased some land under the Texas Veterans Land Program, down payment for which was acknowledged, as was notification as to when the next payment was due. I couldn't understand how he was unaware of the transaction. Surely if someone had committed himself to purchase land he would be aware of the consequences, but this evidently was not the case. I made notes. I would check it out when I got time.

I still did not make the connection between the gathering at the country club and a strange notice from the Veterans Land Board that Battles owed money on land he claimed he had never bought. There might be a small, local story concerning Battle's situation, merely playing on the ineptness and bungling of a state agency that would send out a notice of that kind to an obscure veteran. I would get around to it someday, when I had the time. In the meantime, the paper had to be gotten out.

By now it was sometime in October. Our spies in the courthouse relayed word that strange men were running in and out of the county attorney's office. They had made visits to the district clerk's office, poring over records involving veterans' discharge papers on file there. I went over to check it out.

The DeWitt county attorney at that time was Wiley Cheatham, a young, rather humorless son of an old family in the area. He had a reputation for impartiality, a rare trait among elected county officials. He also had a reputation for tenacity and stubbornness. His father, Tom Cheatham, was a member of the Texas legislature. The elder Cheatham was a local attorney, working out of a small, cluttered office. He was a stirring orator at July 4th celebrations, replete with string tie and flowing white hair. He was a veteran of World War I, and, legend had it, one of a small group of veterans who helped found the American Legion. In today's politics he would probably best be described as an exceedingly conservative populist. The son had never, to my knowledge, taken an active part in partisan politics. He ran for office, of course, as a Democrat, but at that time in Texas there was no other way to go. The Democratic Party controlled the state's political establishment, from justice of the peace to governor. An aspiring politician, or even an aspiring public servant, ran as a Democrat or he did not run.

Wiley was not a talkative sort, and he clearly was not ready to change his ways on this occasion. He did acknowledge that he and others were inquiring into certain practices involving the sale of land to some local veterans. I brought up the Elmo Battles matter, as well as the still unsolved (to me) gathering at the country club. He was aware of both; they were part and parcel of the matter being investigated. And he thought, but was not then certain, that the "irregularities" might extend across county lines.

I got the feeling that Wiley was a worried man. The reasons for his worries, if indeed he had worries, were not long in becoming apparent.

I returned to the paper, not knowing exactly what to do. Certainly I had enough to go with a local story revealing the fact that an inquiry was being made, and I could buttress the story with the Battles angle. Perhaps that was the route to take. And perhaps, I reasoned, that was all there was to it in the final analysis, for surely if it was anything big, and if it was centered in Austin, there would have been some hints of it from that quarter, where reporters representing great papers were in abundance.

I wrote the story and sent it upstairs to be set along with all the other copy that goes to fill space in a paper, large or small. It never got published. Two men from the Department of Public Safety, who had been present in the county attorney's office the previous day, came in to talk to Howerton. They were concerned, they said, that any public mention of their activity, at that stage, might have an adverse effect. They asked that we hold off for at least a little while.

Howerton said it was my call, but he was inclined to agree to their request. I, needless to say, was perplexed. On the one hand I wanted to go with the story. My fears were that if the story did lead somewhere, it might be broken in Austin. So I made a proposal. We would pull the story in return for their assurance that we would be treated fairly in the matter. We wished to be kept abreast of developments. They agreed, and the story was pulled.

In the days that followed I kept in more or less constant touch with Cheatham's office. By then rumors were rife in the small city that something unusual was going on. Reports came in about veterans being interviewed. The district clerk's records of veterans' discharge papers were being perused. Names were being mentioned, names of friends and acquaintances.

On November 10 the break finally came, though not in the manner I had anticipated. Cheatham and at least two others, men from the Department of Public Safety, were in his office when I arrived. We had discussed the matter at some length when Cheatham said, "Ken, let's go out in the hall."

One of the others present said, "Yes, we can't hear this." Which I thought was strange, for the moment. Obviously, they knew what was about to transpire.

We walked out in the hall. Cheatham said something to the effect that "we are just not getting the kind of cooperation up in Austin I think we should be getting." We continued the discussion. He was worried that roadblocks were being placed in the way, possibly because it now appeared the story "might go all the way to the top."

But where was the top? The Veterans Land Board at that time was composed of the governor, Allan Shivers, the attorney general, John Ben Shepperd, and the state's commissioner of the General Land Office, Bascom Giles, all, in the structure of Texas state government at that time, exceedingly powerful men, exceedingly respected men, and all of whom, from that distance, might have an interest in the outcome. In a mood almost of frustration, he told me I was free to write whatever I wished.

Next day the paper carried a small story on page one indicating an investigation was under way concerning certain suspected irregularities in the sale of land under the Veterans Land Program. My thinking was that it would provide a certain amount of protection until I could decide a more definitive course of action. By then I had an idea about what might have been taking place, or, more precisely, what

---

could have taken place. It still appeared to be, from all I knew, a local story. But what if it were not purely a local story? What if it did go "all the way to the top," as Cheatham had come to suspect?

This was not a case of merely "following the story." The story had not yet developed. The path had not yet been beaten. And I, surely, was not yet experienced in matters of this kind. In my ignorance I knew of no other course than simply go to Austin and see what I could find out. I had no fixed plan of action once I got there. Again, in my ignorance, I thought I would merely go talk to the governor, the attorney general, and the land commissioner. Perhaps I could learn something there. But how to go about it?

I knew only one person in Austin, Gen. Kearie L. Berry, adjutant general of the Texas National Guard. I had last seen him as a colonel in Hoten Prison Camp #1, in Mukden (Shenyang), Manchuria. On Bataan he served as commanding officer of the 3rd Infantry, and was generally regarded as a hero of the "Battle of the Pockets." He was taken prisoner with the fall of Bataan and moved to Formosa, along with General Wainwright and other senior officers. From there he was moved, in the spring of 1945, to our camp in Manchuria, ahead of advancing American forces. There we became friends, he a colonel and I, a private.

He had returned to the States, received his promotions, and was now adjutant general, having been appointed to that post by Allan Shivers, one of the men I was concerned about at the moment.

I told Berry, after we had visited about earlier times and friends now scattered, the story as I knew it to that moment. I told him of my concerns and suspicions, and of my intention to try to talk to the men in question. I asked if he had any thoughts on how to go about getting through the doors.

He was clearly astounded. He was unaware of any investigation going on. Our initial small story regarding the probe had not made an impact on the state media. He regarded Shivers as an honorable man and couldn't conceive of his being mixed up in the matter. The other two, Giles and Shepperd, he didn't know and could offer no reports other than that he had never heard anything bad about either. He didn't think I would have much luck just walking in to talk to any of them.

The conversation continued. Berry was a military man, and he made clear he did not know or understand the ways of politics or politicians. From his little office on the ground floor of the Capitol's east wing, it was all very puzzling. Watching the currents and cross-currents of politics made it very difficult for him, he said, to really determine who was honest and who wasn't.

I asked, "Well, do you know a single man here you would put in the category of an honest man?"

He thought for a moment and said, "Yes, there is. I truly believe the auditor would fit that description, and he may be able to help you."

He picked up the phone, made a call, and in a few minutes I was visiting with the state auditor, C. H. Cavness.

I, too, got the impression I was talking to an honest man. He was as forthcoming as he could be, but he did not know the answers to my questions. His office did indeed do audits of the General Land Office, but by law they were unable, at that time, to go beyond the books and records kept by that, or any, agency of state government. And those appeared to be in order. Beyond that, though, he did report that certain members of his staff had the impression that "something strange" was going on over there. He suggested I might want to check the property tax rolls for certain counties, particularly those of Zavala County, near the Mexican border in South Texas.

Interesting information, but nothing here I could use. The only thing left was to belly up to the bar. I went downstairs to the attorney general's office, then located on the ground floor of the Capitol's west wing.

The attorney general was out, or busy, or something. I was directed to the first assistant, a man named Robert Trotti, who represented the attorney general at meetings of the Veterans Land Board. The meeting was unproductive. He knew little, indeed next to nothing, about the workings of the board. He just represented the attorney general at the meetings. Why did the attorney general not attend? Well, he was on a number of boards, in an ex-officio capacity, and he couldn't attend all of them, so he designated certain assistants to represent him. About all they did, according to him, was meet and approve those applications for land purchases which had previously been approved by the Land Office staff and then recommended for approval by the commissioner, Giles.

Next stop, the governor's office. The governor was also out, or in a meeting, or something. I told the young lady I wanted to talk to the governor about the Veterans Land Board. Well, then I should talk to the governor's legal adviser, John Osorio, who represented the governor on board matters.

The meeting with Osorio was even briefer and less productive than the meeting with Trotti. Yes, he represented the governor on the board, for the same reasons put forth by Trotti. The legislature had placed the governor on some forty boards. It was impossible for him to attend them all and still be governor of the state. Beyond that, he had little to say. Besides, it was lunchtime and he had an appointment. I should come back when we had more time. And, of course, if he could ever be helpful, please let him know. He obviously understood the world of politics, which I was yet to learn. But I was learning.

Next stop, the General Land Office. I got a bite to eat and showed up immediately afterward. By then I was tired, somewhat frustrated, and not entirely happy. After being ushered from one office to the next, and finally arriving in the commissioner's office, I made my wishes known. The commissioner was not in. When could I expect him? The secretary did not know. He would probably be out for quite a while. And besides, quite often he did not return to the office after lunch. Perhaps another day would be better. I suggested she get in touch with him, tell him my name, tell him I was from the *Cuero Record*, tell him I thought he should show up as soon as possible, and tell him I was going to take a dim view of his failure to appear. She went into an adjoining room, and, I presume, made a call. Within twenty minutes Giles strode into the room.

I had no real plan of action for the interview. I merely thought I would insist upon answers to the Elmo Battles matter, ask him if he knew anything about an investigation of land sales to veterans, if he had ever had any association with certain people, and have him explain the complete workings of the Veterans Land Board.

The interview took a turn I did not expect. Far from being noncommittal, Giles was expansive, even loquacious. He was completely prepared. It was as if he had been waiting, expecting a session like this to develop somewhere along the line. I brought up the Battles matter. He picked up the phone and within minutes the file arrived. He looked at it. It appeared perfectly in order to him. The veteran had made an application to buy land under the program. His discharge papers accompanied the application. The application designated the tract of land he was interested in buying. The land had been appraised. The veteran had signed the application before a notary public. The application had been approved. That was all he could go on. He had no memory of ever having discussed the matter with the elder Cheatham, who had told me he had made a trip to Austin for just that purpose.

He could see no reason for corporations not to make the down payment for the veterans, or to give them a "bonus" for signing their names. Why should they not do this, since it would be a good thing all around? And one shouldn't worry about potential losses to the state. The program was designed and administered in such a way that it could lose $30 million and still come out on top. A retired appraiser was stirring up all the trouble. And besides, it was all just a matter of politics, someone trying to embarrass the governor because he sat as a member of the board. So it went, on point after point. There was an answer for everything. There were even answers to questions I had not raised, as if he felt he could lay the matter to rest in one fell swoop.

Eventually, I took my leave of the general land commissioner and returned to the Capitol, where I wanted to peruse the tax rolls of Zavala County. When that was finished, I began the drive back to Cuero, sick at heart.

Sick because I had previously regarded Giles as something of a hero. Obviously I knew him not, for country newsmen have little or no contact with people in high places. But he was regarded as the father of the Veterans Land Program, a program that would allow people like myself an opportunity to have, someday, a small piece of Texas, a piece that would ordinarily be denied us. With a small (five percent) down payment, with low (three percent) interest payments, and with forty years to pay off the mortgage, it would someday be a dream come true. And it was obvious, as I made the late evening drive back home, that Giles was a liar, a fraud. Why would he show up so quickly when he found out where I was from and the small paper I represented? Why would everything be so pat, so readily explained? Why would he say some of the things he did, other than as predicate to potential legal and political problems?

And sick because I knew that had he run for governor two years earlier, as he had planned to, I would have voted for him. Giles had been commissioner of the General Land Office since January 1939. He had remained in that position throughout the war, and, in terms of political security, was entrenched. As hundreds of thousands of Texas veterans returned from the war, Giles hit upon the politically popular idea of providing a way they could own a piece of the state. Or at least he claimed credit for the idea. He hoped, no doubt, to ride it into the governor's chair. In 1952 Giles passed word to close friends that he was prepared to run for governor. Those whispers, in the nature of politics, filtered into the countryside. He reasoned that the sitting governor, Allan Shivers, would wrap up the conservative vote in the state, but that Shivers had made "true Democrats" unhappy enough to give him a chance. His proposed entry into the race was enough to frighten another prospective candidate, District Judge Ralph Yarborough, out of the race, at least temporarily. Yarborough, seeing the potential governor's race as being essentially between Shivers and Giles, decided to opt for the race for attorney general.

Then a curious thing happened. Giles dropped his plans to run for governor, choosing instead to remain in the General Land Office. Yarborough then entered the race for governor against Shivers, and was beaten. Giles easily won his bid for reelection.

The drive back home took some two hours, affording time to ruminate and formulate. And to worry. I could see now why Cheatham might be worried.

We had a Veterans Land Board composed of probably the three most politically powerful men in the state. One was a sitting governor. The other two wished to be governor, if not now, soon. Each had his supporters and backers, as well as his detractors, throughout the legislature and throughout the body politic, both at the state and local level. Each was already the nominee of the Democratic Party, which, for all practical purposes, assured election to another term. But the terms of state officeholders, at that time, were only for two years. Another two years would roll around quickly. The net effect of all this was that the top echelons of Texas politics were more or less in a state of constant campaigning, under one guise or another.

And at the local level things didn't look much better, from the perspective of the moment. The elected sheriff had made it known he was going to have no part in the investigation. He had friends "on both sides." Without the active help of the sheriff, Cheatham had recruited one of the sheriff's deputies, Norman "Cutter" Dietz, to help, along with a local highway patrolman named F. R. Byrnes. But Dietz was serving under appointment from the sheriff. I had no idea how long the sheriff would tolerate his deputy knocking on doors of people who had helped elect him to office. Byrnes was not likely to be touched, since he served under a man named Homer Garrison, head of the Department of Public Safety, who was himself politically untouchable by virtue of his reputation for professionalism and perceived honesty.

Then there was the case of our district attorney. It was general knowledge that he was a close friend to one of those under investigation. How determined would he be when the chips were down, and the cases, if there were to be cases, had to be tried?

Even the situation surrounding the district judge, a longtime political power throughout the district, posed concerns. Generally regarded as an honest jurist, he had one fascination that might, I thought, create problems. He loved the game of poker, and signs were already evident that some of his poker playing buddies might well be involved in the story before it ran its course. How would this affect the course of events? Everywhere one looked, it seemed, there were potential problems and potential roadblocks.

It had not been a happy day. Nor were there many happy days to follow. By the time the trip was finished I had formulated a general line for the story that would follow. Obviously, Bascom Giles knew the operation from top to bottom. Obviously, he was aware of the most minute details of the transactions, and was quick to justify the policy under which they took place. But that did not mean, by itself, that he was in league with others engaged in fraud. Indeed, at that stage fraud had not been proven. It had not even been alleged publicly. There were strong indications of "irregularities" that were being investigated, and there was strong evidence that those irregularities could not have taken place without a certain amount of fraud being involved. But despite my suspicions I was in no position to make accusations.

The only course I could think of, in the final analysis, was simply to quote the commissioner extensively, knowing, or believing, that his comments would ultimately prove his undoing. Particularly if I could include, or attach, some factual data that might raise questions concerning his comments, and allow a discerning reader to put two and two together.

I wrote the story on the following day. Our morning Sunday edition was actually prepared late Saturday for next morning delivery. That allowed the day to sandwich preparation of the story with all the other things that had to be done in getting the paper out, but in the end it was done. I turned it over to the typesetters and composing people, and left the paper, worried beyond measure. I did not want to be, for reasons difficult to explain, standing by the presses when the edition came off. I usually was.

I wandered somewhat aimlessly around town, eventually stopping by Bauer's dry cleaning shop to pick up a dress Louise wanted to wear to church next day. There I was told that Howerton was looking for me. He had called there, and several other places. I returned to the paper full of apprehension about what might happen.

The day was done. It was dark. The press run was finished. Most of the staff was gone. Jack's wife, Polly, was finishing up work in her office. She told me that Jack wanted to see me. I finally found Howerton out back, getting in his car to leave. I asked if he wanted to see me. He did.

"I just wanted to tell you that is the best story that has ever run in the *Cuero Record*," he said.

I had written, under a byline:

"I'd like to own all the land mortgages in the State of Texas that are carried under the Texas Veterans Land Program," Land Commissioner Bascom Giles told me in Austin Thursday.

Giles was using this illustration to explain his feelings about his operation of the vast program which has expended $90 million of the $100 million given him by the legislature for the purchase and resale to veterans of land in the state.

"Oh we have made mistakes, a great many mistakes, but the program is so designed or is managed in such a way that I could sit right here and lose $30 million under the program and we would still come out okay at the end of 40 years." Giles was using this statement to explain that the bonds which are sold by the state to obtain money to finance the operation are sold now at slightly less than 2 percent. The veteran pays 3 percent interest and over a period of 40 years the difference between the two figures would amount to the sum in question, according to Giles.

Giles made the statement above after I had asked him about the possibility of the State being left holding the proverbial bag in the event some tracts were appraised too high and the veteran, after some three years, decided he no longer wanted the land. Questioned specifically about the sale of large tracts of land by promoters to large groups of veterans wherein the veteran had never seen the land, and had no means of paying for the land after purchasing it, the Commissioner stated that in order to assure that payment, his office made it absolutely mandatory that the seller, in some cases a promoter who had owned the land only a matter of weeks, agree to take a three year lease on the land.

"What I am particularly interested in, Commissioner, is what will happen to the land when the three year lease is up. The way I understand it, at the end of three years the land will be eligible for resale. Is that right?" I asked.

"That is right and a lot of these boys who think they have a bonanza or a gift from the state are going to be surprised at just how tough I can get. I am going to give them 30 days and if they don't pay any delinquent notes or payments due they are going to be booted out. Now I don't mean to sound cruel, but I am just being realistic about this," he told me.

"Supposing they are forced off their land, what then," I asked. "Will it become eligible for resale?"

"The land will be put for sale to other vets, and then if no veteran wants it, it will be sold to others," he answered.

"Will the original owner or promoter of the deal be eligible to buy under these circumstances?" the Commissioner was asked, "and if so, what will be the terms of payment be? Will he be able to carry on with the same low rate of interest to which the veteran is entitled?"

The Commissioner hesitated a little and said they would, or the state might have to make the best kind of deal it could under whatever circumstances prevailed at the time of resale. If a depression was in progress, the Commissioner said, they would simply wait until the price advanced. And in addition there would always be the possibility that oil would be discovered on those tracts of land the state had taken over in the transaction and this money would be used to pay off the loss on all the other tracts.

Referring back to the sale of large tracts of land to groups of veterans, the Commissioner was asked if it would not be advisable to have the veteran pay the five percent down, as the law requires, or at least a small down payment as a token that the veteran was at least interested in the place.

The Commissioner said, "Why should they, when these corporations will pay the down payment for the veteran in the form of a bonus and then lease the land back from them for enough to make the semi-annual payments?"

Becoming more specific I told the Commissioner that I had heard a few rumors that the land program had been abused in some cases, where veterans became owners of land without even the knowledge they had purchased the land. I told him of one particular case in Cuero where a Negro veteran had received a semi-annual statement concerning a tract of land on which he, according to the statement, had just made a payment. The vet took the note to his boss, who in turn took it to Rep. Tom Cheatham, who in turn took it to Commissioner Bascom Giles for an explanation on the matter.

The Commissioner could not remember Rep. Cheatham

visiting him on the matter and a search of the records of the veteran failed to retrieve the statement from the Land Office.

Asked if he thought the alleged irregularities were of such nature that his office should investigate, the Commissioner said, "It's mostly politics down there. You have a few people who want to embarrass the Governor and goodness knows there is nobody further removed from this than the governor. While the governor and the attorney general sit in on the general policy making decisions they have nothing to do with the administration of the program.

"I'll even name names," the Commissioner told me. "We had an appraiser down there by the name of Wofford for about 4 years. A few months ago he was let out because he became 70 years of age. He has been extremely bitter toward me and is responsible, I think, for going around and stirring up these Negroes and making them dissatisfied with the program. Why even one of the men in public life from your area told me just this morning that it was mostly politics."

Unable to quite understand the connection between a Negro veteran who became the owner of land, leased the land to another party and somehow received credit for making payment on it, and politics, I took my leave of the Commissioner and returned to the capitol where, after more checking I found that the veteran in question was not listed on the tax rolls of Zavalla County. This was understandable since there is a great deal of time lag between the purchase of land and its being rendered for taxation.

While checking the tax rolls of Zavalla I was reminded of another Negro in Cuero by the name of Herbert J. Franklin of 512 West Morgan Street. I had asked this vet if he had ever received anything in the way of a title to lead him to believe he had purchased land in the Wintergarden Development Company. He said he had not. He said he had nothing but an $11.70 check he had received some time ago. I asked if he had ever seen the land in question. He said he had not and didn't even know where it was. For Franklin's information his land is in Section 121, Lot 14, out of the Cross S Ranch. It is 31.2 acres and it cost him in the neighborhood of $7,000. It has a tax evaluation of $567.

(There will be more tomorrow.)

From a man who had grown up in the paper, and whose father had owned it before him, I found Howerton's comments high praise indeed. Never mind that they might have been, and probably were, highly exaggerated. I appreciated it then and still do.

He went on to tell me I was free to follow the story wherever it might lead. "All I ask," he said, "is that you don't get us in a lawsuit. We just don't have the money to defend ourselves."

Terribly relieved, I picked up a copy of the paper and started home. On the way I encountered Elvin Wright, head of the press gang, who told me in passing, "Mr. Towery, if you keep this up you are going to end up with a lot of poor friends and rich enemies."

I know now that the story was not all that good. Very few good editors would have allowed it to run as written. There would probably have been changes in style, changes in structure. The story was not written as well as it should have been. It lacked the polish it should have had. But it did have the effect of opening up the story to public attention and setting the stage for what would follow.

ELEVEN

In Pursuit of Truth

There would be many more stories to follow, very few of which would have passed muster by academic journalists, but most of which contributed in some way to the unfolding of the story. Unable to say flatly that fraud and corruption existed, or that people in high places were being influenced by the illegal transfer of money, we merely proposed a dummy corporation on the front pages of the next day's paper, inviting our readers to join as partners or stockholders, and explaining how, by operating under policies defended by Giles in our interview, we could make millions operating on state money, provided, of course, we could get certain people to look the other way at critical moments. A series of stories followed in that vein, along with interviews of some of the veterans involved, as well as continuing reports on the pace of the investigation.

The stories generated attention beyond the local arena. Wire services picked up the story. Newsmen from the state's daily papers visited the scene, the first of which was Sam Kinch, Sr., of the *Fort Worth Star-Telegram*. The story took on a life of its own. Politicians got in the act, as they are wont to do when they see the need to get on the side of the angels, or on the side of a substantial voting bloc. Some, I felt, had a genuine desire to do right. Others, I felt, were more concerned with political ambition, with cameras and newsprint. Nevertheless, in any battle, one welcomes support from wherever one can get it. And by then I felt I was in a battle.

Certainly, I felt by then that Cheatham was in a battle, a battle against great odds. For months he had conducted a quiet and rather lonely struggle, enlisting a little help as his investigation progressed.

But there were limits to his capabilities. Legally he could not enter other counties and compel response from residents of that locality. He had no legal authority to subpoena corporate bank accounts, certainly not on suspicion of wrongdoing. That was an authority reserved, at the time, for the attorney general's office. Any real chase down the corporate money trail would have to be done under color of that office. But the attorney general sat as one member of the Veterans Land Board. At what point would one feel comfortable in broaching the subject with him?

With the opening up of the story to the general public it would no longer be possible, I thought, for political roadblocks to be placed in the way of a complete investigation. Even if there might be an inclination in some quarters to do so. Fortunately, some of my own worries proved unfounded, and I think, but do not know, some of Cheatham's worries as well. The attorney general, John Ben Shepperd, did indeed come into the investigation, providing indispensable help and support. Shivers was completely supportive, as far as I could tell. That did not prevent me from chasing down every lead I could find, however, to prove or disprove his involvement.

There were rumors, for instance, that Shivers and Giles had business connections. With the help of attorney James Cross of Yoakum, I pored over all the records we could find in the Travis County Courthouse (Austin), but found no record of any such involvement. In the process, though, we did come up with Giles' business transactions with, and close ties to, C. O. "Booster" Hagan and others involved, one of whom, B. R. Sheffield of Brady, would ultimately go to prison for five years. I had heard there was a picture in existence of Shivers and Hagan hunting together on a ranch supposedly owned by Hagan. That would be a great story, since by then many signs were pointing toward Hagan as the overall mastermind in the affair. I could never find it. Indeed I could never find anyone who ever saw it. I was forced to conclude the governor had no part in the scheme, and said so publicly.

In furtherance of my political education, however, I was to find that the governor's political opponents did not share my conclusions. I even received letters accusing me of "selling out to the establishment." He had to be guilty. After all, he had turned his back on our beloved party and supported the Republican Eisenhower for president over the tidelands issue. Anyone who could commit that ultimate act of political betrayal, even if done to benefit the people of Texas, was certainly capable of, and prone to, lesser crimes. How could I defend such a person?

The Democratic Party, I would discover, was, to some people, truth. And anyone who gave aid and comfort to its political enemies was at war with truth. That included, by extension, anyone who gave aid and comfort to those politicians like Shivers, who abandoned "real Democrats" in 1952 when the chips were down. I would have to get my head screwed on right.

Some anonymous, well-meaning soul even saw to it that I begin to receive, in a plain, brown wrapper, a subscription to *Political Affairs*, the American Communist Party's ideological magazine, in which their "draft resolutions" were presented and debated under the aegis of a "chairman" named Gus Hall. And in which, after much "debate," their slogans were published. The slogans had to reflect their agreed upon resolutions. They were great for slogans. Slogans had to be simple, short, and to the point. They must lend themselves to placement on placards, and to chanting at rallies. They must "lead the masses." And for guidance in that leadership they must refer to the teachings of Lenin and Stalin. *There* was truth.

I suppose I have always been a slow learner, even slower in politics than most things. But I was learning. And in truth I am forever indebted to whoever it was that was gracious enough to introduce me to *Political Affairs*. I read it religiously for several years. Through it I was introduced to the thinking of various party wheelhorses, and "non-party" guest writers, some of whom would later surface on the American political scene. And it was through their pages that I was introduced to the writings of one Andrei Vyshinsky, then the Soviet Union's *"nyet"* man at the United Nations. The editors of *Political Affairs* referred to him as "the leading authority on Soviet law," a description that quite often showed up in the American press as well. Long after I had left the *Record* I obtained a copy of his book *The Law in the Soviet State*. Therein was the familiar argument, with a new twist. Western bourgeois capitalists, he said, often pointed out what they called lies in Soviet media and Soviet legal teaching. This, of course, was utter nonsense. There were no lies in Soviet media or in Soviet teaching. Why? Simply because socialism was truth. Anti-capitalism was truth. Marxism was truth. And whatever was required to defend truth and advance truth was truth. A lie told to advance truth could not be a lie, since if it advanced truth it must be, by definition, truth. Soviet law, according to Vyshinsky, had to be, and was, predicated on this thinking and this truth.

One would have to admit this novel approach did not remain confined to the borders of the Soviet Union, nor did it evaporate along with the Soviet Union. Nor, for that matter, did it remain the exclusive preserve of the Communist Party. Despite the mental gymnastics required, it ultimately would find a comfortable home in segments of American politics, in American media, and in the American academic community, under the rubric of "political correctness."

The story ultimately ran its course. It truly never "moved" from Cuero to Austin, it merely expanded from Cuero to Austin and many other counties. Our district attorney, after some initial attempts at prosecution, resigned his office and moved to Victoria. Shivers appointed Cheatham to fill the office. The investigations and prosecutions went forward with what might be called "vigor." Cheatham continued to investigate and to prosecute, and I continued to hammer away. But by then we both had a great deal more help than had been the case the previous fall. Teams of investigators combed the state. District attorneys from various counties picked up the matter in their own bailiwicks. The state's newspapers kept the story alive with continuing reports on the investigation and prosecutions.

In December 1955 the attorney general and the state auditor were able to reveal the overall talley to that time. The auditor reported that his office had examined every transaction involving four or more veterans, and anything else that looked suspicious. His office concluded that transactions involving 591 veterans purchasing land from 39 different sellers for a total of $3,554,994 would have to be classified as "fraudulent in whole or in part." Shepperd reported that the state had recovered a total of $381,000 in civil suits, including some $50,000 from Giles. Still later, in August of 1956, the new land commissioner, Earl Rudder, who had been appointed to the post by Shivers, reported that various settlements had resulted in $1,210,524 being returned to the state. By then Giles had paid back $79,435, and B. R. Sheffield had paid back $393,557.

Giles had refused to take the oath of office, despite being overwhelmingly elected shortly before our first story. He was indicted, tried, pled guilty and went to prison for three years. Hagan was indicted, tried on conspiracy, and ultimately went free. The paper trail could not be proven to the satisfaction of a DeWitt County jury.

Our sitting congressman, John J. Bell of Cuero, who had ushered the authorizing legislation through the Texas Senate while a member of that body, and who had been a guest of Giles' hospitality, was indicted for his part in the scheme. It was an interesting setup. In some of the deals he was invited to participate as a partner. He declined, but suggested a better course. They should just figure out how much his share would be, and pay it to him in "legal fees." Which they did, down to the penny. He said it was in return for standing ready to provide legal help if needed.

After the indictment, and before the trial was to begin, a curious thing happened. It was "discovered" that one of the grand jurors had not paid his poll tax, thereby making him an ineligible juror, which of course negated the indictment. That possibility was overlooked, conveniently or otherwise, when the grand jury was impaneled. The district attorney of Guadalupe County, where the indictment was brought, never got around to taking the case back to another grand jury. Besides, there was the question of possible double jeopardy. And besides that, he and the congressman were university chums.

The congressman stood for reelection and was soundly beaten. People had a different view of politics and politicians then. Bringing home the bacon, while important then as now, had not yet become the overriding criteria by which politicians were judged. Things like perceived honesty and personal integrity weighed heavily in the selection of public officials. The congressman couldn't stand that test.

But other curious things also surfaced in the course of the story. I could never understand how the lesser lights, the leg men, the midlevel operators, notaries public, could end up being represented by one of the highest priced and most prestigious law firms in Texas. At that time the firm of Looney, Clark and Moorhead was generally regarded as one of the best in the state. Everett Looney, who handled much of the firm's criminal defense work, was a former head of the State Bar. Dean Moorhead was generally regarded as one of the best oil and gas attorneys in Texas. But it was through Ed Clark, and business interests the firm represented, that much of the firm's political influence was exercised in the Texas legislature. The interests of Brown and Root Construction Company, of Houston, was only one example. There were others.

Looney usually headed the Austin defense team when it showed up for work on matters concerning the veterans land scandal. The problem was that it seldom showed up for work. There was one "continuance" after another. The defense team, usually made up of Looney, another attorney in the firm named Donald Thomas, and Looney's son, R. E. L. "Bob" Looney, would frequently be absent when a case was called for trial. They seemed to have their plate full somewhere else, and the local defense attorney was left to do the explaining and incur the judge's wrath.

Once, tiring of the routine, I called the firm's office in Austin to inquire of Looney if they intended to show up for trial the following day. I wasn't trying to be obnoxious; I simply wanted to schedule my own time and the time of others in the office. He wasn't at the office. They didn't know where he was. I called his home. A lovely, gracious lady answered the phone. Everett wasn't there, she said. Did she know where I might get in touch with him? Oh sure. "He's out at the ranch." Did she have the telephone number at the ranch? Sure. She gave it to me.

I called, assuming it was Looney's ranch. Someone answered the phone. It was Lyndon Johnson's ranch. There was a booming voice in the background.

A startled, flustered Looney came to the phone. Was he going to show up for trial in Cuero the following day? Oh, ah, uh, yes, they planned to, but they would have to see. He wasn't sure they would be completely prepared. They were working night and day, but there was much to be done. By then I suppose I was becoming obnoxious. Well, then, why was he at the LBJ ranch? Oh, he was discussing some matters with Lyndon. Who all was there? He wouldn't say. Could he tell me what they were discussing? No, sorry.

When the case was called for trial there was no one there from Looney, Clark and Moorhead. The "local attorney" for the defense, a rather rotund young lawyer named Burt Kirk, was called on by the judge to explain the situation. In open court Kirk expressed his exasperation. He couldn't really explain it to His Honor. All he knew was that they were supposed to be there, they had told him they would be there. He also knew that they had already collected $75,000 in fees on the case. He would like His Honor to know that he shared His Honor's unhappiness. There was nothing the judge could do except set a new date, and instruct the local attorney to inform the Austin firm that it would be in their best interest to show up.

Time, of course, is on the side of the defense, and they were fighting for time. By and large they did a good job. In the lower echelons of the scheme, where outright fraud and misrepresentation were relatively easy to prove, prosecutors had a leg up. But as prosecutions moved up the ladder, the element of conspiracy weighed more heavily in cases, and convictions became more difficult. That was the case with Hagan. Many trails led to his doorstep, but the jury could not be convinced they crossed his threshold.

In Pursuit of Truth

Now, just in case the reader needs a break, or a chuckle, let us move forward some thirty years.

The scene is a ranch west of Austin, owned then by U.S. Circuit Court (5th Circuit) Judge Tom Gee. The occasion was a more or less annual Halloween costume party, to which Louise and myself were often invited, and which we sometimes attended. It was customary for guests to show up in some sort of costume, Bluebeard the Pirate or whatever. When we went, we did not arrive in costume. Neither of us is really the type. Nor, on this occasion, was Ed Clark, who also attended sans costume. Accordingly, Clark and I found ourselves sitting in a corner away from the crowd, reminiscing.

Years had passed. After Cuero I had gone on to other things, as had he. Clark, who had been a confidant of Lyndon Johnson's for many years, who had helped "arrange" the votes Lyndon needed in his "victory" over Coke Stevenson in the 1948 Texas Senate race, who had later served as President Johnson's ambassador to Australia, and who, for that matter, had served as Johnson's ambassador plenipotentiary wherever needed around the world, was in a reflective mood. By that time we had both had a drink, possibly two or three.

Our trails had crossed many times since those days. Clark had always been a supporter of Johnson, and for that matter Ralph Yarborough, who eventually became U.S. senator with his help. In time, for good and sufficient reasons, he became a supporter of John Tower as well.

Those unfamiliar with the machinations of American politics might find it strange that a rich and powerful man such as Ed Clark could support such diverse politicians as Lyndon Johnson, Ralph Yarborough, and John Tower. But Ed Clark was exceedingly practical in the art of political influence. Tower was on the Senate Banking Committee. Clark, in addition to being a lawyer and representing powerful business interests, was a banker. In fact, he was chairman of the board for Capital National Bank in Austin. After Tower's first reelection, when it became apparent that he might become a fixture in Texas politics (and on the Senate Banking Committee as well), Clark underwent a public conversion. He became a Tower supporter, even assuming a leadership role in the senator's subsequent political endeavors. During those years we became quite close, and Tower came to regard him as a staunch friend.

Clark, in fact, became chairman of the "Texans for Tower"

committee in 1972 and chairman of Tower's finance committee during the 1978 Senate race, which I ran for Tower. In that capacity we talked a great deal. It was in the 1978 race that he first laid out to me, complete with names and details, the effort to assure Lyndon Johnson the South Texas votes he required to win the 1948 Senate election. He spoke of a secret bank drawer, the amount of money usually kept in it, the four men who knew of its existence, the two men (including himself) who had access to it, how and when it was used, and for what purpose. He spoke of a "task force" that was sent here and there, armed with cash to oil troubled political waters. ("It wasn't just Duval and Jim Wells counties," he said, "it was Nueces County and places like that.") He seemed, quite simply, to want to get some things off his chest.

He spoke fondly of all involved in the operation, as if they were doing the Lord's work. All, that is, except John Connally. In fact, I never heard Ed Clark speak so disparagingly of anyone else in politics. Clearly he was irritated that Connally seemed to claim a closeness to the throne during that episode that Clark thought he didn't deserve. Connally, he told me with some heat, "was nothing but a little shirt-tailed lawyer running around on the fringes, thinking he knew what was going on."

So there was much for us to talk about at the Halloween party. While others admired their own plumage, and the plumage of others, we visited about days of yore. Eventually the conversation got around to the land scandals of thirty years before, plus or minus a year or two. Hagan was dead. The statute of limitations had run out. One could speak freely. I told Clark there were still some unanswered questions, from my own standpoint. I do not remember now exactly what triggered the comment, but Clark said: "Well Ken, I'll tell you. Booster [Hagan] came to us when that thing first broke, and he said 'Look, I got all these boys involved in this thing and I feel like I ought to stand good for their legal expenses. Will you take it on?'"

Ed said they agreed to do so, and, in retrospect, "We did all right."

I never asked whether he was talking finances or success at the trials. My suspicion is both.

Hagan, as indicated earlier, had been tried on a conspiracy charge and acquitted. Now, at long last, the truth finally came out. It laid to rest, at least in my own mind, the question of whether the entire operation had been the result of some sort of scheme, or whether it had just grown, like topsy, from the fertile minds of opportunists.

To me, that wrapped it up.

It explained many, many things. It was in 1952 that Giles suddenly changed his mind and decided not to run for governor, but to remain as commissioner of the General Land Office. It was in 1952 that some of the first block transactions involving the fraudulent transfer of land took place. It was that year the money started flowing.

The man, Bascom Giles, who claimed to be the "father" of the program, who claimed it was all his idea, was obviously involved in the scheme, along with Hagan, from the very beginning. John J. Bell, the state senator who sponsored the legislation in the Senate, and who rode the matter all the way to the U.S. Congress, was obviously involved from the beginning. It was friends and associates of both men who perfected the scheme and devised the technical, mechanical means of carrying it out. And while it was not Bascom Giles who carried out the dirty work of rounding up and misleading hundreds of black and Mexican-American veterans, it was Bascom Giles who must have devised and approved the "legal" documents that made such fraud easily possible, who devised "policies" that gave the color of legality to the manner in which the fraud could be committed and defended, and who was paid for his services.

Despite its seeming complexity, the scheme was simplicity itself. In an ideal world a veteran would have simply located a tract of land he wished to purchase, he would have obtained the proper application form, filled it out, had it notarized in his presence, submitted that application along with proper identification papers (a copy of his service discharge) to the Veterans Land Board, and awaited their pleasure. The board would have dispatched an appraiser to view the land and determine if it was essentially worth what the veteran had agreed to pay.

(The state's role in appraisals, of course, was one of several critical links in the matter. Since the state would be buying the land in the veteran's name, and would become the mortgage holder, the state must be satisfied the land was not inflated in price.)

Another critical aspect of the fraud was the structure of the application form itself. It contained a paragraph stating that the named veteran had agreed to purchase the land "described immediately below." Here there was a blank space in which the legal description of the land in question was to be set forth, metes and bounds, and all that. Under rules then operating, the veteran need never set foot on the land before purchase. In this manner the application to purchase land became more than an application to buy land. It became, once approved, a contract binding the veteran to purchase the land described in the document above. The state, operating through the Veterans Land Board, would then buy the land from the seller and the veteran would be obligated to repay the state over a period of forty years.

At its lowest level the scheme involved simply getting veterans to sign the application itself. This was achieved through a variety of misrepresentations. The state, the veteran was told in some instances, had some free land it was ready to give away to veterans as a "bonus" for their service. In some cases they were merely paid for their signature. One veteran told me he knew there was no free land, and he didn't want any land anyhow, but he agreed to sign in return for a set of tires for his car. So it went. It then became a simple matter, once the "application" was signed, to fill in the paragraph requiring the legal description of the land in question, take that form to a notary public, and have it notarized in the absence of the one who signed it. Any number of "applications" were obtained in this fashion and submitted to the Veterans Land Board in bloc.

While this was going on, others higher up the ladder in the scheme were busy locating large tracts of land that could be purchased relatively cheap, theoretically "divided" into many smaller tracts with inflated prices, each tract with a "legal description" that could be used to fill in the blank space on some veteran's application. There was no real question of the promoters having the deal go sour. That issue had already been settled. The man who sat at the head of the table, and who would ultimately make the decision, was part and parcel of the operation.

One more thing was required to place the color of legality on the scheme. It was necessary to see that the appraiser was one who would agree that the new, inflated, price was fair, or at least that he be one who would not quarrel with the commissioner of the General Land Office if the commissioner said the price was fair in his own opinion. And what lowly appraiser, a paid staffer, would choose to dispute the word of the man who was supposed to know more about the value of land than any other man in the state? The commissioner not only sat as chairman of the Veterans Land Board, but as head of the General Land Office supervised the vast land holdings of the state of Texas, including its oil rich tidelands. Who should know more about the value of land than he?

If everything went well, there would be enough money in it for just about everybody—except, of course, those veterans who were defrauded, and beyond them, the state of Texas and its people. The perpetrators, usually formed into a "corporation," could, if they so wished, make payments on the land for a period of time. This would help cover the scheme. In some cases this took on the form of "lease payments" that were supposed to go to the state to make payments due on the land. At the end of the "lease," or at the pleasure of the perpetrators, the payments would stop. The veteran would then discover he was in fact the owner of land he had never seen and did not know he had ever purchased. If he did not pick up the payments, the land would become property of the state. Promoters of the scheme would have their money, and the state would have thousands of acres of land for which it had paid a highly inflated price.

What then? And it was on this point that I had pressed the commissioner in our first encounter, in November of 1954. The land, he said, would first be offered to other veterans. If none were found who wished to pay the price, it would be entirely possible for those who "sold" the land to the veteran in the first instance to end up buying it back at a greatly reduced price. And selling it again. That would have been a decision made by the commissioner at the proper time.

One might ask how they thought they could get away with so massive a fraud. In truth, had it not been for a number of "ifs," they could very well have gotten away with it. "If" they had not gotten in such a hurry, "if" they had not gotten so greedy, "if" clerks in the General Land Office had not mistakenly sent documents to veterans that should have gone to the shyster promoters, "if" there had been no Wiley Cheatham, with his sense of fairness and dogged determination, and "if" there had been no "Cutter" Dietz, the deputy sheriff whose devotion to his oath of office was greater than his loyalty to his boss, chances are very good that the scheme could have succeeded in the time frame allotted to it.

And if, self-serving as it may sound to some, there had been no *Cuero Daily Record* or no Jack Howerton who told me, in so many words to "have at it, just don't get me in a lawsuit."

Every reporter should be so lucky.

But it is those little "ifs" that seem so often to trip up wrongdoers. And it is the little "ifs" they try so hard to avoid, sometimes successfully and sometimes unsuccessfully. We would see the pattern played out in later stories involving Ben Jack Cage, Billie Sol

Estes, Milton Addison, and many others. It is, I suppose, the story of human nature, or rather the story of the nature of some humans.

There is always the question of "why." Why on earth would a man who seemingly had everything embark on such a course? He was the beneficiary of a wonderful family and wide public acclaim. Of all people in high state office at that time, I admired him most.

Why indeed?

Once, during the course of the story, and on one of my many trips to Austin to pore over records, I stopped by the old Driskill Hotel at the end of the day. The meal was served. I was eating alone. The nearby table was occupied by four men. They were discussing the matter, as many people were doing then. They did not know me, and I did not know them. Obviously, all were friends or acquaintances of Giles, who had been indicted but not yet tried. One asked of his fellow, "Jim, you've always been close to Bascom, has he ever said anything to you about this?"

"Well, yes, as a matter of fact we visited a couple of days ago, and I asked him that very question. I asked, 'Bascom, why did you do it?'"

"He just kind of shook his head, and said, 'Ah, Jim, I don't know. It was just there.'"

It was just there.

I do not know how to properly evaluate my own involvement in the affair. I do believe it should probably not be used as text material for aspiring journalists. I have never believed an artist ought to stand in front of his own painting, thereby obscuring the fruit of his labors. Nor have I ever believed that reporters should thrust themselves into the foreground of stories they are covering, lest their personality, or their obvious political bias, obscure the worth of their work. The nature of this story, however, and the nature of its revelation had the effect of thrusting us into the foreground, uncomfortably, whether we wished it or not.

The story consumed my waking moments. While I tried to be fair and impartial in presenting "the other side," I was anything but impartial in terms of long range objectives. Once convinced that veterans were being defrauded, and that they were being defrauded with the help of people who had been elected to uphold the law, and who had sworn to uphold the law, I could see no proper end until wrong was made right. I developed the mindset that no quarter should be given. That Cheatham and I were on a sort of crusade, assisted by those of like mind. That is a dangerous, risky attitude for a reporter to take. But the veterans had gone off to war to defend their country, putting their very lives at risk in the process. In some cases their friends, even their kin, had been left to rot in some obscure corner of the globe. The system they had fought for was being corrupted by one who had not shared those dangers, but who, in the nature of some politicians, had wrapped himself in their hopes and dreams for his own benefit, merely to feather his own nest, and secure, he hoped, his own political power. What other course was there? I saw none.

Perhaps the memories of Corregidor and of prison camps were too fresh in my mind. Perhaps I had not yet seen enough of the ways of the world to become sanguine about such matters.

Nor were extraneous circumstances surrounding the story conducive to a relaxed attitude. During the early stages of the story I was visited by a member of the Department of Public Safety's Intelligence Division, who told me they had become aware of a "contract" being let on the life of Cheatham, and while they had received no such information relating to me, I should at least exercise caution. At about the same time the attorney general received a death threat, as did Raymond Brooks, a reporter in Austin.

As far as I was concerned, the only problems along those lines were anonymous, ominous, threatening telephone calls. And that simply goes with the territory. I had no real worries, or real fears, involving those in the lower echelons of the affair, most of whom, it seemed then, had merely gotten caught up in the desire to make a few fast bucks. But who knew how far the story went, or what kind of people might be out there, worried that investigation, exposure, prosecution, might cause ruin? I took solace in the fact that now the story was in the public domain, for which I gave myself credit, and any such violence would be foolhardy indeed. However, I was assured by the DPS that they took the threat against Cheatham's life seriously.

Then there was the case of a Brady attorney, Sam McCullum III, who entered his car one morning and turned on the key only to be seriously injured when a bomb exploded under the hood. He was defense attorney for a minor figure in the story, and speculation immediately centered on potential testimony as a possible cause for the blast. The culprit was never found, despite lengthy investigation in the matter. The fact that the incident occurred well after the story had broken only served to reinforce the apprehension.

So perhaps when academic journalists peruse the story in the future, if they ever do, they will understand a little better the tenor of the times and how that might have affected, and afflicted, the way we handled our own involvement.

A year or so later I would visit Giles in the state prison at Huntsville. I was then on my way to the Alabama-Coushatta Indian reservation in East Texas, where trouble between the tribe and the state was brewing, and decided to stop by the prison to see if he would talk. He had been silent since entering prison. I asked the warden if he would relay word to Giles that I would like to visit with him, and also said I would understand if he refused. I asked that the warden not lean on him concerning my request.

Much to my surprise Giles showed up in a matter of minutes. The story was still fresh in Texas politics. I wanted to see if he had any second thoughts, if he had anything further to say. He did not say he shouldn't be in prison, but he couldn't understand why "others" were out there running around free who were no better than he. They were doing the same things he did. Well, I had done the very best I could, I said, and asked him to give me some names. I would get on with it. No, he answered, it wouldn't do any good. He implied it was "just everywhere." I thought it was a very strange mindset.

As the years passed I would find, in my continuing political education, that corruption indeed did not begin or end with Bascom Giles, or those who helped, aided, and assisted in that sordid affair. The Texas legislature, for instance, did make important and needed changes in the program itself, making it much more difficult to carry on the practices of the past. But as far as their own operation was concerned, they merely gave the color of law to legalized shakedowns, that which before could be condemned as illegal. Legalized "office accounts" came into being, to which interested parties could contribute, indeed to which interested parties had to contribute if they wanted a voice in government. And from which senators and legislators could draw funds for the operation of their office, and for expenses attendant thereto.

But what did that mean? Who was to make the determination of what passed muster in terms of legitimate expenditures from the funds? Obviously, the people who created the situation in the first place. It meant, in practical terms, that the purchase of a home could, and would in some cases, become somehow associated with the expenses of office. Or the purchase of fur coats, or college tuition. Or the purchase of apartments. It would also mean, in practical terms, that legislators caught in such obvious wrongdoing could rightly claim, "We have broken no laws, we have broken no rules of the Senate or the House."

Certainly.

But who wrote the laws, who wrote the rules?

Shades of the Congress of the United States, circa whatever.

Back to the *Record*. Sometime in the spring, Howerton submitted our stories to the Pulitzer Committee. I appreciated his thought, but felt it was an effort that would bear no fruit. That was not an arena in which, I thought, little papers could play. Besides, I was not after a "story" when the effort began. In fact, I had no real appreciation for what a Pulitzer nomination meant, or might mean if it were successful. But he was insistent, saying, "Hell, it's just as good as a lot of the stories they give that prize for."

As subsequent awards proved, I suppose he was right.

While it was being considered by the Pulitzer Committee Ed Murrow and Fred Friendly sent a team down to Cuero for a CBS program called *See It Now*. They wanted to do a story on the paper and its efforts. It turned out to be an interesting program, I was told. Our TV couldn't pick it up well. We were eighty miles from the nearest station, and about all we got was snow on the screen. While the cameras were there the Pulitzer Committee made its decision. A reporter for the *Houston Post*, Jim Mathis, called with the information that we had won. Murrow's team recorded our reaction.

Later, when the team of Murrow and Friendly published a book with their choice of the best programs they had done, our little effort was included.

Eventually a check for $1,000 came in the mail. Regular mail, with, I believe, a five-cent stamp on it. I thought they were being very careless with my money. It amounted to three months' pay. It would come in handy.

The story had consumed me. Throughout the months I had lost weight, and now the tuberculosis, which I had thought was arrested, flared up in both lungs. Two months after the Pulitzer was awarded I was back in the hospital, a ward, as it were, of the Veterans Administration. No job. No payroll. One son six years old. A new daughter, Alice Ann, three months old. A good wife. The prospect of my old job back if I made it through.

TWELVE

The Politics of Reporting

Vast changes had been made in the treatment of tuberculosis since my last sojourn at Kerrville. A variety of potent drugs were now available and in use. While they had some undesirable side effects, the drugs did wonders in reducing the time needed for recovery, and they also had the effect of quickly, or relatively quickly, rendering the bacillus inactive. This time it would only be a year.

A year to rest, eat well, curse Tojo and the Emperor for taking still another year out of my life, read the daily press stories about the aftermath of the trials, acquittals, convictions, reversals, prison sentences handed down, and fume about no longer being part of it.

A year to watch. To worry. And to speculate, from afar, on the obvious impact the story was having on the political landscape in Texas.

Politics in Texas during those years was normally in a state of flux. In the absence of a genuine two-party system, the politics of the day normally revolved around the strength of personalities, with philosophy and issues thrown in as window dressing. One of the tactics used, indeed the time-honored tactic used, was not only to promote oneself but to do all that was possible to cut any potential opponent off at the pass. An aspiring politician must never say anything good about another aspiring politician, lest he be reminded of it someday in some future race. Each day was devoted to preparing the fields for the coming harvest, and, in this respect, laborers in the field were many.

Allan Shivers was then in his third term as governor, one term more than usually accorded a governor in Texas. While he was then strong enough to stand for, and probably win, a fourth term, the general assumption was that he would not. If he bowed out, what then?

Bascom Giles, the man who would be governor, and perhaps could have become governor, was removed from the scene.

Ralph Yarborough, a former district judge who had opposed Shivers in the previous election, and around whom the state's liberal-labor forces had coalesced, was an almost certain candidate. He had been beaten badly in the race, but his candidacy did help solidify the liberal wing of the party. Certainly he could count on that support in the future. He was thoroughly capable of giving vociferous support to those who believed that evil forces were out there somewhere, intent on doing "little people" in.

It was generally assumed, by those of us in the hinterlands, that the Shivers mantle would pass to John Ben Shepperd, the attorney general. He had acquitted himself well in the most recent affair concerning the politically corrupt George Parr and his associates in Duval County. He was a politically attractive young officeholder who had not gotten terribly involved in intra-party bickering. His presence engendered no emotional outpouring of support that I could tell, but politically there were no "flies" on him. Not, that is, until the veterans land scandal came along. No matter how well he performed his duties after the matter erupted, he was certain to be confronted with the charge, however relevant, that he was asleep at the switch.

There were others. Jimmy Phillips, a state senator from the Texas coast country south of Houston, and a member of the Senate committee that inquired into the scandal, was busily positioning himself for the race should lightning strike. His role, highly vocal but largely inconsequential, was one of constant criticism aimed at Shepperd, whom he saw as a potential opponent. Phillips was quick to get on the bandwagon, and quite effective in garnering media attention. Indeed, a late arrival in Texas could be forgiven for thinking he uncovered the whole thing almost single-handedly. So it went across the board.

Against this backdrop I received a call from the attorney general, Shepperd. He wanted me to join him in Cuero for a visit with the publisher, Howerton. He would like to review the land scandal situation. I suspected it was more than that. He was apprised of my situation. I had no means of transportation to Cuero, and there was little likelihood the doctors would approve the trip even if I did. The new drugs had done their thing, I was no longer a threat to society, but the doctors would probably determine the 150-mile drive too taxing in any event. Not to worry, he would fly to Kerrville in a private plane, we could fly on to Cuero, visit with Howerton, and they would fly me back to the hospital. It should be no strain. The doctors agreed, and the trip was made.

The first part of the discussion did indeed deal with a review of the story. But as I suspected, and as I imagine Howerton suspected, it turned to politics. Shepperd did not say he was going to run for governor. I do not remember him even saying he wanted to run. He merely asked how we would view his candidacy, if he should decide to run. He would be very foolish, he said, to enter the race knowing the paper would oppose him. In fact, he did not think a victory was probable unless the paper actively supported him. He was in a flattering mode. But there was a touch of political reality in his argument. He anticipated that should he run, his principal opponent would almost surely be Ralph Yarborough, who had already shown himself to be a tireless campaigner, and one who, in the heat of campaigning, sometimes inadvertently allowed a touch of irresponsibility to enter his rhetoric. It made good politics, Texas style. Shepperd was politically astute enough to appreciate the difficulties ahead.

Howerton turned to me. At first I declined to comment. After all, I was no longer on the payroll, and while I had acquired a small financial stake in the paper, it was Howerton's paper and his call to make. But he insisted that I give my views. As far as he was concerned I was still part of the paper.

Well, if it were up to me, I would probably support Shepperd. I thought he had gotten a raw deal in much of the political comment, especially that coming from State Senator Jimmy Phillips. Judging from what we knew at the moment I could see no validity to suggestions of criminal wrongdoing on the part of either Shepperd or Shivers. Perhaps they should have attended board meetings, rather than sending subordinates, but even if both had attended every meeting there would have been no way to detect, at the board level, fraud in the field or collusion between Giles and the promoters without ordering a full field investigation of the program just to see if everything was on the up and up.

It appeared to me that Giles ran the operation. By the time the veterans' application to purchase land got to the board for approval, the fraud had already been committed. Giles merely had to say "I have before me applications from forty veterans. Staff has done the checking. Everything is in order. What is the pleasure of the board?"

Someone would automatically say, "I move they be approved." It was not likely that an employee of the attorney general or the governor would say to a person of Giles' stature, "Now wait a minute Mr. Commissioner. I'd like to run a field check on a random sampling of those applications." In retrospect they should have, but that's not the way it worked at the time.

As the discussion drew to a close, Howerton told Shepperd the paper would actively support him if he ran. My memory is that Shepperd was not urged to run by Howerton. He was told that should he decide to run, the paper would support him. On the trip back to Kerrville, Shepperd appeared considerably less apprehensive than on the trip down. No doubt he had many other things to consider, and many others to check with, but both Howerton and myself felt, given his response, he would make the race.

A few months later another call came, this time from Washington, D.C. The junior U.S. senator from Texas, Price Daniel, would like to visit. Could Howerton and I come to Austin for the upcoming meeting of the Texas Press Association, where he was to be a speaker? He had a very important matter he would like to discuss with us.

I had never met Daniel, but Howerton knew him well. Daniel, too, had a newspaper background. He was an established political figure. He had served in the Texas legislature, became Speaker of that body, served as attorney general, and replaced the aging Tom Connally in the U.S. Senate in the elections of 1952. At that time Connally was one of the longest serving senators in Texas history, having been first elected in 1928. In the nature of Texas politics then, Connally could be expected to live out his days in the Senate. But, unfortunately, he had become chairman of the Senate Foreign Relations Committee. In that capacity he became impressed with his importance, an affliction that seems to go with the territory. After all, he had been there when the United Nations was formed. He could bask in that glory. He was a presence in the Senate. A caustic-tounged presence, to be sure, but nevertheless a presence. The only thing he overlooked was where he came from. By the time the 1952 elections rolled around he was generally assured of retirement at the ballot box. Faced with probable defeat, he retired.

Price Daniel essentially walked into the Senate. Of nearly 1.3 million votes cast, Daniel got more than 900,000.

But rumors had been circulating that Daniel was not entirely happy in Washington. Actually, he had hardly been there long enough to get his feet on the ground. That was evidently long enough to convince him he was in the wrong place. Could it be that this was what he wanted to talk to us about?

We met in a suite on the topmost floor of the old Commodore Perry Hotel in Austin, at the corner of Brazos and 8th streets, overlooking Brazos. Daniel and Howerton greeted each other warmly. A few functionaries darted in and out, in the nature, I would someday learn, of a senator's entourage. Then I knew none of them. As the years passed I would know most of them. Then it was all very strange, but the furniture and carpets were very, very nice.

Basically it was the same story we had gone through with Shepperd, with a twist. Daniel actually said he wanted to give up his Senate seat and run for governor, but he wanted first to know if he could have our support. He went through the same arguments. He held out the specter of Yarborough, and what that would mean to Texas and the Democratic Party. Sorry, said Howerton. They were friends, and all that, but he had given his word to Shepperd that if he ran, the paper would back him.

Daniel said he had firsthand knowledge that Shepperd was not going to run, that he had decided against it. We did not go into how that came about. We took it to mean he and Shepperd had discussed the matter. Very well, said Howerton, if Shepperd was out of it, and if the alternative was Yarborough, he would back Daniel. The senator seemed very happy and said he would make his announcement the following day, when he addressed the statewide gathering of newspaper publishers and editors.

There was a good bit of anticipation among the assembled clan as to what Daniel was about to do, and a good bit of smirking when he had finished his presentation. He had evidently run enough traps, and made enough inquiries, to convince many in attendance that he was going to forthrightly make his announcement. It didn't work that way. Rather, in what I thought was a chicken way to approach the matter, he announced that he would run if he received 25,000 cards and letters from his fellow Texans urging him to run. I returned to the hospital, feeling I had been in the presence of a man who didn't know his own mind, who had difficulty making a decision. After a period of time he announced, Howerton said predictably, that he had achieved his goal, that a sufficient number of Texans had responded, and he was in the race. I don't know of anyone who ever counted the response.

During the course of the story I had received what I could only describe as "feelers" from larger publications. An emissary from the *St. Louis Post Dispatch* visited. He wanted to know if I would like to work for them. The answer was no. I felt I would be completely lost in big city reporting, and I had no desire to move my family there. Besides, from what I had heard about their politics, I wasn't sure it would be a harmonious relationship. The same was true with *Time* magazine. Their emissary was somewhat vague. They were a big outfit, and if I would like to come with them, they were sure they could find a place somewhere. The answer was the same. In fact, I had no way of knowing if either offer was directed by someone in authority, or if they were merely musings. I didn't ask. I still had the offer of my old job back, with an increase in pay to $75 per week, so it was not as if I would be on the streets.

But one offer was intriguing. Harry Provence of Waco, then editor-in-chief for a chain of newspapers owned by the Fentress family, approached me concerning a position on their Capitol staff in Austin, covering state government and politics. I would be part of a staff headed by Sam Wood and including Raymond Brooks, both seasoned newsmen. We would service daily papers in Austin, Waco, and Port Arthur, but would not be on the staff of any particular paper. It seemed a challenging situation. And the pay was good, a boost to $125 per week.

Louise and I discussed the matter at some length, and in the end the decision was made to move. It was a most difficult decision. When the doctors decided I was again ready to go back to work I returned to Cuero for a few months, affording other staff members time for vacations and for a replacement to be found, and joined the new team in Austin in the fall of 1956.

The parting was very friendly. Jack asked me to stay, but the paper simply could not afford a bigger payroll. And he knew, he said, it was only a matter of time. From my standpoint I was worried about the physical demands imposed by my old job. I had no idea what would be required in the new job, but I knew it couldn't be worse, from that standpoint. It is one thing to have the responsibility of covering the waterfront on a daily basis in a small town. I hoped it would be quite another to cover selected topics in a news organization with sufficient reporters on hand to dispatch hither and yon as needed.

In the final analysis it would prove a somewhat unhappy decision, but for the moment it was exciting and promising. Both Wood and Brooks were older, more experienced newsmen. Most of those who made up the Capitol Press Corps then were in the same category. Each one had come up through the ranks and achieved some success in the trade. The *Dallas Morning News* bureau was headed by Dawson Duncan and included men like Richard Morehead and Jimmy Banks. The *Dallas Times-Herald* had Margaret Mayer, who was usually outgunned but seldom beaten on news stories. The *Houston Chronicle* had Dick Wall, who somehow appeared out of place, as though he should have been a member of the British House of Lords. He was an excellent reporter and writer. The *Chronicle* also had Ed Ryder, an older, experienced newsman plagued by failing eyesight, and Bo Byers, whom I regarded as an energetic and observant reporter. The *San Antonio Express and Evening News* had Jon Ford, pound for pound the most prolific writer and, in my own opinion, one of the best reporters in the lot. He was the antithesis of the pack reporter. Bill Carter headed up the old International News Service, before that operation was folded into United Press, becoming United Press International. United Press was headed in Austin by O. B. Lloyd and later, after Lloyd left to work for Lyndon Johnson in Washington, by Lloyd Larrabee. The *Fort Worth Star-Telegram* had Sam Kinch, Sr., who had traveled to Cuero for stories on the land scandal. Dave Cheavens, a short, nervous worrier, was then finishing his newspaper career as chief of the Associated Press bureau, to be replaced by Garth Jones, who, with due respect to everyone concerned, was a much better, more balanced newsman. The *Houston Post* bureau was headed by Bill Gardner, who had long experience in both newspapering and government. Stuart Long headed up his own operation, furnishing service to a number of smaller papers across the state, as well as specialized information to private clients.

By and large they represented papers still in the hands of long-time Texas owners, papers that had not yet become part of giant out-of-state media chains or conglomerates.

While the political spectrum was fairly well represented throughout the group, my own impression was, journalistically speaking, they were a comparatively objective lot judged by today's standards. Few seemed to have political "agendas" that colored their stories. Long was probably the most politically active, both he and his wife being involved on the liberal side of Democratic Party affairs. Surrounded by people of such experience and stature, it was easy to feel out of place. There was much to learn, but many to learn from.

And it was an interesting time to make the change. Allan Shivers was completing his reign as governor, though he would remain a political power for years to come. In January of 1957, in an emotional farewell before a packed legislative chamber, he said his goodbyes, officially. Price Daniel, who had eventually eked out a victory of less than 4,000 votes over Ralph Yarborough in the Democratic primary runoff, would become the new governor. A special election would be needed to fill the Senate seat left vacant by Daniel's resignation.

During the course of the governor's campaign, Yarborough was fond of holding up copies of bonds that had been sold to finance the Veterans Land Program. There, right on the bond, was the name of Price Daniel. In the world of politics that proved, as explained by Yarborough, that Daniel and Daniel's friends had a hand in the operation. Actually the only reason Daniel's name was on the bonds was because he was the attorney general when the bonds were sold, and by law had to sign them. Nevertheless it was a charge Daniel had to continually defend himself against. And it was a charge that fit well with Yarborough's general theme that the people of Texas were afflicted by a cabal of established special interests, of which Price Daniel was part and parcel. His suggested solution, quite naturally, was his own election.

Despite Yarborough's defeat, his campaign did position him well for the special election called to fill the Senate seat vacated by Daniel. At that time a special election could be won by simply being high man in the vote totals. Yarborough's election to the Senate appeared a sure thing.

Enter the Texas legislature. It was probably not the most disciplined of such bodies in American politics, but it is doubtful if any other had as much fun. Even so, the legislators did occasionally get serious, and one of the first serious endeavors of that session was to try to deny Yarborough the Senate seat. One of the earliest bits of legislation introduced was by Rep. Joe Pool, a short, rotund, conservative Democrat from Dallas. The legislation, which became known as House Bill 4, would change the election law to provide for runoffs in special elections. The argument was made by Pool and his supporters that this terribly important legislation was needed to prevent some evil Republican from sneaking into office with a mere plurality of the votes in some future election. The argument was, of course, transparent. Republicans were no force in the state at that time, and even the dumbest legislator saw the effort for what it was — an attempt to keep Yarborough from walking into the Senate with less than a majority of votes. Theoretically, a runoff would give the dominant conservative forces time to coalesce behind an acceptable candidate.

Of the 150-member House, some 30 or 40 members generally passed for "liberals" of that day. Theirs was mostly a motley, disorganized group that could be expected to come together in a coherent fashion, primarily on those issues that moved decision making to Washington, where their philosophical brethren were in a much stronger position. The candidacy of Ralph Yarborough fell in that category. He could be expected to strengthen the liberal bloc in Washington, where more and more decisions were being made that affected those issues the liberals were most concerned about. Also, it would have the effect of keeping Yarborough alive politically, and provide a base for the liberals to build on within the state.

The Pool bill quickly changed from a skirmish to an important, heated battle. It ultimately passed, but with insufficient votes to put it into immediate effect. The little band of opponents managed to scrounge enough votes to place the effective date of the legislation beyond the special election, which allowed Yarborough to win a Senate seat with 364,805 votes out of a total 957,298 votes cast. Twenty-three names were on the ballot.

There were certain ironies in the matter. The argument throughout the debate, however fraudulent, was that the legislation was aimed at some unnamed Republican, not at Yarborough. In fact, that is the way it worked out. The first special election to the U.S. Senate to which the law actually applied was the race of John Tower, some four years later. To the astonishment of the electorate Tower, a Republican, led a field of seventy-two candidates, winning a runoff with Democrat William Blakley, for whom I voted.

The debate also placed liberals in the seemingly uncomfortable position of arguing against, in this instance, the principle of one-man, one-vote, majority rule. I was learning quickly that the Texas legislature was a good place to observe but not absorb politics, that in politics principle is a suit of many colors. There is always a higher principle that can be used to justify the abandonment of an immediate principle. For the liberals, having Yarborough in the Senate was a higher principle, in this instance, than assuring that the winning candidate be one who had a majority of the votes cast.

If I was surprised, I should not have been. After all, there was no outcry from the left in Texas when Lyndon Johnson assumed a U.S. Senate seat with less than a majority of the votes legally cast. And there was no general outcry from that portion of the press that had supported Johnson in that race. A higher principle was operating there as well. Johnson would be "good" for the state. Coke Stevenson, while an honest, honorable man, was an old fogy who would have done nothing but sit in the Senate, voting against "progressive" legislation. So what, if a few votes were illegally cast and Stevenson was denied the seat? So what, if a few votes were counted that had never been cast? If those people had actually voted, they probably would have voted that way, anyway. It was all for the better.

Actually, I found Yarborough to be an honorable man—sometimes blinded by ideology, sometimes carried away by his own rhetoric, but honest in his approach to issues as he saw those issues. And in this instance he was playing by the rules of the game and the law as it was written. While I completely approved of the general thrust of Pool's legislation, I found it somewhat distasteful that the rules should be changed simply to deny to one candidate the potential advantage that had applied to all candidates before him. I felt the same when Lyndon leaned on the legislature later, causing his toadies to change the rules in his favor, in order that he might run for two federal offices at the same time.

Years later, in Washington, Yarborough and I visited at some length about this and other things. It was at one of those annual Texas picnics, where displaced Texans gathered to play games, break bread, and generally renew acquaintances. He had heard I was present and sent a staff member to fetch me. Past and present differences, of which there were many, were laid aside as we reminisced in his tent. I suppose it was there that the final irony of the matter was laid out.

"Isn't it strange," Yarborough said. "Here we both are in Washington. I never wanted to come here. I never had any desire to be a U.S. senator. I always had a burning desire to be governor of Texas. It's strange how things work out."

Indeed it is.

The new job in Austin, the new people, the new surroundings, proved an interesting experience. My assignment was to cover the House of Representatives while the legislature was in session, and generally cover the goings-on of state government when it was not.

Brooks covered the Senate and Wood divided his time between the two, generally coordinating the stories that flowed from both bodies. Brooks also had the responsibility of covering the State Supreme Court. The Court of Criminal Appeals was mine, as were some lesser courts plus a number of state agencies and departments.

In most respects we enjoyed an enviable arrangement. In terms of reporting on our areas of assignment, we were essentially given a free hand. We reported our offering through a teletype connecting all three papers, two of which had both morning and afternoon editions. The third, Port Arthur, was an afternoon paper. The editors were free to use, or not use, what we reported. They were also free to write their own editorials, or they could use the offering of a "chief" editorial writer stationed at the Austin paper. For good and sufficient reasons they seldom did so. He was exceedingly prolific, exceedingly dull, exceedingly predictable.

While we operated as an independent bureau, our paychecks came from the Austin paper. Under normal circumstance one would think we would also receive a certain amount of guidance and editorial support from there, but such was not the case. One reason, I suspected, was that our bureau chief, Sam Wood, stood taller in the eyes of the Waco home office than did the local editor, a man seemingly more interested in society, poetry, and the finer things of life than in the machinations of politics or the humdrum of state government. A certain amount of jealousy may also have been at play.

The paper's editorial stance was, of course, Democratic, but it had not yet been turned into a campaign brochure for the Democratic Party. That would have to await the coming of new owners, and new times. Since Republicans had not yet appeared as a force on the state political scene, most of its battles, to the extent there were any, were carried out in the nature of taking sides in a family squabble. Generally speaking it supported, half-heartedly, candidates from the "moderate" side of the party's two wings. But it did so, it seemed to me, almost apologetically, as if it would really rather be on the other side, wherever the other side was. It was a paper that seemed bent on proving that extremism in the pursuit of moderation was no vice, nor was conviction in the pursuit of principle a virtue.

Lyndon Johnson was the exception—the exception that perhaps proved the rule. When Lyndon zigged, the paper's editorial stance zigged. When he zagged, the paper's editorial writers zagged. In short, Lyndon Johnson could do no wrong. I would find out later he thought that was the way it was supposed to be, and that he had good reason to think so.

For the first few years none of that concerned me. My own plate was full. The process of learning and reporting on affairs of government left little time to worry about such matters. I merely accepted the fact that it was a different kind of newspaper than what I was used to. I would try to do my job and let them do theirs. Besides, I took comfort in knowing that the other two newspapers for which we reported were much more akin to what I thought a newspaper ought to be. Two out of three wasn't all that bad.

As the years passed, however, the situation grated. It became apparent that the Austin paper was not terribly interested in becoming involved with any sort of controversy that might require them to come down on one side or the other of a divisive issue. I did not regard myself as any sort of crusader, nor even as a good "investigative" reporter. And we had plenty to do just trying to keep up with the normal routine. But my involvement in the veterans land scandals seemed to act as a magnet for any number of "tips" and leads on other matters that some citizen thought should be examined. Every reporter will recognize the situation. Once he or she becomes known as one who might be willing to try to correct a perceived wrong, the telephone calls never cease. Most of the time the calls don't pan out. Most of the time they turn out to be somebody with a personal axe to grind. But not always. And because of that we were able to get in on the ground floor of stories involving Ben Jack Cage, the insurance swindler, Milton Addison, in my opinion the premier con man of our generation (outside politics), and assorted stories of various kinds.

But all this was done with very little editorial support from the paper downtown. Not that it was necessary, or critical. It merely would have made the job easier and more rewarding. And it was, after all, the capital city's newspaper. On occasion I spoke to Wood about the seeming lack of interest on the part of the Austin paper with what we were doing at the Capitol Bureau. He took a more philosophical view. We should count our blessings. If they got mixed up in it, we would probably be more unhappy with the results. He was older and wiser. His counsel was taken to heart.

An accumulation of events over the succeeding years finally determined it would be better, from the standpoint of personal peace, to go elsewhere. Perhaps I was just not suited to the situation. Perhaps I expected too much from newspapers. Perhaps I simply still did not have the capacity to adjust properly. Some of the things that rankled me were matters I probably should not have been concerned about at all. But they were matters that in my ignorance and naiveté I thought were important at the time.

A few small items and one or two larger ones may illustrate the point.

Eisenhower was president. Lyndon Johnson was majority leader in the Senate. Trouble erupted in Little Rock, Arkansas, over integration of a school there. A federal judge had ordered the integration, but the governor and state authorities were resisting. Eisenhower moved troops into the area to enforce the federal court's orders. Johnson was in Austin, addressing a group of Democratic women in the State Senate chambers. The story moved over the wires. Clearly it would be a major story, given the tenor of the times, with the potential of having major political repercussions. The Senate majority leader was less than 100 yards away. A small group of reporters, of which I was one, hastened to get his reaction.

Johnson had not heard the news and therefore was understandably cautious and noncommittal. Fine. No problem. But then he said something which rubbed me the wrong way. In his most condescending manner he said he would go back to his office, and if he had anything to say later he would send his comments to us. He was not going to answer any questions on the matter.

My response was, "Well, Lyndon, if you ever decide what you want to say, why don't you come by the press room? Perhaps that way you will be able to help *us* some." I emphasized the word *us*, hoping the implication would be clear. I suppose it was.

Before the day was done he was in the press room. He wandered from one desk to another, exchanging pleasantries, and finally sat down with me. He was not ready to elaborate on Little Rock. He just wanted to talk, "off the record." He had all sorts of problems in the Senate, riding herd over a fractious group. His job was very difficult. We had to understand. In many respects his hands were tied. As long as people like Richard Russell of Georgia and John Stennis of Mississippi were in the Senate, he really couldn't get done those things that needed to be done. We simply had to increase the black vote throughout the South. They would take care of that problem. They would "get rid" of people like Stennis. I had the idea he thought he was talking to a sympathetic soul. Why else would I be working for the Austin paper?

Again, fine. If that's the way he felt, no problem. Next day he dispatched an emissary to repeat much of his message and to plead for understanding.

But now we jump forward a few years. Johnson is laying the ground for his run at the presidency, though as yet he has made no public statement to that effect. We, along with three or four other reporters, are summoned to the LBJ ranch, some sixty miles away. The downtown paper thinks he may have something important to say. A dozen or more guests are in attendance, along with what turns out to be the guest of honor, Senator John Stennis of Mississippi. Stennis, generally regarded as one of the Senate's most honorable men, had recently returned from a trip to the Soviet Union. He was to give the assembled guests a report on his travels.

He is introduced by Johnson as one of the stalwarts of the Senate, a man of the highest character, as "one of the greatest living Americans." Could this be the same man whom Johnson had told me earlier, in private, that must be gotten "rid of"?

I know, I know. In politics hypocrisy and duplicity are much admired by true practitioners of the art. Therein lies success, and success breeds followers, and a larger following breeds still more success.

Forward still. Kennedy and Johnson have just been elected president and vice-president, but have not yet been sworn in. It is shortly after the election. The new president flies to Texas to visit with his vice-president. A number of planes are involved for the newly elected president, his entourage, and a number of newsmen. A reporter on the Austin paper, Robert Sherrill, is assigned to do the story for the following morning's paper. There's not much to write about, in a substantive way. Kennedy merely landed at Bergstrom Air Base and went immediately to the ranch. Sherrill, possibly seeking to add a little color to his story, asked the base public information officer why so many planes were needed on such an occasion. The PIO said he didn't know.

Unfortunately, the story left the impression that the officer, a major, volunteered the comment. In fact it had the PIO saying something like "I don't know why they need all those planes." That story appeared in a Tuesday morning's paper. For the afternoon paper of that day Raymond Brooks picked up and rewrote the earlier piece, and added whatever recent developments had occurred, if any. Again, unfortunately, he used the same comments. It was this paper that made its way to the LBJ ranch, with Raymond's byline.

Early Wednesday morning the phone rang at our desk in the Capitol newsroom. The operator had a call for Raymond Brooks. She had a very nice voice. I told her that Raymond was not there at the moment. I intended to finish the sentence by saying he would be back shortly, and ask if I could take a message. No such luck. A loud, angry voice interrupted, shouting, "Well get him!"

The tone precipitated the same sort of response on my part. "Well, you can't 'get' him. This is court day. Raymond is over at the Supreme Court and he won't be back until he's back."

"Are you connected with the *Austin Statesman*?" he shouted. Yes I was. What was my name? I told him.

He then identified himself, saying, "Ken, this is Lyndon Johnson."

For a moment his tone became entirely conciliatory. He wanted to talk about a story in his paper. Fine. He identified the story. It had Raymond's name on it, and that was why he wanted to talk to Raymond. I explained where Raymond was, and told him I would be happy to have him call, or, I added, "I'll listen to you." I figured it would be a one-way conversation, which it largely turned out to be.

As he talked his fury returned. He couldn't understand why that damned paper had to write anything about the matter anyway. I tried to explain that the editors probably thought it was incumbent on them to have a story about the newly elected president visiting his vice-president. That argument got nowhere. People were tired of politics, they had seen and read enough about politicians flying around in the sky. He didn't know why every time he came back to Texas he had to read about it in that damned paper. It went on. Then he turned to what was probably his chief source of irritation.

"And about that guy at Bergstrom. What business is it of his how many planes we use? That son-of-a-bitch ought to be back behind a plow."

Shortly thereafter, both Sherrill and the PIO left their respective jobs. The story was that the PIO was "transferred" and that Sherrill was "let go." He began work with *The New York Times*. My last contact with him was during the campaign of George McGovern for the presidency. My only passing comment would be, though I regarded him as much a liberal as I was a conservative, that I always found him to be an intellectually honest man.

Perhaps Sherrill's story should have been written differently, if in fact it was as the PIO explained the matter, that he was merely responding to an inquiry and his response got translated to a statement on his part. That was considered a no-no in those days. But I hardly saw why it should invoke the kind of response it got, either from a man who had just been elected vice-president of the United States, or on the part of the newspaper. And what did this say about the future? Was this to be the response, and this the result, when something appeared that invoked Lyndon's wrath? However minor? Was this a straw in the wind?

To others those small incidents might seem little cause for concern. And in truth they did not interfere with my own work. It was merely somewhat embarrassing to be associated with a paper that seemed to stand in such trembling awe of a politician so duplicitous and self-centered. In time I would find this was not an altogether unique situation in what is now called "the media," but at that time, coming out of the Howerton tutelage at Cuero, it was exceedingly strange.

The real reason I determined to look elsewhere had nothing to do with Lyndon Johnson. It had to do with what I thought, rightly or wrongly, impinged on my own ability to follow a story I thought ought to be written. I was visited by an engineer then employed in the development of a municipal water district in the hill country west of the Austin city limits. He was a friend of my older brothers, having gone to school with them in Raymondville many years before, not far from the Mexican border in the Rio Grande Valley. He knew of my involvement in the land scandals and thought I might be interested in what he had to say.

Austin at that time was a city of some 160,000. The city was not officially encouraging development to the west, perhaps because the cost of utility emplacement there was so expensive in the limestone rock that underlies the area, and perhaps for other, more political, reasons as well. To get around this roadblock developers had begun to encourage creation of independent water districts, standing on their own bottom and funded by bonds floated against property within the district and to be paid off by owners of property within the district. The district would develop its own water source or purchase that water from an existing authority, such as the city.

The engineer had a problem, a moral and ethical problem. According to him they were using pipes, valves, and related material that were inferior to what design specifications called for, and for which the district was being charged. His boss, the chief engineer on the project, took the view that once the material was in place, well below ground, no one would know unless they went in and dug it up. That might take years to discover.

The engineer's view was that this was not only morally wrong but legally wrong as well. And he had a longer range view. The material being used would surely deteriorate sooner than planned, which would cause massive replacement costs, which would increase taxes within the district, and which might even cause bankruptcy for the district. He envisioned the city ultimately having to take over the district, with a corresponding cost to citizens of the city. In any event the property owners were going to end up paying more than they had been led to believe.

I asked for proof. He brought it. Copies of invoices for what was purchased and put in the ground. Design specifications for what should have been put in place and for which the district was charged and for which they had paid. He agreed to sign a sworn statement, if needed. He was prepared to take the consequences.

I worked on the story for some three months, quietly, after hours, when I could get a few hours here or there. The plan was to follow, somewhat, the pattern used in the land scandals. Publish a series of stories, beginning with a history of how the district came into being, lay out the fraud that might be possible, and finish with the evidence turned over by the engineer. At the very least we could put citizens within the district on notice and let them clean up their own affairs.

No such luck. The story languished somewhere within the Austin paper's bureaucracy for weeks, bouncing from one desk to another. Inquiries were met with the explanation that it was "being studied." It was finally turned over to the paper's lawyers, who, of course, were paid to keep the paper out of trouble, and who, quite naturally, had the safest of all answers: Don't publish.

I was furious. I could have, and probably should have, appealed to the home office in Waco. But it was an Austin story and the Austin editors were entitled, by my lights, to make a determination on what they were prepared to live with, and, if necessary, fight for. Had they decided to run the story, they would have had to become involved. They could hardly have left it out there hanging, merely as a contribution from their Capitol Bureau. They chose not to do so.

(A couple of years later, in Washington, I read a small item moved on the AP wire: An engineer had been indicted by a far West Texas grand jury for having tried to bribe a city council. The name rang a bell. It was the same person who had been in charge of the water district project. He had approached a member of the council. The councilman and his brethren had placed a tape recorder under a table and called him in to hear his proposal. The indictment followed. I do not know the result.)

The handling of that story, standing alone, would hardly have been sufficient reason to make a change. I simply had to accept the fact that it was their call, they were responsible, and with that I did not quarrel. But it could do little other than create a feeling of uncertainty relative to any future stories of this kind. Why worry, if this would be the result? That, combined with what I regarded as slavish devotion to selected politicians, did not portend a life of fulfillment or happiness. I finally decided to make a change when and if the opportunity presented itself.

It was not an easy decision. I could see no life outside the news business. I had convinced myself there was no higher calling in life than simply being a good reporter, recording the events of the day as honestly as possible. I had been involved in that task long enough to know it is a most difficult assignment even in the best of circumstances. The best of reporters, it seemed to me, were always looking through the glass darkly, always trying to see more clearly, always trying to understand the "why" of things, as well as the what and when of things. Always determined to do a better job on the next story. Perhaps I had been influenced by the teaching of Alvis Hannah in chemistry laboratories. There, if results varied from what had been anticipated, the answer was always, "Take the crucible back to the oven and bake it more." If that didn't work, maybe our calculations were wrong in the first place.

Or perhaps I had been influenced by Howerton's philosophy about newspapering, one I came to agree with completely. His view was that a newspaper ought to have certain fundamental principles of its own, and to the extent any politician accepted or approached those principles, he should be supported. When he departed those principles, he should be opposed. No matter who. No matter what party. Any symbiotic relationship with a politician should have that understanding as its base.

Also, I had to realize that my problem might not be elsewhere.

Perhaps it lay within me, that I was still having difficulty adjusting to a world in which I did not grow up. In prison camp a man's worth was not determined by where he stood; his standing was determined by his worth. If he were fortunate enough to be surrounded by a cadre of friends, it was because they saw in him something worth protecting and supporting. It was not because they thought he could afford them any degree of power or any degree of material comfort. All those factors were controlled by the Japanese, and any man who sought power and material comfort from that quarter at the expense of his fellows was regarded as the lowest of the low. And he suffered the consequences, which, in those prison camps I inhabited, were not pleasant.

The world outside prison camps, it seemed, did not work that way. Here a man's worth was determined by his position, his position by where he sat, as was the worth of those who sat close to him and called him friend.

Increasingly, I began to worry about the role of the media in the whole political process. It was not that there was any conscious effort to do wrong. Indeed, there was, in most cases, a conscious effort to do right. But the sheer mechanical process by which we went about our task, was, it seemed to me, fraught with danger as far as getting at the truth was concerned. Truth does not normally come calling. Truth is seldom ushered in by the sounds of chirping crickets or braying jackasses. Truth normally must be searched for, quietly, as one seeks the white-tailed deer or the wild turkey. But the nature of our job made it much easier, even imperative, that we listen to and report the chirping of crickets and the braying of jackasses.

It can be argued, and is argued, that crickets and jackasses are also part of the scene and ought not be ignored, simply because they exist.

But raging rivers and quiet ponds also exist. Life and death goes on within each. I began to believe we paid too much attention to chirping crickets, braying jackasses, raging rivers, and too little to life in the quiet pond. Nevertheless, I could see no solution to the problem.

Other things as well troubled me about the way we, as reporters, went about our business. This had nothing to do with talent or philosophy. It had to do with the nature of groups generally, and groups of reporters specifically. It had to do with the dynamics of the business. The Capitol Press Corps was then a relatively small group, compared to what it would become. But even then there were nascent signs of pack reporting. If an individual reporter did not show up at his desk for a few days, there was worry on the part of others that he might be off working on a story, which, when published, would precipitate a message from the home office: "Why didn't you have this story?" This led, understandably, to reporters devoting time and energy to what other reporters were doing, rather than exploring for original work. It also led to the tendency to find new angles, or new details, for stories that had appeared elsewhere. The one beneficial aspect of this dilemma was that it could do nothing but enhance the value of the truly independent and aggressive reporter, for whether he wished it or not, he became a leader in the group simply by understanding and not ignoring the unwritten but governing procedures.

Even more troubling to me was the psychological effect of the assignment itself. We, in company with our fellows, were assigned the task of covering and reporting on government and politics. In order to do that properly one must not only understand the process, one must have contacts within the institutions of government and politics. In time those contacts become friends, since they assist the reporter in doing his job. They become, in a very real sense, part of the reporter's team. The longer the time involved, the wider the circle of contacts and the more steadfast the friendships involved. This can become, also in a very real sense, part of the problem all reporters must guard against. Or at least should guard against. The contacts are, after all, part of an institution the contacts want to see protected since it is their livelihood. And since they assist the reporter, or journalist as it is now defined, in his own livelihood, there is the danger that symbiotic relationships develop—that the contact's own protective instincts find expression, unwittingly, through the reporter's pen.

The natural extension of this problem is that journalists covering government and politics may become instinctively protective of their sources and those institutions that feed, clothe, and house their sources. The citizen out in the countryside, the person who foots the bill, is in danger of being forgotten in the process. A story involving increases in expenditures for welfare or education, for example, was and is generally couched in terms of benefits to recipients of those expenditures, seldom explained in terms of its cost to those paying the bill. And I was troubled that I could see, in my own case, a gradual transition from the country newsman who had always looked askance at government to one who looked sympathetically at the problems of government. The problems of those in the hinterlands began to take a back seat to the problems of those in government. It was not a healthy situation, as far as I was concerned. Still there was not much I could do about it, other than try to remember, as best I could, my own roots.

No matter. Life and work went on. The legislature went through many battles, great and small. The truck lobby took the legislature away from the train lobby. The size of trucks, and the weight they could carry, increased accordingly. Governor Daniel lost his battle to prevent enactment of a state sales tax. Lyndon Johnson decided he wanted to be president. Or rather, he finally decided to let people know he wanted to be president. There was only one small problem. State law said a politician couldn't run for two federal offices at the same time. According to the law, Lyndon would have to give up his Senate candidacy in order to run for the presidency. No sweat. Just get the legislature to change the law, allowing him to run for both offices at once.

The governor was not keen on the idea, but in time he saw where the votes were. Rather than go down in complete defeat, the governor salvaged a degree of face by convincing the legislature to also change the date for spring primaries, moving them forward into somewhat cooler weather. The proposal, a brainchild of a legislator named Marshall Bell of San Antonio, had been hanging around for years. Bell thought such a move would be generally beneficial to conservative voters and politicians supported by conservative voters. Daniel finally adopted the idea, feeling it would be helpful to his own endeavors as well, since that was the community he relied upon for his own support.

During debate on that particular bill, I walked over to the Senate chamber to check on the legislation's progress. There, on the floor of the Senate, I encountered Jake Jacobsen, whom I had always regarded as a completely devoted associate of Price Daniel. He was one of the party's principal fundraisers among well-heeled contributors, and, as befits the occupation, was often involved in legislative matters.

Somewhat surprised, I asked, "Jake, what are you doing here?"

"Oh, I'm carrying a little water for Lyndon," he said.

"I thought you were working for the governor."

"That's what the governor thinks too." And he giggled.

My political education took another small step forward.

The legislation passed. Lyndon went on to become vice-president, then president, and Jake went on to the White House. Our trails would cross again.

Johnson's Senate seat, given up when he was elected vice-president, was filled by John Tower.

Daniel served another term as governor and then, seeking a fourth term, finished third behind John Connally, who succeeded him, and Don Yarborough, no relation to the senator and a relative newcomer to politics trying to capitalize on the same surname, in the Democratic primary of 1962.

THIRTEEN

Tense Times in Washington

On an autumn day in 1962, a phone call from Senator John Tower relayed a startling inquiry. Would I be interested in coming to work for him in Washington?

I had never met the senator. His 1960 race against Lyndon Johnson for the U.S. Senate was not a high priority for our papers. His campaign was reported, but most of the copy was furnished by wire service reports. Our own staff reporters, reflecting the concerns of the newspaper's owners, concentrated most of their efforts on the Democratic primary's gubernatorial race between Jack Cox and Price Daniel and the general election's presidential race between Richard Nixon and John Kennedy, with Johnson on the ticket as vice-presidential nominee. There was probably the feeling that the Senate race, at that point, was unimportant from a public interest standpoint, since Johnson was probably going to win it hands down, which he did. Tower ran a surprisingly strong race against Johnson in the Senate race, however, and his party picked him to carry its banner in the 1961 special election called to fill the seat vacated by Johnson. He led a field of seventy-two hopefuls and won the runoff against William A. Blakley, a politically naive conservative Democrat of considerable wealth and modest demeanor.

The idea of going to Washington, even for a reporting job, had not entered my thinking. Even further from my thinking was going there to join the staff of a Republican senator whom I did not know. My reaction was probably not what Tower expected, nor what wisdom would have dictated. I told Tower, "Senator, I didn't even vote for you. I voted for Blakley."

Tower was very gracious. That was of no concern to him, he said. Many people didn't. He was interested in my joining him, he explained, because he thought I knew the Texas political scene, and his staff was woefully short on that experience. The only person on his staff with any extended exposure to Texas politics was Herschel Schooley, a former Texas newsman who had spent many years in Washington, some of those years at the Pentagon. He was retiring and Tower wanted me to replace him as his press secretary.

I told the senator I'd have to think about it. In a week or so he called again. I still had no certain answer. It would be a terribly big step, one I wasn't sure about. We enjoyed our home, the children were in school, and the prospect of uprooting the family was not appealing. I did not want to leave the field of reporting, though I was increasingly unhappy with some aspects of my job. Perhaps I could take a leave of absence, go to Washington for a couple of years, and come back. I reasoned that would make me a more knowledgeable reporter in the workings of government and politics. I knew the paper had a policy along those lines, for it was not at all unusual for midlevel, and what might be called upper midlevel, people to leave their reporting or editorial positions for the campaigns of selected, acceptable Democratic candidates, and return to those posts when the campaigns were over. Indeed, there were even instances where certain employees were allowed to "moonlight" for acceptable candidates.

Sometimes this took strange turns. Once, while covering the campaign of John Connally in his 1962 race for governor against Republican Jack Cox, I found myself in El Paso near midnight. It had been a long, exhausting day. The story was written. I took it to the local Western Union facility, only to find it was closed for the night. I telephoned the Austin desk, apprising them of the difficulty, and asked for someone to whom I could dictate the story. Never mind, I was told, just find where the Connally entourage was staying, take the copy there, and they would send it in via their own communications system. I was told "we have an arrangement with them." I demurred, but the incident stuck in my mind as one more straw.

I called Bill Brammer, a friend in Washington who had made the change from journalism to politics, to ask his opinion on the matter. Brammer had covered state politics for the *Texas Observer*, a small journal of liberal opinion, before joining the staff of Lyndon Johnson in Washington. While Brammer and I were not on the same political wavelength, I had always thought of him as an honest reporter.

He never, to my knowledge, took the position that he was an unbiased observer. He was a liberal, seeking to further the liberal agenda, and was honest enough to say so.

Brammer advised that I accept the job. It would be a learning experience, he said, and no matter what happened next would probably be worth the move. The switch might be more difficult for me than it was for him, since he had been more intimately involved in partisan politics than I, but he saw no real problem with me going to work for Tower. We would probably get along reasonably well, he thought, since we shared the same basic political views. I asked how he, whom I had always regarded as being in the camp of Ralph Yarborough, got along with Johnson.

"Oh, he's still a son-of-a-bitch, but he's not as big a one as he was before I went to work for him," he replied with a laugh.

With that sage advice I approached the paper. How would they feel about my taking a two-year unpaid leave of absence to work in Washington?

Who for?

John Tower.

The exact response was "Not that guy."

Whereupon my mind was made up. If Tower called again I would take his offer. He did call, and I accepted, not having the slightest idea of what I was getting into. I thought I would go for two years and then leave. Surely I could find something after that. Howerton had a standing offer for my return to the *Cuero Record*, and when the two years were up I would look at that again.

It was with a great deal of trepidation that the change was made. I did not know the man I was going to work for. I knew of his stated policies, and had no quarrel with them. I knew he had a reputation for intellectual honesty, which, from where I stood at the moment, had a certain appeal. I had never been to Washington and had no idea what the job of a senator's press secretary entailed. I had avoided any active involvement in partisan politics. I had voted for Tower's Democratic opponent in the special election, but in the general election contest for president had voted for Richard Nixon over John Kennedy, simply because Lyndon Johnson was on the ticket with Kennedy. I was not knowingly going to reward someone whom I felt had corrupted the political process.

I arrived in Washington at the end of January, a few days after my fortieth birthday, to begin work for a senator two years my junior. Louise and the children were to remain in Austin until classes ended for the summer. I took an apartment within a three-block walking distance of the office, in a place called the Jefferson House, across the street from the Supreme Court building. My window overlooked the Court's rear entrance, where each morning Chief Justice Earl Warren arrived, driven by a black chauffeur. The chief justice did not ride up front. The area was patrolled by policemen in pairs, accompanied by trained dogs. Even that did not prevent a burglar entering my room one night, making off with wallet and anything else he could carry, while I slept soundly. I was left, temporarily, in a strange city, and I mean a really strange city, with no cash, no credit cards, and no identification. It was not exactly the scene I had envisioned for our nation's capital.

My first day on the job was Schooley's last day on the job. Together we walked from Tower's office in Suite 141 of what is now the Russell Office Building to the Senate and House press galleries, where he introduced me to the proper authorities, and where he left me. He wanted to get back to the office, clean up his desk, and depart. He was anxious to begin his retirement. It was only with some difficulty that I found my way back. The labyrinth of passageways, would, in time, become most familiar, but on that first day the entire building took on the aspects of a bewildering maze.

I did not meet Tower immediately upon arrival. Despite being low man on an exceedingly short totem pole (there were then only some thirty-two Republican senators in a body of 100), Tower was very much in demand as a speaker at various events around the country. He was the only Republican senator from the South. He was something of a celebrity because he replaced the Senate's majority leader, and he was articulate in giving voice to the nation's growing conservative movement, then in the early stages of convincing Barry Goldwater he should run for the presidency. When we did meet, a few days later, it was mostly a matter of courtesy, without anything of substance being discussed. I told him as long as I was on his staff I would try to give him the best advice I could, but I cautioned that I knew nothing of Washington or the inner workings of its politics. Whatever advice I could give him would have to be weighed in the context of his own party's position on issues, then determined largely by the legendary Everett Dirksen of Illinois, leader of Senate Republicans. He seemed to appreciate my comments, and suggested that he hold a small reception at the Capitol Hill Club, a Republican watering hole, to which we would invite those members of the press that normally covered Washington for media outlets in Texas. The purpose would be a sort of "get-acquainted" affair. The thought was appreciated and welcomed, since there were many in that category I had never met.

The results, however, were entirely unanticipated and set the stage for the relationship between Tower and myself for years to come.

It was a very relaxed, informal affair, which was supposed to be, after the fashion of such functions in Washington at that time, "off the record." Tower introduced me and recounted for his guests the conversation between he and I, wherein I told him I voted for his opponent. It was a nice touch. Drinks were ordered and served. I do not remember members of the press being bashful in this regard. Tower ordered rye whiskey, which struck one of the reporters as strange, since his usual drink was Scotch. Food had been ordered and was being served. Tower had ordered Oysters Rockefeller.

At that moment in history skirmishes were under way between the Rockefeller forces, representing the old, eastern Republican establishment, and the coalescing conservative forces backing Senator Barry Goldwater of Arizona, primarily in the South and West. Tower, reflecting the prevailing mood among Texas Republicans, was identified with the Goldwater effort. Goldwater had not given his blessing to the effort on his behalf, nor would he for months to come. In the meantime there would be much jockeying among politicians and much reading of tea leaves by the press.

When Tower's plate was served one of the reporters at his table humorously asked, "Senator, is there any political significance to the fact that you ordered Oysters Rockefeller?"

There was laughter, to which Tower responded by holding up his glass of rye and remarking, "Not in the least. You will note I am drinking pure Goldwater."

More laughter.

The event, insignificant as it was, almost passed quietly into history. A week or two later a report on it appeared in the column of a reporter who was not present at the event. The account was accurate in all details save one. It had Tower holding up a glass of Scotch, rather than a glass of rye.

Tower was both horrified and terrified. He simply could not understand. The affair was "off the record." Everyone understood that and agreed to that. Why would they violate the understanding? Now he was going to be flooded by thousands of letters from irate citizens. I was instructed to prepare a letter of response in anticipation of that flood. The letter needed to deny the authenticity of the report.

I tried to reason with him. That would be the very worst thing we could do. In the first place, I did not think the report would stir up any hornets' nest. I doubted we would receive more than a few letters, if that many. If we received any letters at all we could respond to them on a case by case basis. Beyond that, it would be far better to take our lumps than to surface the entire matter in the press over a quarrel concerning the difference between rye and Scotch. Or the hypocrisy of an unknown reporter who would voluntarily take part in an "off the record" gathering and then pass the information along to someone who would use it.

My argument was made somewhat easier by the fact that the incident was reported in a column written by a reporter generally known, along with his wife, as a lap dog for Lyndon Johnson or any other Democrat for that matter. He had a number of media outlets in Texas, by virtue of his wife's closeness to the Johnson family, but his readership was very limited. The best we could do, in my opinion, was let it alone. The story was essentially true and I was not going to write a letter for the senator's signature saying it was not true.

The senator insisted I prepare a letter. I did. It was entirely unsatisfactory, deliberately so. He wanted another. Another was prepared. This too was unsatisfactory. In the meantime weeks went by. The flood of letters never materialized. (In hindsight, it might have been better had they done so.) We received two that I remember, one from a family member chiding the senator, and one from a minister. Both were sympathetic and understanding. The family member worried about what the senator's father might think, should he read the account. The minister, a friend of the senator's minister-father, was worried about the influence such a story might have on young people.

The entire matter died a natural death. It had proved to be, as I suspected it would be, a very small tempest in a much smaller tea pot. Welcome to the world of Washington politics. Tower never indicated he had been wrong in his assessment of the affair, and I tried to never indicate I had been right. But from then on, for as long as I was with him, he might sometimes question, but never disputed, my own assessment of the relationship between politics and the press, or, for that matter, the relationship between practitioners of the two arts. As tense as the atmosphere became during the standoff, it was, in the final analysis, a useful learning experience for both of us. I suspect he had quickly decided he made a mistake by asking me to come to Washington. I know there were moments when I had doubts myself, when I was prepared to quit and go back to Texas.

Thus began my association with John Tower, an association that would last until his death many years later. Sometimes close — too close. Sometimes distant — too distant.

I cannot say I ever completely understood John Tower. To me he was a riddle, an enigma, at times a contradiction. He was at once the most complicated yet simple of men. At times he enjoyed immensely the company of others. At times that same setting would find him cold, aloof, distant. Sometimes he would be most grateful and appreciative for small favors. Other times he would be completely oblivious to far greater favors. He seemed to enjoy the relaxed camaraderie of men, particularly men in uniform, but could be most uncomfortable in groups of men he did not know. And, like most men, he appreciated the attention of women. Perhaps more than most men he wanted other men to notice that attention. He was, it seemed to me, an exceedingly private man, seldom given to public displays of emotion. He had no use for what passed as political liberalism of that day, given as it was to incessant attack upon those who spoke ill of socialism, yet he yearned for approbation within that same liberal camp. One of his most admired senators was Eugene McCarthy, whom, he once confided to me, he found "the most intellectually honest man in the Senate."

More than anything else, it seemed to me, he wished to be accepted. He wished to be a member of the Senate club, respected by his peers. A few words of advice or praise from men like Richard Russell, or John Stennis, or Everett Dirksen, clearly gave him great happiness. I do not know how many times he quoted to me the advice given him by Richard Russell when he first arrived in Washington: "Now John, you are new here. You've got six years before you run again. You will learn that you can be a statesman for two years, then you must be a politician for two years, then for two years you are going to have to demagogue a little." Tower never really got around to the demagogue bit. He was then a believer, one who stood in awe of the Senate's traditions, of its rules, its history.

He was not given to badmouthing its members. In fact, the only senator I ever heard him express utter contempt for in private was Teddy Kennedy, whom he regarded as not only dumb but unworthy of his office. Tower was, as far as I could ever determine, an honest man in his dealings with fellow senators and the people of his home state. It would have been alien to his nature to use his office for the purpose of increasing his personal wealth, despite the fact he was probably one of the poorest, if not the poorest, member of that body. Still, he affected trappings that led others to think he was well off. His graduate studies in London had turned him into something of an Anglophile, and he flaunted British tailored suits, English cigarettes, and a brass cigarette case that members of the press seemed to think was made of gold. He sought to maintain, at least in public, what he regarded as the presence, the dignity, of a senator.

As the months went by we became friends but not chums. We spent much time together, but he remained the "senator" as far as I was concerned and was addressed in that fashion by me. A degree of mutual respect developed between us, based, in my own opinion, on an understanding of the strengths and weaknesses of each. Tower was a man of deep intellect, and, at that stage of his development, of sustaining conviction as well. But there were also times when he appeared a deeply disturbed, insecure man, worried beyond measure, seeking reassurance, even solace. Perhaps because I was older than he, perhaps because both of us had served in the Pacific war theater, he began the practice of calling me into his office at the close of day, before we went our respective ways. Customarily he would say, "The sun is over the yardarm. Come on in."

He would pour a drink for himself and one for me, and we would go over the day's activity and plan for the morrow. Usually the sessions did not last long. He was anxious to get home before the children were tucked in for the night. Sometimes, however, it seemed he simply wanted to unburden himself. Then the talk would turn to other things, to personal things. This usually happened when he was worried about his own future and the future of his family. He didn't know what he would do when his term was up, where he would go, how he would make a living.

On one such occasion, in his cups and in a mood of despair, he claimed he had been "a failure in everything I've ever tried." He wanted to be a lawyer. That didn't work out. He wanted to be a pilot. That didn't work out. He had even failed as an insurance salesman, he said, finally ending up as a teacher at Midwestern University in Wichita Falls, Texas. Even then, he confessed, he was plagued by a feeling of failure, of not being noticed. He bought a new De Soto automobile, he said, and would drive upon the streets of his beloved city, for no purpose other than the all too human failing of hoping to be noticed.

"I needed that car like I needed another hole in the head," he said, but it served the purpose of making him feel an accepted part of the larger group, that he was not a failure.

It is probably unwise to speak to a senator in the manner I sometimes spoke to Tower. But on that occasion I told him he was just plain silly. How could he count himself a failure, I asked, when here he was, sitting behind a big desk in Washington, as one of only 100 United States senators? Surely that would count as a success.

Politics didn't count, he said. That was no real achievement. Real achievement took place out in the private world, where men were doing things, creating things. Success in politics was largely the result of the labor of others, he said; it was not the result of one's own labors.

I found his comments on this occasion exceedingly strange, given his obvious love of the processes of government and politics, and his recognition of the impact both have on the lives of people. He was not a man given to frequent forays into the fields of hunting or fishing, or of afternoons spent at golfing. His life, it seemed to me, was wrapped up in ideas and the relative, practical value of those ideas in man's fate.

At that point he did not really believe he would be reelected when his Senate term was up. He tried, and largely succeeded, in keeping up a public image of supreme confidence, but he understood the makeup of Texas politics. He understood the big picture, even if he was not then well versed in all the brush strokes that made up that picture. It was his feeling that the conservative business establishment would simply not support him for reelection despite the fact that they could have no quarrel with his voting record. He felt the same about dominant newspapers in the state. He had grown up, he said, reading the editorials of the *Dallas Morning News*. They had a very profound effect on his political thinking and political development. And he had looked to the paper for guidance on many issues since coming to Washington, and voted accordingly. Still, he said, the paper would no doubt endorse any Democrat who opposed him.

The senator had good reason for his concerns. The state's political and business community was then more attuned to events in Austin than Washington. The burden of taxation and regulation emanating from Washington was not nearly so great as it would become in later years. There was not so much need to worry over things in Washington.

Also, there was a growing fight among Texas Democrats over the issue of "cleansing" the party of those whom the left thought should be driven out, in order that they might take their rightful place among the Republicans. One of the leaders of this "cleansing" effort was Frankie Randolph, wife of a wealthy Houston banker and founding benefactor of the liberal *Texas Observer*. She, at that time, was the crusty leader of a faction called the Democrats of Texas, or the "DOT." She and her followers regarded themselves as "true Democrats," champions of Ralph Yarborough and not to be confused with the holdover "Shivercrats" who then dominated the state Democratic Party, and whom they regarded as Republicans in disguise. Her argument, and consequently the argument of the *Observer*, was that those who could not be counted on to be loyal to the party ought to go elsewhere.

This could have the effect, argued people like Dick West, chief editorial writer for the *Dallas Morning News*, of eventually turning the state Democratic Party over to its liberal-labor wing. Obviously the Republicans could only grow by attracting conservative Democrats made unhappy by constant attacks from the left, or by disillusionment among conservatives with the leftward movement of the Democratic Party nationally. In this scenario there was bound to be a transition period in which state government would be controlled by the Democratic Party's left wing. The Dick West solution: discourage growth of the Republican Party, thereby keeping the Democratic Party in conservative hands.

The argument against growth of the Republican Party also found support in the network of lobbyists that influenced the Texas legislature, both left and right. Many took the position that two active political parties would simply drive up the cost of doing business. Money which then flowed to either side of one party would likely have to flow to either side of two parties, and no doubt increase if both parties were able to field viable candidates. Most of the lobbyists were former Democratic members of the House or Senate, and had a natural, normal bias in that direction. But even those who might be sympathetic to the idea of a strong two-party system realized they made their living working with, and trying to influence, a Democratic House and Senate. They could hardly give the appearance of being sympathetic to a two-party state.

My own position, during those infrequent periods of Tower's gloom, was that all was not lost by any means. Certainly, on balance, the deck was stacked against him. It wasn't just the position of the "establishment" in Texas. Even the votes didn't look good. During the 1960 race in which he contested Lyndon Johnson, a total of 2,253,784 votes were cast, 926,653 for Tower. But in the following special election, in which Tower ran against Blakley, only 886,091 votes were cast, with Tower getting 448,217. Clearly, Tower had some obstacles to overcome, but he would next come up for election in 1966, an "off" year, a year in which the presidential election was not held, and traditionally a year in which fewer votes were cast. If he could hold what he had, and perhaps add to that number, it was not impossible that he be reelected, no matter how the "establishment" reacted. And once he was reelected he would have no problems holding his seat.

I agreed that the dominant political forces in the state would be against him, but my argument was that this was chiefly because they saw him as a one-termer, not because they had any argument with his stance on political issues. Deplorable as it might be, that is generally the position taken by economic interests. They wish to be on the side of the winner. And it is a position also taken by an unknowing and unthinking segment of the electorate. All he had to do was get over that one mountain, to demonstrate he was a winner in an election not influenced by the peculiarities of his win against Blakley.

While there were discussions concerning the problem, there were practically no discussions on what to do about it. One reason was that Tower simply would not focus on the subject. The witching hour was a long way off. In the meantime, to look at the problem was to look at potential disaster. Besides, there was a more pressing problem to be addressed. And it was one in which he could be a major player.

For decades both major political parties had been controlled by political and financial interests in the northeastern United States, the Democratic Party by its heavy reliance upon industrial labor unions, with attendant support in liberal and minority areas, and the

Republican Party by its reliance upon support from financial and corporate business interests. The farm states of the Midwest furnished a good part of the Republican electoral base, but much of the money that oiled the wheels came out of the East. As population and wealth shifted westward and southward, so did political power. This move prepared the arena for a confrontation in which the awakening conservative forces would be a major factor, provided, of course, they could find someone to carry their flag.

There was such a man, some thought, though it would require a lot of convincing for him to hold up the banner.

By the time I arrived in Washington, in January of 1963, efforts were already under way to secure the 1964 Republican nomination for Barry Goldwater. Tower was more than a willing participant in that effort, as was Peter O'Donnell, state chairman of the party in Texas, and national chairman of the Draft Goldwater Committee. Goldwater had campaigned for Tower in his Senate race and was much in demand as a rallying point for conservatives across the country. He was generally ignored by the media, but political activists within the party were well aware of his presence. In the effort to help secure the nomination for Goldwater and move the party's center of gravity to the South and West, Tower would find an outlet for his own political expression, as well as his energy.

It was bound to be a most welcome situation for Tower. At that time he was a freshman Republican senator in a Senate run by Democrats, and by seniority. Neither of his committee assignments was particularly appealing to him. One, the Senate Committee on Banking and Currency, had a subcommittee on housing which he found interesting, and to which he contributed. But the Committee on Labor and Welfare was, to him, a waste of time. It was a committee stacked with liberals, both Democrat and Republican. There he was a voice in the wilderness. When the opportunity came he would move to a committee more to his liking.

I was completely happy with Tower's support of Goldwater. I felt then, as now, that political parties have only one legitimate reason to exist, that being the crystallization of political thought and the presentation of that thought to the American people. How else can the people make an intelligent decision on directions their government ought to take? And how can they express that decision unless the choices are laid out for them in terms stark enough to understand?

Goldwater's public comments, as well as his votes in the Senate, seemed to lay out those thoughts in honest and understandable terms. That made him a frightening figure to those who believe politics and government can operate best when voters are confused, uncertain, who believe the task of political leadership is made easier and therefore more desirable by confusion in the ranks. It made him a frightening figure to those politicians in both parties, and to many in the media, who sought to maintain a liberal status quo. Or, failing that, hoped at least to prevent a rightward shift all the way to the "extremes" represented by Goldwater. Had Goldwater's enemies in his own party and the press understood then how reluctant a candidate he would be, and how good a foil he would be, they would have had fewer worries.

In recent years it has become somewhat fashionable for history to be rewritten in order that political myths be perpetuated. Nowhere is this more apparent than in the myth of Camelot, presided over by a wise and benevolent Arthur, aided by the noble and pure Galahad, graced by the beauteous Guinevere. The myth of John F. Kennedy as a great, invincible, political leader has become firmly established in American media folklore, despite all facts to the contrary. In truth his party was showing signs of fracture in many parts of the country, not the least of which was in Texas, without which his future election was most questionable. There the party was riven by struggles between the Yarborough and Connally forces, with each side insisting it was closer to the throne, Yarborough by virtue of his support for, and ideological ties to, the Kennedys, and Connally by virtue of his long association with Lyndon Johnson, plus the fact that, as governor of the state, he felt a certain deference was owed him. In Washington an increasingly isolated Johnson sought to keep a foot in both camps, protecting his flanks as best he could from assault within the Kennedy palace guard and from erosion of his home base. Standing alone, Kennedy had very little support within the Texas body politic. Most of his support was dependent on the good graces of the factions within the party. In the final analysis, that is what led to his last, ill-fated trip to Texas.

Nor has Goldwater's candidacy escaped historical rewrites. It now seems accepted that Goldwater's candidacy was doomed from the beginning, that Kennedy would have won any contest between the two. It is, of course, impossible to prove the case one way or another, but the grass roots movements on Goldwater's behalf, combined with the fracturing of the Democratic Party in parts of the South and West, were then conspiring to cause great problems for Kennedy and cause worry in strange places about the potential of a Goldwater presidency.

A case in point: A rally of the "Draft Goldwater" forces was held on July 4, 1963, at the District of Columbia National Guard Armory. Its purpose was to demonstrate to a reluctant Goldwater that he had enough support to at least get in the race. The rally was the brainchild of Peter O'Donnell, chairman of the Draft Goldwater movement. O'Donnell asked that I set up the press room, providing the usual array of typewriters, telephones, and certain amenities for whatever press might show up. The event was well organized and surprisingly well attended by an enthusiastic crowd. It received a great deal of media coverage.

Shortly thereafter, I was approached by a representative from one of the largest magazines in the country. He and some of his fellows desired a meeting with Tower. He was authorized to extend an invitation for Tower and myself to meet with them at a place called the Cosmos Club. They did not want any public notice given, nor would any public notice be given if we should agree to attend. We were given no agenda. It was merely to be a meeting to discuss politics. Tower agreed and we attended.

The Cosmos Club turned out to be a place that had apparently seen better days. Either that, or it catered to a membership with an exceedingly high regard for tradition, that tradition having been established many, many years before. The place was very, very quiet. Paintings were upon the walls. Well-worn Oriental rugs were upon the floor. Exceedingly correct waiters were in attendance. I somehow expected a dozing member to bestir himself and hold forth on wars in India, or perhaps bemoan the fact that an ungrateful British electorate had turned Winston Churchill out of office in favor of the laborite Clement Atlee. In short, it was a good place to read. It was also a good place to hold the kind of conversation that took place.

Approximately ten people attended, in addition to Tower and myself. At the head of the table in a secluded room sat the editor of the then-largest circulated magazine in the United States. Arrayed around the table were representatives of some of the largest, most influential "slick" magazines in the country. Also in attendance were people who claimed to have the speaking and listening proxy for certain newspapers and newspaper chains. I recognized most of them as people representing institutions that had been very supportive of

John Kennedy. They had certain concerns which they wished to discuss with the senator.

It soon became obvious that there had been a meeting of minds before this gathering took place. The lead spokesman used the term "we" and was not disputed.

They were concerned with what was happening and what was likely to happen under John Kennedy. They were concerned about the lack of decisive leadership he had shown in the Bay of Pigs fiasco. They were concerned with the ineptness and inexperience shown in his first meeting with Khrushchev. They were concerned about certain unstated things within the White House itself, things they seemed to know about but did not wish to discuss and which might ultimately prove embarrassing to the president and do the country no good on the world scene.

Kennedy was not showing the degree of political sophistication they had expected of him. They were concerned about "the direction" the country was taking under Kennedy. They were aware of the fact that the Kennedy–Johnson ticket had won with less than a clear majority of the votes cast in 1960. Above all, his political ineptness was likely to turn the country over to Goldwater, about whom they had many concerns as well. A Goldwater presidency, unless he modified his more "extreme" positions, would polarize the country and cause untold problems.

But they had a solution.

If Tower would write a political treatise, setting forth the rational, philosophical argument for an alternative to Kennedy, they would collectively see that it got widespread distribution and attention. Perhaps such an article, calmly stated by a rising star from a state as important as Texas, could have a beneficial, moderating effect on the thinking of Goldwater and the movement supporting him. It would be a contribution to the American political process.

Actually, Tower had already written a paperback book setting forth his thoughts. But, he told me, it was not something he was proud of, and a work to which he had actually contributed only one chapter, that being an elaboration of a letter he had previously written to Ronnie Dugger of the *Texas Observer*. The rest of the book was put together by a staff member, Jim Clay, then the senator's legislative assistant, before that position was taken over by a young Texas lawyer named Tom Cole. Most of the book was boiler plate, rewrites of previous speeches or position papers. It was not the caliber the assembled guests thought useful, and rightly so.

I had been in Washington long enough to realize some modification in my earlier, somewhat romantic, view of the press (and of politics) was warranted and called for. Here the political nerve was much closer to the surface than I had ever dreamed would be the case among people who publicly proclaimed their independence and objectivity. Here, to properly read and understand a story, one first needed to read the byline. By knowing who wrote the story, and knowing his or her politics, one could more readily evaluate its contents. Still, I was surprised by the nature of the meeting. It was my first experience with a potential "laying on of the hands" exercise, and I did not know quite what to make of it.

I did know one thing, however. If Tower decided to accept their offer, it would be my responsibility to draft the article. When the meeting broke up, and on the way back to the Capitol, I asked Tower what he proposed to do.

Absolutely nothing, he replied. The entire exercise was nothing but an attempt to torpedo Goldwater's candidacy. Any difference in nuance concerning a stated position would be interpreted as a challenge to Goldwater's leadership in the realm of conservative thought. No doubt Tower was correct, but I saw it somewhat differently at the time. Believing that in politics, even more than in war, there is "strength in numbers," I argued the movement would benefit by more political leaders speaking out on its behalf. Tower was certainly doing his bit in this regard, but there is a difference in making a speech that might be heard by several hundred, even several thousand, and committing to print an article that might be read by millions. Perhaps such an article would encourage other leaders to examine the conservative position more closely.

The senator was adamant and the subject was dropped. As far as I was concerned, the event was instructive in two areas. It indicated to me the degree of Tower's commitment to Goldwater's candidacy, and the degree of worry on the part of some high-level media barons concerning that same candidacy.

From that point forward the potential Goldwater candidacy took up more and more of Tower's time and energy. He continued to do his bit in the Senate, but more and more of his public appearances were couched in terms of helping generate support for the conservative movement generally and for Goldwater specifically. He wished to be seen as someone close to Goldwater, as someone who had the ear of Goldwater. And in truth he did. There appeared to be a measure of friendship between the two which Tower cherished. Still, it appeared to me that Goldwater kept his distance, perhaps because he did not wish to be seen as someone overly influenced by those seeking to thrust him into a race he did not want, or was not sure he wanted. At that point only one thing was certain. Whatever Goldwater decided, it would be his decision. In the meantime, the effort on his behalf would continue.

Life in the Senate went on as well. A bored Lyndon Johnson occasionally roamed the floor of a Senate he had so recently dominated. Now the Senate was mostly his escape hatch, away from the White House, where the two Kennedys, John and Bobby, held sway. For one so proud, so desirous of power, so accustomed to power, it must have been a humiliating experience indeed, occasionally relieved by attempts at humor, or by nostalgic sessions designed to remind his guests he had been around and was still around. Once, when I had gone to the Senate floor in Tower's absence, Johnson spied me, crooked his finger, and beckoned me to his presence. At the moment he was trying to look busy, escorting a small group of Peruvian senators around the Senate floor, introducing them to others and giving them a feel for life in the World's Greatest Deliberative Body.

Johnson, much to my consternation, introduced me as "the senator from Texas," and then, with a grin on his face and a twinkle in his eye, stood back to see how I would handle the situation. Obviously, I could not tell the visiting senators that the vice-president was making a joke, that he was pulling their collective legs and mine as well. I merely stammered out a welcome to them on behalf of the "people of Texas," shook their hands and quickly departed. Johnson appeared to enjoy the episode immensely. My own brand of humor runs in a different direction.

On another occasion his office called Tower's office with a request that the senator attend a small luncheon he was giving for certain members of the press and a few congressmen. The luncheon was to be held that same day. Tower was in Texas and unavailable. His secretary wished to talk to me. The same reply was given. She would check. Then Johnson came on the phone. The senator really ought to be represented, he said, so why didn't I come in his place? I had other plans, but the vice-president insisted Tower should be represented. In the end I went.

At that time the vice-president had an office just off the Senate floor. The table was long and narrow. Lyndon sat at the head of the table and I to his immediate left, where Tower would have been had he been there. Johnson was great for protocol. To his immediate right, and across the table from me, sat Congressman J. J. "Jake" Pickle, who occupied Johnson's old House seat, having replaced another Johnson crony, Homer Thornberry. Pickle sat where Senator Yarborough would have sat, had he attended. In fact, I do not know that he was even invited. Down both sides of the table sat two or three congressmen and eight or ten reporters and columnists, primarily people whom Lyndon could count on to put the proper spin on matters involving him. At the far end of the table sat Doris Fleeson, a columnist who could always be expected to properly bash political conservatives and praise political liberals.

It soon became apparent that the luncheon was something quickly thrown together for the sole purpose of providing an audience. It had no agenda, nor rhyme or reason other than that Lyndon was simply bored and wanted to reminisce. He spoke of days gone by, when he would visit the White House during Roosevelt's reign, of his conversations with Harold Ickes, of the days when the New Deal was remaking the American political scene. As he spoke his voice progressively became lower, to the point where those sitting beyond three or four chairs away were unable to hear. People further away first strained to hear. Then, on occasion, unable to hear, they would begin conversations on their own, among themselves. Clearly, this irritated Lyndon. He would cast anxious glances toward the end of the table, and then, seemingly absent-mindedly, pick up a knife and begin tapping on his water glass, all the while continuing his soft-voiced monologue as if the tapping was merely a nervous reflex. This was extremely important. People ought to listen. This was history.

He did not address himself to the growing political problems in Texas, and none of the assembled press brought up the subject. He did not address himself to his continuing problems with Senator Ralph Yarborough, nor did anyone bring up the subject despite the fact that it was a matter of some interest throughout the Texas political community.

Eventually the luncheon ended and I returned to the office, none the wiser.

It would have been interesting if someone had brought up the subject of his running feud with Yarborough. I doubt he would have responded, but still it would have been interesting.

It is customary in the Senate for important federal appointments to be cleared through the homestate senator involved. In fact, an appointment cannot go forward with active opposition from that senator. The process is usually made easier when both the president and the senators involved are from the same political party. When Lyndon Johnson gave up his Senate seat and became vice-president, the normal process would have been for that prerogative to pass automatically to Ralph Yarborough, who then became the senior senator from Texas, and the one through whom those appointments must pass. Among politicians all this becomes very important. It is one way senators keep their supporters happy, or at least hopeful, and keep their political organizations intact. It is one indication of power.

The problem in this case was that Lyndon did not wish to give up what he considered his right, his own prerogative. Moreover, he claimed that his continuing involvement in Texas patronage matters was by virtue of an understanding he had with John Kennedy when he "agreed" to go on the ticket as vice-presidential nominee. He didn't want to be cut out of the loop. Otherwise, what did he have left? The vice-presidency, in his case, was not exactly an active, involved position.

After much jockeying and no small amount of ill feeling, the two men had reached some sort of compromise. The appointments would be divided between them, with each being the lead horse in certain areas. One could propose, the other agree or blackball. Yarborough got East and West Texas, and Johnson got the rest.

No vivid imagination is required to see that problems would quickly arise. They did. Yarborough was still the senior senator, and had the support of the chairman of the Senate's Judiciary Committee, Jim Eastland of Mississippi, who, according to Yarborough, was instrumental in working out the deal. No matter what Johnson thought, the appointments still had to have Yarborough's approval, tacit or otherwise.

In an effort to keep the agreement on course, more or less, periodic meetings were held with Bobby Kennedy, then attorney general, presiding. At some meetings the proposals put forward by Lyndon were considered, with Yarborough approving or disapproving. At other meetings the reverse was true, with Yarborough proposing and Lyndon agreeing or disagreeing. On one particular occasion Yarborough returned to the office elated. He had won an argument with Lyndon.

The entire episode was relayed to me in living color by Chuck Caldwell, then a member of Yarborough's staff. The Yarborough staff and the Tower staff got along well together, as did the two senators. The senators seldom voted together on the floor of the Senate, but their philosophical and political arguments did not extend beyond that. Tower was no threat to Yarborough, nor was Yarborough a threat to Tower. Each had his constituents to please, and in the matter of political appointments Tower did not then figure. There was a Democratic president, vice-president, and senior senator. It was their fight.

After hours it was another matter. It was not unusual for senior members of both staffs to gather at some watering hole at the end of the day to compare notes, to laugh or moan over what had transpired during the day. On this occasion Caldwell called. He had something he wanted to share. We went across the street to the seedy Carroll Arms hotel, downstairs from Bobby Baker's infamous "Q Club."

According to Caldwell, Yarborough had just returned from a late afternoon session at the White House. He relayed to Caldwell what had transpired. Bobby Kennedy sat behind his desk, with a stack of folders at the ready. One involved a Yarborough proposal that Woodrow Seals, a Democratic liberal activist and longtime Yarborough supporter, be named United States attorney. It was supposed to be Yarborough's call. But Lyndon objected.

Seals, Johnson said, was nothing but a "toadie for Frankie Randolph," the crusty matron of the liberal Democrats of Texas (DOT). Randolph was also a longtime supporter of Yarborough, a bitter opponent of Allan Shivers, and not too trusting of Lyndon Johnson either. Lyndon was, after all, a "Brown and Root man."

Yarborough insisted. Lyndon resisted. Finally, Bobby said he had to overrule Lyndon. His family owed Seals.

It was Seals, said Caldwell, who had set up the meeting of Protestant ministers with John Kennedy in Houston, an event that proved most beneficial to the Kennedy presidential effort. It was Seals' idea, and it was he who put it all together. Now was time for the payoff.

Seals not only got the appointment, but in subsequent months he made certain that Lyndon come to think kindly toward him. So much so, in fact, that Johnson, when he was president, approved Yarborough's proposal that Seals be named a federal judge.

Needless to say, the meeting did not last much longer. Yarborough returned to his office happy as a lark. He had stood his ground, made his point, and won the battle — if not the war.

Bobby Kennedy got another taste of Texas politics and Lyndon got another taste of Kennedy politics, which, after all, were not much different from each other. (Yarborough told me nearly thirty years later that he and Johnson never managed to settle their squabbles over what each regarded as his rightful privilege.)

The strains were still evident when Kennedy reluctantly departed for Texas in November of 1963 in an effort to please Lyndon and shore up his flagging support there.

In fact the strains within the Democratic Party were so pronounced that the senior senator, Yarborough, and the state's governor, John Connally, were hardly on speaking terms. It was not at all unusual for the Democratic governor to communicate his thoughts concerning governmental policies to the Republican John Tower, rather than the Democrat Ralph Yarborough.

Usually this came in the form of a telephone call from a member of the governor's staff to me. Sometimes it was from the governor himself. Once I was rousted from sleep at our home in McLean, Virginia, by a call from Connally, at that moment in the Governor's Mansion in Tennessee. I have long since forgotten the substance of the call, but I do remember it was a lengthy conversation, most of which was devoted to a critical review by Connally of Yarborough the senator and Yarborough the person.

Nor was the Connally–Yarborough relationship, or the Johnson–Yarborough relationship, or the Johnson–Bobby Kennedy relationship the only problem besetting the party in Texas. While Camelot reveled in the glow of an adoring media, the Texas Republican Party, under the leadership of Peter O'Donnell, was showing signs of becoming a force in state politics, taking on more and more of an indigenous character and becoming more of a worry to those Democratic leaders concerned primarily with maintaining control within the state.

Indication of that worry had surfaced as far back as the National Democratic Convention in Los Angeles in 1960. I, along with Sam Wood and Raymond Brooks, covered that convention for the newspapers we represented. The papers' primary concern, of course, was the fate of Lyndon Johnson, whose fortunes they had always promoted. Following Kennedy's capture of the nomination, a breakfast meeting of the Texas delegation took place, with Johnson the centerpiece. There was much unhappiness, confusion, and depression among a delegation sent to Los Angeles for the express purpose of nominating Lyndon Johnson for the presidency. In that setting I was struck by the nature of Johnson's address to the delegates. He went through the formality of thanking them for standing with him. But then he began what I regarded as a somewhat disjointed, rambling talk that seemed to have no real purpose, as if he had other things on his mind that he was unwilling to share with those who had stood with him. Not long after the meeting broke up we picked up rumors that the vice-presidency had either been offered him, or would be offered him, and that he was considering the matter. I immediately went to the suite of Speaker Sam Rayburn and asked him if he knew anything about it. I told him I had heard Lyndon either had agreed to it, or would agree to it.

"I hope not," Rayburn replied. "I have advised against it. I hope he doesn't take it. It will be terrible for us in Texas."

Those same thoughts were echoed by Governor Price Daniel, leader of the Texas delegation, and the next person I turned to after Rayburn.

Daniel was even more emphatic. In a visibly upset mood, he said he, too, had heard the rumor, but he just couldn't believe Johnson would leave his position as majority leader for the position of vice-president under Kennedy. Daniel went even further than Rayburn had gone, saying such a move "would be disastrous for the party in Texas." It would, said Daniel, "cause all sorts of problems down the line."

Those "down the line" problems were now evident.

All of which is to say that those who now hold that a Goldwater candidacy was doomed from the outset, that John Kennedy would have won in a cakewalk, are, in my opinion, living in a political dream world. First of all, the Kennedy–Johnson ticket had won in 1960 nationwide by the narrowist of margins, even then on the strength of disputed (and questionable) ballots in Texas and Illinois. The ticket would be going into the 1964 elections with fractures evident in many places. A politician, even a sitting president, simply cannot survive if his generals are divided and his troops are at war with each other. And, given the development of American politics, the coalition of forces that make victory possible must be maintained if that victory is to be lasting.

Events did transpire, of course, that changed the existing equation, that did doom the Goldwater candidacy. But those events were not then evident. They soon would be.

FOURTEEN

A Campaign Killed by Assassination

Sometime about the middle of November of 1963 we were visited by a professor from the School of Law at Harvard University. He laid out his identification and credentials. He was a Ph.D., a refugee from Cuba, and he urgently needed to talk with the senator. Tower was in Texas.

Could I help?

No, this was something he could only talk to the senator about. It was most urgent.

Very well, I would try to set up such a meeting if he could give me some idea what the meeting would be about. He gave me the outline of what he wished to discuss.

The Cuban community in South Florida was suddenly in great turmoil. Rumors were flying through the community that Kennedy, during the Cuban missile crisis, had entered into an agreement with Khrushchev whereby Castro was not to be molested, either by American forces or forces operating out of America. His contacts within that community said their information was that this agreement involved Soviet Premier Nikita Khrushchev's decision to remove missiles from Cuba. In return for our moving certain U.S. missiles out of Turkey, he, Khruschev would move his missiles out of Cuba, if the U.S. also agreed to leave Castro alone.

The Cuban community had, of course, lived for the day when Castro would be gone, and was in fact still living and agitating for that day. If this information was correct, they could only see a lifetime of exile from their homeland. The rumors were creating panic. Anything might happen.

217

Tower, by virtue of his stance as a conservative anti-Communist, was highly regarded within that community and was a frequent speaker before Cuban refugee groups. That was why, the professor said, he had turned to Tower. Someone needed to ascertain the truthfulness, or untruthfulness, of the rumors quickly and put a lid on the situation.

I told him I would set up the requested meeting, but that I simply could not believe that Kennedy, or any American president, would agree to such an arrangement.

Dumb. Dumb.

When Tower returned, he was briefed on the meeting. He was skeptical. It seemed so farfetched. But he agreed to meet with the professor when we could work it in on the calendar. The meeting was never arranged. Within days the whole subject became moot.

Kennedy left Washington for Texas in an attempt to shore up his own support, and Tower left Washington shortly thereafter for Missouri in an attempt to gain support for Goldwater. Tower was still in the air when an excited Jerry Friedheim, a former Missouri newsman and recent addition to our staff, called from the Senate floor with news that the president had been shot in Dallas.

I couldn't believe it. It seemed so implausible. I thought he might be making a bad joke, except that Jerry seldom joked about anything. But he insisted. He was standing by a wire service teletype machine that was reporting the event. At that moment there was no word that the shooting had been fatal, but that information followed shortly. Connally had been shot as well.

Literally within moments our office became flooded with telephone calls. The calls followed a pattern that in turn followed the irrational and disgraceful pattern of early news reporting on the event. Kennedy had been killed in Dallas, a conservative Republican bastion, therefore Republicans must have been responsible for the murder. Tower was a leading Republican conservative, therefore Tower was culpable in the killing of the president. The calls were abusive, threatening, hysterical. We received reports of car windshields and windows being smashed in various parts of Washington, solely because the automobiles bore Texas license plates. The decision was quickly made to move the senator's family to a safe haven, away from their home. We had placed urgent calls to Tower, then still on an airplane approaching his destination in Missouri. Once on the ground he called from the airport and was informed of the tragedy.

In the meantime, press reports indicated Dallas police had apprehended someone named Lee Harvey Oswald as a suspect in the slaying. That was good news, but my own fears were that he would be found to be exactly what the news reports were suggesting must be the case, a right-wing, political activist goaded into action by anti-Kennedy sentiment in Dallas.

Within moments after the name of Lee Harvey Oswald moved over the wires, the senator's personal secretary, Linda Lee Lovelady, from the West Texas town of Odessa, stopped by my desk with a startling bit of information, if it proved to be true. She had served for a while, before I came on the staff, as a case worker in the office before being promoted to her current position. She thought she remembered handling mail from someone named Oswald when she was a case worker. A hurried search of the files proved her memory accurate.

The office had received a letter from Oswald, then in the Soviet Union, expressing his desire to return to America and requesting Tower's help. The letter was forwarded to the State Department for advice and guidance. Rather than reply in the usual manner, by mail, the department sent an official to talk with her. They were thoroughly familiar with the Oswald matter. He had gone to the Soviet Union as an avowed Marxist. After a time there he had approached the American Embassy in Moscow, threw his passport on the desk, and renounced his American citizenship. It would be better, the official said, if Tower's office did not get involved. The advice was taken, no reply was sent to Oswald, and no further action was taken by Tower's office.

This, to me, was important information that ought to be made public quickly. It would afford the first public knowledge of at least a smattering of Oswald's background and his political orientation. And it would surely, I thought, change the focus of the irrational media and public comment surrounding the death of Kennedy in Dallas. It would, I thought, redirect the understandable public grief and wrath, influenced as it was by early media reporting and early political comment, to a more legitimate target.

The first persons called were Roy McGhee, then United Press International's man who covered Texas politics in Washington, and "Tex" Easley, who performed a similar function for the Associated Press. I wanted to get the information on the wires as quickly as possible, in order that it might be shared by all reporters and writers covering the event and its aftermath.

McGhee responded quickly. He chose not to wait until we had made copies of the letter and delivered them to the press room. He showed up immediately, helping with the process of copying and collating. Easley showed up later, appearing hurt that his competitor was on the scene and had gotten a "break" on the story. There was no effort, or thought, on our part to show any such favoritism. McGhee was simply the more aggressive reporter.

A facsimile of the letter was moved nationwide, with an accompanying story giving the details. Then more problems erupted.

In many papers the facsimile of the letter appeared on one page, with the cutlines indicating this was a copy of a letter written by Oswald to Tower. The explanatory news story appeared elsewhere in the paper, and was often overlooked by those who had seen the letter. The natural assumption was that Oswald wrote Tower, that Tower interceded on his behalf, and as a result was able to return to America. Therefore, a reader who went no further would conclude that Tower must have had a hand in bringing Oswald back.

In the hysteria of the moment this only compounded our problems. Even Walter Winchell, then a much listened to radio commentator, noted that Oswald was able to return to America after writing Tower. The implication was plain. This merely proved the point that there was a right-wing conspiracy afoot to assassinate the president, and Oswald was merely an unwitting tool in that conspiracy. In my effort to get the truth out, we had only succeeded in compounding a lie.

Nor did later revelations that Oswald was an active member of the Communist-front Fair Play for Cuba organization do much to change the general thrust of commentary about the event. So what if Kennedy was killed by a Marxist or Communist? It was really the fertile soil of anti-Kennedy hatred created by right-wing conservatism that set the stage for his slaying, that "created the climate" for the tragedy.

A long, rambling, incoherent editorial appeared in the *Austin American-Statesman* seizing upon the occasion to condemn the political climate brought on by opposition to Kennedy and issuing a warning to all Democratic officials that they could no longer feel safe in Dallas.

The emotional irrationality of the moment was perhaps best manifested when a Republican candidate for the U.S. Congress suddenly appeared in the Capitol Press Room in Austin to announce his withdrawal from the race, ashamed and humiliated as he was that his party had caused a climate to exist in which the president could be slain.

There was no great loss in the Republican candidate's emotional withdrawal from the race. It was, in fact, good riddance. Anyone capable of becoming so unhinged as a result of spur-of-the-moment media commentary had no business being in the Congress in any event.

The days following were traumatic beyond measure for the office. The phone calls slowed, but the accusatory mail increased. I remember one letter in particular, highly emotional from beginning to end. It was from a Methodist minister. He knew the senator. He knew the senator's minister father. Because of that he had supported the senator. But now he was ashamed of the support he had given. In fact, he was so ashamed that Goldwater, Tower, and the Republicans had "created a climate" that led to the president's death that he would henceforth oppose the senator in all respects, even promising to denounce him from his pulpit. The minister made clear that he believed Tower bore a major responsibility in Kennedy's death. A day or two following the assassination, Linda Lovelady, the senator's secretary, brought a package to my desk and asked, "Ken, what do you make of this?" The package had arrived in the form of a book, wrapped in brown paper and addressed to the senator. That was not at all unusual. People were always sending the senator this or that book, with the instruction "You really ought to read this." She had unwrapped it and observed something of which she was not at all familiar. I looked at it. It was clearly a bomb. There was the timer, with wires connected to what appeared to be two sticks of dynamite. I placed the parcel on the desk, somewhat gingerly, and asked her to advise all staff members to quietly vacate the office, saying nothing about what was transpiring. I also asked Friedheim, who sat one desk in front, a scant four feet away, to vacate as well. He said he would stay. My own feeling, and I'm sure Friedheim's feeling, was that any show of panic on our part would only cause pandemonium. The post office's bomb squad arrived, took the parcel away, and later reported that it was perfect in all respects save one. The dynamite was fake. The post office officials asked us not to say anything of the event, that it would only point out how easy it was to get such a package through. Their view was that the sender was merely telling the senator he could do the job when he really wanted to.

Nor were the problems confined to the office. Our teenage son came home from classes at McLean High School, terribly hurt over being approached by his most-favored girlfriend. Weeping, she said, "Roland, I hope you are satisfied. You Texans have killed our president." In this fashion did we exist in the first few weeks after the assassination.

In time the hysteria quieted. The new president took office in a calming, dignified manner. A reasonable moratorium on political comment was more or less agreed to and observed with the usual honesty Americans have come to expect of their politicians.

But it was clear to me that the die had been cast as far as the next election was concerned. When the bullet struck John Kennedy the next election, for all practical purposes, was over. The left wing in American politics, along with the left in American media, was not about to abandon a good thing. They had the right on the defensive, and, the hypocrisy of their own position notwithstanding, they meant to keep it there, one way or the other. There would be no apologies on their part for the unwarranted finger pointing that occurred immediately after the assassination. They would simply move next to the task of perpetuating Camelot. That could never be achieved under the reign of a Barry Goldwater.

In politics, as in war, there is a time to attack and a time to defend the fort. In all battles there is a time to sally forth and a time to await a better day. To my mind this was a time to hold the fort, to await a better day. With that in mind I argued with Tower and other Republican leaders that the Goldwater candidacy ought to be abandoned. No matter who the Republicans came up with as a presidential nominee, he was sure to go down in defeat. I would much rather see that defeat handed to the entrenched liberal wing of the party than to the conservative Goldwater movement.

The scenario I saw was a bitter fight with the Rockefeller wing over the nomination, in which Goldwater would win and in which the Rockefeller wing would then abandon the field, offering no help in the general election. Liberals in the press and in politics would mount a massive campaign against Goldwater. All Lyndon Johnson would have to do was appear presidential, to maintain the appearance of being above the fray. His campaigning would be done for him. Most Americans, not caught up in partisan politics, would simply want to keep the ship of state on an even keel, following the trauma they had undergone with the Kennedy assassination. Johnson, not then identified with the divisive civil rights agenda or the Vietnam conflict, would be elected, probably in an overwhelming fashion, and liberals would blame the defeat on Goldwater's message.

Not only that, following the election there would be a calculated, steady drumbeat in the media reminding the electorate that conservatism had been rejected and therefore discredited. The Rockefeller forces, in and out of the media, would constantly remind the conservatives that they had had their chance, it was now time for them to abandon the field. I saw nothing but disaster for the conservative movement, from which it would take years to recover.

Tower saw it differently. He acknowledged the problems, but he said, "We've got to go with our best man. Lightning may strike."

Lightning did indeed strike. But it was the kind of lightning I was worried about, not the kind of lightning he was hoping for.

In truth it made no difference what either of us thought. The troops in the field were committed to a Goldwater candidacy, whether the opponent was John Kennedy or Lyndon Johnson. It mattered not one wit what John Tower thought, or what Ken Towery thought. Goldwater had captured the imagination of those who thought government had grown too big, too expensive, too burdensome, too intrusive upon the lives of citizens. They were going to make the fight, no matter what. The lay of the battlefield mattered not to them. I applauded their courage and honesty, even as I worried over the outcome.

The scenario played itself out much as I had feared. Despite the best efforts of the Rockefeller wing, and the early fence-straddling of people like Richard Nixon, Goldwater won the nomination. And then went down in defeat, tagged as an "extremist," as one who would expand the war in Vietnam, as one who would play fast and loose with the nation's nuclear arsenal.

The American media, in large measure, simply took the position that Goldwater ought not be elected. Some were simply trying to further the liberal agenda. Others, equally honest, were of the opinion that it would be best for America if the country did not have to undergo the problems inherent in "changing horses in midstream," that the country needed some breathing space.

There were still others who took the position that Goldwater was a dangerous man to have at the helm, and that any means of keeping him from that position were not only justified but obligatory.

One illustration: A young reporter for the *Dallas Times-Herald*, John Schoellkopk, stopped by my desk in Washington on one occasion in furtherance of his duties. It was my understanding that he was an heir to a family of great fortune, then in a training mode for later, upper-level management duties at the paper. It was also my understanding that his Washington assignment was part of that training.

The conversation turned first to matters of pending legislation and the senator's position on that legislation. That out of the way, the conversation turned to a discussion of the campaign. It was a friendly discussion, even after I made the mistake of saying I thought media coverage of the campaign was somewhat biased. He became immediately defensive, even aggressively so. He did not take issue with my comment, but took the position that the media was merely fulfilling its responsibilities by pointing out what a dangerous character Goldwater was.

I had no quarrel with the idea that the press had an obligation to assess, analyze, and provide guidance in such matters. But I thought this should be done in editorial comment, not through news columns.

Not so, he said. If the press was convinced that a candidate would be dangerous for the country, it had a moral obligation to "use all the resources at its command" to achieve the desired ends. The desired end in this case was the defeat of Goldwater, whose election would be disastrous for the country.

For a moment I was speechless, the reason being that my mind flashed back to the land scandals, wherein I did essentially the same. In that story I used news columns to achieve a desired result, that result being the prosecution of people so obviously guilty of betraying the public trust.

But I saw this differently. In this case there was no question of any betrayal of public trust on Goldwater's part. There had never been a question raised about any sort of moral meandering on his part. There had never been a question raised about vote thievery on his part. There had never been indications of Machiavellian tendencies on his part. He was essentially an honest, straightforward proponent of a rather honest, straightforward political philosophy. His sins, to the extent they were evident, were wrapped up in the single sin: He was politically incorrect. He could be a stumbling block on the road to a welfare state.

The press was by no means alone, among the politically powerful institutions of the time, in opposition to Goldwater. Major financial institutions located in the Northeast were, as expected, cold to his candidacy, as were many major corporate interests. While some paid lip service to his candidacy, in the trenches it was a different matter.

On one occasion an officer in the giant IBM Corporation dropped by our office to check in with his wife, a member of our staff. His corporation was interested in certain legislation, and I took the occasion to chide him ever so gently. As we visited I told him of my continuing education on the ways of Washington, how things were not always as they seemed in the world of politics, how I was beginning to see things differently from what I had always been led to believe.

For instance, I told him, while the people of corporate America might talk a conservative line, pleasing to the ears of those who loved liberty and appreciated competitive free enterprise, the end result of much of their legislative endeavor was a more centralized government, a bigger government, a more expensive government, a more regulatory government.

"You people may vote for Goldwater," I said, "but some of the legislation you are backing goes completely counter to what Goldwater is preaching."

His response was a surprising, "Ken, I don't know of a single, solitary person in management levels of IBM who is going to vote for Goldwater."

He wasn't either, despite the fact he felt a certain pull in that direction by virtue of his wife's position on Tower's staff.

I asked why this was so.

"It is simply not in our best interest," he said.

Shades of Bob Wheeler. It was not the first time I had heard the point made.

Wheeler was a delightful, nervous, highly excitable member of the Texas legislature during the 1950s, a member of the little band of liberals then exercising somewhat limited influence over the course of legislation. He was a son of some wealth, so much so that his parents could afford to keep him comfortably ensconced at the University of Texas law school while the years went by, and while he pursued his other interests as a member of the legislature.

Sometimes referred to fondly as "Whiskey Bob" by his colleagues, he was nevertheless something of an intellectual type, given to reading *The New York Times* and taking pleasure that somewhere in the world there was a newspaper with its eyes on the big picture, as were his own. In company with his fellow liberals he was also given to championing "the little man," to publicly bashing the accumulation of great wealth, unless, of course, that wealth happened to be in the hands of enlightened individuals or corporations run by enlightened individuals. Occasionally, however, problems arose.

A battle had erupted between big oil and little oil, or between the major oil companies and the smaller, independent oil operators. The battle spilled over into the legislature, posing major problems for people like Bob.

As the battle raged on I walked out for a cool drink of water at a fountain located just outside the House chamber. The area was swarming with lobbyists seeking votes and legislators seeking guidance. There was Bob, nervous, agitated, hands shaking as he bent over the cooler. I asked how he might vote on the pending legislation. He didn't know just yet. He would probably vote with the little companies, the independents, but he really didn't want to.

Why not? I asked.

We would be a lot better off, he said, if we could just get rid of all these small operators. We would be a lot better off if we had just a few big oil companies, rather than a multitude of small companies.

Why so? I asked.

A few big companies would be a lot easier for government to deal with, he said. A plethora of little companies just made things more difficult.

Then, realizing what he had said, Wheeler quickly added, "Ken, I didn't say that. Don't print that. I'll deny it."

I didn't print it. It seemed of little consequence at the time. Besides, he was a friend.

The comments from the IBM executive were merely cut from the same cloth, the other side of the same coin. Big government would be easier for them to deal with than would a host of small competing companies also clamoring for government attention. And the Goldwater candidacy represented the opposite of big labor, big business, and big government. Still, the defeat of Goldwater cannot be laid exclusively at the feet of the press or those economic interests seeking a more regulated, more centrally managed society. There was, in my opinion, the overriding public concern about embarking on a new path so soon after the assassination of one president and the swearing in of a new president. Also, the Goldwater campaign was an exercise in political ineptness, the likes of which would not be seen on the Republican side of American politics until the campaign of George Bush in 1992.

Surrounded by a small cadre of people who had little to do with his gaining the nomination, Goldwater made repeated blunders in terms of both strategy and tactics. He seemed to delight in bearding the lion in his own den, in going into Florida and pointing out impending problems in Social Security, in going into Tennessee and attacking the huge TVA bureaucracy, in going into the Pacific Northwest and raising questions about the fairness of subsidized public power. It was a campaign that seemed, from where I stood, more concerned with making people think than it was with winning an election. The conservative message was there, but it was couched in terms that offered little in the way of hope, which, to me, is an indispensable part of national campaigning and ultimately in the art of governing. The only bright spot in that regard during the entire campaign, as far as I was concerned, was a speech given by one who was not even the candidate, Ronald Reagan of California. It was as if the nominee, Goldwater, realized he was not going to win, but would, in the end, have the satisfaction of knowing he did it his own way.

Tower was an active participant in the Goldwater campaign nationally as well as in Texas, despite what I regarded as rather shabby treatment of him by those who ran the campaign. In the spring of 1964, for instance, Tower was proceeding under the assumption that he would be the floor leader for Goldwater forces at the National Convention in San Francisco. I do not know who told him that, but he and those of us on the staff understood that to be the case and Tower was delighted with the assignment.

A few months before the convention, however, Tower was visited by one Denison Kitchel, whom Goldwater had brought in from Arizona for a leadership position in the campaign. Kitchel informed Tower that a change had been made, that they were going to ask Rep. John Rhodes of Arizona to be floor leader. Tower was deeply disappointed, even crushed over the move, unable to fathom a reason. In the depths of his despair, when I counseled retaliation, Tower merely responded, "No, in this business you just take your lumps and move on."

Occasionally I traveled with him on the Texas trips, and argued my point concerning the lack of "the hope message" coming through as a fundamental part of the overall campaign. Tower was a good soldier. He defended the strategy, arguing the classic position that in a national election those out of power must rally dissatisfied voters affected adversely by the policies of those in power. That is what the textbooks taught. I did not contest his point, so long as it was used as a campaign tactic for organizational purposes, but I never retreated from my own position that such a tactic, when elevated to the realm of strategy, overlooked what I regarded as an essential element—the element of hope—in the process of political campaigning, and governing as well.

And while I no longer argued the point, I never retreated from my own thinking that the conservative movement would have benefited from allowing the Rockefeller wing of the party to suffer the defeat that seemed inevitable.

On one of those swings through Texas, during the final days of the campaign, Tower asked how I thought it might come out. I really didn't want to answer, knowing how much energy he had invested. Trying somehow to bolster his spirits I answered finally that perhaps we had a chance, a small chance.

"I think we're going to get our butts kicked," he said.

It was a crushing defeat. Not just for Goldwater, but for many other good men as well. The party's fortunes in many parts of the nation, including Texas, suffered a tremendous setback. Peter O'Donnell asked for a meeting of the party's leadership in Austin. A shaken John Tower asked me to accompany him.

The flight there, in the same twin-engined Beech he had used to log many thousands of miles on behalf of Goldwater, was very quiet. Tower spent most of the time gazing out a window, in a most pensive mood as the rolling prairies of Texas passed beneath us. It was not a pleasant flight.

We met upstairs in the Commodore Perry Hotel overlooking Brazos Street. It was a small gathering of the old guard, not all of whom I can now recall. There was Peter O'Donnell from Dallas and retired Air Force General John Bennett from San Antonio. There was Anne Armstrong from the Armstrong Ranch in South Texas, and Al Fay from Houston. There were a few, very few, others. All had been instrumental in Tower's own election and had been ardent backers of Goldwater as well.

There was not much small talk. All knew what lay behind and before them. Behind lay the wreckage of what they had worked long and hard to build. Across the state the fledgling party had suffered crushing defeat. In front lay no prospects of immediate recovery. A Texan would occupy the White House, probably for eight years. The state would be governed by John Connally, made politically untouchable by his own experience during the Kennedy assassination in Dallas, as well as by his closeness to Johnson. Those divisions within the Democratic Party, so evident during the reign of John Kennedy, all but buried with his passing, would now likely be buried for good. It seemed a reasonable assumption.

Democratic leaders, led by an exuberant House Speaker Ben Barnes, were chortling over their victory. It was only a matter of time before they took care of the one remaining fly in their ointment, that fly being John Tower.

Tower laid out his thoughts to the group. He was not long in coming to the point. It might well be that his close identification with the Goldwater effort would be an albatross around the party's neck. Perhaps it would be better if they found another standard bearer for the next election to the Senate, a scant two years away. If that was the decision of the group he was prepared to accept it.

I was stunned by his comments. He had not even hinted at such a course during our flight to the meeting. Others appeared stunned as well.

After a moment of silence O'Donnell spoke. He did not want to hear such talk.

"Hell, John, you're all we've got. We'll rebuild."

With that the discussion turned to the future, bleak as it was.

(Many years later, when Tower was writing his own memoirs, his researcher phoned me about this incident. It had been reported in the book *Two Party Texas* by John Knaggs, but Tower could not remember it having ever taken place. The researcher wanted to know the details. I assured him it did in fact take place, that I was there. I relayed to him the words exchanged. It appeared in Tower's book *Consequences*, which was devoted primarily to his trials and tribulations over being nominated by President George Bush as secretary of defense and having been rejected by the Senate for that post amidst allegations of drinking and "womanizing.")

It is somewhat ironic, in passing, that four years after the Goldwater defeat the political landscape would not faintly resemble the one foreseen at that time. Johnson would be driven from office over the Vietnam issue, and Democrat Connally would be quietly giving aid and a degree of comfort to a man running for president on the Republican ticket, Richard Nixon. Tower would have been reelected by more than 200,000 votes. Such are the uncertainties, and the vicissitudes, of politics in America.

After the meeting was finished, Tower and I returned to Washington and duties there. Shortly after the Kennedy assassination Tower had named me his administrative assistant, replacing Ed Munden, his longtime friend and college classmate, who had resigned to go back to the private sector. At my urging Jerry Friedheim replaced me as press secretary, a job he held until he left the office for a Pentagon position as assistant secretary of defense for public affairs, before going on to head up the American Newspaper Publishers Association.

Ed's only advice to me, on leaving, was "Don't get too close to him." It was good advice, impossible to follow. The nature of the job, and the characters involved, dictated otherwise.

FIFTEEN

Trials of a Campaign

Defeat in battle is not the worst of man's fate, though it may seem so at the time. It is possible, though difficult, to learn from victory. It is much easier to learn from defeat. Still, the process takes time. And the daily grind of political life offers little time. Little time for reflection, little time for learning.

Fires must be constantly brought under control, the first always being those closest. It is only then that anticipated fires can be dealt with. As can be easily imagined, the recent defeat caused some smoldering fires to erupt and even ignited a few new ones. Advice is not a rare commodity in politics, but it seems to flow more freely in times of distress than otherwise. It was now 1965. A year hence, Tower would campaign for reelection. This was clearly a time of distress for the party faithful.

The first few months after the Goldwater defeat were not particularly happy for our office. Tower maintained a certain air of private stoicism about the matter, but there was no denying the depths of his despair. What happened to Goldwater was now likely to happen to him, in spades. While he kept up a public persona of confidence in his own reelection, in private it was a different matter. At times he seemed to question what had been his philosophical bearing, worrying about a sense of direction concerning matters and issues that formerly would have caused no such soul searching. It was as if the Goldwater defeat, and his closeness to it, had shaken his own belief in the rightness of convictions previously held.

In some ways his seeming ambivalence was understandable. It was, in fact, exactly what I had expected from many within the party, but not from Tower. It was true that he was much more of a party person than myself, and I much more of a "movement" person than he. I could never understand, for instance, how he could, in good conscience, travel to New York to campaign for Senator Jacob Javitts, a liberal Republican who voted against Tower on practically every issue. Or why he would travel to California to campaign for the reelection of Senator Tommy Kuchel, who consistently tried, as far as I was concerned, to balance himself somewhere between Javitts of New York and Goldwater of Arizona, and who otherwise had no political compass.

In our not infrequent arguments on such matters, Tower explained it away as the lesser of evils. Javitts was better than any alternative we were likely to get out of New York. Kuchel was better than any alternative, Republican or Democrat, we were likely to get out of California. The alternatives, as he saw it, being liberal Democrats from both states.

I saw it differently. As far as I was concerned, if New York or California were to be represented in the U.S. Senate by liberals I would rather they be Democrats. How could conservatives from either state have a voice if their only choice was between a liberal Republican and a liberal Democrat? How could they get themselves organized into a coherent political force, despite their numbers, if the ground was being cut from under them by recognized and respected conservative leaders urging them to vote for people who would never represent them once they were ensconced in the Senate? And how could our own conservative positions be enhanced within the party, or within the government, when our arguments were being disputed and diluted by people we had helped to positions of influence? To me it appeared a self-defeating exercise.

For the moment all those arguments were pushed into the background. It was time, indeed past time, to begin preparations for his own campaign. It was to be an exercise he approached with a marked lack of enthusiasm. In one of our late evening sessions, when I was trying to focus his attention on the need to prepare for his reelection, he indicated his belief in the utter futility of it all. Harking back to what he regarded as the biased news coverage of Goldwater contrasted to the favorable coverage of Johnson, he referred to those he called "the whores" in the press, and, lapsing into somewhat melodramatic rhetoric, claimed "they will crucify me with a crown of thorns. They will pour vitriol upon my brow."

It was a bit much. I told him I didn't really think it would be quite that bad. The fundamentals of Texas politics had not changed all that much. True, Johnson was still president. But the only difference was that now he was president in his own right. The feeling of euphoria that gripped the Democratic Party at the moment was not likely to be a permanent situation. The Connally–Yarborough differences would still be at play, as far as I could determine. The right-left differences would still be evident among the state's Democrats and could be exploited. In terms of the press there were two aspects, as I saw it. One dealt with those reporters who normally covered our activities. Here I saw no real problems. Tower had a generally good relationship with those reporters who covered his Senate activities. A few shared, in a general way, Tower's political posture. Others did not. But he was usually open and above board in his dealings with the press, despite whatever private misgivings he might have had concerning the lack of intellectual honesty he saw in some.

The matter of future editorial positions by most of the state's papers was another matter, yet to be determined. Here the picture was admittedly not too bright, but aside from those papers that could be counted on to blindly support any Democrat on the ballot there were others that I felt could be reasoned with. Despite all the rhetoric about political principle, most publishers were (and still are) concerned about the economic growth and vitality of their own community. And most publishers in Texas would at that time have called themselves conservatives, though they considered themselves squarely in the Democratic camp. My argument was that we had to convince them it was in the long-term interests of their community, and consequently in their own self-interest, that Tower be reelected.

Fortunately, a circumstance arose that would prove to be of tremendous benefit in this regard. In the spring of 1965, after the Senate convened following the Goldwater defeat, an opening occurred on the Senate Armed Services Committee. Tower was offered the assignment. It was an assignment Tower longed for, but which had always seemed out of reach.

Now he would be able to leave the Committee on Labor and Welfare, which, for someone of Tower's persuasion, was a complete dead end. That committee was stacked with liberals, both Democratic and Republican, and Tower paid scant attention to its deliberations.

The new assignment would mean a place on a committee having tremendous impact on the economy of Texas, home of numerous military installations. It did not go unnoticed by us that such an assignment could have, and probably would have, exceedingly beneficial results among a politically powerful segment of Texas opinion molders, as well as hundreds of thousands of potential voters. Any publisher, right or left, could be counted on to support a military installation that poured millions of dollars into his community, and would think twice before openly opposing a senator who might have some influence on the continuing viability of that base. This would be true even among those publishers and editors who generally took a liberal position on social issues, as well as those who generally took a conservative position on economic issues.

Tower asked what I thought of the prospective assignment. Clearly, he wanted the change. The staff was unanimous, as I remember it, and I urged its acceptance, but only after he had discussed the matter with supporters in Texas. No need to surprise them, and they would be flattered if he asked their opinion. I do not know that this was done, but it was recommended. At any rate he took the new assignment.

The move to Armed Services Committee was probably one of the best things that happened to Tower, politically and psychologically, during the time I was with him. It provided a socially and politically secure base in many Texas communities and, more broadly, among the state's electorate. But just as important, perhaps even more important, the move had the effect of rejuvenating Tower. He quickly became absorbed with work on the committee, which in some ways became his hiding place, the place where he found comfort and inspiration. Here he was dealing with the big picture, not squabbles growing out of competition among various economic interests within the body politic. Here he could vote his basic convictions, knowing that he would be applauded for doing so, not editorially castigated for a lack of compassion toward unwed mothers on government welfare.

It would be honest to say, in my own opinion, that Tower not only loved the work but also loved the trappings of the work. The constant parade of high-ranking military officers, pleading for support for this weapon or that weapon, this project or that project, could not have gone unappreciated by a former enlisted man in the U.S. Navy. And it would also be honest, in my opinion, to say that he was most supportive of the military's concerns, seeing those concerns as being in the best interest of the nation. In turn the military was most supportive of him. At that time the nation was mired in the Vietnam conflict, and Tower was publicly and politically supportive of the Johnson Administration's position in the matter, even if he was privately critical of how it was being run. His move to Armed Services placed him in the center of an arena where his basic philosophical instincts relative to the purposes of government and his political instincts relative to self-survival could mesh.

The move to Armed Services served another useful purpose. Tower, a student on such matters, would often hold forth on the "geo-political" aspects of world diplomacy and considered the Senate Foreign Relations Committee, then headed by the dovish William Fulbright of Arkansas, as an exceedingly weak link in the chain that held America's interests together. Indeed he saw it as an impediment in the proper conduct of American policy, not recognizing the utility of military power as the final arbiter in either the protection or projection of the nation's interests. Now he would have a seat at the most important table, for, in time of war or crises approaching war, the Senate's legislative center of gravity moves to the Armed Services Committee, not the Foreign Relations Committee.

Important as the new committee assignment was, however, it was not the be-all and end-all of Senate service, nor was it a guarantor of ultimate success at the polls. The problem still faced us: how to take what we had and translate that into success during the upcoming campaign. This involved both strategy and tactics, neither of which he was prepared to devote time to at the expense of his new interests on Armed Services. The result was that we had many long hours of inconclusive discussions concerning what to do and when to do it. And in the final analysis it became apparent that we would have to draw our own campaign roadmap in conjunction with party leaders in Texas, principally Peter O'Donnell and Anne Armstrong.

The strategy was simple enough. Utilize his position on Armed Services as a vehicle for frequent visits to military bases in Texas, where he could be received by local officials in a nonpartisan manner in a nonpartisan setting, and where he could defend his support of the country's moral commitment in Vietnam on the same basis. The strategy also involved trips to Vietnam, where he could receive first-hand briefings on the course of conflict there. And it should be said, in all honesty, that care was given to see that cameras were on hand to record the event.

It is sad, but that is the nature of American politics. American politicians rushing off to Israel, immediately before a fundraising

---

event, for a picture with whoever happened to be prime minister at the time, or traveling to Rome for a picture with the Pope, were and are a part of the scene. We had no legitimate reason for making a trip to Rome, and even less for visiting Israel. But America's sons were fighting and dying in Vietnam, and there were legitimate reasons, in my view, for a member of the Senate Armed Services Committee to go there, to talk to and lend support to the troops and commanders in the field. He was called upon constantly to make decisions affecting their lives, and he could do no less, in my view, than show up occasionally, doing whatever he could to show support for those carrying out the nation's policies. We realized a certain amount of political risk was involved, for quiet rumblings of discontent were already being heard concerning America's involvement there. This was particularly true within the president's own party, but we were beginning to hear criticism from some of our own supporters in Texas, pointing out that we were, in effect, helping pull Lyndon Johnson's chestnuts out of the fire. No one knew what the picture would be one year or two years hence. But from our own standpoint the die had been cast. Tower was morally committed to the effort.

Tower became consumed with his work on Armed Services, so much so that preparation for his reelection fell to the staff and his supporters in Texas. Many, many things are involved in a statewide campaign — things other than a candidate's committee assignments or his general posture on issues or matters that are likely to become issues. This is particularly true in a state as racially and economically diverse as Texas. And it was those matters, the nitty-gritty details of organization, the mundane work of pacifying various interest groups, that Tower expressed little interest in. Still, he was the one who had to agree with what had been proposed and in that sense I do not remember him ever saying no, finally, to a recommended course of action. Sometimes, however, it took a lot of convincing.

In one of our late evening sessions, for instance, I brought up the subject, again, of the impending campaign and some of the problems we needed to address. We needed to make inroads in traditional voting groups other than those generally regarded as conservative Democrats, many of whom I felt we could already count on. The only other sizable voting bloc that held promise, as far as I could see, was in South Texas among the Mexican-Americans, where I had grown up. They were traditionally a conservative people, placing high values on such things as the church, family, work, education for their children, local communities. Many of their sons were in the military. A strain of patriotism ran through the community.

Tower was skeptical. He was a child of East Texas. He had grown up around blacks and whites. At that time Hispanics were practically unknown in that part of the state, being a political and cultural influence only in South Texas and along the border as far west as El Paso. Besides, they were of a different culture, relying traditionally upon their *"jefes,"* or recognized leaders, for political guidance. And those leaders, acting the role of Judas goats, had traditionally been in the pay of Anglo Democratic officeholders, whether left or right. He could see little promise there.

The discussion, perhaps even the argument, went on. Finally, in an almost plaintive response, he said, "Ken, what can I promise them? I'm not going to change my position just for a few votes."

Even if it meant his election.

It was a comment by Tower I have always remembered. A most pleasing comment. It set him apart from the vast majority of those occupying public office. And it was said in a setting and with a tone that indicated its sincerity.

No change in any position was necessary, I told him. Indeed, if he started changing positions I would no longer be with him. This was simply a matter of trying to convey to that community the similarity of our views on many issues affecting their lives. It would mean a commitment on his part to spend time and effort among a people then generally ignored by those seeking national office. It would mean trying to bypass the local leadership, tied as it was to corrupt state and local officials. If we were successful in that effort, I thought, the "leaders," always anxious to please their followers, would at least take a somewhat less belligerent position toward us. That in turn should allow us an opportunity to have our message considered within a community previously considered off limits.

He finally agreed, with "Okay, we'll try it."

We began to move him about that community when time and circumstances permitted, first merely to indicate he had no horns and then to explain his message. Our first, feeble attempts were met with a degree of resentment, even derision, on the part of the "leaders" within that community. Obviously, and understandably, they did not want to see outsiders intrude into what had been a cozy arrangement. They did not want to see any diminution in their ability to deliver a bloc of votes, or at least to have the appearance of being able to deliver a bloc of votes. A reduction in that ability meant a reduction in the value of their own coin.

Those first, somewhat experimental steps finally led to an expanded effort that played an important role in the campaign. Tower later told me he was surprised at how much he enjoyed the process and the people involved in the process.

I have thought many times of that particular discussion with Tower. During the two years we had been together, it was the first conversation we had held that had any sort of racial or cultural overtones. It was clear he had a fixation concerning black people, one he would never get over. Like many Republicans he could not understand why they were not more supportive of the "party of Lincoln," which, after all, was instrumental in their freedom from slavery. Or why they would give their votes to a party that had kept them, as he saw it, in political bondage for so many years. Surely one day they would see this and would "come home." Surely political freedom should mean more to a people than welfare doles. After all, man did not live by bread alone.

Even with the recent defeat so evident, he was still living in the world of what should be, the world of the theorist rather than the world of what is and what will be. But he was a quick study, and he was learning. The period between Goldwater's defeat and Tower's reelection two years later was a time of much learning for a former college professor, who, by any standard, would have to be considered "a learned man." In my own mind there is no doubt that the defeat of Goldwater, sad as it was, contributed to the political growth, indeed the political longevity of Tower. It forced him to realize, political textbooks notwithstanding, that politics is not a "science" at all, that it is a mixture of art and mechanics, with the art sometimes resembling Picasso and sometimes Rembrandt. And with the mechanics sometimes resembling those of the Swiss watchmaker, sometimes the assembly line of Henry Ford. In the broadest sense it plays upon the basic hopes and fears of people. In its narrowest sense it plays upon greed, revenge, lust for power over fellow humans.

I do not believe Tower ever succumbed, while I was with him, to using politics in its narrowest sense, but he at least began to realize its presence in the world in which he operated. It was as if he was finally beginning to realize that he, as a preacher's son, was bound to live in that world his father warned about, and in which he, in his own right, was going to have to make up his mind concerning how he would operate.

In that respect he was no different from any of us.

In time the campaign was upon us. We had set up a campaign operation in Texas. The state party organization was geared to the reelection of Tower, under the assumption that if it lost him it would have lost everything, and if it were successful in keeping him it would have something upon which to build. In theory the campaign organization would work closely with the state party organization, and both would take their cue from positions and statements emanating from Washington. It proved, in operation, to be a somewhat less than perfect arrangement. Problems arose in communications, sometimes because of the mechanics of the arrangement, sometimes because of the personalities involved. Tower suggested that I take leave and return to the state to oversee the operation. I was reluctant to do so, fearing my presence would only further confuse the situation since I would have no power to change anything. Finally he insisted, adding, "What is writ in Austin will be writ in Washington."

With that assurance I took leave of my duties in Washington and assumed new ones in Austin.

The prospect before us was not entirely happy. Our own polls showed us in a precarious position, largely because of the party identification factor, but not completely so. We had drawn Waggoner Carr, a three-term former Speaker of the House of Representatives and former state attorney general, as the Democratic nominee. He was at that time the state's highest vote-getter, a respected and extremely popular person among the electorate. It was expected that he would have a built-in cadre of supporters across the state, based on friendships with members and former members of the legislature. And it was expected that he would ultimately receive the support of the governor, John Connally, who at that stage appeared to be taking a largely hands-off position in the whole affair.

In the final analysis I would have to say it was a well-run campaign in terms of both strategy and tactics. It was not without its frustrations, its moments of despair and doubt. Many obstacles had to be overcome, but certain fundamentals redounded to our favor. Among the nonpoliticized electorate, Tower was generally seen as doing a good job in the Senate, and there was no overriding reason to turn him out of office. Among the politically active there were mixed minds. The Republicans were basically united, while the Democrats still suffered from the right-left split that had marked the party in recent years. That ideological split, and the differing personalities of those who headed up the various factions, were to stand us in good stead.

Tower was initially a somewhat subdued campaigner, still suffering from doubts expressed to me much earlier. It was only much later in the campaign, following a speech in Corpus Christi which received prominent news coverage, that he became truly energized. During the early stages he seemed to have difficulty escaping the notion that an enlightened electorate would simply weigh the relative merits of each candidate and make their decisions accordingly. That would be the "civilized" approach to politics and government. He did not wish to be placed in the position of an attack dog, lest it demean his position as a sitting senator. Laudable as that might be, it had the effect of causing widespread apprehension in the ranks. Many saw our campaign as lacking enthusiasm. And if there was no enthusiasm at the top, how could there be any in the ranks?

The problem finally reached a head when I was visited by a delegation of longtime Tower supporters from Fort Worth, men who were not only heavy financial contributors but personal friends as well. It was a long, involved, even emotional discussion, but in the end the message was clear. They understood my problems, but if I could not get the senator to carry the fight more aggressively they would pull out of the campaign and issue a press release stating their reasons. I felt it would be a devastating blow, one I was determined would never fall.

We had scheduled Tower to attend a community celebration in Columbus, to ride in the parade and later address a rally of supporters. I wrote a rather hard-hitting speech, one designed not only to enthuse the troops but to portray the candidate as a courageous fighter standing alone against an entrenched establishment. There was little doubt that in the end most lower-level officeholders, and perhaps higher-level officeholders as well, would be rallying around the other side, seeking to create the image of a politically isolated Tower, hence an ineffective Tower. If they were successful in that argument, then our own argument that Texas needed a voice in both parties would go out the window. What benefit would Texans derive from having a voice among Senate Republicans if that voice was ineffective? The only thing we could do, I thought, was preempt the battle and attempt to crown necessity with virtue.

THE CHOW DIPPER

I drove to Columbus with a copy of the speech, determined that he should deliver it there. CBS had moved camera crews into Texas to cover segments of both the Tower and Carr campaigns, and had selected the Columbus appearance as the place they would cover Tower. It seemed like a good place to deliver the speech.

Arriving in Columbus, I immediately encountered Roger Mudd, CBS-TV's man on the scene. "Ken, where's your candidate?" he asked.

"He's riding in the parade," I answered.

"The parade is over. His car came by, but he wasn't in it," Mudd said.

I was furious. I went immediately to the motel where we had him booked. There, after much pounding on the door, I was admitted by a young lady who informed me that the senator was not there. When would he be back? She didn't know. She was looking after the phone, she said.

"Well, I'll just wait." I walked past her and sat in a chair near the unmade bed.

After some twenty minutes Tower arrived through a door to an adjoining room, the lady left, and we began our conversation. I told him of the visit by his friends from Fort Worth and gave him a copy of the speech with the urging that it be delivered there, or if not there, somewhere soon. He looked at it, put it down and said, "I'll think about it."

I told him he had to do more than think about it — he had to deliver it. If we didn't do something to energize the campaign we were going down the tube. He didn't see it that way. He was deeply troubled by the position taken by his friends in Fort Worth, but he thought things seemed to be going well, despite what our polls said and despite our reports from the field.

It would not be an exaggeration to say that the conversation, at least from my side, became heated at times. We had blown an opportunity to get free exposure on national television at a time we were having difficulty finding money to move him from one place to another. Beyond that was the attitude. He took the position that very few votes were influenced by politicians riding in parades, which of course is true. But it can have the effect of letting one's own supporters know he is out there, at least trying. How could we expect our supporters to break their own backs when they could see little evidence we were willing to do the same? If we weren't willing to be part of their parade, they might not be willing to be part of ours.

I suppose, also, that my ire was increased by the simple knowledge that his wife, Lou, was a trooper in the campaign, putting in long hours to out-of-the-way places in an effort to be helpful. I may have been wrong, but I always felt that Lou simply tolerated politics, rather than revel in it. She tolerated it, I thought, because it was her husband's life and she was part of that life. Still, she was, and is, a friendly and gracious human being to whom people warmed. During the campaign we were moving her from place to place in largely "non-partisan" social settings, to which the wives of Democratic county officials flocked, right along with the wives of Republican farmers and businessmen. The stories of her comings and goings usually ended up on the society pages of newspapers, which tend to be read by the community's movers and shakers, and talked about in subsequent gatherings. It was one area where a certain amount of political symbiosis could take place. A county judge, for instance, or a county commissioner had no objections to seeing his wife's name in the paper as having attended a tea given for the wife of a United States senator, even if that senator was a Republican. It might be politically risky for the Democratic politician to attend such an event, but his wife was another matter. In fact, it might even get him a few votes.

I took my leave and returned to Austin, still angry and still not knowing that the speech would ever be delivered. He insisted he would continue to "think about it," and at one point even said "All right, I'll say it, but I don't believe it." This was at a point where I had played down the importance of party loyalty, knowing that if that was the determining factor in the election we were lost.

Admittedly, the subject of party loyalty was a difficult one for Tower to address in the context of a campaign. He had no problem in welcoming the votes of disaffected Democrats, or in pointing out that conservative beliefs were better represented in his party than in the other. But party loyalty was so much a part of his own makeup that he had difficulty in raising it as an issue. He had difficulty in paraphrasing John Kennedy's "Sometimes party loyalty asks too much." He had deep intellectual problems with calling on all members of his own party to stand fast, no matter the philosophical bearing of a nominee, while asking members of another party to desert their own nominee.

I had no such difficulty. To me party loyalty, on the part of the voter, has validity only so long as political parties have loyalty to ideas and ideals, and so long as the candidates reflect those ideas and ideals. Otherwise "party loyalty" is simply a means to entrap the ignorant for the benefit of politicians.

He was scheduled to appear the next morning at a breakfast in Corpus Christi, before members of the Corpus Christi Yacht Club. It was not to be a large gathering and I did not expect much from it. Breakfast campaign events are not usually very productive and seldom given much play in the media. This one proved the exception. For reasons I never really understood, he chose this forum to deliver the speech. Later I had dark suspicions that he felt it might not be noticed, and he could say "I told you so." Or perhaps he just couldn't think of anything else to say that early in the morning. But I prefer to think that he finally psyched himself up for the task ahead. That would not have been unusual. I had seen him many times worry with an issue like a dog with a bone, chewing it, worrying with it, trying to make up his mind what to do with it. Usually, when he finally made up his mind, he could become a tenacious fighter indeed.

At any rate his speech was played prominently in the *Caller-Times* and picked up in other papers. The reaction seemed to breathe new life into the campaign and in Tower as well. He emerged as a far more aggressive campaigner, a far more focused campaigner. And it gave the entire campaign a focus we were able to maintain, with various nuances, to the end.

It also took some of the rough edges off our meeting in Columbus. We never discussed it again, though I suspect neither of us ever forgot it.

In truth there was not much difference, if any, between the fundamental positions of John Tower and Waggoner Carr. Both would have to be considered as coming from the conservative side of the political spectrum, both believing in a less powerful, less intrusive, less costly federal government. Other than that the problem was very simple. There were two candidates in the race for only one Senate seat. Given the fact that both candidates were honorable men, one the now experienced incumbent and the other an experienced leader in state government, the argument essentially boiled down to two questions: Would Texas be better served by having a voice in both political parties in Washington, and would Tower be effective as one of those voices?

It was a debate more prevalent among editorial writers and the political intelligencia, but the question did filter down into the ranks of ordinary voters, primarily on the strength of our own campaign efforts and our own arguments. There the argument began to take hold, slowly but perceptibly. For many it was an intriguing argument, one Texans had not seriously faced before. The campaign's task was then to provide credible evidence of the argument's plausibility. Over the course of the campaign I believe we did that.

Even so, there is always a sizable segment of the electorate whose vote is determined by matters completely unrelated to fundamental political issues in any election. This race was no exception. The supporters of Senator Ralph Yarborough, who considered themselves the keepers of the keys in terms of Democratic "purity," now saw no urgent need to elect another Democrat, particularly a conservative Democrat who would provide an avenue for conservative influence in Washington. Indeed there were valid reasons, as they saw it, to discourage such a course. Tower posed no problems to Yarborough in the all-important area of political patronage. An additional Democratic senator, liberal or conservative, would have to be taken into consideration and could only dilute the senior senator's influence. Yarborough had enough troubles in that regard already, by virtue of Lyndon Johnson's insistence that he also be part of the patronage process. Too, as they saw it, the election of a conservative Democrat would give aid and comfort to John Connally, with whom the Yarborough forces were conducting a running battle. All things considered, it would be better, from their standpoint, that Carr not be elected.

Out of this concern there grew a close-knit, highly motivated liberal cabal known as the "Rebuilding Committee," in a theoretical sense dedicated to the continuing orientation of the party along liberal lines, but in this instance having the practical goal of defeating Carr and protecting the interests of Yarborough, and their own as well.

Leaders of the group were men like Chuck Caldwell, at various times a member of Yarborough's staff with close ties to organized labor, Dave Shapiro, an activist liberal Democratic lawyer, and Tom Bones, a tall, lanky liberal activist who made his living, as I understood it, in the wholesale furniture business. It was Bones who seemed to call the shots for the group's activities. Certainly it was he who maintained the closest liaison with me, and who wheedled money from our own campaign for certain projects they thought might be helpful. They understood they were unlikely to cause many "crossover" votes, where longtime Democratic Party stalwarts could be convinced to actually vote for a Republican, but they believed they could be successful in encouraging a "stay-at-home" vote, which, from our standpoint, would be just as well.

The group's principal effort was among labor unions in the Gulf Coast region, where organized labor was then a disciplined, potent political force. Their work had the blessing of the state's AFL-CIO leadership, regardless of the public stance taken by those leaders. In fact, the AFL-CIO's political action committee paid for some of the Rebuilding Committee's mailings to key political activists within the unions. And while I do not know that the group came into being at the behest of Yarborough, it certainly operated with his knowledge and acquiescence. A few weeks before the final vote, Bones came to my office (from Yarborough's office) to happily report he had finally gotten Yarborough to make some calls for them. Until then Yarborough had resisted being tied closely to the process of actually trying to get Democrats to vote for a Republican. He still wouldn't go quite that far, but now he was on the phone to key operatives, telling them, "We want an honest count this time." People on the other end of the phone, according to Bones, understood this to mean they shouldn't be too concerned about turning out the vote "for the ticket." Members of the Rebuilding Committee then made follow-up calls explaining in more detail the import of it all, saying things Yarborough couldn't say. It became, in effect, communication by code. It was the best they could do, but Bones was pleased with the development, as was I.

Much has been written about the significance of the Rebuilding Committee efforts during the 1966 campaign. In most cases the usefulness of the effort in that particular campaign has been over-rated. But in terms of the long-range political development of Texas, I believe the Rebuilding Committee's efforts have been largely under-rated. Their work had the effect of eroding the "yellow dog" syndrome that then affected and afflicted many Democrats in Texas, and to an extent still does. It had the effect of speeding the exodus of conservatives from the Democratic Party and the growth of the Republican Party.

It also contributed mightily, in my view, to the long-term effort aimed at more clearly defining the basic difference in political philosophies in the state. That may be a development not greatly appreciated by some who run for political office, and who seek constantly to "fuzz" the issues before the electorate, but it is one that should be appreciated by the rank and file of all parties.

The group's efforts did, no doubt, draw off some political energy that would have been detrimental for us had it been directed against us rather than against Carr. But as a positive force for adding votes to the Tower column, I have never believed it contributed very much. Of far more benefit to our campaign, in my view, were two factors that have drawn little media or historical attention over the years. One dealt with John Connally. The other with Lyndon Johnson.

Throughout the campaign I expected the governor to finally throw his support to Carr, unequivocally and with force. That would have been very damaging to us, for Connally was at that time the political commander of many troops in the field. It is true, of course, that Connally was then engaged in his own campaign for reelection, but it was against a very weak (politically) Republican opponent running with little help from his party, that help being concentrated on the reelection of Tower. He did make known that he was a Democrat and would support Democratic nominees, but he never issued that clear call to arms that one might expect from the leader of the party. And as far as I could determine he never sent those early, private signals to his troops that the election of Carr was a matter of highest priority. Perhaps it was because the Tower and Connally offices had developed a comfortable working relationship over the years. Perhaps it was because he saw, like Yarborough saw, that another Democrat in the Senate, a Democrat around whom the state's conservative establishment could rally, might detract from his own political position as unquestioned leader of that force. Or perhaps he was simply determined, as was rumored, that Carr must come to him on bended knee and beg for the support, which Carr was unwilling to do. And perhaps all the "perhaps" assumptions are wrong. But for whatever reason, the support was not forthcoming to the degree I feared it would be.

The Lyndon Johnson factor was more understandable. Tower had opposed most if not all of Johnson's "Great Society" programs. That was of no great consequence, since Johnson, given the tenor of the times, had the votes he needed in that arena. But the Vietnam War was another matter. Johnson needed all the support he could get, and Tower was solidly in his camp. In fact, during the time leading up to the campaign, we had produced a 30-minute documentary on the war with Tower as the centerpiece, explaining why it was important that America prevail in that effort and calling on the nation to support the government's position. The program gave a coherent philosophical underpinning to the effort, something that had been sorely lacking to that point. Johnson was so appreciative that he called Tower, thanking him profusely and saying he wished some of his own people would do the same, rather than running for cover at every opportunity. The language used, Tower told me, was typical, earthy Johnson.

Johnson was the consummate politician. As such he had an appreciation of the political risks involved for Tower in supporting policies that might prove unpopular, particularly when he was surrounded by so many "nervous nellies" in his own party. He would gain nothing, as I saw it and probably as he saw it, in the defeat of Tower. The defeat, at the polls in Texas, of a strong supporter of the president's Vietnam policies would do nothing to strengthen Johnson's hand in the Senate. On the other hand the presence in the Senate of a strong supporter, a member of the Armed Services Committee in the opposition party, could be very helpful indeed in the dark and difficult days ahead.

At any rate, and for whatever reason, we saw little evidence that Johnson was a significant factor in the race, as he certainly could have been. And we did not see Connally marshal the kind of support for Carr that he certainly was capable of doing.

In fact, one of the few times Connally publicly associated himself with Carr proved to be politically damaging to Carr. It was unintentional, even inadvertent, but nevertheless it cost Carr support in the important Democratic stronghold of South Texas.

The story had a strange, somewhat humorous beginning and a stranger, not so humorous ending.

One day, while the campaign was in full swing and after the Rebuilding Committee had come into being, I was visited by Bones with a proposal. I was told that in San Antonio there was a Catholic priest who might prove helpful. He was then a "barrio priest" (some said a "political priest") involved in West Side organizational activities on behalf of labor unions. Organized unionism was not popular among the predominantly Mexican-American citizens of San Antonio, or South Texas for that matter, and the priest's job was to make it more acceptable. He was not himself an "organizer." He would, according to Bones, merely show up at organizational meetings, bless the gatherings, say kind words, and generally put a good face on the efforts, indicating the Catholic church did not stand in the way of union activity.

Perhaps, Bones said, he could do the same for us. It was not likely that he could convert many San Antonio West Siders to Republicanism, but perhaps he could neutralize some of the latent hostility toward a party many local inhabitants regarded as merely a bastion of rich Anglo Protestants, thereby reducing the turnout among those with a tendency toward straight-ticket voting. At the very least he might be able to convince some of them that Tower was "not like all those other Republicans." I was warned, however, that he would expect to get paid for his efforts. Would I agree to meet with him and discuss the matter?

It was not the first time I had been approached on behalf of "men of the cloth." Many black churches in Houston had refined the process to an art. There one could make a "charitable donation" of some two or three thousand dollars to the preacher's "building fund," in return for which the candidate was promised glowing recognition in the church's newsletter. That was supposed to be the signal of who was friendly and, by implication, who wasn't. If one believed the sales pitch it was almost a sure thing. Many votes would flow automatically. My problem was that I didn't believe the sales pitch, though many in the political world did and much money was thereby wasted. Actually, I suppose I should not say the money was "wasted." It would, after all, contribute to the preacher's financial security.

But this might be different. After all, there were no great promises made. There was no assurance that a single vote could be changed. We did, however, need someone saying a few kind things about us in a setting where traditionally very few kind things were said. I agreed to meet with the priest.

It went about as I expected. The Reverend Antonio Gonzales showed up in the company of one or two members of the Rebuilding Committee for the discussion. He was certainly not an imposing figure. Rather, he was a small, somewhat nondescript individual bent on pleasing. But he had the necessary credentials, including the robe, the collar, and the connections. There was nothing new or different from what I had been told by Bones. Finally, I asked what salary he would expect if we put him on the payroll and gave him free rein to roam San Antonio's West Side, being helpful where he could.

He hesitated. He didn't know what to ask. I offered him $400 per month, which I thought we could probably afford, about as low as he would probably accept and also what Bones had suggested I offer him.

He thought the figure was completely adequate, even generous, but he would have to clear it all with his bishop. In a week or so he was back.

His bishop said no. He could not go on the payroll. That would be wrong. But the bishop did say he could accept an expense account.

I asked how much he thought his expenses might run.

He did not hesitate. He said they would be $400 per month.

For some reason I was not surprised.

Agreed. I heard no more concerning the matter and assumed our new agent was soon happily spreading the word throughout San Antonio's West Side.

However . . .

In my old home of the Rio Grande Valley, on the Mexican border in South Texas, a dispute erupted between farmers and melon pickers over wages and working conditions. It was a little more serious than those things usually were, for the dispute was now being used as a vehicle to unionize farm workers. In an effort to attract media attention and dramatize their fight, union leaders decided to march the 300 miles north to the State Capitol, where they would rally with sympathetic supporters and demand an audience with state political leaders. Ultimately, they hoped to force a confrontation with the Democratic governor, John Connally.

As a media event it was a natural. There would be nightly TV clips of bedraggled marchers, holding up placards demanding justice. There would be sympathetic stories concerning how many miles the workers had progressed that day, along with a few choice comments about the alleged greed and inhumanity of the farmers. As the days passed, and as media attention increased, the dispute began to take on significant political overtones. At first it seemed not to involve us. We were, as could be expected, sympathetic to the position of the growers but at that stage had not been drawn into the dispute. Unfortunately, that enviable position did not last forever.

Tower flew into Houston after a day on the campaign trail, no doubt tired and not at his best. The local campaign organization had scheduled a press conference so he could report on the progress of the race. But for reasons I never understood, the location of the press conference was moved to a rather swank country club. There Tower was queried about his position on the dispute. He sought to defend the growers, pointing out some of the problems they faced at the time, with crops rotting in the field and markets gone. In the process he made a comment that would dog his campaign trail, at least for a while.

The first reports I received on the conference were in the next

---

morning's newspapers, where Tower was pictured as being unsympathetic to the workers, noting that "eighty-five cents an hour is better than nothing." He spoke the truth, of course, since the dispute resulted in both lost crops and lost wages, but truth and logic act as small defense where emotions hold sway. It was a politically damaging development that tended to undercut much work we had done throughout that community. And in politics, one candidate's loss is another candidate's gain.

Tower's comments also tended to politicize the story even more, which pleased organizers of the strike but distressed us. Now we were faced with the task of trying to distance the campaign and minimize the damage.

However, just as chance can place a monkey on one's back, it can also take it off and place it elsewhere.

The farm workers' trek wended its way northward, bent on a Labor Day confrontation with the governor on the Capitol grounds in Austin. The governor, John Connally, perhaps thinking to diffuse the political impact of such a meeting, decided to intercept the march in New Braunfels, some thirty miles north of San Antonio. There were also reports he planned to be out of the state when the marchers reached Austin, and did not wish to leave the impression he was reluctant to meet with the workers. For whatever reason he showed up in New Braunfels in company with House Speaker Ben Barnes and Waggoner Carr. There the three were met with, of all people, a crucifix-wielding Father Antonio Gonzales, whom I thought was busily spending his expense account on San Antonio's West Side. Naturally, press people were in attendance, including a wire service photographer.

Gonzales, in his role as a champion of the oppressed and a facilitator of unionization, had emerged as something of a spokesman for the marchers. In that role he confronted the three state political leaders, one presumes to air the workers' grievances. Somewhere in the conversation he suddenly thrust a large crucifix forward almost in the face of a startled Connally, the image being recorded for posterity and politics by the waiting photographer. The expression on the faces of both Carr and Barnes was no less startled, and understandably so. It was not a picture of adoration; it was a picture that was grist for the mills of the Rebuilding Committee, who saw to it that it was widely circulated in selected communities in South Texas, replete with accompanying commentary. The monkey was off our back.

It was a small thing in the world of politics. A small thing on the order of Gerald Ford trying to eat a tamale with the shucks on, or a television picture of a helmeted Michael Dukakis riding around on an army tank, looking like Snoopy in search of a downed Red Baron. It was not helpful to Mr. Carr's campaign.

Unfortunately there are thousands of people, indeed hundreds of thousands of people, whose political decisions are afflicted and affected by such things. But who was I to argue with a potential voter, especially when the net result was votes for the candidate I was trying to get elected?

Finally, the matter was over. A day before the election Tower asked how I thought the vote might turn out. I thought we would win. He asked the margin. I ventured it would be on the order of 200,000. He looked at me as if I had lost my senses. In truth it was merely an educated guess, but I never told him that. Better, as it turned out, that he regard me a genius. Actually, I would have been happy with 10,000.

We sat in his family's Wichita Falls home and watched the returns come in. The margin between Tower and Carr was 198,746.

Next morning the state's newspapers recorded the victory under bold, black headlines. Few, in my opinion, had anticipated the victory. I know of none who had harbored the thought of a margin of that magnitude. All, one way or the other, paid tribute to Tower and in effect noted the historical implications of the victory. He could no longer be considered a "fluke" in the annals of Texas political history.

For me it was a time of subdued satisfaction. The long ordeal was over and it had played itself out largely along lines planned in the beginning. Even so, I knew that things would never be quite the same between Tower and myself. He would return to the Senate as an established figure, to the congratulations of his peers. The periods of self-doubt would be gone, replaced by I knew not what. Nor did I know how I would fit into the new scheme of things.

One would think that in such circumstances Tower would have been supremely happy. All across the state, headlines told of his victory. Publicly he said all the right things, but privately he fumed that the "slick" magazines would probably ignore his reelection, concentrating instead on the election of Charles Percy of Illinois. It was Percy who would get the buildup as the rising star.

He was right, of course. Percy, coming out of the liberal or "moderate" wing of the party, was just exactly the kind of Republican the dominant national media would champion. And did champion. But what was new about that? Why be concerned about it, especially at this moment? Why not simply savor the victory?

I've never understood the fascination politicians seem to have concerning the so-called "slick" press, the weekly *Time* or *Newsweek*-type publications. Their value, in a political sense, lies not in their influence upon the voters, but in their influence upon lazy reporters and lazier editors who in turn do have influence upon the voters. Still, a politician seems to think he has "arrived" when he sees his name in company with all those other names of national import. Especially if he has ideas of future greatness.

Somewhat the same situation prevails relative to television. Politicians seem to get some sort of vicarious pleasure out of seeing their image on television, as do a host of political journalists. But I've never seen a successful politician who did not, upon arising in the morning, grab the morning papers to see how his previous day's activities were reported. While they may be fascinated by their own presence on the tube, they are well aware of the lasting value of the printed word. Therein lies the magic of print, the fodder of campaigns, of history as influenced by partisans and taught by academicians.

Nevertheless, the deed was done. The battle was fought and won. It was, in a way, a new beginning.

A somewhat different attitude on the part of his peers greeted Tower upon his return. He was now looked upon as someone who was likely to be there. This attitude also affected the power brokers and lobbyists who clutter the scene in Washington, most of whom had never bothered with our office in the past. The office began to be visited by people other than the party faithful, the old guard of Tower supporters, the conservative "movement" people. There was now a steady stream of people obviously bent upon establishing their credentials as longtime, if secret, supporters. That is, of course, the way of politics, especially Washington politics. Still, it was interesting, and I imagine for Tower it was heady stuff. In the past, during the Goldwater effort, the national attention given Tower was primarily from the media, since he was considered an articulate spokesman for conservative thought. Now the attention was coming from that other permanent fixture in Washington, those representing the status quo, the hangers-on.

After all, the hangers-on must have someone to hang on to. There's no need to waste time and energy trying to latch on to someone who might not be around long. Now it appeared Tower would.

In some respects the following two years were the worst two years I ever spent in the world of politics or government. I know it should not have been that way, but it was. Many things contributed to that state of unhappiness, but basically there just seemed to be no big or immediate worthwhile challenges ahead. At least none that I could see at the moment. Many, many small problems needed attention, to which Tower's response was always, "Ken, take care of it."

The prospect of going to work each morning became less and less appealing. There would be, almost certainly, the worrying about some senseless fight between warring party factions in Texas over which "side" was going to win which obscure post, then fending off complaints from unhappy participants from both sides. There would be listening to those who worried about rumors that the senator sometimes engaged in activities not calculated to earn him a priesthood. And there would be those occasional staff problems, minor in themselves, but nevertheless emotionally draining.

Once, for instance, one member of our staff, an attractive young lady from San Antonio, caught the eye of Senator Teddy Kennedy, then a younger man-about-the-Senate. She had headed for the Senate gallery during her lunch period, one presumes to observe proceedings. On the way she had picked up an ice cream cone, and was awaiting the arrival of an elevator reserved for senators and staff when an interested Ted Kennedy took note, wondering who she was and what she was doing. She replied she was trying to put on some weight, whereupon the distinguished senator gazed for a moment, finally observing (as the two rode the elevator by themselves) that there was nothing wrong with her figure, that it was just perfect the way it was. Her little heart went pitter-patter and thus began an acquaintance that finally led to her leaving the staff. She would go to the gallery when she had word he was to be on the floor, wave to him, he would leave the floor, and they would ride up and down the restricted elevator. He, according to the young lady, referred to her as Miss Texas, which thrilled her mightily. Personally I did not care how close she and Teddy became, but she insisted on relaying it all to other staff members in living color and during working hours. Eventually other members of the staff approached me, insisting that something be done, that her frequent recounting of the latest episode was becoming a disruptive distraction during working hours. I called her in, we discussed the matter, and I suggested she might be happier working somewhere else. She moved downtown, going to work for a stockbroker.

I am sure the entire affair was entirely innocent. She, no doubt, was merely trying to further her education in the working of the Senate, and the senator, always concerned with furthering the education of young women, was fortunately happy to be of help.

But most distressing of all during that period, there would be the phone calls from mothers or fathers distraught over losing a son on the battlefields of Vietnam in a war growing increasingly unpopular. We had an arrangement in our office where late night telephone calls were bounced to our home in Virginia. It is not pleasant to be awakened to the voice of a sobbing mother who had gotten word that her son was killed in a war she did not understand in a country she knew nothing about, but the gory details of which she had witnessed nightly in her living room.

And I could do nothing about it.

It was as if our role was changing, from being part of the battlefield force to the Army of Occupation. I realize, as much as anyone, that the goal of politics is to become and remain the Army of Occupation, but it is a role that has never appealed to me. It is a necessary role, in politics even more than in war, but it is a role to which I am not well suited.

Also, I had gone to Washington with the intention of staying two years, learning all I could about the intricacies of that place, and then returning to the world of newspapers and newspaper reporters. It was important to me that I did not allow myself to become entrapped by the system, so dependent on it, so enthralled by it, that I would be willing to compromise my own beliefs in order to stay. I was so determined to follow that course that I had not even entered into the Senate's lucrative retirement system for its employees. I did not want any extraneous influences exerting pressure when the time came to leave. But now that time had passed, with a year to spare. Should I not now begin looking for other things to do?

I suppose it could be argued that I had the best of worlds, a world in which I should have been content. The senator did his thing. He immersed himself in his Armed Services Committee work and left the running of the staff, and the worries of the mundane political world, to me. He had never really enjoyed the hands-on, nitty-gritty details of politics or government unless they dealt with what he regarded as the bigger picture. Now, with the election behind him, he could devote his time to that bigger picture. From the standpoint of a staff member in Washington, it should have been an ideal situation. He was not prone to second guessing how I ran the staff, and I was generally happy with his political posture in the Senate. I should have been content, but I was not.

One reason was that we had a somewhat different relationship after his reelection. The campaign had left a few raw nerves that would take time to heal. There were times I had to lean on him rather heavily during that effort. There were also times I had to make changes on the staff he did not appreciate. In the political world, that does not make for happiness. In my own view they probably contributed to his continuing in office, but I'm not sure he saw it that way. Even if he did, the end result was the same. We no longer had those long, intimate and rambling conversations at the end of the day, where he was sometimes wont to pour out his personal trials and tribulations. His thoughts, particularly as they related to the future, were now much more closely held. I would not say our relationship was strained; it was just not as close as it once was.

Another reason for my unhappiness was that I could not determine how the senator wanted to posture himself in the political struggles ahead, or indeed if he had an interest in such things. I could not determine whether he intended to be a leader in the cause with which he had so recently been identified, that being the conservative movement that had nominated Goldwater, or if he hoped merely to be a passive beneficiary of that movement. To me it was important, since it would determine how we might respond to political developments in the state, and in the nation for that matter. But in this area I got precious little guidance.

Shortly after we returned to Washington following the election, I was visited by a man of some influence in the national party and in Washington. He had been a figure in the Cabinet of former President Eisenhower. He was not a "lobbyist," per se, but his firm represented, legally, what might be called the backbone of America's industrial might. He wanted to discuss a matter with the senator.

We met at a newly opened watering hole on the House side, called, if memory serves, The Rotunda. The food was good, the drinks were satisfactory, and the waitresses were very pretty. He paid the bill, which made it even better.

It was not my first visit with the gentleman. Not long after I arrived on the scene in Washington he had asked for a meeting, during which he had expressed his disappointment with certain aspects of the senator's service, and urged me to do what I could to make matters better. He said, for instance, that when Tower first came to the Senate, "there were many of us who were very happy. We thought we had in Tower the ideal choice for a vice-presidential nominee in the near future. He was intelligent, articulate, he was from the South, he had all the credentials." But Tower's early months had indicated to them that he, like many senators, was more interested in the fanfare, fun and frivolities of the Senate than in the work of the Senate. He was just not giving out signals that he wanted to be, or would be, around long enough to be taken seriously. I should try, he said, to be helpful in this regard.

But now things were different. Tower was on the Armed Services Committee, where he was earning a reputation as an interested, involved, hard-working member. He had, as they saw it, "buckled down." He had won reelection against a respected opponent. He now appeared in a different light.

His proposal was simple enough, but it was one with profound implications. He had been a supporter of Goldwater, as had Tower. Goldwater was gone. The conservative cause now had no clearly defined standard bearer at the national level. It needed one. In the absence of that there was danger, in his view and in the view of those for which he purported to speak.

Tower was the logical choice. He hoped Tower would claim that ground. If Tower would agree, if he would write an article suitable for magazine publication, he would then see to it that the article was widely published. Such an article would, by implication, claim that ground. In fact, groundwork for that had already been laid. *Reader's Digest*, with a circulation of many millions, had agreed to its publication. It was bound, given the politics of the moment, to receive widespread notice.

I was struck by the similarities between this conversation and the one we had had a couple of years earlier in the Cosmos Club. But this individual had not been part of that meeting, and, as a supporter of Goldwater, would have been appalled that it was taking place. Now times were different. A different situation confronted us.

Tower and I returned to the office and discussed the matter. At first he seemed inclined to move in that direction, but he wasn't sure.

I hoped he would. But I told Tower he should think the matter through, understanding that once he raised the flag it could not be put down "except in defeat." There well might be others who, in time, would want to hold up the standard, and unless he was prepared to defend his position he ought not raise it in the first place. To claim the ground and then abandon the field would do him no good in the long run. And I warned that it would be a consuming endeavor, many demands would be made upon his time. He would have to decide what course he wanted to follow, how he would achieve his own goals.

The conversation ended with him saying, "I'll think about it."

During the following days I would occasionally check with him to see if he had made a decision. He hadn't. Finally, he said "Aw, Ken, just write 'em something."

I took that to mean he had made no firm commitment to see the matter through. I wrote nothing. He never asked about it. It was never discussed again.

I have no way of knowing what thinking went into his decision. I felt he had decided, for the moment at least, to devote his time and energy to matters of the Senate, to his position in the "club." That was where he was most comfortable. From his perspective it probably was a wise decision. From mine it was something of a disappointment.

SIXTEEN

In the Trenches of Party Politics

The next two years would hold tremendous historical import for the nation, but, as earlier mentioned, they were perhaps the unhappiest, personally, of all my years spent in Washington. To watch, helplessly, while the nation's universities passed from bastions of learning to havens for draft dodgers, to see the flag of the Communist Viet Cong paraded down the streets of our cities while the cream of America's youth fought and died in Vietnam, to see a beleaguered American president essentially held hostage in the White House save for occasional visits to military installations, was, to be honest, almost more than I could bear. Each time I witnessed the American flag being desecrated, there reappeared the prison camp scenes of grinning, conquering Japanese soldiers unrolling our flag, spreading it on the ground and using it as a tablecloth for their evening meal, in full view of defeated, starving prisoners.

I thought a lot about leaving, of going back to the world of private citizens, but there always seemed to be one more problem to deal with. Not big problems, nor important problems, only problems that loomed large and important in the eyes of the beholder. In the world of politics or government, there are many beholders.

In some ways I felt trapped. The senator followed his own star, or stars, and I ran the office as best I could. It was not the easiest of chores, given the fact that about the only guidance I had been given along those lines was an allegorical story from his navy days. He recounted that his ship's captain had told the executive officer, or the second in command, that his principal duty was to see that the captain got credit when things went right, and the executive officer got blamed when things went wrong. The comment was relayed with good humor, but I got the message, with which I had no quarrel. In the final analysis it meant his best interests were my best interests, though the reverse of that was not necessarily true.

Nor did we always agree on what was in his best interest.

Several events of a political nature stand out in my memory as being relatively important, to me, during those years. One involved the handling of the Vietnam War, during which I lost whatever lingering respect I ever had for Lyndon Johnson as anything but the compleat politician.

Another involved a secretive, ultimately aborted, attempt by Tower to run for the presidential nomination in 1968.

Another was the selection of Paul Eggers to be the Texas Republican gubernatorial nominee for that same year.

Still another involved the nomination of Richard Nixon for president, and my selection to run his campaign in Texas.

In August of 1964, after Johnson had been in office for some nine months, the Vietnamese attacked, or were alleged to have attacked, ships of the U.S. 7th Fleet in international waters. Johnson seized upon this incident to push through the so-called "Tonkin Gulf Resolution," giving him broad powers to conduct essentially unlimited military operations against North Vietnam.

Until that time there had been a large question in my own mind concerning the legality of American operations in Vietnam. I had no quarrel with the idea of helping a small, struggling nation defend itself against the clear designs of its Communist neighbor. But I thought the effort should have been clothed in constitutional legality, which I did not see as then being the case. And I felt, and still feel, that any time American servicemen are committed to foreign battlefields, they should go there wrapped in the American flag, sustained by the moral commitment of their own nation.

I felt the same way about America's involvement in Korea under Harry Truman. Merely calling the Korean War a "police action," as Truman did, did not satisfy my own understanding of what a war was. And the Constitution clearly gave Congress the power and responsibility to declare war, as I read it.

(Tower and I did not see eye to eye on this issue. He felt the president had ample legal authority under the Constitution, by virtue of his responsibility as commander in chief, to commit American troops to battle in accordance with treaty obligations.)

But those "legalities" aside, I felt some congressional expression of national commitment was needed to sustain the Vietnam effort over the long haul, rather than a continuation of the piecemeal escalation begun under Kennedy and continued under Johnson. Without that expression of national commitment, there was a danger, as I saw it, of the effort becoming known as "the president's war," embroiled in politics, rather than the country's war, sustained by patriotic endeavor.

So I welcomed the Tonkin Gulf Resolution, which passed the Congress with only a few dissenting votes and, as far as I was concerned, then gave American involvement in the war a color of legality and national commitment. The Tonkin Gulf Resolution was essentially a declaration of war, even if it fell short of saying so in so many words. At that time the country was overwhelmingly supportive of the Vietnam effort, as reflected in the congressional vote. I hoped the resolution would give the president enough political backbone to prosecute the war and get it over with quickly. I hoped it would take politics out of a war that threatened to divide the country, prolong it, and cause many more casualties than would otherwise be the case.

Passage of the resolution had the desired effect, at least for a while. The lopsided vote in favor of passage tended to mute both congressional and editorial criticism, and gave needed political strength to those of us who wanted to win the war quickly and get out. It did little, however, to change the mind of America's left, those fundamentally sympathetic to a victory by the Communist regime of North Vietnam and the defeat of their own country's policies in Southeast Asia. And that goal of America's left, in my view, was aided and assisted by an unfair and inequitable national military draft policy which allowed hundreds of thousands of young men to hide out in universities at home and abroad while their less affluent and less cowardly peers slogged through the jungles of Vietnam, doing what their country asked of them, so long as they lived.

Passage of the Tonkin Gulf Resolution also seemed to do little to change the fundamental nature of Lyndon Johnson or the way he ran the war. Trapped by those in his administration whom he termed "nervous nellies," he cowered at the prospect of the Chinese entering the war on the side of North Vietnam. The fact that the Chinese were then embarking upon a long "cultural revolution" that would engulf that country, rendering it incapable of massive intervention abroad, seemed to escape the president's thinking, and that of his policy advisers as well.

The result was that in time the grumbling, and the opposition, increased. Senator William Fulbright, chairman of the Senate Foreign Relations Committee, a constant critic of the use of American military might anywhere in the world (and the benefactor of a young staff member named Bill Clinton, who would one day become president of the United States), complained that Johnson had misled the Congress concerning the nature of the Tonkin Gulf attack on U.S. ships. Fulbright began making noises on the Hill that he would hold hearings on the matter. I felt if he did that, and if he were able to cloud the issue, nothing but disaster would ultimately ensue. No matter if he were successful in proving his own point that Johnson had lied to the nation concerning the attack. The result would be a more divided country, a longer war, and more casualties.

I called the White House and talked to George Christian, an old friend from days in Texas and at that time Johnson's press secretary, telling him I had a subject I wanted to talk about, and one to which I attached some importance. He said he would have someone get in touch, and within a matter of hours I received a call from Jake Jacobsen, then acting as the White House legislative liaison with the Senate. This was the same Jake Jacobsen whom I had run into on the floor of the Texas Senate, "carrying water" for Johnson many years before, at a time when the governor, Price Daniel, thought that Jacobsen was "carrying water" for him. And it was the same Jake Jacobsen who would ultimately charge John Connally with accepting a bribe for influencing the price of milk subsidies for American dairymen, a charge for which Connally was ultimately tried and acquitted.

I laid out my concerns to Jake, telling of the rumblings I had heard among fellow staff members in the Senate. I thought there was potential for danger. There was still overwhelming support in Congress, I thought, but it would be wise for them to send us another resolution along the lines of the Tonkin Gulf Resolution. Then the Congress could debate the matter and pass it, again overwhelmingly. That should put the matter to rest, or at least put to rest the question of congressional support. We could get on with the war and get it over with.

Jake listened patiently. We had supported the president's handling of the war, sometimes to our own detriment. I suppose he figured he owed us the courtesy of at least listening. Then he said, "Ken, we've already considered that. In fact we've discussed it at great length. But we've got problems."

He then explained. Many Democratic congressmen didn't want the issue raised again. They would have to run in their primary with Vietnam around their neck. They wanted it left alone. Mostly, he said, the problem was from the congressmen "up East," among the liberal Democrats. While their districts, taken as a whole, were supportive of the president's Vietnam position, within their own Democratic Party primary it could prove a divisive and troubling issue. That might cause the seat to be lost to a Republican.

The president needed their votes on other issues, particularly his Great Society programs, and he was not willing to put them at risk. The liberal congressmen felt the president, as leader of the party, "owed" them his support in this since they had stood with him in a cause they were not particularly fond of. In the end the president agreed. Either that or his advisers agreed and convinced him accordingly.

I put down the phone in a deeply troubled state. It was no surprise that politics loomed large in Johnson's thinking. That had always been the case. He had demonstrated as much in the circumstances surrounding his "defeat" of Coke Stevenson, in his willingness to accept victory on the wings of fraudulent, stolen votes. But that he was willing to risk the lives of thousands of men in what was surely to be a protracted struggle simply for the sake of protecting the fortunes of self-serving members of his own party, thereby protecting his own political security, struck me as being completely beyond the pale.

In effect, as I saw it, liberal support for the troops in Vietnam was being held hostage by Johnson's Great Society programs. And Johnson, unwilling to see his domestic priorities placed in danger, was willing to pay the price. After all, it was not his life, not his blood.

I have no way of knowing, but I suspect there came a time when Johnson wished he had handled things differently during those critical days. At any rate, my lasting impression of the character of Lyndon Johnson was determined by that episode and its ultimate aftermath.

The war finally played itself out. A divided, confused nation saw its troops politically abandoned at home and stalemated on the fields of battle. Not because of any lack of valor on their part, but because of a lack of valor on the part of political "leaders" at home worried about their own survival. Worried that if they were defeated for office they would be thrust back into the world from which they had come — a most unwelcome thought. Before it did run its course, however, Lyndon Johnson would be driven from office, a deserving victim, in my view, of the kind of politics he had nurtured and that had nurtured him.

Perhaps if Lyndon Johnson had grown up in war, as had I, he would have seen things differently. And perhaps if I had grown up in politics, as had he, I would have seen things differently. I suppose each of us must view the scene from our own corner of the street.

And it is somewhat ironic that Johnson was driven from office by people like Bill Clinton, who would one day occupy his place in the White House, lauded and fawned over by many of the same people who lauded and fawned over Lyndon Johnson when he was there.

The months passed. Tower immersed himself in work on the Armed Services Committee, took more trips to Vietnam, and became increasingly active in speaking engagements across the country, quite often in California for reasons I did not then understand, other than for the "honorariums" involved. It was a time in which he increasingly kept his own counsel. We visited occasionally about the political scene in Texas, but seldom about the national political scene. He voiced concerns about what might happen relative to the governor's race in 1968 and who the candidate might be, but voiced no preference to me about the matter. On one occasion, in what I took to be mostly idle speculation, he even toyed with the thought of running for the office himself. He voiced the opinion that if he did run, and if he were successful, "I would probably be regarded as something of a liberal." I asked why. There was just so much that needed to be done, he answered. Primarily in the field of education, and in the Texas tax structure. Anyone who tried to change things, he said, would probably be portrayed in the press as something of a liberal. I found that somewhat strange, since conservatives in the Senate were in such a minority, and they were always trying to change things, mostly without success. I also found his occasional preoccupation with the subject somewhat strange, since he normally seemed so consumed with things on the national level.

On the national scene it was becoming apparent within political ranks that Richard Nixon was going to make a run for the presidency, a development that left me with mixed emotions. Even though he had contributed yeoman service during the congressional elections of 1966, he had, I felt, played footsie with the Rockefeller forces in 1964. I then saw him as one who would not stand hitched to those political ideals I thought any aspirant for that office ought to treasure, as one who was motivated by a desire to be president only for the sake of being president. In that regard I did not see much difference between him and Lyndon Johnson, or others who would come later and whom I saw as being driven by the same affliction. I still had strange ideas about the office of president and who should seek to occupy it.

Nevertheless, the party's leadership in Texas coalesced around Nixon, primarily, I thought, because he was likely to be the more "centrist" potential candidate, and that such a candidate was needed to pull the party's factions together. Or, if not pull them together, at least let them live together for a reasonable period of time.

It was against this backdrop that I got a call from a highly disturbed Peter O'Donnell in Dallas, the state's party chairman. Never one to waste telephone time with idle chit-chat, Peter came directly to the point.

What was this business of John Tower running for the presidential nomination?

I didn't know what he was talking about, and said so. I got the impression quickly that Peter didn't quite believe me.

"You mean he's made a decision like this without talking it over with the staff, or with us?"

I repeated my comments that I didn't know what he was talking about, that Tower had never mentioned anything like that to me. Not only that, there must be some misunderstanding, for I was sure nothing like that would happen.

He said he had received phone calls from friends in California telling him that they had been contacted by Tower or agents of Tower, soliciting financial backing for a run for the presidency. They were confused. They thought the Texas leadership was backing Nixon. They were seeking guidance.

I could offer no help. I told Peter I knew Tower had been spending a good bit of time in California on speaking engagements, but as far as I knew that's all it was. I knew he had developed some contacts there, one of which was an actor named Drury, but I assumed that was primarily for the purpose of assuring future campaign financing.

"We'll see about that," he said.

And within short order he did. Another of those meetings was called in Austin, attended by Peter, Tower, myself, and some six or eight of the party's political and financial leaders, including, if memory serves, Anne Armstrong. All were capable, if so inclined, to speak directly. It was not a pleasant affair, at least not at first. Tower was, in effect, put "on the carpet." O'Donnell told him he was "muddying the waters." He was asked to explain.

The senator did not deny that O'Donnell's reports were accurate. He went on to say that he knew he could not, and would not, obtain the nomination, but he felt a campaign effort would "provide a forum" to get his thoughts considered in the national political arena.

At that point O'Donnell turned to me and asked for my thoughts. I suspected he expected me to support Tower in his arguments, which I might have been willing to do. After all, I had always encouraged him to be involved in shaping the party's thoughts.

But first I asked, "Senator, what forum would it give you, in terms of getting your thoughts considered, that you do not already have by virtue of being a United States senator?"

The question was not asked to humiliate the senator, nor to cut the ground from under him. It was meant to give him an opportunity to expand on his explanation that he intended to make the move in order to have a forum for his views. He had, after all, turned down previous opportunities to do just that.

It did not have the effect intended.

There was a momentary silence. Tower seemed to be struggling for a rationale. Then, in an unhappy scene that stuck in my memory, he seemed to wilt, and said merely, "Well, nobody can say I surround myself with 'yes men'."

He went on to say he would drop the effort. It had died aborning. The meeting went on to other matters. As far as I know it was never discussed again, at least not in my presence.

It soon became necessary for the party's leadership to address the question of who would be the "official" candidate for governor. Voting in Republican primaries had increased to the point where nominees had to be selected by primary, rather than by convention, but the rank and file still looked to the leadership for guidance in such matters. Also, any serious candidate knew he, or she, would probably need organizational and financial help. There was still no real cadre of potential candidates with statewide name recognition or following who could stand on their own, or who felt they could successfully challenge a candidate endorsed by the party's leadership.

There was one, Jack Cox, who had run a nearly successful race against John Connally for governor in 1962, and who would have won the race, in my view, had it not been for the Cuban missile crisis. I had covered that campaign and found him to be an enormously able candidate, every bit the match of Connally in terms of crowd appeal and in articulating his position on issues. But to that point he had given no real indication he was interested in the 1968 race. That is not to say that he would not become interested, nor is it to say that subsequent events proved at least some of the leadership was not concerned that he might become interested. In fact I had gained the impression, during my years of either following politics as a reporter or as something of a participant in party affairs as a member of Tower's staff, that Cox was not generally included in that group one might call "the party's leadership," despite the fact that he had been the party's standard bearer in some very difficult races. Seldom, if ever, was his advice asked, and seldom, if ever, was it given. Despite his grassroots Populist following, or perhaps because of that following, he was generally treated at arm's length.

I never really understood the reasons for what I regarded as the somewhat strained relationship between Cox and those who made up the party's leadership. He and Tower, for instance, seemed to have a personally cordial relationship. When in Austin, Tower quite often stayed at the 40 Acres Club, then run by Cox. There the visits were always friendly, but seldom ventured far into politics, at least when I was present.

A number of names were floated within party ranks, and even in the press, concerning potential candidates, but just as quickly faded away.

So still another of those meetings was called. This time the participants, roughly a dozen in number, and consisting of the national and state committee men and committee women, plus Tower and myself, O'Donnell, the state party's executive director, Marvin Collins, and a few traditional financial backers, met in a room on the ground floor of the old Driskill Hotel in Austin. It was in that area of the hotel occupied at one time by the Headliners Club, before it outgrew its quarters and moved elsewhere.

To the meeting were invited those few people who had indicated they were, or might be, interested in the party's nomination for governor. This was to be, in effect, a "screening" process. The party had grown to the point where candidates no longer had to be dragooned into offering themselves up as sacrificial lambs, although everyone understood that anyone who got the Republican nomination for governor would go into the race in a decidedly underdog position. John Connally had indicated he did not intend to run for a fourth term, but there was always the possibility he might change his mind. If he did not run the probability was great that the Democratic nominee would be the lieutenant governor, Preston Smith, who, while not exactly a forceful campaigner, was generally acceptable to the state's dominant conservative community. And that community, of course, was where any Republican candidate for governor would have to look for support. It was not the most propitious time to be running for governor on the Republican ticket.

Nevertheless, three potential candidates did show up, each at his scheduled time. There was B. K. Johnson, a South Texas rancher and part of the King Ranch extended family, former Democratic Attorney General Will Wilson (who had also served as a member of the State Supreme Court, as well as district attorney for Dallas County), and Paul Eggers, a Wichita Falls tax attorney and former Republican county chairman in Wichita Falls.

All were asked essentially the same questions: What did they consider their basic political strengths and weaknesses? Who, in a general sense, would be for them and who would be against them? How much money could they expect to bring into the campaign, either from personal wealth or in the form of help from friends? (The latter question was not so crass as it might sound. Those assembled knew they would be responsible, in the final analysis, for raising the money needed to run the race. The more the candidate could bring into the pot, the less they would have to raise.)

I do not remember the sequence of appearances before the group. But I do remember my impressions of the individuals as potential candidates. B. K. Johnson was, I thought, the more aggressive, the more determined of the lot. He could, he felt, bring $300,000 into the race, either in his own money or from his friends. Of the three, he was clearly the most financially comfortable. No doubt he had the resources to lead the charge, as far as I was concerned. But he had one caveat: He was a friend of John Connally, and would not oppose Connally should Connally decide to run again. The information around the table was that Connally would not run again. He understood that, but should Connally change his mind and decide to run we should be aware that he would not oppose Connally.

Will Wilson was clearly the most knowledgeable, the most thoughtful, but most reticent of the three. He was also exceedingly honest with the group. He thought they ought to know, for instance, that as attorney general, as district attorney, and as Supreme Court judge, he had made decisions that offended many groups. We could expect those people to oppose him in any race he joined, and that such opposition might rub off onto other candidates on the ticket. It was a degree of honesty I had not come to expect among politicians. In fact, it was left to me to wheedle from him the admission that for every group he made unhappy, he made another group happy; that he had strengths as well as weaknesses. Yes, that was true. But . . .

The impression I got from Eggers' presentation was that he thought it would be nice to be governor of Texas. He was a nice, cleancut sort, a native of Indiana with a good sense of humor, but he didn't know enough about state government to give the assembled group any indication of what he would do or which direction he would take. In terms of state government, he didn't know from Adam's off ox. As far as I was concerned, he brought nothing into the equation. No money, no experience, no ideas, no troops. His mind, as far as the details of state government were concerned, was essentially a blank slate. He would have to begin from ground zero. As matters would develop, that message was music to the ears of at least one member of the group, who would present his arguments later.

Eventually it came time to take a break. The presentations were over. Next on the agenda was to discuss what had transpired and then to vote. Tower and I went aside. I told him I really did not believe I should vote on the matter. I was, after all, merely a hired hand. I would not be called on to contribute any substantial sums of money for the cause. I would not be held responsible for decisions made that turned out to be bad decisions; therefore I did not think I ought to vote on the matter. And by the same token, I did not think any other staff member, or hired hand, ought to vote on the matter (and here I was thinking of the party's executive director, Marvin Collins). Tower readily agreed, and indeed jumped at the suggestion. When the group reconvened he offered a motion along those lines which was also readily accepted, that when it came time to vote, the vote would exclude paid staffers. It had the practical effect of saying that Collins and I could not vote, which was entirely satisfactory to me.

In the meantime the small group milled about, drinking coffee and weighing what had gone before. Tower and I returned to the group. One of the women, I cannot remember now if it was Anne Armstrong, or Virginia Streeter (who later became the wife of Paul Eggers), or Rita Bass (who later became the wife of Bill Clements), approached me and asked how I was going to vote. I told her I did not think I was going to vote, but if I had a vote it would be between Will Wilson and B. K. Johnson.

"The first person I would scratch would be this guy Eggers," I said.

I saw nothing in him, at that time, that would add strength to the party, much less win the governor's chair. He knew next to nothing about state government. His highest political office had been party chairman in a county not then known for any Republican proclivities. My own choice would be to lean to Wilson.

We reconvened. Anne Armstrong told the group she had received a call from B. K. Johnson, wishing his name to be withdrawn from consideration. He had had second thoughts, whatever they were. The choice was then between Wilson and Eggers. Much talk ensued. Finally, Tower took the floor. His own choice, he said in a long and impassioned speech, was Paul Eggers. He was a fresh face. He had no scars. He could and would learn. True, no one had heard of him. But that was Tower's own situation when the party leadership picked him to run for the Senate against Lyndon Johnson. Yes, it would take a great deal of money to introduce him to the electorate, but we would just have to find that money somewhere.

Finally, Tower added, as if an afterthought, "and he will be amenable to the wishes of the party leadership." He was very skilled about such things.

The vote was taken. I was happy I had no vote. The decision was to go with Eggers, largely, I thought, on the strength of Tower's impassioned plea. And the strength of Tower's plea, I thought, was based largely on three factors: Eggers was a friend, he was a "fresh face," and he would be "amenable to the wishes of the party leadership."

What then?

They had a candidate for governor. Nothing could exclude anyone else from offering his or her name in the primary, but this was the one they had settled on, for good or ill. His name would go out as the anointed one. It was not likely the endorsed nominee would face serious challenge in the upcoming Republican primary.

But what would happen when the man was introduced to the press? What sort of an impression would he make when he started answering questions? Clearly, he had to be brought up to speed, or at least as close to speed as possible. He could perhaps be forgiven for not having any vast plans at that date for his governorship, should he ever arrive at that point. But he could hardly be forgiven for exhibiting total ignorance of the office he sought.

I was assigned the task of trying to rectify that situation. He proved an exceptionally willing, intelligent, and inquiring student. He readily admitted he was operating in the dark, but he seemed to truly want to learn.

After a few hours, however, it became apparent that much more time would be needed. Besides, I had to get back to Washington. We called in John Knaggs, a former newsman and then an Austin-based Republican political operative, to take over the task. I don't know how John did it, but within a reasonable period of indoctrination Eggers managed to get through his initial presentation to the public without too much embarrassment. Knaggs obviously had more patience with such matters than I.

The selection of Eggers did not end the matter. The Austin meeting took place during the latter part of January, leaving a week or so until the February 5 filing deadline for governor.

Tower and I returned to Washington, leaving the political education of Paul Eggers in the hands of Knaggs and whomever he might find necessary to include in the instructional process. Tower seemed very pleased, somewhat like the cat that had swallowed the canary. I was very worried. I thought we had selected the weakest candidate. I still feel that way. For, while Eggers did go on to be a reasonably good candidate, losing to a conservative Democrat, Preston Smith, by about 400,000 votes out of nearly 3 million cast, he did little to identify the party with anything other than better management of whatever was in place. That is an affliction that still plagues many Republican politicians.

Within a few days of our return to Washington, I began hearing rumblings in the ranks. Jack Cox, who, as far as I know or knew, had not been consulted about who should be the anointed candidate, was unhappy with the leadership's choice. He had told friends he might just run for governor himself. I told Tower. He put it down as insignificant, as the understandable thoughts of someone who had had his day in the sun but who wished to remain a player. He really did not think it would amount to much.

The weekend came. The office was closed down. When we

returned to work on Monday morning, February 5, which was also the filing deadline for candidates for governor, our reports from Texas were that Cox was indeed serious. He intended to file before the midnight deadline.

Tower was furious. I had never seen him in such a state.

"Why is he doing this to me?" he shouted rhetorically. "I throw a lot of business his way," he said, referring, I supposed, to his frequent stays at Cox's 40 Acres Club. Somehow he saw it as a betrayal, a challenge to his own leadership. He determined he would just go to Texas and file for governor himself.

I tried to reason with him. That would be the worst possible thing that could happen, I argued. But no amount of argument on my part made any difference. So agitated was he that he picked up pencils from his desk, broke them in pieces, and flung the pieces about the room. He was, in short, beside himself. It was completely unlike Tower, who had always maintained an air of stability and calm in almost any situation.

But now, I suppose, he saw his best laid plans going out the window. If Cox entered the race he would no doubt beat Eggers in any Republican primary, which would be a reflection upon his own strength since he had championed Eggers and persuaded the party leadership to endorse him. If Cox beat Eggers the party would be bound to support him. But Cox had indicated privately he preferred Ronald Reagan over Richard Nixon in the political maneuverings of the moment. If Cox won, the party's standard bearer would be at odds with the party's leadership, who had determined to support Nixon. It would be an intolerable situation, one he was determined to prevent.

Tower had a secretary arrange airline passage to Austin. There was time. He could arrive there minutes before the midnight filing deadline, and he was determined to make it. No arguments of mine could prevent it. He left for Dulles Airport to catch his plane.

I immediately called Austin and talked to Marvin Collins, asking him to contact his chairman, Peter O'Donnell, and apprise him of the situation. It was my hope that they could put an end to the matter. I also called Nola Smith, who was in charge of our Austin office, informing her of the situation, telling her Tower was on his way to Austin, and asking her to do all she could, once Tower reached there, to persuade him of the folly of his actions. She promised she would.

Fortunately, by the time Tower arrived at Dulles Airport some thirty miles west of Washington he had cooled down somewhat, and was a little more receptive to rational argument. A phone call was waiting for him from Marvin Collins, who told Tower, according to what Collins told me later, that his proposed course of action was unthinkable, that it would tear the party apart in Texas, that it was the worst thing he could do.

For whatever reason Tower decided to abandon his plan to run for governor. He returned to Washington. Cox decided, in the final analysis, not to run either, and Eggers went on to win the primary over two little known challengers, John Trice and Wallace Sisk, before losing to Preston Smith.

Things returned to normal, but only for a very short time. The Tower–Cox affair had not yet run its course. There was still the matter of the upcoming State Convention in Corpus Christi, where delegates would be chosen for the National Convention in Miami that summer. Richard Nixon had emerged as what is called "the apparent front-runner" for the nomination, and support for him had firmed among those in the party who influenced such things. Given all the givens I assumed the party would send a delegation to Florida pledged to work for Nixon's nomination.

Cox, however, saw it differently. Still smarting from the recent flap concerning the gubernatorial thing, he let it be known he would oppose such a course of action at the convention, where he was likely to find many kindred souls who were less than enthusiastic about Nixon. My own view was that he was hoping to send an uninstructed delegation, which would provide time for the Reagan forces to gather their strength; that is, of course, if he finally decided to make the race. At that time a small cell of devoted followers, men like Lyn Nofziger, Tom Reed and others, were busily pushing the California governor but were not getting much help from Reagan. Time was important to them, and I felt Cox, who preferred Reagan over Nixon, was at least hoping things would work that way even if he was not a part of their team. And, I would have to admit, it is possible that Cox had other motives. It would, after all, demonstrate that he still had significant strength among the party's grassroots, to the chagrin of the party's leadership. Unless something was done to put a lid on the situation we were facing the prospects of a bitterly divided, acrimonious convention on the eve of what should be a harmonious show of support for Nixon.

I suggested to Tower what I thought would be a way out. Why didn't he work toward having the delegates pledged to him as a "favorite son"? Surely the delegates would go for that. Cox could hardly oppose having Tower lead the delegation in that capacity. My reasoning was that it would serve the purposes of both Tower and Cox. Tower could keep the delegation together until Miami. Cox could save face and at the same time feel he was instrumental in a measure of peace. It should enhance the ego of both, which, in politics, is no small consideration. Indeed, for some it is the only consideration.

Tower seemed pleased with the suggestion. It would solve many problems. But he was in no position to make it work. That would be up to Peter O'Donnell.

In truth it would. O'Donnell was then the party's wheelhorse. Not only was he a master organizer, he understood strategy and tactics as well as any and better than most. By the time the delegates gathered in April the details had been worked out. There was a flurry of support for Reagan, but it was contained. Cox gave a rousing, emotional "unity" speech which brought the delegates to their feet. It must have been most satisfying to him. He endorsed the resolution naming Tower as the favorite son, with the delegates pledged to support him "until released after consultation with the delegation," and pledged his support. He said all the right things. A degree of harmony and peace prevailed.

The convention concluded. I returned to the hotel suite, where Lou Tower and a few staff members awaited Tower's arrival. He showed up shortly, having been delayed to accept the usual congratulations and that sort of thing. He seemed very pleased, and understandably so. With a little help he had, after all, contained the Jack Cox problem. And the Ronald Reagan problem.

Then Tower announced, to no one in particular, that "at the appropriate time" he intended to announce that he was throwing his support to Nixon.

Lou asked, "What's the appropriate time, John?"

"I figure in about seven or eight days," he answered.

Lou looked at me and I at her. Neither of us said anything.

It was not what I expected. There had been no doubt that eventually Tower would make that move, but I anticipated it at the Miami convention or much closer to it than seven or eight days after the Corpus Christi gathering. It would be seen by many, I thought, as a betrayal of trust and would likely cause bitterness where just a few hours earlier harmony had prevailed.

The terms of the resolution said Tower was to head the delegation as a favorite son nominee until he released them from that pledge "after consultation with the delegation." It was now apparent he was going to make a personal endorsement of Nixon "within seven or eight days." But was he also going to release the delegation from their own pledge to support him as the favorite son nominee? And did he intend to consult with them first, as the resolution demanded? If he consulted with them, and if the consensus was that they did not wish to be released, what then?

These were matters we discussed once back in Washington. It was clear Tower hadn't thought it all the way through, which would have been somewhat unusual for him when it came to politics, or he had thought it through very carefully and determined to use this tactic to demonstrate his command of the situation.

He was a great believer in the philosophy that says, in effect, "There's no reason to have power if you aren't willing to use it." Now he had the power and he proposed to use it. I had no quarrel with the philosophy. Within reason it makes good sense, in both politics and war. There is an ancient Chinese maxim, for instance, that says, "You kill the chicken to frighten the monkey." Which means, I presume, that the watching monkey gets the message. The message being that one is willing, even anxious to use power — so beware.

But my own view is that power used simply for the sake of demonstrating power tends to dissipate power in the long run. We talked. In the end he delayed his endorsement for an additional week and released the delegates from their pledge. How much actual consultation he did is unknown to me.

Actually, by then it didn't make that much difference. The political tea leaves said Nixon was going to get the nomination with or without the Texas delegation and with or without Tower's endorsement. But by coming out for him in May, some three months before the August National Convention in Miami, Tower did earn some political brownie points with Nixon, which stood him in good stead with the future president, even if it did cause rumblings in the ranks of the delegates.

I attended the Miami convention in the capacity of observer, more than anything else. Some months earlier O'Donnell and others in the leadership asked if I would agree to take leave from Tower's office and come to Texas to direct Nixon's campaign in the state. It appeared then that Nixon was probably going to get the nomination, and O'Donnell wanted to hit the ground running when it happened. I was reluctant to take on the assignment. I wasn't all that enamored of Nixon, for reasons indicated earlier. I wasn't opposed to him. I just wasn't enthusiastic about him. He was an ardent anti-Communist, which I thoroughly agreed with. But once that political factor was laid aside, it was difficult for me to determine just what he stood for.

On the "social issues" of the day, he seemed prone to carry water on both shoulders, and I've long since learned to look askance at politicians of that stripe. Too, there was real concern on my part that we could carry Texas for Nixon. There was no great reservoir of popular support for him. In a two-way race with Hubert Humphrey, Nixon would win, according to polls I had seen, simply because Humphrey was so poorly thought of. But it wasn't going to be a two-way race. George Wallace would be in the race as a third-party candidate and would carve out a large segment of socially conservative voters Nixon needed to win.

Still, when O'Donnell said, "Ken, if you can't pull it out, I don't know of anyone who can," I succumbed. After all, few of us are immune to flattery. I agreed, pending Tower's approval, which he gave after some hesitation. So in time I took leave from my Washington duties, and from my Washington payroll, and began the task of trying to pull the campaign together in Texas. In that capacity I went to Miami to watch, but to have no official part of the proceedings.

Most of the Texas delegation was lodged in a hotel owned and run by the Teamsters Union, a fact that afforded a rather close up view of arrogant, surly service. The waitress who brought the water could not bring the butter. The waitress who brought the butter could not bring the water. Neither could bring the silverware. It was "union rules."

A dead cockroach on the floor of my room when I checked in was still there when I checked out several days later. The bed would be made daily, but the person whose responsibility it was to remove dead cockroaches was evidently on leave, or resting somewhere. I started to undertake the task myself, but then decided I would just wait and see how long it took for the hired help to get around to the matter.

It never happened. When I checked out of the hotel the cockroach was still there.

In the Trenches of Party Politics

The official convention proceedings, which I watched on television in my room, went about as planned. Nixon got the nomination, and the next order of business was selecting the vice-president. Tower sat in with the little group of "advisers" Nixon chose to help him determine who that would be.

The group was meeting for that purpose when I decided to walk over to the convention arena, for no particular purpose. Our own hotel was largely devoid of people, most being over at the convention site. I pushed the elevator button and was waiting for it to come.

The door opened and there stood George Bush, then a congressman from Houston, alone in the elevator with two packed suitcases at his side. He was clearly unhappy.

I spoke a word of greeting, which went unanswered. I then said, "George, where are you going? This thing isn't over yet."

What I didn't know was that it was, as far as George was concerned.

Without a word he picked up his bags and walked past, leaving me perplexed. This was entirely unlike George. Normally, he was the friendliest of people, always ready to exchange pleasantries. Now he had a steely look in his eyes, oblivious to the present moment.

I walked over to the convention site and discovered the decision had been made, that Spiro Agnew had been selected as vice-presidential nominee by Nixon.

A few days later, back in Washington, Tower asked me, "Ken, what's wrong with George?" He went on to say that Bush, for some reason, was acting very cool toward him.

I told him "the word I get in the corridors" is that Bush felt Tower blocked his consideration for the vice-presidential spot. When Bush's name came up for consideration, rumor had it, Tower interposed objections, indicating he (Tower) thought Bush would add little or nothing to the ticket. Bush was, after all, much less known than Tower, and much less of a political influence throughout the South than Tower. There were dark insinuations, of course, that Tower felt if Nixon was to select someone from Texas, or the South, it should be Tower, not Bush.

"That's not the way it was at all," said Tower. He went on to explain.

Each time a name came up for consideration, said Tower, Nixon would channel the discussion into a comparison of that name to Agnew, who was a border state (Maryland) governor, and thereby should be acceptable to both North and South, had run and won a race against a Democrat who championed the peculiar, old-fashioned notion that "a man's home is his castle." (Which was, at that time, a sort of code phrase in the ongoing battle over "civil rights.") Many Maryland black voters had supported Agnew, despite the fact he ran as a Republican. Nixon thought this support might spill over into the presidential race. It should also cause a warm feeling on the part of many liberals in the media.

A futile hope.

It soon became apparent that Nixon wanted Agnew, although he wouldn't come straight out and say so. "So everybody just folded," said Tower. "He was the nominee, and if he wanted Agnew, the rest of us just said okay."

He did acknowledge that Bush's name was mentioned in the discussion, but he insisted he took no part in it.

I asked where Bush's support came from, for it struck me as somewhat strange that a young congressman would have the kind of support necessary to be considered seriously in such circumstances.

"Oh, it came mostly from that Chase crowd," Tower said, meaning, I presumed, from what we generally referred to as the "Eastern establishment," influenced heavily by the Chase Manhattan Bank headed then by David Rockefeller.

Nixon may well have figured he already had that support sewed up.

Tower went on to say he would talk to George and straighten the matter out, which I suppose he did, for after a while things returned to normal.

The way things turned out with Agnew, I suppose Nixon would have been wiser to select Bush, or almost anyone else. But in retrospect it seems he gave as much thought to the selection of a running mate as is usually the case. The Goldwater selection of Bill Miller, a little known New York congressman, or the Bush selection of Dan Quayle seemed to make no political sense to me.

Both were fine men, but neither, I thought, brought much in the way of political strength to the ticket. In many respects I thought Quayle stood on firmer philosophical ground than Bush, but if Republicans could count on carrying one state in the Union during that presidential race, it would have been Indiana, with or without Quayle. His selection also had the effect of placing a Senate seat at risk, which was subsequently lost. Quayle acquitted himself well as vice-president, but in a political sense he did not add much, if anything, to the Bush victory in 1988. By the same token, Miller's selection did nothing to prevent the magnitude of Goldwater's loss. I suppose a careful reading of history would indicate this is usually the case. Only rarely has a vice-presidential nominee figured in the ultimate victory of the winning ticket, the Kennedy–Johnson duo being an exception. More often than not in recent years, the vice-presidential nominee has served as campaign fodder for the opposition.

There are good and sufficient reasons for this.

In the first place, there is the human element. It would not be natural for any candidate, having emerged as the winner of his party's nomination, to deliberately go out and select an individual who clearly overshadowed him, or was even on a par with him, as his running mate. That would clearly be dangerous. Unless it is absolutely critical to his own election, the nominee will usually be looking for someone who does not detract from his own perceived lustre, who will serve, at best, as a dedicated neuter.

Secondly, there is the element of the American press. Along with other elements of what has become known as "the media" in America, the dominant press generally reflects an overwhelming liberal bias. And since the vice-presidential nominee is, almost by definition, the politically weaker of the two on the ticket, he becomes, if he has any conservative tendencies at all, the more tempting target, the comparative weakling only a heartbeat away from the presidency.

At any rate the Agnew selection proved a drag on the ticket and for other reasons a blot on the White House.

The next stop, as far as my own involvement was concerned, was back to Texas to begin work on the campaign.

THE CHOW DIPPER

SEVENTEEN

The Nixon Campaign

We entered upon the Nixon campaign in somewhat less than fortuitous circumstances. There were, to be honest, problems galore.

In the first place, trying to organize and run a statewide campaign as part of a national campaign is not the most enviable of jobs. Policy is set at the national level, and usually those policies are not designed for the benefit of any particular state. Positions taken at the national level, reflecting the candidate's position and a watered down "consensus" of ideas in many states, act to prevent the state organizations from championing policies that would assure victory within the individual states.

The result is that state campaigns, as part of national campaigns, are relegated primarily to explain and defend policies taken elsewhere. That and raise money, most of which flows to the national effort.

That was certainly true of the Nixon campaign. Nixon, for instance, had determined that he was going to run the kind of campaign that would make him acceptable to black (and centrist or "moderate") voters in the electorate without alienating fiscally conservative voters. That reflected not only his own personal stance on the civil rights battle then going on, but also reflected the presence of George Wallace as a third-party force in the election. It reflected as well on the political shrewdness of Richard Nixon and a degree of subservience, or "hush money," to the liberal Rockefeller forces who had helped torpedo the Goldwater campaign four years earlier.

Perhaps as an indication of the importance of this factor in the campaign, I should point out that as I was preparing to leave Washington for Texas to head up the campaign, I was asked to go to the

National Republican Committee to talk with the head of the party's "minorities" section. I was told we were going to make a push for black votes. And since I was regarded as the resident "reactionary," I might need a certain amount of indoctrination. I should talk to him to determine how it might be possible to attract large numbers of black voters to the Nixon banner.

This bright, delightful black man had a large office with plush carpets and a rather large polished desk. I could not help comparing it with my own quarters, where my secretary and I were confined, along with two desks and filing cabinets, to a space of approximately eight feet by ten feet, alongside the senator's office, which was considerably larger. It is my understanding that things have changed somewhat on Capitol Hill since then, but that is the way it was when I was there.

He leaned back, put his feet upon his desk, and we discussed the situation. He was aware of my problems, indeed very sympathetic to them. But he was honest and frank enough to say straight out that not many black folks were going to vote for Richard Nixon, especially with Hubert Humphrey on the ticket. He didn't want to discourage the effort, but he warned against getting our hopes up.

"Now, you'll go down there, and you'll organize a group of 'black people for Nixon,' or whatever name you give to it, and they will be with you right up until election time nears," he said.

"But when that ball starts rolling, they are going to desert you. We have many black people down there in the River Oaks section of Houston, who live in $200,000 homes [this was in 1968] and who ought to be with us. They are successful businessmen. But when that ball starts rolling they are going to desert you. They have to go get in the parade. They will have to identify with the masses, and who can blame them? That's where they make their living."

Without putting too fine a point on it, that is exactly how things turned out. We did have such an organization. We even had a number of bright, young volunteers from a local, and predominantly black, university in Houston who involved themselves in passing out campaign literature in that city's black community . . . until, that is, they were accosted, threatened with having their "legs broke" if they ever came back on the streets.

The leader of the troop explained to me, with tears in his eyes, that they were pulling out. He and his fellows were mere students. They were no match for street thugs. They were afraid, and anyone who understands the cultural and political life of Houston's East Side can also understand their fears. To put it mildly, our message did not receive widespread distribution within the black community of Texas' most populous county.

I could understand, from a political standpoint, Nixon's reluctance to clearly enunciate conservative positions. The party was still trying to come together after the Goldwater defeat. The press was still doing its thing in trying to discredit conservative political thought, and Nixon had no desire to raise those issues again. Besides, he had made his peace with the Rockefeller forces long before the convention. The best approach, from his standpoint, was to fuzz those issues that might tend to divide the party if they were met head on.

Such might have been possible outside of the South, but in the South it posed a problem. George Wallace was in the race, and he was no shrinking violet when it came to issues, social or economic. While he had neither the organization nor the money needed to sustain a viable nationwide campaign, he at least had the message needed to make him an influence in the South and in working neighborhoods elsewhere. So while I could understand Nixon's national strategy, it did not take long to see that it would be a major problem for us in Texas.

Our own campaign in Texas was not alone in facing this dilemma. Throughout the South, state campaign managers were complaining that Nixon's reluctance to face the Wallace problem was likely to cost us the election. Their pleas for a more aggressive approach to the issues on which Wallace was campaigning were first met with silence. But eventually the clamor grew so great that a meeting of Southern campaign managers was called at Callaway Gardens in South Carolina. So sensitive did the Nixon people view the subject that we were not to publicize the gathering or our attendance at it. Obviously it didn't, and couldn't, work out that way. It finally was billed, more or less, as merely a review of the campaign throughout the South. In point of fact it was a little more critical than that.

Wallace, despite his detractors, was a shrewd politician and an effective campaigner. He not only had rapport with his audience, he believed, or at least gave the appearance that he believed, his own message, something of a rarity in politics. He had tapped into the widespread resentment against federal "social planning" policies, both legislative and judicial, which many saw as potentially destructive of community schools, around which so much community cultural life centered. And for the record, the widespread decline in academic standards for public schools since that time suggests that those who worried did so with adequate cause.

The Nixon campaign team at the Callaway Gardens affair was headed by Fred LaRue, who would later go to prison for a minor part in the Watergate matter. He was a son of the South, originally from the Louisiana/East Texas country, and was completely familiar with the problems that worried the assembled managers. But he was also a completely loyal soldier for Nixon. We were just going to have to live with the policy. Nixon was not going to make concessions on account of the Wallace factor. There was nothing he could do that would "out-Wallace Wallace" even if he were so inclined, which he wasn't.

Nevertheless, by the time the meeting ended we did have from LaRue the promise they would look closely at one theme that kept coming up: that having to do with "freedom of choice" in public schools. The idea was resisted at first, as was even the use of the word "choice." But in the end Fred evidently became convinced it was something the Washington campaign management might find politically viable; that is, it might not cause too much backlash among the party's "moderate" wing. In time it did surface, in a sort of back-handed way, providing us a little breathing room.

I do not mean to sound so harsh on Nixon. He was a calculating politician, which was one of the keys to his success as a political leader. He had more to worry about than just the concerns of the South. But from the standpoint of those of us in the trenches, it was a most difficult situation. Humphrey on one side of us. Wallace on the other. The middle ground, in politics, fails to excite many troops. Especially if that middle ground is arrived at by virtue of reactions to dedicated positions on either side, rather than as a result of firm political convictions. In the end it may sometimes elicit the most votes, but it is rarely the most exciting place to be.

Given the constraints placed on us by the national campaign, our own effort in Texas was forced into the awkward position of trying to hold Wallace at bay without drawing too much attention to him, while pointing out the political sins of our principal opposition, Lyndon Johnson's vice-president, Hubert Humphrey, of which there were many.

Aside from organized labor, where Humphrey was popular, and the political left, where he was regarded as something of a godfather, Humphrey had little personal support in Texas. He was considered something of a loudmouth. As a senator from Minnesota he had actively and vociferously opposed the Texas claim to its oil-rich tidelands. He had always championed the political agenda of unions, a position not exceedingly popular in Texas generally, but one which stood him in good stead along the densely populated upper Gulf Coast region. He could expect, by virtue of his association with Lyndon Johnson (and, by extension, the politically corrupt George Parr regime), strong support among traditionally Democratic Hispanic voters in South Texas. He would be the beneficiary of the Democratic Party's strong control of county courthouses, as well as those state politicians still smarting over Johnson being driven from the White House by his party's divisions elsewhere, and anxious to demonstrate their support for the politically exiled architect of the Great Society by elevating his vice-president to the presidency. In short, we were up against a formidable foe, despite his own lack of a personal following in Texas. Circumstance made it so.

Our campaign went slowly forward, or sometimes forward. It seemed to me we spent more time being hammered than doing the hammering. We had an able state chairman, oilman John Hurd of Laredo, who ultimately served as ambassador to South Africa, and a young, highly dedicated finance chairman in Sam Wylie of Dallas, one of the early-day computer whiz kids. Sam had his work cut out for him, for problems with money were not long in coming. Looming in the background, of course, was the presence of Peter O'Donnell, the state party's chairman who shared the unenviable responsibility of seeing to it that the state not only went for Nixon, but that it also elected Paul Eggers as governor.

The first order of business in politics, as it operates in America at least, is money. Without money, there is little hope of getting the message out. Without the message, there is little hope of organization. Without the organization to deliver the message, the candidate is left to the tender mercy of his opposition, not the best position in which to be.

Shortly after arriving to begin the Nixon campaign I was greeted with the information that the Eggers campaign, to put it mildly, was "strapped for funds." That was exactly what I thought would happen when he was chosen back in January in the Driskill Hotel. At that time I could see no possibility that he could come up with the money needed to mount a viable campaign for governor.

In politics "little" money may follow conscience, but big money follows power. A presidential campaign would be under way, and most money would flow in that direction, for both Democrats and Republicans. In terms of the governor's race, most of the "big money" would be committed to the Democratic side. The Democratic nominee, Preston Smith of Lubbock, then the lieutenant governor, was acceptable to the state's monied interests, who saw no need to back a politically unknown Eggers. Money for the Eggers campaign was simply not forthcoming. It was a problem that not only plagued the Eggers campaign, but one which, by extension, impacted our own as well.

But it was worse. The Eggers campaign had entered into an agreement with a politically potent liberal Democratic Hispanic operative in San Antonio to work that community on behalf of Eggers. I do not know who had approached whom. I suspect the deal was brokered by a newly reconstituted Rebuilding Committee of activist liberals who had little love for Smith. At any rate the Eggers campaign had been convinced that for a certain and substantial amount of money (actually in the tens of thousands of dollars) the West Side political organizations, where County Commissioner Albert Pena held sway, could do wonders for Eggers. They did not particularly like Smith, whose political history was that of a conservative Democrat, but the denizens of San Antonio's West Side knew nothing of Eggers. Hence they were ripe for education — theoretically speaking, of course.

The problem now was that the Eggers campaign found itself with no money with which to honor the agreement. They looked to us for help, arguing that the money being taken out of the state for the Nixon campaign made it impossible to raise sufficient funds needed to sustain their own effort. It was a legitimate argument, but I did not see where that was my problem. I had entered into no such agreement. Besides, there was nothing in it for us. We had our own campaign to run.

Ah, but it quickly became my problem. There were dark hints out of the "organization" in San Antonio that if the money was not forthcoming they would go public with charges that "the Republicans" had approached them with offers of political bribes, and that they, being pure of heart and noble of spirit, had of course turned down the offer. In a practical sense there was no way we could come out of the matter looking even halfway innocent. The resulting furor would reflect on all Republican efforts, including that of Nixon.

THE CHOW DIPPER

So we negotiated. My position was that since no services had been performed, it would be best to agree to call it all off and everyone could go about his business. But they understood as well as I the position we were in, and they wanted the money.

Even Collins acknowledged that the West Side organizations could do nothing for Nixon, in a positive sense, but they might be able to help Eggers, which could possibly spill over into help for Nixon. On the other hand much adverse publicity might flow.

There is, of course, a name for such things in any arena other than politics. In politics it is merely politics. Struggling for time and a way out, I said I would see what I could do.

I called LaRue in Washington and laid out the problem, asking not only for some guidance but for some money as well, should they decide we ought to go that route. I was not inclined to give them anything. We had no money to offer. And besides, I felt any money given them would be wasted, that it would be used merely to oil the wheels of the West Side organization with no political benefit coming our way in the final analysis. Still, there was the implied threat.

LaRue counseled patience. Keep 'em on a string and drag it out as long as possible. He had a small fund for such emergencies, but it wasn't anything like the figures mentioned. How much could I expect? He figured about $18,000. No more. Even that would be in small increments.

There were more "discussions," all of which fortunately took time. As far as the campaign itself was concerned, the West Side problem did not loom large. It was merely a worry, a nagging problem that took up time that should have been devoted to other worries. In the end a few "transfers" of money were made, on the order of three or four thousand dollars each, usually in an office in the old Littlefield Building in Austin. For the record, the principal leg man in the affair, and the one to whom the money was delivered, was a former Democratic member of the Texas legislature, a man generally regarded in the world of Texas politics as being a loyal soldier in Pena's army. I trust (I am a trusting soul) he delivered the money to the appropriate operatives in San Antonio and that it was used to spread the word, or the wealth, on behalf of Eggers, with Nixon possibly receiving some ancillary benefit. Were I not such a trusting soul, I would have dark suspicions that much chortling took place all the way to the bank.

But that could not have happened. West Side politics is, after all, an honorable business.

The money must have helped. Otherwise we would have been wiped out totally there, rather than merely being wiped out.

Aside from such distractions the campaign went on. Political positions began to jell, and Nixon's fortunes in the state began to appear much more favorable. The Wallace vote reached a point at which it appeared to stabilize. We were able to convey the message that he couldn't win, that a vote for him would be "wasted," and that the result might be Hubert Humphrey. The argument had little effect on the base of Wallace's support, but it did have the effect of preventing its growth much beyond that. As far as Humphrey was concerned there was no great groundswell on his behalf. His support remained about where it had been — among organized labor, the political left, and those voters who traditionally voted Democratic because their grandfather voted Democratic, completely ignoring the sea change that had occurred in Democratic politics since their granddaddy lived and breathed by that party as the protector of home, flag, and "states' rights."

In the face of Humphrey's lagging support we got word that he was coming to Texas, where a gathering of the clan would make a final push on his behalf. It was to begin with a giant rally in Houston, replete with the usual bevy of Hollywood stars and starlets, known far and wide for their deep devotion to the national interest, good government, and all other things good and decent. This would be followed by a tour of the state, where local officeholders would voice their undying support for the ticket. Perhaps the big man himself, Lyndon Johnson, would be part of the process. It was a worrisome development.

Against this backdrop I received a call from Peter O'Donnell in Dallas. I should come to Dallas the following morning, to a certain room at a certain time in a certain hotel, for a meeting with unnamed people. "No matter what you are doing, just drop it and be in Dallas," he said. "It's important."

I walked into the room, high above the streets of downtown Dallas, to see O'Donnell, two or three other men I did not know, and, of all people, the Democratic governor of Texas, John Connally, whom I did know.

One of the others present represented Ben Carpenter, leader of a group known generally as Democrats and Independents for Nixon. I knew Carpenter but he probably didn't know me, considering his

THE CHOW DIPPER

lofty position in the financial affairs of Texas and the South. Carpenter was at one of his ranches, or in a business meeting, or somewhere and couldn't be there on such short notice. The other man was a short, stocky, rather aggressive individual introduced to me as Bill Clements. I understood him to be in the oil well drilling business. I had heard of him but had never met him. He was, shall we say, "different." He exhibited no awe whatever at being in the presence of the governor, whom he addressed as "John," not as "Governor." Nor was he bashful. I would learn years later this was not at all unusual for William P. Clements, Jr.

I was never told, nor did I ask, who had called the meeting. To me it seemed that in the background there was O'Donnell. In fact, it seemed he was always there when Republican politics or money were discussed. At least in this instance it was he who seemed to say, "Let's get this thing under way."

The thrust of the meeting was simple enough. They wanted Connally to stay away from the scheduled Houston rally for Humphrey. They did not want him, as governor of the state, to even lend an "official welcome" since it was strictly a Democratic Party affair. In fact, they would be much happier if he would simply come out and endorse Richard Nixon, where his sympathies clearly lay. My memory is that it was Clements who said something like "John, you know as well as we do that guy ought never be president of the United States."

To which Connally replied, "I know that. I've seen him break down and cry. Shed tears over little things. He has no business being president."

"Well, why in hell don't you just come out and say that?"

"I can't."

"Why not?'

"Good lord. I'm the elected leader of my party. I just can't do things like that. I have responsibilities to my party."

It was at this point that Clements said, with some heat, "Well then, John, why don't you just get on a boat and go out in the Gulf and go fishing? This is not your fight. Just go fishing."

The governor said he couldn't do that. It would just be too obvious. (Which was indeed the point.)

If he couldn't do that, argued Clements, why couldn't he find somewhere else in the state he had to be at that moment? He could just send official greetings, and all that.

That, too, would be obvious.

Well then, would he pass the word privately to his own lieutenants via a written communication, outlining where his sympathies really lay, in order that they might join the team? Connally didn't want to do exactly that, but he would give us their names and we could contact them. They would know. A number of names were passed to us, verbally. (My own feeling was that he didn't want anything in writing.) I doubt that any names fell in a crack.

We left the meeting with the understanding that Connally's participation in the Houston affair would be strictly low-key, and that would be that. It didn't work that way.

The Houston rally took place. It was a rousing success, a gathering of not only the clan but various, frequently warring factions of the clan, bringing to mind the ancient adage that "there is one thing upon which two robbers may readily agree, that being how to rob a third."

What followed, however, was of much more importance, politically, than the rally itself. Humphrey then began a tour of the state, accompanied in the northern half by John Connally, where Connally was popular, and in the southern half by Ralph Yarborough, where Yarborough was more popular. Whether that was a carefully calculated political ploy, or whether it merely represented the political realities of the Connally–Yarborough situation, is unknown to me. Nevertheless, it had the effect of propping up Humphrey and making him look acceptable to the various factions. Finally, there began to be some movement in the opposition camp, which was not good for us.

I have thought many times of the Dallas meeting. And why any man would say Humphrey "had no business being president of the United States," and then would go out and campaign for him. I suspect in this case it was a matter of the sitting president, albeit a lame duck president, holding a club bigger than one's own conscience, or bigger than any other club that might have been held by those in attendance. Or, it might have simply been that Connally could not then make up his mind where his future lay. Lyndon would soon be an ex-president. He himself would soon be an ex-governor. Humphrey might win. Or Humphrey might lose. Nixon might win. After that, the wheels of fortune, and all that. After the governorship, what would it be? Would it be business, or law, or politics? Or would it be all three? There were men present who could help in all three potential fields. (Indeed, if these worries did not play a part in the meeting, why would a sitting Democratic governor even agree to meet with leaders of the opposition camp during a critical stage in the campaign?) Perhaps it was a good time to carry water on both shoulders.

He would, in a few weeks, be out campaigning for Humphrey and against Nixon. Then, after his own preferred candidate lost, he would, in due course, serve as secretary of the treasury in Nixon's cabinet, that innermost circle of the man he had sought (publicly) to defeat.

Still, in all honesty I would have to say he was among the ablest, as well as the most loyal, of those who served in Nixon's cabinet.

I have thought of that meeting for other reasons as well. It was my first, although brief, encounter with Bill Clements, who would one day become governor of Texas in his own right, but who even then indicated he was not awed, or even slightly impressed, by the earthly power of others. I had followed Connally as a reporter when he was running for governor. Even then, people seemed to treat him with a certain amount of respect not usually afforded an aspiring political candidate. He had a "presence" about him. He had walked with Lyndon. People tended to fawn over him. Even more so after he became governor. And still more after he suffered grievous wounds at the hand of Lee Harvey Oswald while riding with John Kennedy. But here was a meeting of equals, excluding my own presence of course, in which no quarter was asked and little given. I was unprepared to hear a governor, any governor, spoken to in the manner Clements spoke to Connally. And O'Donnell, while much quieter than Clements, nevertheless made his points in a forceful manner. I was forced to conclude, not reluctantly, that neither Clements nor O'Donnell felt, as men measure men, they were in the presence of their better.

A few years later I got another, somewhat similar view of Clements. By then he had become governor, served one term, been defeated by Mark White, then won the governorship again. It was near the end of that term and others were jockeying to succeed him. I received a call from Norman Newton, executive director of the Associated Republicans of Texas (ART). He had heard rumors that Clayton Williams, from Midland, was thinking about running for governor and was due to arrive in Austin that evening to discuss the matter with Billy Clayton, a prominent lobbyist, consultant, and former Democratic Speaker of the Texas House of Representatives. Newton asked if I would accompany him to the meeting. The story I got was that he wished to ascertain Williams' intentions, if possible, since there were other friends and contributors within the ART organization who also had designs upon the governor's seat. I agreed.

Newton and I went to Clayton's office, where we were shortly joined by Clayton Williams and his wife, Modesta. It was the first time I had met either of them. They had recently returned from an extended big game hunt in Pakistan, or some such place. There was some preliminary discussion of the possibility that he might run for governor. He indicated he was thinking about it. Then, out of the blue, he said he had an appointment with the governor, Bill Clements, and that we should all just go over and talk to him about this matter.

So we all trooped over to the Capitol, where Clements and his staff were still at work. It was dark by then, and most state employees had left their posts some three hours earlier. Through curious glances, we walked through outer sanctums to the inner sanctum, where we found a clearly unhappy Bill Clements. He had thought he was to have a private conversation with Williams. Here came a group. It was not on his agenda, and, as I would learn, Clements very much liked to keep control of his agenda. So the meeting started on a sour note.

Williams, pointing to the rest of us, said, "Governor, these people are trying to get me to run for governor. I'd like your own opinion on the matter."

I resented the comment that "these people" were trying to get him to run for governor. My only involvement was in accompanying someone who was trying to learn whether Williams intended to run. I had no thoughts, pro or con, on whether he should run for governor.

And that feeling of resentment was made even deeper when Clements, after staring at us for what seemed like a full minute, but which was probably only a few seconds, turned to Williams and, in a tone bordering on contempt, said, "You can't listen to these wise owls. If you want to know about running for governor, talk to me."

Somewhat chastened, Williams responded, "That's what I'm doing, governor. That's why I came to you. I'd like your thoughts."

With no hesitation, Clements obliged. "You can forget about running for governor unless you are prepared to dig down in your pocket and come up with ten million dollars," he said. "It will cost you nearly that much to get through the primary. You'll get a lot of promises, but you're not going to get much help unless you win the primary. If you do that, you'll get some help. But until then you're going to have to depend on yourself."

There was more advice along the same lines, all given in a somewhat authoritarian, slightly irritated manner. I translated it, in my own mind, to mean "You're not going to get any help from me unless you win the primary. Then we'll see."

Williams seemed nonplussed. Then he wanted to know how much time he would have to devote to the job.

That seemed to tick Clements off even more than the money thing.

"I'll tell you one thing. There won't be any of this business of going off on six-week hunting trips, or even long fishing trips. You'll be lucky if you get some weekends. This job is not like it was when Shivers was governor, or even when John Connally was governor. The state has grown. The problems have grown. You'll have to devote time and energy to it."

Williams thought for a moment, and said, "Well, I don't know. The money [$10 million] doesn't bother me. But I'll have to think about the time business. I'm not sure about the time."

After the meeting broke up, and Williams returned to Midland, I thought we had probably heard the last of it. But a few days later, after having thought the matter over, and having come, I suppose, to the conclusion that he could devote the time as well as the money, he passed the word he would be in the race.

He ended up winning the primary and losing the election, with the help of a few mistakes of his own and a media that generally wanted his opponent to win.

The Dallas meeting had shown me that Clements did not stand in much awe of people with political power. The Austin meeting indicated he also was not overly impressed with people who had financial power. He was indeed different, somewhat strange — in fact, unique, in the world of politics.

The Houston rally and the subsequent tours by Connally and Yarborough had the desired effect for Humphrey. Without doubt, it caused many Democrats to go to the polls who otherwise would have stayed home. The movement toward Humphrey, or more accurately the coalescing of Democrats, was noticeable and worrisome. Nixon had gone as far as he was willing to go to meet the Wallace threat—indeed, much further than he wanted to go. In the absence of help from the top there was little we could do to erode the Wallace vote more than we had to that moment. And there was little we could do to counteract the combined political clout of Johnson, Connally, and Yarborough. In a few days the matter would be settled.

Will Davis and I met for coffee at the Driskill Hotel a couple of days before the vote. We were longtime friends. He had the same responsibility for the Humphrey campaign I had for the Nixon campaign. Davis was generally thought of as a "moderate" or even "conservative" Democrat, but he was Democrat. Both could feel the closeness of the race.

"I wish this election had been last week," I said.

"I wish it was next week," he replied.

Humphrey beat Nixon by 38,960 votes in Texas. Wallace received 584,269.

Within a few days of the vote we went back into the field with a survey, for which I had set aside $13,000 during the campaign. The question, asked of those who had voted for Wallace, was essentially this: "If Wallace had not been in the race, who would you have voted for?"

More than seventy percent of those who responded said they would have voted for Nixon had Wallace not been in the race. In which case Nixon would have carried the state hands down.

Still, although Nixon lost Texas, he won the presidency. The prize he had sought so diligently for so long was now his. He could now go about the task of staffing his new administration. My own future was considerably less certain.

I had assumed in the beginning that, win or lose, I would resume my duties in Washington. But the campaign had seen Tower and myself on different sides during some critical discussions and decisions, primarily over funding of the Eggers race. At Tower's insistence a portion of the money raised for the Nixon effort was diverted to the Eggers campaign, causing financial problems in our own. Tower took the position that "the party" was responsible for Eggers getting in the race, therefore the "party" was responsible for helping fund it. It was true, of course, that in the final analysis Eggers did win the primary and became the party's nominee, and as such was entitled to its support. But I had, or felt I had, the responsibility of delivering the state for Nixon. Any diminution of our own resources worked against that possibility. So we differed. As could be expected, and as should be expected, his position prevailed. The result was that our own financial condition became so perilous that at one point Sam Wylie, our finance chairman, took me aside and informed me, with some emotion, that beginning at that moment I would have a

$250,000 "line of credit" for the Nixon campaign, none of which was to be used for anything else. In those years that was a lot of money.

Still, it was not the first time the senator and I had differed and remained friends. He asked me to come back to Washington and take over my old duties.

Before I left for Washington, however, Peter O'Donnell asked what I wanted in the new administration. My answer was that I did not feel I deserved anything. I had lost Texas, and in politics losers are not generally rewarded. I had no claim, the way I saw it, for any consideration.

"Bullshit," Peter replied, with some agitation.

"We'll be at that table," he said. "We raised a ton of money for that [national] campaign. We did a whole lot better than New York. They didn't carry New York either, and they had a Republican governor and a Republican legislature. We had a sitting Democratic governor, a Democratic legislature, and we had Lyndon Johnson. We came a lot closer than they did, and we'll be at the table. Make no mistake about that."

I told Peter the only thing in Washington I really wanted was the directorship of the United States Information Agency. I approved of their mission and it was a place where I thought my talents, such as they were, could be utilized. Not only that, I was emotionally committed to the battle against communism. I had long since realized the wisdom of Guh Ching-Yu, that the world was not big enough for communism and liberty to live peacefully on the same planet. All things considered, it was a place I thought I could serve reasonably well and be at peace with myself.

O'Donnell was indeed at the table, as was Anne Armstrong. Not long after the new administration took over, I received a call. The new director of USIA was going to be Frank Shakespeare, who had resigned as vice-president of Columbia Broadcasting System to be part of the national Nixon effort. Frank was one of the few conservative thinkers at CBS then, and was probably one of the last within that organization. He wanted to talk to me about the position of deputy director of the agency.

We had good discussions. He was a man I liked instinctively, with a view of the agency's mission that matched my own. But neither of us had any previous experience in the executive branch of government. He felt at that stage he needed someone in the number-two spot who had that experience. In the end he asked Henry Loomis, longtime head of the Voice of America (which then was a division of the agency) to take the deputy's position. He asked me to take the position of assistant director, in charge of the agency's worldwide radio teletype service, along with the production of a number of magazines around the world, as well as publishing plants in Lebanon, Mexico, and the Philippines. To replace Loomis at the Voice, Shakespeare chose Kenneth Giddens, owner of television and radio stations in Alabama. To head up the agency's movie and television arm he chose Bruce Herschensohn of California, one of the ablest persons, if not the ablest, I have ever known in that field. And one of the most committed to the concept of human liberty.

It was a good team. Loomis was considered an apolitical type, which, by and large, made him persona grata within both the foreign service and the domestic civil service. Since his position entailed primarily the management of the agency's money and personnel, the perceived absence of any strong political ties on his part was no doubt comforting to those worried about the agency being taken over by committed anti-Communist zealots. And while the political convictions of the operating heads of the agency's three principal arms (movies and television under Herschensohn, the Voice of America under Giddens, and the worldwide print and publication service under me) might have caused heartburn among some, no one could reasonably argue we were unfamiliar with, or unqualified for, our own fields.

Shakespeare visited Tower to see if he had any objections to my joining the USIA team. He told me later that Tower became emotional, even shed tears, but said in the end that it was probably time.

I certainly thought it was time, that I had probably outlived my usefulness where I was. Tower was now an established, reasonably secure senator. I had helped in those areas where I could help, but the potential (and apparent) problems he now faced were not problems I could help with. They were personal problems he would have to face and work out on his own.

Too, I wanted to simply get out of it. One statewide race has a way of draining a person. Two races in two years had left me emotionally spent. Two years, as it were, of living on the edge of a volcano. A new challenge, in a field that offered much promise, for a cause in which I believed deeply, just might be the thing.

So I took my leave of the senator and undertook my new duties on the first day of March, 1969. For slightly over six years his life had impacted mine, and mine his. Now it was over. Or so I thought.

EIGHTEEN

Striking a Blow for Liberty

I do not know at precisely what point the Cold War between the Soviet Union and the West could be said to have been at its peak. It began, of course, shortly following World War II, when the West finally realized the full extent of Soviet aims and aspirations, along with their intentions of using the Communist Party and the party's military arm (the Red Army) to achieve those objectives. The issue was brought to a focus, as far as I am concerned, with Churchill's "Iron Curtain" speech in Fulton, Missouri. At that point the public was made to understand what had happened, what was happening, and what would likely happen if the battle was not joined in earnest.

If March 1969 was not at the peak of the Cold War, it would certainly fall within that period's general time frame. American troops were battling Communist forces in Vietnam. China and the Soviet Union were contesting with each other over who could provide the most help to their comrades in Vietnam without having to commit troops of their own. Each hoped that in the end they would be in position to exert their own influence in the region. All across Europe, armies stood at the ready. The Soviet Union, through its agents and sympathizers in America and elsewhere in the West, had stolen American nuclear secrets, and the missile race was on.

Around the world Communist parties, funded and directed by the Kremlin, were doing their bit to undermine and subvert governments friendly to the West. That is where we came in.

At the outset I would have to say that the years I spent at USIA were among the most gratifying "employed" years in my life. And, in a sense, the most enlightening. They were years I could go home at night feeling I had struck a blow for liberty, for mankind, somewhere in the world. And there was the feeling that our labors were directed toward the interests of the nation as a whole, not merely toward the interests of political parties or individual politicians. And those who staffed the agency — right, left, or center — were among the ablest I had encountered since coming to Washington. On my own staff there were even Ph.D.s who could marshal their thoughts and write simple, declarative sentences, a rarity anywhere but an extreme rarity within the government of the United States.

The job was not without its frustrations, of course, or its disillusion, or even its heartaches. There was the bureaucracy, with its built-in frustrations, its occasional time-servers. There were the problems of dealing with certain senators and congressmen who were entirely unsympathetic to our mission, which was essentially to defend the American concept of government, the American sense of justice, in the ongoing battle with the ideas of Marx, Lenin, and Joseph Stalin. And there was the so-called "non-Communist left" within the American media as well as the body politic, who saw our efforts as being an impediment to the eventual establishment of a worldwide "workers' paradise" in which peace and harmony would reign. They were not socialists, or at least few would admit to being socialists; they were merely opposed to all who were actively opposed to socialism. In their ignorance or naiveté they seemed unable to realize it was a distinction without a difference.

Perhaps a word of explanation is in order concerning the agency's structure — how it fit into the scheme of things, who reported to whom. What, in the final analysis, did it do? It would be best to begin, structurally at least, in the field.

At practically every American embassy around the world there existed a public affairs team, presided over by what we referred to as the "PAO," or public affairs officer. The PAO was always the most senior foreign service officer in the USIA team. He usually served as the spokesman for the American ambassador assigned to that country. In some of the larger embassies he might delegate that authority, with the approval of the ambassador, to his own press officer. There was also usually, again in the larger posts, a cultural officer, who looked after the local American library, if one happened to be located there, as well as the exchange of scholars, and, in the case of the Soviet Union, the local implementation of cultural agreements between the two countries. Again, in the case of the Soviet Union, this involved agreed upon exchanges of publications, and the presentation, in various parts of the Soviet Union, of "exhibits" featuring aspects of everyday life in America. (The Soviet Union sent their own exhibits to America, including the Bolshoi, certain art collections, and the magazine *Soviet Life*, among others.)

The function of that team, which was well understood by the host government, was essentially to assist in the overall effort of furthering American interests in that country. And a large part of that effort involved countering international Communist Party activities aimed at tarnishing all aspects of American life — cultural, economic, whatever.

There was also the traditional State Department team reporting directly to the ambassador, who reported through channels to his appropriate desk in Washington. In some embassies, there were commercial officers, concerned with trade matters. And, in some instances, there were the ubiquitous CIA station chiefs, whose home base went unquestioned by me, but who generally showed up when I later went abroad.

The American PAO was assigned his post by USIA in Washington, as were his subordinates. They reported to their regional desks at USIA (the African desk, the Middle East desk, etc.) and their work was evaluated annually by teams made up of peers, plus others from the "outside." Upon those evaluations depended the officer's progress up the career ladder, and accordingly up the pay scale. With luck, perseverance, a clean slate and excellent evaluations, he could expect to reach the rarefied realm of the Class I foreign service officer within his normal career span. Provided, of course, there were sufficient openings at the top.

The operating arms of the agency were charged with the responsibility of seeing to it that officers in the field had the tools with which to work. Those tools were theoretically to make possible the implementation of certain policies, which flowed from the agency's deputy director for policy and plans — policies which in turn had to be coordinated with policy positions taken by the Department of State.

This aspect of the operation proved, in my opinion, to be the most troublesome of all. The traditional State Department type is, or at least was, completely unprepared to do battle in the war of ideas. Their education, their training, the manner in which they are evaluated for promotion tends to produce, whether calculated or not, a certain objective blandness in both thought and action.

This is not to argue that trained diplomats should appear anything other than bland, even if they harbor forceful, controversial thoughts. A diplomat constantly engaged in controversy would hardly be useful in representing his own country abroad. Indeed, one does not normally go up the ladder in the field of diplomacy by being controversial. But one can scarcely engage an opponent in the world of ideas without being controversial.

Their approach seemed conditioned upon the notion that the diplomatic corps had been around long before advent of the Soviet State, that their function was to "negotiate" with the other side. Over the decades, indeed since the beginning of the corps, they had lived with and "negotiated" with governments of all types. They saw no end to this. Many took the position that an aggressive stance toward communism by USIA merely roiled the waters, making their own task more difficult and their life more uncomfortable. The leadership of the agency that came in with Shakespeare took a generally more aggressive attitude. We did not merely wish to hold our own in the battle; we wanted to do the other side in, and do it as quickly as possible.

Needless to say, there were times when this difference in approach caused problems, for while we were an independent agency with a clearly defined mission we were also required by law to take overall "policy guidance" from the Department of State.

In an effort to help us better understand our various responsibilities, Shakespeare arranged for a luncheon meeting with Nixon's new secretary of state, William Rogers. Shakespeare wanted Rogers to meet his new team, and for the new team to meet Rogers. In some respects it proved to be a wasted effort. In other respects, not. My impression of Rogers left more questions than answers. After a couple of hours I could not understand how he ever got to be secretary of state, unless Nixon proposed to be his own secretary of state and merely wanted Rogers as a figurehead. No matter how Shakespeare tried to channel the discussion toward a resolution of our problems, Rogers wandered all over the lot. We learned a great deal, for instance, about his former law practice, and how much he knew about the legal positions, or lack of positions, enjoyed by the three major television networks. We also found that back in his New York law offices he had a telescope, where, at an appointed hour, he could look across town to his apartment, and where, by prearrangement, his wife would wave to him from her window. She would know he was looking, and he could see her wave. Fascinating.

Still, it was a useful meeting. If he was no more concerned about the matter than that, we could at least know we were not likely to be bothered by high-level disputes involving the secretary of state. We would merely have to occasionally argue with State Department underlings, assistant secretaries and the like. With them we could hold our own.

(Sometime later, after I had been kicked upstairs to the position of deputy director for policy and plans, thereby becoming the agency's liaison with all those departments and agencies having to do with foreign affairs, I sat in on the briefing that followed Nixon's meeting in Moscow with Brezhnev. It was a very important summit, and the department's top staff were assembled to get a firsthand review of the matter from their leader, the secretary of state. What we got from the secretary, however, were a few personal glimpses of Mr. Brezhnev. "He reminded me of someone running for president of his local Rotary Club," said Rogers. "Gladhanding everyone he could see." Fortunately, he then turned the briefing over to a senior foreign service officer, who did give us a fair account of what transpired.)

Eventually Rogers left his post, being replaced (some said squeezed out) by Henry Kissinger, who served as head of the National Security apparatus in the White House. That caused no vast change in our own operations, since he played his cards so close to his vest. While we at the agency were seldom privy to his thoughts, his own lieutenants fared no better. This obviously allowed for a certain gray area in policy interpretation within which we learned to maneuver, causing heartburn in some quarters and untold joy in others. The cause of freedom and liberty was served.

In some respects I could not quarrel with Kissinger's obsessive secrecy. The Department of State was riddled with "doves" concerned with Nixon's reputation as a strong anti-Communist. They were of like mind with some in our own agency. They had their contacts, their soulmates, in the media and on Capitol Hill as well, not the least of whom was Senator William Fulbright, chairman of the Foreign Relations Committee, and mentor of numerous anti-anti-Communists in the "intellectual" community, one of whom was a youngster named Bill Clinton. Fulbright was not merely opposed to American involvement in Vietnam, concerned as it was with aiding a struggling ally in its fight against Communist North Vietnam. He was essentially against the extension of American power, or even the expression of American power, anywhere in the world. He even developed a theme he called "The Arrogance of Power," with an arrogant America, of course, being the chief villain. This was seized upon by the left in America as intellectual justification for their own opposition to our involvement in Vietnam, and their own apologies for the misdeeds of Communist aggression around the world. If America would merely stand down, the left's argument ran, the "other side" would do likewise. If America would first throw all its missiles into the Potomac, the Soviet Union, overcome with guilt, would then throw all its missiles into the Volga. Peace would reign forever and ever.

It is no wonder Kissinger sometimes acted the way he did. He may have been obsessed with his own intelligence, or blinded by his own ego, but he was nevertheless aware of the struggle then going on in the world, and America's place in that struggle. And, unlike Fulbright, he had an appreciation of the value of American military power in the world of that time.

I'm no authority on Henry Kissinger. For a few years I was merely thrown into the mix where he operated. Only rarely did I attend, as a representative of our agency, top-level State Department staff meetings at which Kissinger presided. (Most of my meetings at State were with people of lower rank, assistant secretaries and the like.) I was struck by his ability to speak in lucid, organized paragraphs. But I was also struck with the thought that it would have been very difficult for him to adopt any idea, any plan of action, unless he could somehow be convinced it was his idea in the first place. Once he reached that point he was very good at convincing others of the soundness of his thoughts.

In time Nixon and Brezhnev entered into the understanding called "détente." Stripped of all its intellectual verbiage, it essentially meant the two sides would try to live together without war, or at least without "hot" war. The contest would go on, but those problems that might cause physical confrontation would be dealt with in a manner designed to defuse the dangers of actual combat. Certain rules of engagement would be entered into, particularly between military forces on both sides. Efforts would be made to keep active military forces at something approaching arm's length, lest small incidents become cause for major confrontation. Efforts would be made to enhance peaceful contact between the two sides. Soviet efforts at jamming Western shortwave radio broadcasts, notably those transmitted by the Voice of America, would be eased.

It was, in a way, a buying of time. The move was generally hailed in America and the West by those on the left, who were convinced time was on the side of socialism, and approved somewhat grudgingly by those of us on the right, who also thought time was on our side but who worried about the rapid buildup of Soviet military forces and the tendency of the Soviets to ignore agreements previously entered into. If the Soviet military threat could be contained there was no doubt, among those of us on the right, that the Soviet empire would eventually crumble, predicated as it was upon a system that refused to accept any concept of human dignity as a basis for its laws or its actions.

But when that happened, what would replace the Soviet system and the ideology that underpinned it? Would it merely be an economic variation of the existing system, with the ideology and the Red Army left intact? Or would the ideas of freedom and individual liberty hold some attraction for them? Our job, as I saw it, was to see that it did.

At any rate, and for good or ill, those were the ground rules that generally governed during the seven years I was at USIA, as assistant director for press and publications, as deputy director in charge of the agency's policy and plans, and, ultimately, as acting director for a brief period before returning to Texas in 1976 during the presidency of Gerald Ford.

After a few months of learning the system, we were able to identify and bring in a top team of foreign service officers who generally agreed with our approach, and as a result had been banned to somewhat obscure posts around the world by the agency's previous leadership. The ball had bounced in favor of those who had kept the faith and had been punished for it.

Even that was not easy. In fact, it is never easy to make changes in a bureaucracy. The agency, made up as it was of both civil service and foreign service personnel, posed peculiar problems in this regard. So many, in fact, that Shakespeare despaired over the prospect. When we took over the agency there were some 12,000 employees in Washington and around the world. In time that figure was reduced to some 9,000, mostly by terminating "local employees" on bloated staffs in places like India and Brazil. That, we figured, was an improvement, since it created a much more efficient operation worldwide. It not only saved money, but made it possible for the American PAO to get a better handle on his operation. Yet that did nothing to solve the problem of how to assemble a staff in Washington that would carry out what we regarded as the will of the American people, expressed through their action at the ballot box. That would take some doing.

Hoping to gain some insight from someone who had engaged the left since his days at Yale, Shakespeare suggested we go up to Connecticut, or wherever, to the home of William F. Buckley, who had been appointed to a nonpaying agency advisory council created by Congress. That group's function was to keep an independent eye on the agency and report to Congress annually on its findings. I doubt that many in Congress read the advisory council's report. Nevertheless, many prestigious Americans served the council over the years. People like Buckley, Frank Stanton, James Michener. They tried to do good things and sometimes succeeded.

It turned out to be a delightful occasion. Shakespeare, Giddens, Herschensohn and I, along with Buckley, repaired to a spot overlooking a body of water, most likely a sound, to discuss our problems. The more they were discussed, the more intractable they seemed. Finally Shakespeare, almost in an air of resignation, opined that in the end the bureaucracy would win, that about all we could do was go forth with what we inherited and do the best we could.

At that point Buckley said something that has stuck with me since: "Frank, if we don't strike a blow for liberty when we have the chance, what will we tell our grandchildren?"

There was a brief moment of silence while it sank in. Shakespeare spoke next.

"We'll do it. Somehow, we'll do it."

The machinery was put in motion. It took time, but we brought back people like Hoyt Ware and Lyle Coopman from South America, Art Hoffman from Western Europe, and Walter Bastian from Turkey or somewhere. Frank Harmon, a former CIA spook who had long since come in from the cold, moved into the policy shop, along with Rob McLellan and Dan Hafrey and Richard Monsen. We moved people sidewise, we moved them up. We couldn't move people down, but we could do what the previous administration had done: send them off to the Central African Republic, or Ethiopia, or even Tanzania, where they could savor the fruits of Kenneth Kuanda's tribal socialism up close. Or, if they really deserved it, we could always hold out the threat of reassignment to beautiful downtown

Ouagadougou in Upper Volta, only a few days' camel ride from Timbuktu. Before too long we had assembled a team that was not embarrassed to champion American thoughts and American interests in the Cold War we were then about, détente or not. The stage was set.

Our task was not easy. But those in the field, the trench officers, faced even more difficult challenges. It would be easy to surmise that our own side held all the trump cards. After all, truth, freedom, liberty, all those good things, ought to have no trouble in any battle with communism or any other dictatorial form of ideology. The logical Western mind would think any system of government that gave its people the right to move about freely, to entertain differing political thoughts, to acquire and hold property and pass that property on to one's children, to worship one's own God in one's own way, would have no problems in any ideological struggle with a government, or an ideology, that would criminalize all those things.

Given those thoughts, it would appear that we were, or should have been, playing on a field tilted in our favor. It didn't work out that way. In fact, the field was tilted against us.

Lyndon Johnson, mired in the Vietnam conflict, had proclaimed his celebrated "war on poverty" in America as part of his Great Society program. Whether that was a deeply held conviction on his part, whether it was more of his one-upmanship with the Kennedy clan, or a means of pacifying the left with displays of public compassion and gifts of public money while the Vietnam struggle went on, is immaterial for this illustration. But in order to justify his war on poverty, he had to prove the need for that war. This meant that facts and figures had to be brought forth, the worse the better, in order to convince the American electorate, and through them the Congress, that vast numbers of Americans were "living in poverty," and were, in fact, on the verge of starvation. His Great Society would correct that. The implication to those not steeped in American politics was that the American system had failed.

Johnson's "war" was, of course, accompanied by a great deal of domestic propaganda, in the nature of American politics. It was an easy message to sell, since there were many in the media who honestly believed it and wanted something done, and there were many others in the media who knew better but saw this as a means of attacking the capitalist system.

In terms of domestic politics it was a very shrewd ploy on

Johnson's part. Never mind his ascent to power. Never mind Brown and Root. Never mind George Parr and Box 13. Never mind the means by which Johnson arose to power. To be opposed to his solutions meant to be against poor people. And the dominant American media, rich and powerful that it is, likes nothing better than to be seen as fighting for the poor and powerless. It creates a good self-image.

All of which would have been fine and understandable in terms of American politics, if the issue and the stories could have been confined to the American body politic. But they couldn't. When the president of the United States speaks, the message goes worldwide. Even the Haitians listen, as a future president, also ignorant in the field of foreign affairs, would learn.

With only minor adjustments by the Communist propaganda apparatus, Johnson's message became: America was a land reeking of poverty-stricken people, living under a capitalist system where the rich (mostly white) got richer and the poor (mostly black) got poorer. The president of the United States was himself the authority.

Hardly the kind of a system to be recommended for struggling new Third World countries, where emerging leaders were looking for role models after which to pattern their own societies.

Compared to the utopian, socialist societies described in Communist propaganda, where there was no unemployment, where people were well fed, where modern, up-to-date medical facilities were available to all, where housing was available and affordable, where workers were voluntarily and constantly striving to better the "norms" (for the benefit of the Soviet state and the new "Soviet Man"), the capitalist system must have looked bleak indeed to those developing nations seeking a way out of their misery.

It did not help, of course, that America was then involved in the Vietnam conflict, that Johnson seemed unable to articulate compelling reasons for being there, and that vocal segments of his own countrymen were in the streets (or in Canada or at Oxford) publicly protesting his policies. It required no great imagination on the part of our adversaries to point out that while the American government presided over a system that had failed to properly provide for its own people, it was nevertheless attempting to force that system upon others, killing hundreds of thousands of little yellow people in the process.

How would you, gentle reader, defend your own country under those circumstances?

That is the situation we faced abroad when we took over management of the agency. That is what our foreign service officers faced every day when they went about their task of trying to represent America in Country X, Y, or Z. Truly, it was not a job for the faint of heart. And fortunately, we did not have terribly many faint-hearted people manning the barricades. A few, but not many.

In large measure, by virtue of decisions flowing from the clandestine meeting with Buckley, we managed to neutralize the few. They were around, hither and yon, mostly yon. But they did not direct the working lives of others, except, usually, in some remote corner of the globe.

But it was not just a matter of contesting propaganda emanating from the Kremlin, from Tass, or Pravda, or the multitude of Soviet government publications and broadcasts. There were, in academia and in the media at home, those who sympathized completely with the idea that man was merely an economic animal, that socialism was merely another economic system, like capitalism, but that unlike capitalism socialism sought improvement in the lot of the common man as a matter of official policy. They were the ones, many of whom were educated in the "better" schools of that day, who at best took a neutral position in the ongoing struggle, and at worst came down on the side of the Soviet Union, the Vietcong, or anybody else who opposed America. Their reports and lectures on life and politics in America were grist for the mills of Communist propaganda. Our people in the field had to contend with not only the Soviet Union's worldwide propaganda apparatus, but also what was being written and broadcast in their own country, then picked up and distributed by the Soviet propaganda apparatus as reinforcing proof of their own message.

Lest there be those who would say that I, by outlining some of the problems faced in the Cold War struggle with the Soviet Union, seem to be advocating a fettered press in America, I can only say "nonsense." I believe deeply in a free press, fettered only by a devotion to duty, that duty being a devotion to truth and fairness. The question for a free press is, and always has been, what is truth and what is fairness? It is normal for people, even journalists, to differ on what is truth. But even people who differ on truth can recognize fairness, or the lack of fairness. And in the world of ideas, fairness requires a degree of objectivity and honesty.

Again, lest some think I overdraw the picture, let me recount two small incidents, illustrative of many.

The first:

I was attending one of those obligatory embassy functions in Washington, which I hated but which was occasionally required. Present were the usual attendees at such functions, politicians, staff, and members of the press. In short order I found myself off to the side, in conversation with a Washington-based political reporter for the United Press International news service. He had arrived earlier than I. The drinks were free, so he was possessed of good spirits and a loose tongue. I was familiar with his writing, so it was no surprise to find him completely in tune with those who opposed the American effort in Vietnam. Nor was it a surprise to find him possessed with decidedly anti-capitalist views.

He had many good friends at USIA, he said, but he always felt so terribly sorry for them, forced, as they were, to "send out all that propaganda." He could never work under those circumstances.

I replied that I didn't think that was the way it was at all, that a good deal of our work was trying to bring some balance and objectivity to the propagandistic reports of others. In terms of pure propaganda I did not think we were any more guilty than many members of the press. I took as an example the issue of unemployed people in the United States. When stories in the American press were sent around the world pointing out the number (as opposed to the percentage) of people out of work in the capitalistic United States, we had an obligation to also point out the number of people who had jobs and were gainfully employed. In a foreign country of 10 million, for instance, a story indicating 5 million Americans were unemployed would take on an entirely different meaning were it not also pointed out that 60 million were working.

Even the word "poverty" was and is a relative term. Poverty in the world's wealthiest nation is entirely different from poverty in the Philippines or India. The poverty-stricken people of Calcutta would think themselves most fortunate to suddenly find themselves among the poverty-stricken of America. Use of the word "poverty," without some explanation as to its meaning within the society being described, is obviously subject to differing interpretations. All we were asking for was some fairness and balance in order that truth might be served.

He became livid. That was exactly the point. The story, he said, was not about the employed, it was about the unemployed.

"If one American, if one single American is out of work, that is the story you ought to be telling the world. That is your story," he said.

Senator Tower being briefed on pressure chamber research at the USAF School of Aerospace Medicine, by Col. Harold V. Ellingson, commander of the school. Also pictured is Col. Frank M. Townsend, vice commander, Aerospace Medical Division.

Southwest Texas Junior College students, Senator Tower, and Ken Towery at the Annual Citizenship Assembly.

Tower's staff, ca. 1967. Front row, left to right: Carolyn Ely, Barbara Curtis, Carolyn Poteet (behind Curtis), Janie Maxfield, Nicki Papanicolas Ward, unidentified, Rose Mary Butler, Jeanie Cole, Kay Sealy, Linda Lovelady, and Carolyn Bacon. Back row, left to right: Kent Spann, Tom Wise, Phil Charles, Tom Fahey, Pierce Langford, Jerry Friedheim, David Martinez, Tom Cole, and Ken Towery.

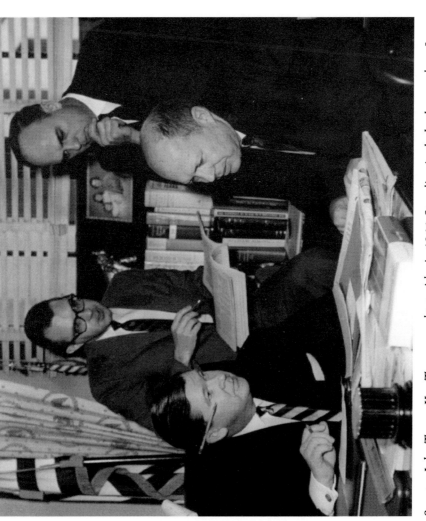

Senator John Tower, Ken Towery, and top aides in 1966. Standing in the background are Jerry Friedheim, then Tower's press secretary and later assistant secretary of defense for public affairs; and Tom Cole, Tower's legislative assistant, now an attorney in Houston.

Senator Tower (center) during a briefing at Headquarters Air Training Command, Randolph AFB, Texas, March 1965. General Momyer, commander, standing left; Major Hammock, briefing officer, standing center.

Mrs. Raymond Tapp of Lubbock, Mrs. Rose Farmer, and Ken Towery with Barbara Bush and a younger George Bush as a Texas congressman in the 1960s.

With Goldwater — Left to right: Jerry Friedheim, Ken Towery, Barry Goldwater, and Tom Wise, the legislative assistant to Senator John Tower. This picture was taken in 1967, when Barry Goldwater was returned to the Senate following his losing 1964 presidential campaign.

Senator Tower with General Momyer during a visit to Headquarters Air Training Command, Randolph AFB. Also pictured are Charles Cheever, Jr., president Broadway National Bank, San Antonio; the author; and Captain Prophett, General Momyer's aide.

Ken Towery (right) and Louise Towery (left) with Vice-president George and Barbara Bush in Dallas in the early 1980s.

Ken Towery met President Ronald Reagan in the Oval Office of the White House in 1988 to mark the 20th anniversary of the Corporation for Public Broadcasting. Reagan appointed Towery to the CPB Board after assuming the presidency in 1981.

Ken Towery, then deputy director (policy and plans) for USIA, and President Gerald Ford, then in the process of requesting top administration figures to remain in the White House to advise him in his new administration.

The author with the American ambassador to Argentina, John Davis Lodge, in Buenos Aires during the early 1970s.

Lt. Gen. John B. McPhearson, USAF, commandant of the National War College, and Ken Towery, following a lecture by Towery at the War College in October 1972, during the Vietnam War.

The author examining the presses of USIS Manila's printing plant. The plant was production center for a number of publications that circulated primarily throughout Asia during the period of the Cold War, chief among them being the Agency's Horizon magazine. The plant occasionally assisted in production of the agency-produced magazine America Illustrated, which circulated in the Soviet Union. At that time the Agency had similar plants in Beirut, Lebanon, and Mexico City, all of which came under the author's general responsibility.

Senator John Tower shaking hands with former Vice-president John Nance Garner during a courtesy visit in 1967. At the right is Jack Ware of Uvalde, one of the initial class at Southwest Texas Junior College. The occasion was to recognize Ken Towery as the first student to enroll at the college and for his success in journalism and government.

Texas senators — Left to right: Opal Yarborough, wife of Senator Ralph Yarborough; Senator Yarborough; Senator John Tower and his wife, Lou Tower; Louise Towery and Ken Towery, ca. 1968.

Swearing-in ceremonies at the United States Information Agency in March 1969. On the left is Frank Shakespeare, newly appointed director of the agency, a former vice-president of Columbia Broadcasting System; and to the right is Henry Loomis, the agency's deputy director and former head of the Voice of America. Loomis later served as president of the Corporation for Public Broadcasting.

USIS Public Affairs Officer Jack Gallagher (right) and Foreign Service Officer Terry Kneebone (center) go over documents with the author following a visit to the American Embassy in Lima, Peru in the early 1970s.

Chamber of Commerce "Gold Carpet Greeters" and Southwest Texas Junior College students welcome Senator John Tower and Ken Towery to the Annual Citizenship Assembly, October 1967.

Southwest Texas Junior College President Wayne Matthews presents Ken Towery with an engraved plaque at the Annual Citizenship Assembly, honoring the college's first student for "distinctive merit" in journalism and government.

The author, as chairman of the board for the Corporation for Public Broadcasting.

Untying the ribbon at the CASA Inaugural were American Ambassador to Brazil John Hugh Crimmins (left) and Saraiva Guerreiro, secretary general of the Brazilian Ministry of External Relations. Behind Guerreiro are USIA Deputy Director Ken Towery, Assistant Secretary of State John Richardson, and PAO Hans Tuch.

That is the way he saw it, and that is the way he reported it.

With America having friends like that, who needed enemies? Stories reflecting that attitude, picked up by the Communist Party apparatus and moved worldwide, merely added to the burden faced by our officers in the field.

Needless to say, the conversation degenerated. I was already unhappy about a UPI story that had moved weeks earlier out of Cambodia. There the Communist forces of one Pol Pot had encircled the capitol. The battle raged. Supplies were short. People were hungry. We had flown in relief supplies to the defenders. Suddenly, a UPI story "revealed" that the food was being given out to military forces while civilians starved and died for lack of food. The story was front-page news in Washington. Irresponsible senators and congressmen, of whom there is never a shortage, immediately jumped into action demanding an "investigation." The only problem was that the story was a complete fabrication, a complete lie. The UPI reporter on the scene had been taken in by rumors circulated by the Pol Pot forces. The food was still in a warehouse. Nothing had been given out, to anyone. They were still trying to organize a distribution system while under siege. Within days, after, of course, the wire service story had had its impact, the truth finally emerged. But it was a damaging story, picked up and circulated by the Communist propaganda apparatus. I reminded the reporter of this story. His immediate reaction was to condemn the newspaper publishers. If they would only pay a higher salary to their correspondents they would get a higher caliber reporter, and we wouldn't have errors like that appear. He calmed down only after I told him, in no uncertain terms, that I was a part-owner in a small daily newspaper (the *Cuero Record*) which subscribed to UPI, that we helped pay his salary, and that we were much more concerned about getting a story straight than getting it first but wrong. He went away. I probably only made matters worse.

The second:

Out in California a black woman named Angela Davis, an avowed Marxist and teacher of philosophy at UCLA, was charged with being a principal in the murder of Judge Harold J. Haley during an attempt to free some convicts awaiting trial for assaulting a prison guard. Evidence indicated Davis purchased the weapons that were smuggled into Haley's courtroom by one Jonathon Jackson, younger brother of George Jackson, a figure in the Black Panther organization and a companion of Davis.

Angela Davis had been in the news before. When reports surfaced that UCLA had hired a Communist to teach philosophy, the governor of that state, Ronald Reagan, caused the university regents to dismiss her, under an old policy that then barred Communists from university jobs. (The regents' ruling was contested in the courts and in October of 1969 California Superior Court Judge Perry Pacht found her firing unconstitutional.) Her dismissal caused a great deal of furor among the left on American campuses, which was only exacerbated by the later charge of first-degree murder leveled against her by District Attorney Bruce Bales in Marin County. Davis disappeared and federal "fugitive from justice" charges were brought against her in August of 1970. She was ultimately arrested in New York.

Her fate became an immediate cause for the left worldwide. "Free Angela Davis" posters appeared throughout American cities. Stories appeared in the official Soviet press, decrying efforts of the "racist" American system to convict a black woman for murder simply because she was a Marxist. The worldwide Communist apparatus jumped into the fray. This proved what they had been saying, that the American capitalist system was designed to keep black people down, that they could get no justice under the American legal system. Angela Davis was being railroaded on trumped-up charges because of her race and political beliefs. She was being held incommunicado, the story went. Abroad the left wing press picked up the cause, creating such a storm that even responsible members of the foreign press requested our help in arranging interviews with her in her jail cell, where she was anything but incommunicado.

The issue was doing America great damage abroad, particularly in those emerging Third World countries with no real legal history of their own. Many countries, for instance, were unfamiliar with the American grand jury system. The system they were familiar with was one where a person charged with a crime is presumed to be guilty and must therefore prove his innocence. They were unfamiliar with a legal system that said a person was innocent until judged guilty by a jury of peers.

It became our duty to try to set the record straight. We had no idea whether Angela Davis was guilty or innocent. But the responsibility was there, naturally, for us to explain the American legal system, and to defend the system as it had worked in this case. Then the charge went out through the Communist propaganda network that the American government was trying, through the United States

Information Agency's offices abroad, to convict Angela Davis in the court of world opinion. That charge filtered its way up to editorial management levels at the Columbia Broadcasting System. They decided this might be worthy of a story.

So we were descended upon by CBS. By then I had been elevated, if that is the right word for it, to the position of deputy director for policy and plans. They wished to interview me and various other officers in the agency concerning charges that we were not being fair and impartial in our treatment of the Angela Davis case.

Fine. Have at it. We had nothing to hide. In fact, we were quite proud of our record in the matter.

They set up cameras in my own office and interviewed me for over an hour. They combed the agency, talking with other officers who had responsibility in the matter, going over records of what policy directives had gone out as well as what had flowed from those directives. That went on for three days. Then they went away. We waited for their report.

Nothing.

I finally called the interviewer and asked, in essence, "What happened?"

They had come to the conclusion, he said, that there was "no story." They couldn't find where we had done anything wrong. So they dropped the matter.

Well now, wouldn't it be nice to say so?

You know how it is. People don't write stories about banks that haven't been robbed.

True enough. People don't write stories about banks not being robbed. But my own view is that when a community is flooded by rumors that a bank has been robbed, or rumors of an impending bank failure caused by chicanery on the part of a bank official, and if a newspaper (or even a television network) investigates those rumors and finds them to be false, the very least that ought to be done is reveal the truth. And if they find the basis for those rumors to be a rival bank seeking some economic advantage, they ought to say so. They owe that to their readers. They owe their readers the truth. They ought not just walk away and say "no story," leaving their readers confused or misled by conflicting rumors.

CBS in this instance had no desire to pull truth's chestnuts out of the fire, particularly if in doing so they appeared to be defending an administration headed by Richard Nixon. If baseless charges from the left were damaging a president they wanted to see brought down, so much the better.

I suppose it is difficult for those coming of age now, with the Soviet Union collapsed as a political force, with bits and pieces of the Berlin Wall being sold as souvenirs, with citizens of Eastern European countries free to travel at home and abroad, with intercontinental missiles being destroyed rather than built, to comprehend the tenor of those times, the reality of those times.

It even seems strange to those of us who lived through it and did our bit to keep the faith. Within a few weeks after I joined the agency as assistant director for press and publications, for instance, I was visited by a reporter for *Time* magazine. He requested an interview. Granted, though I did think it strange that one so low on the totem pole would be sought out by so great and lofty a journal. It was a lengthy, and I thought friendly, interview. He was concerned in a small way about my qualifications. He seemed concerned in a larger way about my thoughts, particularly as they related to the Soviet Union and communism. I said I honestly believed communism to be an evil system. (I do not think I used the phrase "evil empire" made famous later, but I certainly would have if it had come to mind.) I explained that to my mind any governmental system that denied its people the right to travel freely in their own country, that denied them access to a free press, that denied them the right to worship a God other than the state, was by my definition an evil system and one that ought to be opposed.

The resulting story, as one can imagine, held out the specter of one of the agency's principal operating arms being headed by something of a rednecked kook who regarded the Soviet Union as being part of an "evil system." There were no explanatory comments in the story as to why I felt as I did. It was merely the standard *Time* treatment, written in such a way as to let the reader know the editors did not approve. The story upset a few in the agency who feared it might be an indication we were to go on the magazine's hit list. And it upset some in the agency who wondered who this new guy was and what life was going to be like under him. The head of the agency's regional desk dealing with the Soviet Union and Eastern Europe, a Foreign Service officer named Kempton Jenkins on assignment to the agency from the State Department, was particularly put out. He fancied himself the agency's authority and spokesman on matters relating to the Soviet Union and Eastern Europe. And, like most

State Department types I would come in contact with over the years, he did not like the idea of anyone rocking the boat — any boat, but especially his. It made things embarrassing. He might have to explain the situation to his counterparts at State.

Jenkins' concerns were of no concern to me. But I did think the interview was poorly reported. I wrote a letter to the magazine, setting forth in more detail my thoughts on the subject. It was printed. Peace and happiness prevailed. Even Jenkins was complimentary. He did say, however, that if I had not written the letter (of which he was completely unaware until it was published), "I just don't know if I could have accepted the situation." I don't know what he could have done about it, other than ask to be returned to the State Department, perish the thought.

NINETEEN

Foreign Service

After a year or two as head of the press and publications division I was asked to take over as deputy director for policy and plans. I was not really keen on the change, since I enjoyed where I was. As head of an operating arm I was not expected to do a great deal of travel abroad. That suited me fine. I did not like to fly, and the older I got the less I liked it. I was encouraged to go abroad a good bit more than I did, and perhaps should have. I went occasionally, primarily to look after affairs at the publishing plants in Manila, Beirut, and Mexico City. There were also occasional trips abroad to attend regional gatherings of our public affairs officers, where I was able to get a grasp of the problems they faced and how we could better serve their needs. But the trips were infrequent.

There were reasons quite apart from the dislike of flying that made those trips unwelcome for me. Certain physical problems had plagued me since my prison days. I was on a strict diet. No sugar. None. Low carbohydrates. Low fat. High protein. That routine. My usual baggage when I went abroad was one suitcase of clothes and one full of sardines, powdered skim milk, and dried fruits of one kind or another. In some countries I could fare reasonably well. In others I relied heavily on my suitcase.

As head of the policy shop the routine changed drastically. It was to this office that information flowed from various parts of our own agency, and it was from here that policy guidance flowed to the agency's operating arms, to the Voice of America, to movies and television, to print and publications, to the office of cultural affairs, and through the regional desks to the field. The Department of State's input took place at various levels, through contact between our regional desks and regional desks at State, and through attendance at various gatherings in the rarefied atmosphere of State's seventh floor. The CIA's input was gained through daily briefings concerning that agency's gleanings from around the world. Our contact with Defense and Commerce usually took place at interagency meetings at one level or another. And, of course, there were Shakespeare's own contacts with the president and members of the National Security Council.

In the field our operation was completely apart from the CIA. Not only were our missions distinctly different, with theirs being the gathering of intelligence and ours the purveying of public information, but there was the matter of political sensitivity regarding the host country. It was just better that way.

Nevertheless, somebody, someplace, had to be aware of what was going on where. Even if we had separate missions, we all got paid out of the same pot and had the same long-range goals in mind, that being to serve the interests of the United States. By and large I was that person as far as our agency was concerned. The daily briefing from CIA provided a glimpse of the problems. It did not give any indication of what was to be done about those problems, if anything. That information came from sources other than the briefing officer. Accordingly, when I now traveled abroad it was not unusual to visit with the CIA's man on the scene. Usually, not invariably, I found the agents to be intelligent, highly dedicated individuals.

I had friends among them long before I went to USIA, back when I worked for Tower. We lived in what might be called a "nest" of them in McLean, Virginia, only a few miles from their headquarters in Langley. Contrary to the general impression abroad, I did not find them to be a bunch of right-wing, reactionary anti-Communists. In terms of politics I would classify many of those I knew as "social democrats." In fact, after I had joined USIA, I was once told, by the then head of all "covert" activities in Central America, that Senator Fulbright's treatise on "The Arrogance of Power" was right on target, that the worst mistake America had ever made was to "predicate its foreign policy on unyielding opposition to communism."

Our conversation took place in one of those small, windowless, barren rooms at CIA headquarters in Langley, where one went for conversations of this type. I had just returned from some weeks in South and Central America, and was concerned about developments there, as was the chief of our own Latin American operations who accompanied me on the occasion. The CIA man's bottom line was "not to worry." Hardly the picture of one obsessed with anti-Communist fervor. That was before things erupted in El Salvador, and before Nicaragua.

In McLean our own backyard joined the backyard of one of their senior agents, Justin O'Donnell, who had served in many locales, the Middle East, Southeast Asia, various other places. We played many, many games of chess together. Next door to him there were others. Across the street and down a few houses was an analyst who spent his time poring over aerial photographs, pinpointing various Ho Chi Minh trails into South Vietnam. O'Donnell, who is now deceased, was once tapped, as I understood it, to neutralize "with prejudice" one Patrice Lumumba in the Congo, whom the Soviets had destined to destabilize that part of Africa. He begged off, and while a suitable replacement was being sought the matter was taken care of locally, in one of those coups that characterized newly emerging African nations at the time.

I was, and am, certainly no expert on that agency or its operation. But I had been around a number of its agents so much that after I had gone to USIA I felt comfortable working with them when it fell my lot. So much so, in fact, that I agreed with a request that I help "turn around" a KGB agent stationed in Washington, posing as a journalist for Tass. He had acquired a taste for Scotch whiskey and American women. Beyond that, and more importantly, he had begun to see some good things in the American society, even living in Washington. He began to appreciate its "openness." Someone in CIA (or elsewhere) had detected that weakening of his dedication to the ideas of Marx, et al., so they began to work on him, subtly and slowly. But his own superiors also began to see that weakening. So they sent him off to Dar es Salaam in Tanzania, which then enjoyed the enlightened leadership of the socialist leader Kenneth Kuanda. I suppose they thought he would be safe there. Either that, or perhaps that's where they sent people who needed reindoctrination.

A conference of East African PAOs was scheduled for Kenya and one for West African officers in Morocco. I was scheduled to attend both. I was asked if I would detour down to Tanzania between the two conferences. They hadn't given up on him, and someone had the bright idea that he might benefit by rubbing shoulders with me. Once a semifamous newsman from Texas, now a big wheel in the agency, that sort of thing. Perhaps if he visited with a former newsman from the hustings, as it were, he could get a better understanding of the things that were troubling him back in Washington.

So when the Nairobi conference ended I packed my bags of clothes and dried powdered milk, with sardines, and went to Dar es Salaam.

It didn't take long to decide why he was banished to that place. The surroundings were, if not delightful, at least interesting. A lovely seashore, with the Indian Ocean washing the beach. Beautiful trees and tropical shrubbery. But it was one of the more depressing places I'd ever seen. (Not the most depressing, for I had seen gray Warsaw in the winter, with its daily flyover of military jets, its uniformed soldiers on the streets, its beautiful, poorly dressed women with faraway looks in their eyes.)

A huge furor was going on within the Indian community when I arrived. The government, under the prodding of the "vice-president," from Zanzibar I believe, had decreed that beginning almost immediately, a black man's proposal of marriage to any Indian girl could not be refused. She must accept. She could not refuse, under penalty of criminal prosecution. The only "out" she had was if she could prove she was already betrothed to someone else. Needless to say, the clannish minority Indian community was upset, and understandably so. They had not yet adopted political correctness as a way of life.

A meeting between leaders of that community and the government had been concluded when I arrived. The next day's press, controlled by the government of course, carried an account of the meeting. When an Indian father, it was reported, protested that parents could not always influence how their daughters felt about such things, he was told by an official it was the parents' responsibility to influence their daughters properly. Otherwise they, too, would be held responsible.

It was that kind of place, the kind of place that brings joy to the hearts of real democrats and fellow egalitarians everywhere. The environment (I will blame it on that) even afflicted some of our local staff there. Our public affairs officer, for instance, was convinced that Kuanda's socialist approach to "nation building" was the proper approach, given the stage of Tanzanian development and the makeup of Tanzanian society. He was also convinced America was wrong in aggressively waging the war against Communists in Southeast Asia. So much so, in fact, that he had told his staff, in a childish display of braggadocio, he intended to wear a black armband to work the morning I arrived in Dar es Salaam. This would silently "make a statement," a practice much in vogue among those who sided with Ho Chi Minh, or anyone else who opposed American policies abroad. After having thought the matter through, however, he arrived at the office sans armband. Asked by his subordinates what changed his mind, he replied, "Well, you will notice I am wearing black socks." Whereupon he pulled up one leg of his trousers and displayed his black socks. That, presumably, made him feel better. Which I suppose was the whole point.

When his tour of duty in Tanzania ended (within a few months, fortunately) he was brought back to Washington, where he wandered agency halls for many months, waiting for another assignment. I helped where I could. His next assignment was no better than his last.

I don't know how the matter concerning the government and East African Indians was settled, but I do know that many came to America and went into the motel business.

The United States played no major role in the affairs of Tanzania at that time. The struggle locally was primarily between the Soviets and China under Mao. As a large player America had lost out when the socialist leader, Kuanda, cast his lot with the Red Chinese. He wanted to exploit the country's copper mines in the interior. America offered to construct a highway, thinking that would be more beneficial to the people along the way. The Chinese offered to build a railroad. Kuanda opted for the railroad. It was then under construction, but the construction site was essentially off limits to all foreigners except the Chinese. Progress in the construction and potential completion of the railroad was understandably of interest to both Americans and Soviets, since it could easily have something to do with world trade in copper.

Under those circumstances it became politically wise for the government of Tanzania to constantly praise China and China's accomplishments under Mao. In fact, while I was in Dar es Salaam the Chinese sent up their first, small, earth satellite, prompting the local press to chortle about the glories of socialism in general and of Mao's society in particular.

They had an interesting line, predicated on socialist logic: The American revolution had occurred some 200 years earlier. The Chinese revolution had occurred within the past 25 years or so. It took the capitalist Americans 200 years to perfect and send up their first satellite. The socialist system of the Soviet Union was able to do this in some 50 years. But it took the Chinese Communists only 25 years to perfect and send up theirs, thereby proving the superiority of their system over all others. And thereby proving the wisdom of Tanzanian leaders in adopting socialism as a way of nation building, as well as proving their wisdom in siding with the Chinese.

And also proving, I suppose, that it is not only in America where political rhetoric sometimes adopts an unreal, illogical, disconnected rationale.

At any rate, our mission proceeded. An embassy welcoming reception had been arranged, featuring the usual invitees from the diplomatic community. It was well attended, and, as hoped, one of those in attendance was the recent arrival from the United States, assigned to the Soviet mission as a press attaché or some such thing.

The reception, more a party than anything else, went well. Good food, plenty of Scotch, a little bourbon, much conviviality. Introductions were made. Long conversations ensued. The Soviet attaché was an interesting, intelligent fellow who seemed to enjoy the occasion. He circulated a great deal. He talked more than he should have.

When it was over and stock was taken, those who had arranged the affair seemed pleased. More than pleased, in fact. There was no way of telling whether they had done much good in their central objective, but they had gained information that seemed to have been a surprise to them.

Relations between the Chinese and Soviets were then undergoing considerable strain. Friction had developed along the frontier between the two countries in northern Manchuria, but they were, after all, still "brotherly socialists." How far and how deep that friction might go was still a question of some interest. It might have impact in other areas, and particularly in other parts of Africa.

In the course of the evening it was learned that people in the Soviet Embassy were quite upset. A couple of Soviet "diplomats" had ventured into the interior to check on the railroad's progress. Until then they had been allowed a good bit of freedom in this regard, where Western, non-socialist governments were not. On this occasion, however, they had been accosted by Tanzanian officials who, it was known, were heavily influenced by the Chinese. The Soviets were asked their reason for being in the area. They replied they were there on "official" diplomatic business, traveling with diplomatic credentials.

How long would it take them to complete their diplomatic mission? They thought about six weeks.

No. Not acceptable. They must complete their mission within twenty-four hours and return to Dar es Salaam. Otherwise, they would be escorted back to the capitol under guard.

This, needless to say, upset the Soviets. They were not accustomed to this kind of treatment. But what upset them more was knowing it would not have occurred unless the Chinese had leaned on the Tanzanians. It was a straw in the wind, the east wind. It was very interesting, and very prophetic, information.

I resumed the trip to Morocco, took part in the weeklong conference there (and heard a career State Department officer expound on how much farther along the road to modern development Africa would be if white men had never set foot on the continent), and returned home. In time I asked, as a matter of academic interest more than anything else, what had happened regarding our "friend" in Dar es Salaam. He was evidently being watched very closely, for suddenly he received orders to return to Moscow. I hoped it was a normal transfer. I feared it was not.

At any rate I felt sorry for him. I had been to Moscow. In fact, I had even been to Moscow during the snows of October. Cold Moscow was not a great place to be during the Cold War. The most enjoyable part of any trip there during those years was the leaving.

The problem was not among the people, whom I found to be good, decent folk interested in a better life for themselves and their children. The problem was with the system, a system regimented in accordance with Bolshevik thought. It was just so screwed up.

Once, for instance, I had to go to the Soviet Union to officially open a cultural exhibit in Donetsk, in the Ukraine some seven or eight hundred miles south of Moscow. It was part of the general agreement between the United States and the Soviet Union regarding a somewhat limited attempt to expose something of the culture of each country to people of the other. Everything had been worked out. It should have been a very simple procedure.

It was not.

First off was the hotel. It was a nice enough place, just off the square near the Kremlin. After we got squared away we became acquainted with a woman who appeared to have fought her way up through the ranks of the Communist Party, which I suppose she had. Sour, surly, overweight, she was our "floor monitor." Upon leaving the room we had to go by her desk, actually a small table, and leave our key. She would log the time, ask where we were going and when we would be back. Then we could go down the elevator. When we came back we were to again check in with her, get our key, and go to the room. Every floor was run in this fashion.

This seemed a strange requirement. They knew exactly who we were, why we had come to the Soviet Union, our destination, what we were to do when we got there. Nevertheless, this was the routine. It could not be altered.

Next morning, while it was still dark and with October snows falling lightly on previous October snows, a car from the American Embassy came to pick us up for the trip to the airport. A young USIA foreign service officer named Andrew Falkiewicz was to accompany us to Donetsk as interpreter. My understanding was that he was a native-born Czech. He spoke Russian fluently and was not particularly fond of the Soviets, knowing what they had done to his country.

The driver was a local, employed by the embassy but furnished to the embassy by the Soviet government. He was burly but quiet. The limousine displayed small American flags atop the front fenders. We bundled ourselves in and headed for the airport.

At curbside, where we were to unload, there were a few unused parallel parking slots evidently for use by various Soviet officials and visiting dignitaries. The driver whipped into the vacant spot so we could unload. Unfortunately, there was a Soviet citizen standing a foot or two from the curb, well inside the reserved space. The driver's lights were on. The man was clearly visible. The driver simply ran into him, knocking him to the ground. The citizen was heavily bundled against the cold, fortunately, and was not seriously hurt. He struggled to his feet and received a tongue lashing from the driver. He stood and stared at us, at the American flags, and finally went his way. He never said a word.

We took our overnight bags and went to the airline ticket counter. Again everything was supposed to be arranged, but Andrew had warned it probably wasn't. In fact, he called our attention to the fact that what followed would probably be interesting. It was.

The young lady behind the ticket counter (well, actually she wasn't so young) could find no record of our proposed flight. There followed many words in Russian as Falkiewicz became increasingly irritated and vociferous.

Finally, she found the record. More words followed. Andrew told us, "Come on, we're going back to the hotel." Which we did.

On the way we asked what it was all about. He translated.

When she finally found what she was looking for, she asked to see our luggage.

"We have no luggage," Falkiewicz told her. "We're just going down for one night and this is all we have."

"You have no luggage?"

"We have no luggage."

"Well, you have no luggage. We have no plane."

"What?"

"You have no luggage, we have no airplane."

"Why didn't you say that in the first place, and save us all a lot of time?"

No answer.

"When will you have a plane?"

She would not say when a plane would arrive.

More words followed. The closest she would come to it was to say, "You may come back this afternoon around two o'clock. We'll see."

All we could do, Falkiewicz said, was return to the airport and "hang around" during the general time frame she had given us.

"It won't do any good to call and ask if the plane is in, or when it will leave, or anything about it. They simply won't tell us."

He had been through all that many times.

We went back to the hotel, went up to our floor, and asked for the key. This naturally upset the floor monitor. We weren't supposed to come back until the next day, she reminded us in forceful terms. We must stick to our schedule.

After lunch we returned to the airport. The plane was there, but the ticket counter didn't know exactly when it was supposed to leave. We should wait. We would be called.

We waited. And while we waited we looked at pictures of Lenin adorning every nook and cranny of the place. Lenin the child. Lenin the youngster. Lenin the man. Lenin the friend of the worker. Lenin the revolutionary. Lenin in company with various party leaders. Lenin the Father of Socialism.

Within a half hour or so another young lady showed up. Since we were on official "diplomatic" business, traveling on diplomatic passports, we had been assigned an escort to take us to our plane. It would not be proper to require us to go to the plane in company with common passengers.

We soon found out that if it were not for the honor of the thing, we would just as soon have ridden. By getting out of the customary bureaucratic loop we were inviting trouble.

She took charge of our little party. But she could command no transportation, so we walked.

Another small problem was that she did not know which plane was going to Donetsk. We walked along a flight line where plane crews lolled alongside their planes. At each plane we would stop and she would ask the pilot, "Are you going to Donetsk?"

We never found a pilot who admitted he was going to Donetsk. But we did find one who said he was going to Volgograd. The escort said, "This is the one, we must wait here."

Again Falkiewicz explained. It was all perfectly normal, he said. For reasons he could not explain it was normal under such circumstances for pilots to indicate only their ultimate destination. They would simply never indicate the cities where they might stop along the way. But the escort knew that the plane that went to Volgograd had to stop off in Donetsk.

The plane appeared to have the configuration of a modified DC 3 with twin prop engines, as were most planes along that particular flight line. It was relatively new, and once we got inside relatively comfortable. But we were not inside yet.

There was no ramp, merely a ladder up to the forward door. We started up the ladder. She stopped us. We must wait. So we stood near the bottom of the ladder and waited. Then she had an idea. We must move back, away from the ladder.

"Why?" Andy asked.

"There might be a woman come down the ladder and it would not be nice for you to look up her dress."

MTV had not yet come to the Soviet Union, or America either for that matter. So we backed up.

Eventually, a signal must have passed. We were told to board. Shortly an airport conveyance showed up with the rest of the passengers. Evidently, the driver had been told which plane was going to Donetsk. An uneventful flight in good weather put us in Donetsk shortly before dark.

We checked in to a small hotel, with small rooms and not much else to recommend it to the weary traveler. We were, obviously, running late. Things that were planned for that afternoon would have to wait until the morrow. Then we would get another lesson in the glories of that most carefully planned of socialist societies.

We were met by an agency officer named Davis, who had been

assigned the task of creating the Donetsk exhibit and seeing it through. He was black, tough, and a thoroughgoing believer in America and the capitalist system, facts we mention only because they had a bearing on what followed.

Before the exhibit would be allowed to open, there had to be a meeting between myself, as the highest ranking American there, and the local government official. I have no idea where he was from or what his rank was. He simply had to get into the act. He seemed to think the entire enterprise had to be approved by him before it could go forward, despite the fact it was already set up and waiting to open. Davis saw in the occasion an opportunity to get some beefs off his own chest and to demand some cooperation on the part of the local officials, who had, he said, thrown all sorts of roadblocks in the way of a successful exhibit.

In the first place we had been given a site far from any population center, nearly one-half mile beyond the end of the city bus service. Visitors would have to walk that distance through terrain not well suited to walking. The exhibit was scheduled to open that afternoon, but any effort to publicize the event had been meager at best. Clearly the authorities had not only made no effort to be cooperative, they had deliberately sought the opposite. Davis was unhappy and wanted to tell them so. So if we had to go through with the routine perhaps we could accomplish something for "our side."

The official showed up, a perfect rendition of the Communist "commissar"—short, heavy, round-faced and round-headed, unsmiling, shaved head, dark suit, a medal or two, accompanied by a bevy of lesser lights.

We drew some tables together into a makeshift conference table, around which all gathered, the Soviets on one side and the Americans on the other. He and I sat directly opposite each other at the center. He had his interpreter. My memory is that all the Americans, except myself, were fluent in Russian.

After welcoming us he launched into a speech about how the two sides needed to agree to some sort of détente. I got the impression he was advocating such a course. It went on and on.

When it came my turn I said I thought those matters had already been settled at much higher levels, by Mr. Brezhnev and Mr. Nixon. There was no need for us to discuss the wisdom, or lack of wisdom, of such a course. All that was left for us to do was get on with it and carry out the agreements between the two governments. And in that vein, I said, Mr. Davis had a few words he would like to express, which he did. The commissar sat and listened, impassively. He said he would look into the complaints. As things turned out there was no need.

By midafternoon local citizens began to trickle in. At the end of the workday they came in droves. Clearly the grapevine was working, as it does in all closed societies. They crowded around the new automobiles, many taking notes on the prices, what the car would cost with or without automatic transmission, air conditioning, radio. They pored over the kitchen appliances, again noting the price range normally charged American consumers. They marveled at the library, small though it was. They gawked at the equipment available for the American sportsman. In short, it was off to a most pleasing beginning.

So much so in fact that certain measures were called for. There appeared throughout the crowd individuals endeavoring to set the record straight, from the Communist viewpoint, of course. They were ostensibly plain Soviet citizens, scattered throughout the crowd, muttering to all who would listen that this whole exhibit was a lie, that it was merely propaganda, that the items on display were not available to plain American citizens who could not afford them in any case.

Our plan called for Davis to welcome the visitors (when and if a sufficient number arrived), explain to them the nature of the exhibit, and answer any questions they might have. We quickly learned we didn't have to worry about the "if and when" part of the plan. The crowd was there in the hundreds. Overflowing, in fact.

Davis stood upon a table, welcomed the visitors in fine style, and went through the routine, ending with an offer to answer any questions they might have. Then the fun began.

Almost immediately, questions were hurled at Davis from various parts of the crowd by those individuals seen earlier acting as "agents provocateurs." He handled them well, calmly, until the questions turned somewhat personal. How could he defend a country and a system where his own people were kept in bondage? Obviously, he was a paid agent of the capitalist society. They knew all about the widespread poverty among blacks in America. It was so bad that even the American government had to acknowledge it. How could people living in that kind of poverty afford a dishwasher or a washing machine? How could they afford a new car?

Davis acknowledged that not everyone in America, black or

white, could afford a new car, and that not everyone had an automatic dishwasher. But we were not saying that. We were saying these things were readily available in America to those who could afford them, and that most could afford them. Others could hope to get there under the American system. When the questions persisted along the personal vein, he appeared to lose his temper. (He later said he didn't, that it was part of the act.) He told them what kind of home he had back in America (a lovely, two-story red brick in Maryland, just outside the District of Columbia) and what kind of car he drove and what kind of car his wife drove. (Both were better than my own, by far. I had been a guest in his home. He was telling the truth.) Then, with his voice rising, he pulled his passport from his pocket, waved it over his head, and all but shouted: "This is my passport. The only time I need it is when I go abroad. In my own country I can go from place to place, from city to city, from state to state, and never show it. I can travel as I please anywhere in my own country. Can you do the same?"

There was silence from the provocateurs and applause from the crowd. There was no need to belabor the point, for all knew the answer.

We spent another night in Donetsk and returned to Moscow. The floor monitor was beside herself. Where had we been? What had we been doing? "Everyone" had been looking for us. We were supposed to be back the previous night. This was entirely unacceptable. We must never do this again. Andrew, who acted as interpreter on these occasions, was completely unsympathetic, for which I was happy.

I spent the next few days in Moscow visiting with the embassy staff and took one brief tour of the Kremlin grounds in the company of John Jacobs, editor of *America Illustrated*, then in Moscow trying to work on some distribution problems.

Our distribution problems were easily identified but less easily corrected. At that time we were allowed to distribute a specified number of the popular *America Illustrated* magazines in the Soviet Union. In return the Soviets were allowed to distribute a specified number of their English-language magazine *Soviet Life* in the United States. Basically the problem was that while *America Illustrated* was much sought after in the Soviet Union, being one of the very few Western publications having even limited distribution in that country, *Soviet Life* was not popular in America. While it was lighter and more colorful that most other Soviet publications, it was still obviously and overly propagandistic. Too, it had to compete with hundreds of other periodicals on American newsstands.

We were caught in a sort of dilemma. The slow sales of *Soviet Life* caused embarrassment for those Communist "cultural" officials having responsibility for such matters. The obvious popularity of *America Illustrated* in the Soviet Union also caused embarrassment to those same officials. Somebody in that branch of the KGB having responsibility in such matters evidently got the idea that one way to increase their sales in America was to exert downward pressure on the sale of *America Illustrated* in the Soviet Union, thus forcing the American "side" to do what it could to encourage sales of *Soviet Life* in America. Their solution was to send agents around to the various kiosks and pick up copies of *America Illustrated* at the designated distribution points before they could become available to the general public. In this manner the "letter" of the exchange agreement could be observed, but circulation among Soviet citizens could be curtailed.

Nobody would admit publicly what was going on, though both sides knew exactly what was going on. The matter simply became "problems in distribution" that had to be worked out. So we gave advice to the other side on how they could make their magazine more readable, more attractive to the American consumer. For us it was a win-win situation. The pro-Soviet message in *Soviet Life* was no different than the pro-Soviet message appearing in much of the Western media, where stories frequently appeared praising the advanced state of Soviet medicine, the peaceful nature of the Soviet state, the secure and happy life of the Soviet worker. In fact, I never fully understood why the Soviets agreed to the exchange in the first place. Their magazine caused hardly a blip on the scale of American political thought. The message carried by *Soviet Life* was certainly nothing new to readers in America.

At any rate Jacobs took time off from his "negotiations" with Moscow officials on our distribution problems to accompany me on a truncated tour of the city, explaining in the process what was legally permissible at the time. With what sounded like perfect Russian he convinced a soldier guard that I was a very important visitor from America on official business with the government of the Soviet Union. I had not had time to obtain the necessary clearance to enter the Kremlin grounds, he argued, but surely the guard wouldn't mind us looking around. It worked. The guard opened the gate and we entered.

Inside the Kremlin walls there was the appalling spectacle of thousands of loyal Communists from throughout the empire and beyond, patiently inching forward for a glimpse of the mummified Lenin, their own personal deity to whom they gave eternal thanks for starting this glorious system, then so much admired and defended by Western liberals.

I didn't get in line, figuring the reward not worth the effort.

As evening approached the question arose of what to do about dinner. A small group of embassy staffers wished to continue our discussions before I left Moscow, and they didn't want to suffer through another hotel meal. One knew of a small Georgian restaurant where the food was reputed to be decent, and where a makeshift band might afford something approaching a musical diversion as we talked. He had been there before and it was, he said, "different."

It was indeed different, at least compared to the hotel fare. But getting inside was another matter. A long line of Muscovites was patiently waiting in the cold of the October evening when we arrived. We got in line, but eventually it became apparent we were going nowhere fast. Finally, the person who had been there before decided he would correct the situation. He got out of line, went to the door of the establishment, and began banging for attention. The door had one glass window which was frosted over. He scraped the frost away and continued his knocking. When someone inside eventually came to peer through the glass, he held up something which I assumed was some sort of identification papers. He came back to the group and instructed us to follow him. We trooped to the door and were promptly admitted.

His identification papers, it turned out, had been a ten-dollar bill, U.S. currency. The meal had to be paid for in rubles, but if one left some American currency on the table, and it was "found" by the appropriate people, nothing would be said. It worked wonders.

The meal was good. The band played something approaching music of the fifties, and many couples danced. Many Georgians were present but they were remarkably well behaved, for Georgians, with only one serious fight erupting during the course of the evening.

For myself the evening was instructive. I was somewhat embarrassed that we had walked from the back of the line, past some fifty or sixty local citizens waiting in the cold, for immediate entry. Not to worry, I was assured. That was the way the system worked. Those inside would remain there until the place closed. There was small chance that those outside would make it inside. Eventually, most would simply leave. It was not exactly my idea of an egalitarian society.

There was one small sidebar, one small aftermath, to the Donetsk exhibit. Even though the Soviet Union was then a "closed" and tightly controlled society, it was imperative for the government to know what the people were thinking. Without that knowledge it was possible that a people's thinking could get out of hand. With that knowledge the government could, through its control of the means of communication, alter and shape that thinking in a politically correct manner.

In the Soviet Union the Communist Party served that function. It not only served as the eyes and ears of the government, it served as the government's strong right arm, or, more aptly, the government's strong left arm, in enforcing governmental policies.

The practice then was for higher ranking Communist officials to visit local communities, call in the local cadre plus an assortment of party workers from the factories and farms, and discuss whatever complaints they were hearing from ordinary citizens. The sessions were closed to all but the "invited," but it was not unusual for our "other agency" to have informants at those sessions. The feedback from this particular session was most interesting.

The commissar opened the meeting in the usual manner, asking those assembled to relay the mood of their constituents. He was told that much grumbling was going on among the citizens over the lack of consumer goods. Pointed reference was made to the recent American exhibit and questions were raised as to why things like that were not available to Soviet citizens.

At first the official tried to blow the whole thing off as "capitalist propaganda." Americans did not enjoy those material goods, he said. Claims that they did were merely lies, designed to spread discontent. The questions persisted. Perhaps it was propaganda, but the people believed it.

Finally, the official exploded. "I'll tell you why you don't have those goods," he said. "You spend too much time with vodka and not enough time working. When you learn to work as hard as the Americans work you can have those things too."

There were more words along those lines. The meeting broke up in disharmony.

Our efforts had not been in vain. In fact, that was the whole purpose of our exhibits in the Soviet Union, to bring pressure upon the system, to try to create so much demand for consumer goods that pressure would be brought on the government to divert resources from the military, which then consumed massive proportions of the nation's industrial output.

From Moscow I had to go to what was then Yugoslavia, where we had certain problems concerning certain matters. In fact there always seemed to be problems there. Nobody liked anybody and we had to get along with everybody. The principal problem at the time, from our own perspective, was the impending (and apparent) winding down of the Tito years and the probable breakup of a diverse nation held together by force of arms. There was little we could do about that. But we at the agency could, perhaps, help create a climate where American influence could be brought to bear when that time came. As subsequent events would prove, however, there is no assurance that the understanding of a political problem will necessarily result in anything constructive being done about it. The Tito years did indeed wind down. The country did indeed fly apart. But when that time came, American influence would be noticeably lacking.

It came time to leave, on a cold, misty, foggy morning, with a ceiling so low I could not imagine airplanes operating. But I had been booked on an Austrian flight, with an Austrian flight crew operating an American-built plane headed for Vienna. That helped some. I figured I was lucky.

The passengers trailed on board. I was an early boarder and got a seat next to a window. Then a large group of Japanese boarded. They were obviously traveling as a group, for they seemed to take instructions from what was probably the youngest member. I assumed they were all good, loyal Communists, come to Moscow to pay their respects. I figured I had probably seen them standing in line to see Lenin the previous day. Suddenly, in what I considered a terrible turn of fate, the young Japanese sat down in the seat beside me. Oh, Lord, was I going to have to sit beside a damned Commie Jap all the way to Vienna? A Japanese would have been bad enough. But a Japanese Communist?

Neither of us said a word.

The plane taxied to the end of the fog-shrouded runway. We waited a few minutes before the pilot pushed the throttle forward. The jets roared, we began to move, and just as quickly the brakes were thrown. Out of the mist a plane passed directly overhead and hit the runway immediately in front of us, on the same runway. Another hundred feet. Another fifty feet.

We waited another few minutes, during which I suppose there was some excited conversation between the Austrian pilot and what passed for Moscow ground control. Quite frankly, I was most apprehensive. Among the passengers there was complete silence, a sort of terrified silence.

Power was again applied and we rolled down the runway.

I have flown a great deal in my life, but I have never been on a plane that climbed to such altitudes in such a hurry. It was as if the pilot stood the plane on its tail and used every ounce of power available, anxious as he was to leave the immediate vicinity as quickly as possible. We hung in that position until he was satisfied. Then we leveled off, and he apologized for the "delay" and told us to relax.

My seatmate turned to me and said, in perfect English and with obvious emotion: "I've never been so glad to leave a place in all my life. It's like a prison there. An absolute prison. I feel free, free."

My astonishment, and my pleasure, knew no bounds. For all he knew I might have traveled all the way to Moscow to view the remains of Lenin. But it didn't matter. He said what he thought. Here was a man after my own heart. This might not be such a bad trip after all.

I asked what brought his group to Moscow.

They were going to Africa on a picture-taking safari. He was the tour guide. They merely came through Moscow because it was the shortest route for them, and stopped over to see the sites. It was a bad choice, he said. He never wanted to go back.

I deduced I had not seen him in the Lenin line.

It was a good flight. My seatmate and I had pleasant conversation all the way to Vienna. I never told him about my days in Japanese prisons.

I have thought about that incident many, many times since then. It has helped in many ways.

I suppose, at this point, and before I go further with this effort, I should lay out my feelings about the Japanese and all other people.

I do not "hate" the Japanese. I do not know that I "hated" them even when they were trying to kill me, and I was trying to kill them. In the heat of battle I was most happy, if that be a fitting word for such circumstances, when they, rather than Americans, were killed. It was better that they die than that we die. I would have felt the same if they were black, or brown, or white. In war the enemy is the enemy. One's friends and comrades are one's friends and comrades. Hate, as I interpret the word, enters the picture only as an element of enduring emotion, not like the time I stood on our gun parapet and cheered when we shot down an enemy bomber and watched it roar, flaming and twisting, into the waters off Corregidor. The fact that five or so people went down with it was then somewhat immaterial. At that moment there was happiness, not hatred.

I am not devoid, unfortunately, of the capacity to hate, though I am much more inclined to "hate" certain ideas and certain individuals than to hate a whole people. I would have no difficulty, for instance, in finding hatred for those American officials who, by accident or design, sat on information that allowed the Japanese to attack Pearl Harbor with relative impunity, if they could be identified.

It is very difficult for me not to hate individuals whose ideas or actions cause the deaths of innocent people. As far as I am concerned, American soldiers and sailors sleeping in their barracks on Sunday morning in peacetime are innocent people, and it matters not to me whether their deaths may be laid to calculating politicians in Tokyo or Washington.

However, it is one thing to harbor certain thoughts, certain "after the fact" thoughts. Whether one would have acted on those thoughts when they were relevant is another matter. For instance:

Would I have killed Tojo in time of war?

Certainly.

Would it have been better if he were killed in time of peace, before Nanking, before Bataan, before Corregidor, before the Bataan Death March, before the prison ships?

Certainly.

Would I have done it?

If I had known what was about to ensue, the answer is probably yes. Not because he was Japanese, but because I remember Nanking, and Bataan, and Corregidor, and the prison ships and the prisons.

But while I do not "hate" the Japanese as a people, I must confess in all honesty that I am still uncomfortable around those I do not know as individuals. I am particularly uncomfortable around groups of Japanese, simply because it brings back so many memories. That feeling is not so pronounced now as it was for many years after the war. In fact, my first trip to Japan, other than an airport stop on the way to the Philippines, was traumatic indeed.

I was chosen to head an agency inspection team slated to examine our operation in Japan. I did not want to go, but I figured I would simply have to screw up the courage and face my own problem. I did not feel I had any right to refuse an assignment that had a bearing on the operation of the agency.

Our Japanese operation was one of the largest, if not the largest, among the "advanced" countries. It was headed by a high ranking foreign service officer named Bill Carter. He had decided he wanted to embark upon a different course, one costing much more money than had previously been allocated to the Japanese operation. Aside from the money, many saw his proposed course as being one of style over substance, as being centered too much in Tokyo, where the bright lights were, and not enough in other parts of Japan. Also, we had reports of some unhappiness, of a personal nature, within the ranks of lower ranking officers and employees. Some regarded the PAO as overbearing, self-centered. Others regarded him as the wave of the future. Before additional monies were allocated to the post, and before any approval was given to the new course of action, Shakespeare and Loomis decided we needed a closer look.

It was the practice then that when inspection teams of this nature were sent to a post, it was to be headed up by foreign service officers of equal or higher rank than the head of the post to be inspected. The team traveled under the aegis of the agency's inspector general, himself a senior foreign service officer. This, I presume, was to take into consideration the personal sensitivities of the people involved. It was also the practice, in such cases, to take along an outsider, someone with no connection to the agency, someone with no axe to grind, someone who might provide an independent assessment.

To take care of that sensitivity our own team was officially headed up by a senior foreign service officer, but all concerned understood the significance of my own presence, as well as the significance of another member of the team.

I was informed that the outsider in this case would be James Michener, who had gained a considerable amount of recognition as a writer. I did not then know Mr. Michener, and I must confess that I groaned inwardly at the prospect of his being a member of the team. Here would be deadweight, someone going along for the ride, someone who would spend his time seeing the sights.

Never was worry more wasted.

Michener proved to be probably the hardest working member of the team and certainly one of the most valuable, although we did differ on one or two occasions. He had a tendency to feel compassion in certain cases where I felt the axe would have been more appropriate. For many days we worked at small desks no more than four feet apart. I gained a great deal of respect and admiration for him, and, at the risk of causing embarrassment to him, will claim him as a friend to this day. Our trails have crossed many times since those days, and when they do it is seldom that the Japan experience is not mentioned.

That first postwar landing in Japan caused untold anxiety for me. Being submerged in a society of Japanese, being surrounded by a sea of Japanese moving hither and yon, all seemingly intent upon some purpose, all seemingly oblivious to my presence, was extremely difficult for me to adjust to. As long as I was back at the embassy, at our own operation, I had no great difficulty. But once out on the streets it was another matter. I could not help thinking of times past.

In addition to the problems at USIS (for United States Information Service, as USIA posts were called abroad) there were problems elsewhere. In fact, in my opinion, the problems elsewhere stemmed in large measure from the problems in our operation in Tokyo, where the obsession with "new directions" and "super graphics" devoured energy that should have been devoted to simple problems at hand.

One such problem was near a place called Fukuoka, on the southwestern edge of Japan in Kyushu, across the straits from Korea. There a large American Air Force base had been built after the war. It was built well outside the city, but in the nature of such things many local citizens, in order to be close to their work, had constructed homes nearby. In fact, many were built as close to the runways as legally permissible. People would sometimes cross the runways directly rather than go the long way around to see Aunt Sadie. Under such circumstances accidents do happen. Planes do fall. People get hurt. People get killed. A great deal of ill feeling had been generated, fueled by leftists who saw an opportunity to sow seeds of anti-American discord. If the base were not there, none of this would happen.

Our small local operation in Fukuoka felt overwhelmed and asked for help. I went there to see if anything could be done.

I went first to the base commander. Not much help there. He had the mentality of a tank commander. So what if he got shot at (figuratively) by small-arms fire? No harm done. He was in charge of running the base. The way he saw it, the base would be there until the twenty-five-year agreement ended, then the base would probably be closed down. Everybody knew the rules; all they had to do was learn to live by them. That was the military way.

I tried to argue that America would be living with Japan long after the base was closed, and that it would be better, it seemed, to leave with good feelings rather than bad. Well, maybe so, but that was not really his responsibility. His responsibilities were plain. Still, he would be willing to sit down with local leaders and discuss the problems.

I next asked for a meeting with the editors of the local newspaper. The Japanese are an extremely literate society, and newspapers have wide circulation with much influence. I thought they could help, if they wanted to. The meeting was arranged. The next morning we assembled, some fifteen or twenty of them and one of me.

I sat at the head of the table and looked down both sides. Unsmiling, impassive faces. Some were older, but many were about my age and I got the idea they were trying to figure out what part I had played in the recent unpleasantness between our two countries. Certainly that thought crossed my own mind.

I understood, I said, that certain problems had arisen concerning the nearby Air Force base. We would like very much to see if we could get to the bottom of the matter and perhaps come to a better understanding. Did they have any thoughts?

Strangely enough, the first comments did not deal with the base at all. I suppose the local USIS people, who arranged the meeting, told them of my own newspaper background. So they were very honored, very pleased, all that good, formal stuff, that I should come to visit them. That out of the way, they gave me their thoughts concerning the situation. They took turns, around the table. All given in a somewhat cold, impassioned manner.

Until . . . Near the end of the table, on my right, one finally asked: "Were you in the service?"

"Yes."

"Where did you serve?"

"In the Philippines."

Silence. Their assumption being, I suppose, that I had served in the invasion forces that recaptured the Philippines.

"I didn't serve in the Pacific theater," he said. "I served in Manchuria."

Now my blood was beginning to run cold. At that moment my sympathies were entirely with the base commander.

"Where did you serve in Manchuria?" I asked.

"I was in Mukden." (The Japanese name for Shenyang.)

I figured I may as well lay it on the table. Get it over with.

"Oh? I was in Mukden too."

Stunned silence. He knew. They all knew.

"Were you, ah, ah . . ."

"I was a prisoner there. I was on Corregidor."

He hastened to say that he was never at that prison, he was merely the information officer for the army in Manchuria, based in Mukden.

There was another silence.

"That war is over," I said finally.

For the first time there were smiles. Even a scattering of applause. The tension had been broken. We had a good, honest discussion.

I do not know how things worked out between the local community and the base commander. I do not know if my visit did any good for them. But for me it did a world of good. I left feeling great about myself, as if I had climbed some high hill, wrestling dragons along the way. A hill from which I could see a little better. A little farther.

I returned to Tokyo, we completed the inspection report, and made our way back to Washington.

If I had been the sole judge of such matters I would have relieved our PAO of his responsibilities and denied the request for new money and a "new" course. I saw nothing innovative in his suggestions at all. To me it would amount to costly wheel spinning. A great deal of showmanship and not much substance. An exercise in self-aggrandizement.

But I was not the sole judge. That, in the final analysis, would be up to Loomis. That was his portfolio. It would be up to him to make the recommendation to Shakespeare.

He called a meeting at his Middleburg farm. Members of the inspection team were there, as was the man in charge of the Far East desk, John Reinhardt, whom we had brought back to Washington from Pakistan or some similar location, and placed in that position because we thought we saw in him a person of some backbone. Without putting too fine a point on it, I argued my position, Reinhardt argued Carter's. In the end Loomis decided in the post's favor.

When it was all over Reinhardt approached me and said, "Ken, you are probably right. I agree with what you say. But I have to defend my PAOs."

The system was alive and well.

In fact, when Jimmy Carter became president of the United States, he named Reinhardt, who was black, as director of the agency. I assume Bill Carter fared well, at least for a while.

THE CHOW DIPPER

An interesting little sidelight occurred during this whole process. After the report had been written but before any decision had been made, before we had the meeting at the Loomis farm, Carter left Tokyo and showed up in Washington. He perhaps had heard that the report might be unfavorable, that there were questions in some minds, particularly mine, for he asked for a meeting to argue his case.

We had the meeting, but the discussion had little to do with the report. He said again what he had said in Tokyo. Nothing new that I could see.

But then he brought up the fact that he was Jewish. His name was originally something else, Cohen, I think it was. He had changed his name, he said, because he had been subjected to so much discrimination as a youngster. He didn't want non-Jews to know he was Jewish.

I found it astonishing. If he wished to cloud the fact that he was Jewish, why tell me? I did not know it, did not care one way or the other. And obviously the fact that he was Jewish had not harmed his career. He had climbed to the top of the foreign service career ladder, and I doubt seriously I was the only person to whom he had ever told this story. I had persons of the Jewish faith on my own staff, persons to whom I listened with great respect. The fact that they were Jewish had no bearing, as far as I was concerned, on the wisdom or lack of wisdom concerning their thoughts or recommendations.

He seemed to be implying that the cause for some unhappiness on his staff in Tokyo was because he was Jewish, and that opposition to his planned course of action in Tokyo might be predicated on the same reason. But, given his stated efforts at concealment, how would they have known, unless he had told them, as he was telling me? All I could do was sit and listen. And wonder. Sometimes I still do.

TWENTY

Hello, Solzhenitsyn;
So Long, Nixon, Allende

The gods of the Cold War ground slowly, but exceedingly fine. Alexander Solzhenitsyn was expelled from the Soviet Union (in handcuffs) and came westward. The State Department went into a tizzy, fearful that we at the agency would attempt to exploit the situation. If State, under Kissinger, had had its way we would have made no more than passing mention of the "defection." They took the position that the word would get out one way or the other and that we in the West should not appear to brag about it, thus proving they had less sense than the proverbial chicken. Even a dumb chicken has enough sense to cackle when she accomplishes something worthwhile.

I was not with the agency when Svetlana Alliluyeva, daughter of the murderous tyrant Joseph Stalin, defected to the West in 1967, but others who were there reported much the same reaction among many at State and some within the agency. One of the excuses given then was that she might prove to be a "flake," that she might turn out to be an erratic individual who would shortly change her mind and go back to the Soviet Union. That worry, if it was legitimate, could hardly be the case with Solzhenitsyn.

The Solzhenitsyn issue posed particular problems for us. Here was a giant of a man, an uncompromising man, an icon to many of us who marveled at his immense physical and intellectual courage, a man who had suffered mightily for his beliefs, now casting his lot with the West. He seemed to embody those qualities we in the West, at least publicly, most admired.

Yet our own policy makers reacted in a state of shock. The first word we got from the State Department desk having responsibility for affairs in the USSR was not to exploit the matter. They were particularly worried about what the Voice of America might say in its broadcasts to the Soviet Union. Retreating into their usual mode, they did not want the waters roiled. This, needless to say, caused great unhappiness among those of us in policy areas at USIA who wished to take a different approach. The result was a sort of holding pattern until we could get things sorted out.

As noted earlier, the law did say that in matters of foreign policy we at USIA were required to take our cue from the Department of State. But who in the Department of State? I was determined that the final word on the matter would not be some career desk officer at State, worried that his future might be affected by a risky decision during politically troubled times. Left to his own devices, the reaction of the typical State Department officer to any sudden change of circumstance is simple: do nothing. As far as I was concerned, unless we could get word from the top at State, i.e., Henry Kissinger, we should be free to act on our own. After all, our own director also had access to the president.

Our differences with State over the handling of the Solzhenitsyn story also became a cause for immediate dissension within our own ranks. There were, obviously, those who would have jumped at the chance to provide Solzhenitsyn a forum to talk to his own people. And there were those who agreed with State that the less said the better. Some thought we were not saying enough, not acting boldly enough. Others thought we were saying too much simply by reporting what others were saying.

Our new director, James Keogh, who had followed Shakespeare as head of the agency, dispatched a "secret" memorandum to Henry Kissinger asking for guidance. (The message, labeled "Memorandum for Henry Kissinger from Jim Keogh," was classified "secret" by Keogh on March 4, 1974, and was "subject to General Declassification Schedule of Executive Order 11652. Automatically downgraded at two year intervals and declassified on December 31, 1982." So I see no reason not to use it now.)

The essence of the memorandum was that Solzhenitsyn, still in Vienna after having been "expelled" from the Soviet Union, asked for a letter requesting an interview by the Voice of America. But in order that the flavor of that moment not be lost, and that I not mislead, the memo is quoted here in its entirety:

SECRET March 4, 1974
MEMORANDUM FOR HENRY KISSINGER
FROM: JIM KEOGH

Alexander Solzhenitsyn has suggested that he might like to be interviewed on the Voice of America. He has asked VOA to send him a letter requesting an interview and listing the subjects proposed for discussion.

An interview with Solzhenitsyn could have such important implications in U.S.-USSR relations that I would like to have guidance from you before we move one way or the other.

The history of Solzhenitsyn's suggestion is this: On Saturday, February 16, the USSR Division's European correspondent, Yevgeniy Nikiforov who was then in Zurich, spoke to Solzhenitsyn's interpreter on the telephone. He said he did not want to ask for an interview but simply wished to pass a message to him welcoming him to the West. The interpreter put Solzhenitsyn on the line and Solzhenitsyn said he was pleased that VOA was interested in him and appreciated the words of welcome. He went on to say that although he could give no interview at the present, he would be happy to consider an interview at a later date. He then made his request for a letter.

Let me review briefly how we have been handling the Solzhenitsyn affair.

VOA—acting under guidelines I have laid down—plays the Solzhenitsyn story as a news story. It reports what is being done and said in the U.S., the USSR and around the world and uses roundups of comments on the issue by journalists and public figures in the U.S. and elsewhere. Under my guidelines, VOA does not do its own editorial commentaries on the case and avoids rhetoric that would suggest that the official radio of the United States is campaigning against the Soviet Union on the issue in the old Cold War style. VOA has not used extensive excerpts from Gulag Archipelago —as Radio Liberty has—although some VOA staffers have pushed strongly for this.

I believe the course we are following is right in line with the policy President Nixon and you have enunciated.

There have been some charges in the news media that VOA is being too soft on the story.

The Solzhenitsyn request poses some troublesome questions.

If we go ahead and get an exclusive interview, it would be a broadcasting coup for VOA greeted with considerable excitement and a great deal of interpretation by journalists around the world. Solzhenitsyn surely would use the occasion to speak directly to the people of the Soviet Union and attack the current regime.

If we do not respond to his request for a letter and let the matter drop, the fact that we took that position will almost certainly leak and we will get more criticism in the media and on the Hill.

The questions I am pondering are these:

Should we send the letter Solzhenitsyn requested?

Should we just let the matter drop and take whatever lumps come our way?

Should we adopt a compromise position and write him suggesting that VOA would like to be included along with other media when he permits interviews? (This, of course, would not be a solution if he responded with a precise suggestion of an exclusive interview.)

I would deeply appreciate your thoughts on the foreign policy implications involved.

For all practical purposes that is the way the matter was left. The interview in question did not take place. Keogh told me Kissinger called him and agreed with the policy as outlined. But as far as I know he never put it in writing. It's safer that way.

I have the feeling that had Shakespeare still been in charge of the agency the memorandum would never have been sent. Rather, I have the feeling that Solzhenitsyn would have received the request for an interview. Kissinger would have heard the interview on the Voice of America.

State did not have its way entirely, however. As every reporter who has differed with his publisher knows, there are ways to get around established editorial guidelines. Still, I must admit I think the "official" West, including we at the agency, did not handle the affair in the manner it should have been handled. The case presented golden opportunities, opportunities which were not properly exploited by virtue of Kissinger's attitude at State, and the law that said we at the agency had to take our cue from State on matters involving foreign policy.

There is the possibility, of course, that extraneous matters were having an influence upon policy considerations at the time. That would be the developing story of Watergate.

Many months earlier I had returned from somewhere, El Salvador I think it was, and heard of a break-in at a place called Watergate. A small item had appeared in the local paper. Evidently, some people having a connection with the Nixon reelection committee (known, unfortunately, as CREEP, or the Committee to Re-Elect the President) had entered the offices of the Democratic candidate illegally. It didn't make much sense, and I shrugged it off. When the whole matter had played itself out in Nixon's second term, it still made no sense. It was just plain stupid. The Nixon campaign was rolling along to a certain victory of massive proportions. I have no idea what the burglars hoped to find, but even if they could have walked into the offices legally they could have found nothing that would have increased the margin of victory. The break-in, and the White House effort to cover it up, has been thoroughly commented upon by others and nothing I could say would add to the body of public knowledge concerning the matter. The only area of that entire incredible episode on which I am any authority is its impact on our own operation abroad and its circuitous impact on our management in Washington.

Strangely enough the story abroad took a different turn. Among our friends there was a certain amount of sympathy, an attitude of "what are you people doing to yourselves?" It must be remembered that at that time the world was essentially divided into two major camps, with a third camp playing it smart and bleeding both sides. Among those in our own camp the United States was looked upon as the leader, the only power strong enough to hold the other side in check. Any weakening of America, any dissension that tore at the fabric of American society, was looked upon as a threat to their own survival.

Even the left abroad found the story somewhat difficult to exploit. It did not fall into those "evils" of Western society they had been trained to exploit. It did not deal with "racism." It did not deal with "capitalist exploitation," or "capitalist imperialism."

I do not mean to say the story was ignored abroad. It was just looked upon differently. It was not exploited in the fashion of the Angela Davis story, for instance. And I am alluding to that period in which there was no thought of a presidential abdication. It was generally assumed that when it was all over, Nixon would still be president, though a weakened president, and he would still be commander in chief of American forces.

Even the Soviet press was comparatively restrained in its treatment of the affair. After all, Nixon and Brezhnev had arrived at a tenuous working relationship, and it is possible the Soviets did not want to do anything that would upset that delicate balance.

In terms of our own agency's output, about all we could do was rely upon our only sources of information, that which appeared in the American press. We did have a limited number of correspondents working the Washington scene, but our principal strength in reporting, in my view, was in our foreign correspondents. The thrust of our commentary from Washington regarding Watergate was that this was a free society working out its problems, that in a free society people had the right and the power to hold their leaders accountable. In the end justice would be served under established law, and the country would go forward.

And in the end that's about what happened. The story did bring down a sitting president, but it did nothing, that I can see, to elevate the level of official morality or ethics in American politics. The spectacle of a humiliated president being driven from office did nothing to keep U.S. Speaker of the House Jim Wright from being Jim Wright. After being caught trying to further feather his nest he merely gave up the lucrative perks of his Speaker's office for the lucrative perks of congressional retirement. It did not cause an embarrassed Tom Foley, for instance, to fly into some public rage and demand exposure of culprits in the House post office and banking scandals. Rather, both Wright and Foley did what Nixon did: they sought to minimize the damage to themselves and their position, dragging their feet until forced to do otherwise. The difference is in the degree. And, in politics, the difference is also in who your friends are and where they are. How else could Teddy Kennedy have survived politically all these years?

Sometime after the story of the break-in ran, but before the election, Shakespeare asked me into his office for a confidential visit. He had, he said, just returned from the White House and a long conversation with the president. He had made up his mind that he was leaving the agency and informed Nixon of his decision. Shakespeare had already served longer than was usual for a head of the agency and wanted to return to private life. But I got the impression that there was more to it than that. I may have been wrong, and probably was. Still, that is the impression I got.

Shakespeare was a deeply religious man, a devout Catholic. He had left a high-paying job in network television to come to government, thinking, I suppose, he could contribute his talents and thoughts to something in which he believed. He was not a "hands on" nitty-gritty director of the agency. He left the actual running of the agency to his two deputies, Loomis, who handled budget and personnel, and myself, as head of policy and plans. But it was Shakespeare who provided the overall guidance.

Shakespeare was also not enamored of Henry Kissinger.

Our conversation revealed a troubled Shakespeare. He told me, for instance, that "they are doing things over there in the White House that ought to be left for the National Committee."

He did not identify what those things were. I doubt he knew, precisely. More likely it was a "feel," for anyone with a modicum of political sense knows it is unwise to mix the actual workings of a campaign operation with that of any government office, particularly the office of president. Any impact the one can have on the other is apt to be detrimental to both.

The president tried to dissuade him from leaving, but when Shakespeare told him the decision was final the conversation turned to the future. He said he told the president he should be concerned about how history would record his administration, that history would record a "Nixon" administration, not a "Kissinger" administration.

Nixon replied, "Frank, Henry is a very important person."

I have no idea how or why Henry Kissinger had become a "very important person" in the eyes of Richard Nixon.

It must have been a very difficult time for Shakespeare personally. He had carved out a portion of his life and devoted it to this administration. But when word passed within the White House staff that he was leaving, he was looked upon as a "deserter." I suppose that alone should have been an indication that something more ominous was brewing.

Again, it must be remembered that at this point in history Nixon was a man in trouble. He was not yet under siege, but in his own mind he must have suspected what might be in store. Indeed, it was only shortly thereafter that I got a call from Anne Armstrong, the ranch woman from South Texas who was then in the White House, and of whom there are few or none more honest. She asked, "Ken, what do you think should be done?"

My reply was "Somebody ought to first find out who has any responsibility in this and then fire them, from the highest to the lowest. I don't care how high it goes, or how low it goes. If that doesn't happen, we are not going to be talking about some burglary, we are going to be talking about the presidency."

At that moment I was still under the impression the whole thing was a low-level operation gotten out of hand. I had no idea it went as high as it did, nor did she.

While all this was going on Henry Loomis was negotiating with the Corporation for Public Broadcasting about assuming the presidency of that organization. They finally came to terms, and Loomis left the agency. Shakespeare left the agency, and I, perforce, became the acting director of USIA while maintaining the position of head of policy and plans. That situation prevailed until Nixon picked James Keogh to fill the vacancy created by Shakespeare's departure.

The "acting" designation is probably the unkindest cut of all, especially in a situation where there is a scent of blood upon the water. The president had not designated a permanent replacement for Shakespeare, and the "acting" title given me clearly indicated to the politically sophisticated bureaucracy that chances of it being me were marginal at best. As could be expected, the ranks of the "loyals" diminished to the loyals indeed.

It was not the best of times. Throughout government that fragile thing that might be called the "discipline of duty" began to break down. People in the ranks saw wounds being inflicted upon the leader. They saw the leader unable to fight back. In the past that leader had been noted for his political shrewdness. Now they saw him floundering, making stupid political mistakes at every turn.

For the life of me I have never been able to comprehend what caused Nixon to handle the Watergate problem in the manner he did. Despite my own unhappiness with some of his domestic initiatives, I had always been impressed by the manner in which he went about making decisions in the field of foreign affairs. The process by which he arrived at decisions in this area indicated, to me at least, an extraordinarily logical mind.

There is a fundamental weakness, for instance, in the manner many decisions are made in any large organization, whether government or corporate. The person at the top of the heap tells his subordinates "we have a problem" in this area or that. He asks what should be done. His staff makes a study. They come forth with a recommendation and arguments to support their recommendation. The person at the top is then confronted with the question of accepting or rejecting the recommendation of his staff. If he rejects that recommendation he will be exhibiting a degree of no confidence in his own staff. His tendency will be to accept, particularly if the problem deals with matters he is not thoroughly familiar with. The net result is that he is run by his staff; he does not run his staff.

Nixon avoided that dilemma by requiring those of us in the departments and agencies concerned with foreign affairs to put forth alternatives to our own suggestions and to argue the case, in writing, for and against those alternatives. He could then take all that to his National Security Council, who could synthesize the pros and cons of various approaches, take all that to Camp David, or somewhere, and make his decision. Nobody felt inhibited in giving it their best shot, and nobody felt humiliated that their position was not finally adopted.

I have no clue as to how a mind so logical in one area (foreign affairs) could arrive at such illogical conclusions when it came to his own personal place in history. It would be easy to simply blame it all on his personal staff, but he chose them. He put them in place. He had a grasp of "the big picture" shared by few in the American body politic. How there could be such a disconnection between that and his own White House operation will probably always remain a mystery to me.

Our agency operated entirely on the foreign scene. We were forbidden to involve ourselves in domestic affairs. We could not even circulate among the American people that material we circulated abroad. The Congress, under whose laws we operated, insisted that they have access to the things we produced, but they, in their wisdom, said the American people could not view, except under certain, restricted conditions, that same material. Under those circumstances it would seem very easy for the domestic turmoil brought on by Watergate to pass us by. But it is the nature of the political beast that it have a leader. If one is not readily available, one will be, one must be, created. Like the frogs in Aesop's fabled pond, those with a political turn of mind will find their king, even if in the end they are gobbled up in the process. So there was a great deal of scurrying around within the ranks.

While it may not have been the best of times it certainly was not, in terms of my own perspective, the worst of times. I simply did the best I could, as acting director, to hold things together at the agency and weather the storm. Fortunately, I did have around me some senior foreign service officers, and some senior civil service officers, who saw their duty and stood with it. While the American body politic was rapidly becoming immobilized, the world did not stop. Our problems abroad remained our problems abroad. So I have been eternally grateful for those who stood quietly and steadfastly at their posts during those days. I would name them now, but some may still be in the agency. No need to place them in jeopardy from the minions of a president who has different thoughts about that period.

In time the president picked James Keogh, a White House aide and former editor for *Time* magazine, as Shakespeare's replacement. Keogh was a stable man, by my own lights a loyal Nixonite, but he was not the most politically sophisticated person I had ever run into. When Jimmy Carter surfaced as a candidate for the Democratic nomination, for instance, he essentially wrote him off. With a certain amount of apology for present company, he noted that Carter was "from the South" and that he was "a Baptist" and that this combination would never sell in the Northeast, the Midwest, or the far west. I thought otherwise. Against Gerald Ford I thought Carter would be a formidable candidate indeed. There was a certain pious, superficial slickness about him that was apt to appeal, I thought, in the post-Watergate atmosphere of the time.

But his lack of political sophistication was understandable. The editors of *Time* frequently attached more importance to informing the electorate of their own views than in learning the views of the electorate. And it is an affliction not peculiar to editors at *Time*. It is difficult, though not impossible, for editors to think, or act, otherwise.

Nevertheless, after a somewhat strained beginning, we got along well together. He knew little about the agency, in fact next to nothing about it, while I had been in its top leadership for a number of years. It became apparent he wished to be a detail-conscious head of the agency. We were about the same age. That is always an awkward position for a new leader to be in. Certain personalities have difficulty coping with situations like that. In the end Keogh shored up his position by elevating Gene Kopp, considerably younger than either of us, and then the agency's general counsel, to the post vacated by Loomis. I stayed where I was, as head of policy and plans. It was a good decision on Keogh's part.

Ultimately, the Watergate ordeal ran its course. Nixon resigned. Gerald Ford was sworn in. He called us over to the White House, asked us to stay on and help in his administration, had his picture taken with us. It was nice, and appreciated. It had never happened during the reign of the previous president.

Hello, Solzhenitsyn; So Long, Nixon, Allende

Keogh was a worrier. Coming out of the Nixon White House, I suppose he had ample reason to be one. He became worried that our agency had somehow been involved in the affair of one Salvador Allende in Chile. Allende, the Marxist leader of that country, had died during a military coup. When Keogh called me in for a discussion, I assured him our hands were clean. We had been very careful to see that this was so. I had been in Chile shortly before the coup, I knew our operation there intimately, and I knew that no one from our agency was involved in the actual military events leading to Allende's downfall. Too, I had daily briefings from the CIA. I knew about as well as anybody who was involved from other agencies, and where.

Still Keogh worried. All those wheels relative to Chile were in motion before he came aboard. Perhaps I should go back and make sure. He did not want something to surface later that would be embarrassing.

There was nothing to do but go.

I went. Nothing I saw or heard changed my view. Our own offices there, scarcely 200 yards from where the final chapter in that event played itself out with the suicide of Allende, bore all the earmarks of a frontal attack. The building itself was pockmarked with machine-gun fire. All that took place while members of our staff, headed by a seasoned foreign service officer named James Halsema (a former newsman on the staff of the old *Manila Times* who had been imprisoned in the Philippines when the Japanese overran Luzon in 1942), huddled under their desks during the Chilean military's surprise attack on government headquarters some 200 yards distant. That was hardly the picture of someone involved in planning or carrying out the attack. Or even someone who had an inkling that it was coming at the time it did.

The left has heaped much blame on America, on the CIA, on everyone but Allende, for the failure of that marvelous effort to create in South America another Cuba, another socialist paradise. I will give them another scapegoat, one which they will not accept, but one which they ought to consider.

If they are really looking for a scapegoat in Chile, they should turn to what was then the Soviet Union.

The plain simple truth of the matter is that Allende's policies were rapidly turning Chile, certainly one of South America's most civilized societies, into an economic basket case. Allende, like Clinton, came to power with much less than a majority of the popular vote. But that did not prevent him from instituting, where possible, socialist policies he had advocated prior to his election. Lacking the strength to install a socialist system overnight, Allende and his followers began a skillful, circuitous, and systematic attack upon the existing private sector. Laws were passed making it all but impossible to operate without government sanction. Regulations were instituted making it difficult for conservative, opposition media to exist, much less prosper. The availability of supplies and various replacement machinery needed to carry on business was made subject to government whim. Marxist labor unions flexed their muscle, urged on by Allende's government. Copper mines were plagued with turmoil and lost production. Large farms were "occupied" and turned into villages of squatters. Large signs were erected around the perimeters proclaiming that the land and the village were "courtesy of Che Guevara," the Marxist zealot and onetime associate of Fidel Castro. Former landowners became displaced persons, their property taken with only the promise that sometime in the future the government would make recompense. A large and thriving middle-class business community was strangled with government decrees and red tape. Production of goods and services plummeted. The entire economy was "redirected" and began a downward spiral from which it was impossible to recover without outside help.

Allende was then receiving financial assistance from the Soviet Union, but it was a pittance compared to his needs. He was receiving moral support from leftists worldwide, many of whom flooded into Chile in order that they might have the satisfaction of helping create yet another socialist paradise. But moral support is of scant benefit in situations like that faced by Allende at that moment.

It was my practice, when I went abroad in those days, to arise early and walk the streets or the marketplaces of whatever country I happened to be in. For one thing, it held a fascination for me, going back to the days when I worked those markets on San Antonio's West Side as a youngster, hawking carrots and cabbages, beans and beets. There is a magic about a city, great or small, coming to life in the early dawn. First there is quiet. Then a small stir as deliverymen make their rounds, increasing activity as dawn comes, and finally a bustle as the populace awakens and goes about its daily chores.

Another reason I followed that practice during this particular period in my life was that the early morning hours tell a great deal about any society, about its energy, about its hopes, or its despair.

Santiago, Chile, was no exception. The picture was there.

When dawn broke in Santiago during that period one saw on the sidewalks of that beautiful city long lines of well-dressed housewives of the "middle class," some sitting and knitting, some in conversation with their friends, some merely sitting quietly, staring into the distance with vacant eyes. All were waiting for the opening of some store they had heard might have a few chickens to sell. Or some fruit. Or some beef. They had taken up their positions in the darkness of night, hoping that when daylight came they might find some food to feed their family.

That may be a picture that brings joy to the hearts of Marxists and their sympathizers, the bourgeoisie getting its just deserts, but it is hardly the picture of a society going anywhere but down. Even Allende and his cadre of fellow socialists could see this. They had to do something to survive. Where to turn?

A delegation was dispatched to Moscow. In a nutshell the delegation's mission was to get long-term financial backing for their efforts in Chile. A little help wouldn't do. Short-term help wouldn't do. They wanted some sort of long-term financial backing on the order of that extended Castro in Cuba. After all, they deserved the help. They were good Marxists.

How do we know this?

We had a "friend" in the delegation.

The Soviets were sympathetic, but they were not in the position, at the moment, where they could take on another financial commitment on the order of Cuba. In order that the delegation not go home empty-handed, they were promised something like $50 million in a one-shot deal.

(My own personal view is that it was a smart move on the part of the Soviets. They had already made the commitment to destabilize Central America with the help of their client state, Cuba, and they saw no need to expend enormous energy and resources in an out-of-the-way country like Chile, on the west coast of South America. There is, after all, an element of practical politics even among socialist "brothers.")

The delegation came home publicly trumpeting success of the mission, but in the world of real politics the die was cast. They would have to make it on their own. That meant, in so many words, the government of Salvador Allende was doomed.

The Chilean economy was now in shambles. It was only a matter of time.

I will make no pretense that the United States was a disinterested observer in all this. Our government did nothing to pull Allende's chestnuts out of the fire. Nor, in my mind, should it have done so. That would merely have propped up, for a short while, a regime and a system that was doomed from the beginning.

On the other hand, I would also have to say that certain policies were instituted, and certain practices followed, that had the effect of hurrying the process along. But it was not the United States that brought Allende's regime down. It was the refusal of the Soviets to provide needed assistance at a critical time. It was Allende's policies. And, in the final analysis, it was the Chileans.

We were well aware, toward the end, of Chilean military intentions. We were not aware, to my knowledge, of the timetable. In fact, until shortly before the coup, I do not know that even the Chilean military had a definite timetable. They even showed a certain irritation at our trying to find out what they were going to do, and when.

A few days before the matter was brought to a head, for instance, an American army colonel, who will not be named, asked a Chilean general, who also will not be named, "When are you people going to move?"

The reply was: "The water is now up to our knees. When it reaches our neck, we will move."

They did, and the rest is history.

Shortly thereafter I received a personal letter, obviously typed hurriedly and without too much editing, dated September 19, 1973, from Halsema in Santiago, Chile. It read:

Dear Ken:
    The long awaited military move did take place and I am sending separately a copy of a letter I wrote to Dorothy Dillon [then the head of the agency desk concerned with South America] to describe some of the things we did during the initial phases of the coup. However, I doubt that she nor some of the members of my staff here would appreciate what I meant by saying that the solution will not be conventional but uniquely Chilean. The junta is not a fascist dictatorship as so many Americans believe. Its head described them as "four tired old generals who would like to be with their families but who feel a sense of duty to their country."

The cynical react with "that's what they all say in the beginning." I think differently.

Certainly what has been discovered has borne out the belief that the Marxists were planning to move beyond their democratic facade into outright use of force. The Chilean military planned carefully and well so that when they moved they caught all this subversive apparatus off guard despite all its talk of civil war. It will take awhile to rebuild the structure. Undoubtedly they will seek revenge and American officials are a likely target. We will have to watch our step. Many Americans here who were strong sympathizers with the Allende regime will want to leave. Even some of my staff who were not feel strongly about what they consider to be the repressive nature of the new government. Many of the Ford Foundation grantees, the Maryknoll missionaries and media stringers are in this category and some are out-and-out supporters of the Marxists.

Our own position is almost embarrassingly well founded. The key radio and TV stations of the post-September 11 era as well as the newspapers are run by people with whom we have worked very closely. The new press secretary to the junta and his wife are old friends. (Our ambassador was initially critical of my talking with him and giving him Wireless File items on the U.S. position about Chile after the coup but now keeps pushing me to more contacts.) The new administrator of El Teniento copper mine is the brother of our senior cultural section local.

One of the big problems the new government is having and will continue to have will be meeting a worldwide propaganda attack by the Left. Already they have launched a series of wild rumors. One remedy will be to invite senior journalists to look for themselves and talk with the junta. Chilean embassies can hold press conferences. We can keep the Chileans informed as to our policies that affect them, and to what the Left is doing worldwide.

These days it seems difficult if not impossible to discuss or claim credit for helping beat back our enemies but I want you to know that we are still very much in the fight.   Signed, Jim

Halsema was completely on target concerning the left's reaction to the demise of Allende's regime. The sense of euphoria they felt when Allende came to power in Chile was now replaced by enormous frustration, by bitterness and anger. Their dreams of another socialist paradise now lay shattered. They reacted accordingly.

God rest his soul. Jim was a good soldier, a good citizen, a good champion of liberty. He had served his time in Japanese prison camps. He had come back and continued the good fight in that arena available to him. While he and his family were fighting the good fight in Chile, while the cream of America's youth were slogging through the jungles of Vietnam, the streets and college campuses of America were wracked by cowards shouting "Hell no, we won't go." It was all very strange.

Eventually it became time to return to Texas. What had started out as a two-year learning experience had turned into a thirteen-year learning experience. The presidential race between Carter and Ford was under way, and it was obvious to me that no matter how that contest came out I would not be head of the agency in the next administration. Moreover, there were family reasons. During the Washington years I had lost a mother and two brothers. I was now the youngest surviving member of a family that had been very close and was not growing any younger. I wanted to return to my roots and be around them.

I had been approached concerning what I considered a lucrative position with Phillips Petroleum Company, but it required living in London and worrying about the company's public affairs in Europe and Africa. It also would require a good bit of travel, of which I had had quite enough. The offer was not pursued.

George Bush was named to head the Central Intelligence Agency. He asked me to go with him to the agency. I asked what he wanted me to do there. He said he didn't know exactly; he just wanted me at his right hand.

It would have been no promotion for me, but that was not the problem. I knew the CIA to be a tightly knit operation, and any outsider coming in at a high level during that particular period of trauma for the agency could well have made the new director's task even more difficult. It was with a great deal of reluctance that I finally decided against it. Besides, I still wanted to go back home. I still wanted to get back to newspapering.

It was probably another of the many wrong decisions I have made in my life. Perhaps I could have helped. But I do know one thing. The director of covert operations for Central America would have had a change of heart, or a change of jobs.

In the end I accepted an offer from Dr. Charles "Mickey" LeMaistre, chancellor of the University of Texas System, to return to Texas as his assistant. I would help raise private "enrichment" funds for the University of Texas System and inadvertently learn something about academic politics.

If you wish a postgraduate course in politics, gentle reader, I suggest you study academic politics. It is a brand of politics that can be practiced only in academia, being too vicious and personal for any other setting. Variations of academic politics are practiced throughout corporate and government bureaucracies, of course, but they pale in comparison to the original. The nature of academic politics is predicated on two factors: Those involved have a great deal of idle time on their hands, and the matters over which they fight are often very trivial, which affords the opportunity to render the entire process more vicious.

I do not wish to leave my years at the agency without one final comment.

It is true, of course, that victory has a thousand fathers and defeat has none. The circumstance surrounding the collapse of the Soviet Union and the discrediting of socialism as a workable alternative to freedom is no exception. Throughout my adult life, for instance, world politics has been divided roughly between "right" and "left." The "left" was either supportive of socialism or apologetic of socialism. The Communists loudly claimed they were the left's "vanguard," and few disputed that claim. Those who opposed communism or socialism in anything approaching a militant manner were labeled by liberals, and those on the left generally, as "conservative anti-Communist right-wingers." People on the right certainly did not reject that appellation.

In America and the West, liberals proudly held themselves out to be left of center. Thousands of words were written about, and much television time devoted to, the proposition that those who actively opposed socialism were "behind the times," that they were "moss backs," or "reactionaries," or "right-wingers."

Suddenly all that has changed. The collapse of the Soviet Union, along with public revelations of just how the Communist Party controlled that country and its satellites for so many years, has resulted in a political "newspeak" in Western media. Now the Communist Party in the former Soviet Union, without ever having changed its ideas one iota, is labeled "right," not "left," its philosophy labeled "conservative," not "progressive." Those throughout the former Soviet Union and Eastern Europe who ended up going to the barricades against the power of the Communist State have suddenly become "liberals" in American media terminology, while their fellow

THE CHOW DIPPER

anti-Communists in the United States and elsewhere are still labeled "conservative" and "reactionary."

Much as we may deplore the twisting of the English language for political purposes we may, in this instance, express a certain amount of satisfaction, even gratitude. If the West's "liberals" now wish to be seen as active "anti-Communists," as champions of the capitalism they long ridiculed, we may put it down to their fundamentally "progressive" nature and count our blessings. If they now wish to be counted as one of many fathers of the anti-socialist effort now going on in Eastern Europe and the Soviet Union, well and good. After all, the battle is not over.

In terms of our own agency I honestly believe that the men and women of USIA contributed mightily to the ultimate collapse of the Soviet Union as a military threat to the Western world, as well as the opening up of that society to ideas of individual liberty and freedom.

It would be foolish and dishonest to claim too much credit. Most of the credit goes, in my opinion, to the resolve of a voting majority of the American people in standing firm during all those years. It was that resolve that resulted in the election of political leaders who could stand firm. Without that resolve, our military could not have stood firm. Without that, nothing else would have mattered.

But the work of the agency in constantly defending Western concepts of liberty and freedom, and exposing those ideas to people who otherwise would have known only the thoughts of Marx or Lenin or Stalin, did, in my view, speed the process along. And, in the doing, contributed its bit in the struggle.

I am not at all certain I would be comfortable working for the agency under present circumstances. I have never been comfortable in any endeavor that has no honest, legitimate, clearly defined objective. During those years we did not have to have endless conferences for the purpose of trying to find out what we were all about, the reasons for our existence. We did not have to study our navel to determine why we were alive. For the most part the men and women who then made up the agency knew why they were there.

By and large they did their work without glory. They had no special constituency in America seeking their favors, their handouts of tax dollars. They went unnoticed on the domestic scene. They did their work under difficult conditions, with duty being its own reward.

I have no hesitancy now in saying I am proud to have been part of that struggle.

TWENTY-ONE

Tower's Defeat from Within

The new job as assistant to the chancellor was relatively short-lived, fortunately.

LeMaistre was a physician by training, a public-spirited man by inclination. He had served on the surgeon general's panel that came up with the finding that cigarettes might cause cancer. I came to look upon him as a kind and decent man, a thoroughly able man, but one entirely unsuited to the task of maintaining his position in the world of academic politics. His job was coveted by, shall we say, "others."

When word passed that LeMaistre had visited with me in Washington about the possibility of joining him in Austin, I received a call from Don Walker, then the system's deputy chancellor. He wanted me to visit when I was next in Austin. The call sounded most urgent.

I went by his office, wondering what the matter was about. He explained things. In so many words he let me know that his office was where all the power lay. If I really wanted to become involved with the University of Texas System I should consider coming with him rather than LeMaistre. I found this somewhat strange, for I had assumed that Walker was number-two man to LeMaistre, that they were on the same team, in a manner of speaking.

Somewhat confused by this turn of events, I visited with former governor Allan Shivers, then chairman of the system's Board of Regents. He was aware of certain problems in communication between the two men, but that was something they had to work out. I told him I had no desire to get caught in some sort of internal struggle if I was to do my job properly, and asked his recommendation. No deal had been cut at that time and nothing said I had to go with either. Shivers suggested I go with LeMaistre. "He needs the help," he said, "and you can help us more there (in the development office) than anywhere else." So I went with LeMaistre. Quite frankly, if the recommendation had been to join Walker I would have passed.

I had my own office and my own staff, in a building apart from both LeMaistre and Walker. It was a nice, cushy job, something I had never had before. About all we had to do was raise money and hold hands with the donors. I had been exposed to the money bit before, in politics, and the staff did a much better job than I at holding hands, so between us we managed to do a semirespectable job.

I did find out, however, that there is a vast difference between raising money for a political campaign and raising money for "good" things, no matter how esoteric they may be. There were many who were somewhat anxious to give in order that they might rub shoulders with others who had also given to "good" things. Then there were others who gave simply because they thought they were helping a good cause. I was never able to see where either benefited in any real material way. That, I suppose, is the essence of giving.

It was the kind of job with which one could have become bored very quickly were it not for the sideshows of academic politics. I watched, from afar, as Don Walker, ably assisted by staff member Bob Hardesty, managed to systematically chop at LeMaistre every chance they got. Eventually LeMaistre left his post, went to Houston to head up the university's M.D. Anderson Cancer Center in Houston, and did good things for suffering people. Walker finally got to be chancellor, and his aide Hardesty, a former LBJ staffer, became president of Southwest Texas State University at San Marcos for a while.

Before that scenario finally played itself out, I was gone. In the spring of 1977, before I had completed my first year in the new job, I got a call from John Tower in Washington. He wanted a few of us to gather in Dallas.

I was surprised. Since leaving his office in the spring of 1969 our contacts had been minimal, at best. Once, during the Church (Senator Frank Church of Idaho) hearings on the CIA, of which Tower was vice-chairman, I had gone to his office with some information I thought he ought to know. It concerned a matter I was familiar with, and one I thought would be beneficial for him to know about as ranking minority member of the committee. I found a different Tower from the one I had known. He didn't have time to talk to me. If I had anything the committee needed to know I should contact his legal counsel, one Curt Smothers. I left and never went back. The only other times I had seen him prior to the phone call were at a Washington reception marking the engagement of his former aide, Nola Smith, then at the White House, to GOP State Chairman Paul Haerle of California, and at one or two staff parties where we spoke briefly, very briefly. It was as if he had simply closed the door. For those reasons I was somewhat surprised by the call.

The purpose of the meeting, which was attended by only a handful of longtime supporters, was to assess his political standing. Within a few months it would be time to gear up for another campaign, if he decided to run again.

At the moment that was problematical. He had gone through a divorce, which did not sit well with many Texans who knew and loved his wife, Lou. Rumors persisted about his drinking. As the couple's marriage crumbled, his home base support had shown signs of crumbling as well. He was aware of all this, and the time was at hand to take stock.

It was a rather bleak session. We looked not only at his political capital but at his financial capital as well. Financially, his capital was in even worse shape than his political capital, a fact that troubled Ed Clark to no end. Clark was a banker, and, having spent many years in close association with Lyndon Johnson, he couldn't understand how a man could be in public office for so long and have so little to show for it financially. That wasn't the kind of politics he was used to. In fact, he urged that the matter be kept quiet. How would people react? They might take the position that a man who couldn't manage his financial affairs better than that had no business managing other people's money.

In the end Tower asked that we make our various assessments and report back. He was not then ready to say unequivocally that he would make another run.

My concern, as we left the meeting, was that he would drag out the decision until late and then say he was not going to make the race. It was the concern of others as well, who asked me to go to Houston and talk with George Bush. (By then George had served his tours of duty as head of CIA and ambassador to China and was back in private life.) They did not wish to be identified then, and I will not do so now. Obviously, they did not wish to appear "disloyal" to Tower, but they also did not wish a vacuum to develop at the last moment, into which a host of candidates might flood with all sorts of bloodletting and a subsequent loss of the Senate seat.

So I went. George and I walked from his office to a nearby eatery featuring hamburgers and barbecue where most of the employees behind the serving counters seemed to know him on a first-name basis. I laid out the problem and suggested he ought to hold himself in readiness for such an eventuality.

He said he would only accept another run for the Senate "if the party came together" and asked him to do it. In other words, if it was some sort of "draft" situation. He had run two races for the Senate (one against Yarborough and one against Bentsen, losing both) and he would undertake another only with a united party supporting him. Obviously, I was in no position to speak to anything like that. All I was attempting to do was lay out the problem as seen by some friends of both he and Tower.

Besides, said Bush, he had made up his mind to run for president.

It was the first I had heard of anything like that. "I have already told both Reagan and Ford of my intentions," he said.

"What was their reaction? What did they say?" I asked.

"Nothing," he said. "They both thanked me for letting them know, but they made no comments beyond that."

At that time it was assumed by many that both Reagan and Ford would run, but neither had made any public statement declaring his intentions.

We visited more and I returned to Austin. I had known Bush for a number of years, but I was still somewhat surprised at his decision to run for the presidency. I had assumed, in my younger years, that anyone wanting to run for the presidency would have a list of things he wanted to achieve. A program, an agenda, something on that order. I was unaware of any such agenda on George's part. My impression of George was that he had always wanted to serve, and serve well, in whatever capacity he found himself. He had done that in the past, but, as William Shakespeare said, "What's past is prologue." Now he was going to try for the roses, but to what end I knew not.

The assessment concerning Tower's campaign was somewhat mixed. A survey showed him still with a substantial base of support, and a substantial base of opposition. There was a large "middle" that could conceivably go either way. On balance, he might have the edge against an unnamed opponent, but the race was there to be won, or lost.

He decided in favor of running and asked me to help. I had not expected that. He did not ask me to come back and run his reelection bid. By then I think we both understood we got along better when we were not thrown together closely. He asked, instead, that I rejoin his staff, in charge of his Austin office, from which vantage point I could give a degree of advice and guidance to the campaign. It was understood that this would be a temporary affiliation lasting only through the campaign. My own personal goal was to become established again in the world of private citizens.

I went back to Shivers. I did not want to leave with any bad feelings between us. I told him of Tower's request. He was quick to urge that I take it. It was imperative, he said, that Tower retain the seat. Both he and Clark would be supporting Tower, who, he thought, was going to "need all the help he can get." Based on that I told Tower I would come back.

Before I made that move, though, I got a call from Carolyn Bacon, then the senator's administrative assistant in Washington. She wanted to alert me to the fact that Tower was to be remarried.

"To whom?"

It was to a Lilla Burt Cummings, a Washington lawyer whom I had never heard of. Carolyn didn't want me to be blindsided by the news, in case it might make a difference on my decision. I had already given Tower my word. I couldn't see a new marriage helping, but maybe it wouldn't hurt. At that point I was considering the news only in a political context. I did not see myself having any active part in the campaign and had no idea of the personalities to be involved.

Little did I know. If I had had any hint about what was to ensue, I expect I could have found a way out. Come down with the flu or something.

My first exposure (poor choice of words there) to the new bride came at a gathering of Texas bankers in Austin, where Tower was to be the principal speaker. I sat in the audience, not as a banker but as an interested observer. Tower delivered his remarks from a podium on a platform with only one other person on it, that being his new wife, Lilla. She sat immediately to his left with a yellow legal pad. As he spoke she would occasionally shake her head vigorously and scribble furiously. When he finished his remarks, while he was still on the stage and before he had even had a chance to mingle with the assembled guests, she engaged him in what appeared to be a lecture, pointing to her notes and making her points. He would nod his head in agreement. Many in the audience had known Tower for years. They looked on in amazement. This was not the "platform Tower" they knew, forceful, self-assured, in command of the situation. As for myself, I suppose I was more puzzled than anything else.

Tower retained Nola Smith Haerle, then living in California with her husband, to run the campaign. Nola had been in charge of the 1972 campaign against Barefoot Sanders. The staff was put together and the mechanism of the campaign began operating. The campaign kickoff took place in January with a traditional tour of the state. I remained in Tower's office in the Federal Building in Austin, keeping the campaign at arm's length. If my advice was asked, I gave it. If it wasn't, I didn't.

The campaign quickly ran into difficulties, both organizationally and financially. The senator had insisted that he have a private, twin-engined plane at his disposal, and at the ready, for the campaign. It was arranged. The problem was that while it sat unused at a Dallas airport, the meter kept running and the campaign kept paying. And at that stage of the campaign the plane was used very little.

There were other problems as well, one of which, in my own view, was that Lilla simply wanted to get rid of Nola. And while it was then not evident, in time I got the feeling she would be happier if all those who had any past connection with the senator's career simply went away.

In the spring Tower called and asked that I meet him in his room at the Driskill Hotel in Austin. It was a friendly, yet somehow strange and awkward meeting. He sat drinking black coffee. We engaged in some informal discussion involving nothing in particular. He seemed to want to talk about something else, but didn't want to broach the subject.

Finally he said, "Ken, I had hoped it wouldn't come to this, but . . ." He stopped again.

By then I had figured what he had on his mind, and I broke in. "I had hoped it wouldn't too, Senator."

We both laughed. He then continued, "But will you come back and run my campaign?"

He had to make a change, he said. Things weren't going well. He did not explain what "things" he was talking about, but it was enough to cause worry on my part. I was reluctant to make the move. I felt that in his present situation there would be problems. Left to our own devices he and I had usually been able to work those matters out, but now there would be a third force involved, one I knew nothing about. I reminded him that the only way I knew to run campaigns was to run them, that I thought one of the problems then manifest in his campaign was confused signals up and down the line. I had no desire to become part of that, if it could not be changed. He assured me we could find ways, that I would be in charge. So we agreed and the change from staff member to campaign manager was made.

In terms of the inner turmoil it caused me, it was another bad decision on my part.

In short order Tower, Lilla, and her twenty-year-old son by a previous marriage came to Texas to discuss the campaign. I picked them up at the airport and we started to the campaign offices on Congress Avenue. No sooner were we under way than she leaned over my shoulder and began what ultimately became little short of a tirade, informing me of all the changes she wanted in staff personnel.

The staff was bloated with unkempt, inept people who did not project the image she wanted for the senator's office. In particular, she wanted a young University of Texas student named Kevin Moomaw fired forthwith. (He was still at his post at campaign's end.)

Not only that, she wanted the young woman in charge of Tower's Houston federal office, Cindy Taylor, dismissed. (She later became Cindy Taylor Krier, state senator from San Antonio before going on to become county judge of Bexar County .) Tower remained silent. I kept waiting for him to defend at least some on the staff she had indicated ought to be fired, but the wait was in vain. (Nonetheless, Cindy remained in her position until she left voluntarily.)

As Lilla talked her son would chime in with supporting comments. It was incredible. Neither of them had any experience in running a large operation, neither had any understanding of Texas and even less about a political campaign. I saw it as nothing less than an attempt to impress upon me where the power lay.

By the time we reached the Littlefield Building, some two blocks from the office, I had had enough. I stopped the car in 6th Street traffic and told one and all that I had barely taken over. I was still taking stock. I was in charge of the campaign and would make decisions concerning the campaign staff. If that wasn't satisfactory, we should know about it now and they could find someone else.

Oh no, nothing like that. They wanted me to stay. Lilla was just making suggestions. We went the rest of the way in silence. And that began my acquaintance with Lilla Tower. Things never got much better between us.

I do not intend to dwell at great length on that particular campaign. Enough has been written elsewhere to give a fair picture of what transpired, not only on our side but on the side of our opposition as well. We won it, and in a way that should be all that is or was important. But the inner workings of that campaign should be a case history on how a campaign ought not be constructed. And, at any level, history ought to be served as honestly as recorders can make it so.

Tower, in his book *Consequences*, made the point that the campaign was not well run, that it made about "every mistake in the books." I disagree. There was only one major mistake made in that campaign. That mistake was his acquiescing to Lilla's demand, of which I was completely unaware, that she would have carte blanche authority to approve all print, photos, news releases, campaign commercials, all public statements, emanating from the campaign. That even included press releases from his Washington office having anything to do with the campaign.

That decision alone caused untold problems for the campaign. Time consumed when advertising material would have to be sent to Washington for her approval, time consumed while we argued over selection of an advertising agency, time consumed as we tried to straighten out problems caused by her interference in decisions arrived at and charted for the next week's activities.

After our encounter coming in from the airport, I heard no more about the staffing matter. I have no doubt she kept up a steady drumbeat of suggestions to the senator, but she said no more to me. In the world of the senator's persona, however, and how he was presented to the public relative to the campaign, it was another matter.

At that point in the campaign the usual practice was to hold early Sunday morning review and planning sessions, during which developments during the previous week would be reviewed and plans made for the ensuing week. If Tower was in town he would attend. Normally, I would call the staff to order, go over some preliminary matters, and turn my seat over to him. We would then get his assessment and usually a little pep talk.

We proceeded along those lines until one morning Tower arrived in the company of Lilla, her son George, and a black attorney from Washington named Curt Smothers.

It was an apparently forceful, decisive John Tower who then marched to the head of the table, sat down, and delivered the message. With Lilla sitting beside him he introduced her as his wife, whom he loved dearly, but who was also his best friend and most trusted confidante. He wanted everyone to know he trusted her judgment completely and that she would have carte blanche authority in the campaign.

He introduced Smothers as a dear friend in whom he had complete confidence, as his "landlord," and noted that he too had carte blanche in the campaign. He also said kind things about Lilla's son George, of whom he was very proud.

The entire proceeding took on the air of an orchestrated, rehearsed presentation, as if he were speaking and acting under orders. There was an element of rote about it.

Whatever the genesis of the presentation, it had the effect of giving Lilla what she obviously wanted—effective control over the most important aspects of the campaign. It also had the effect of causing manifold problems.

There were disputes over policy matters, disputes over campaign media plans, disputes over timing.

In the area of policy, for instance, Tower had been convinced he should remain silent on the subject of statehood for the District of Columbia, then a proposal by the Democratic left in Congress. He told me Smothers and Lilla were close to black politicians in Washington who had promised to be helpful within the black community in Texas if he did not get openly involved against the D.C. Statehood proposal. He didn't want us to raise the issue. He would never vote for the proposal, he said, but he didn't want to be seen leading the charge against it, or even involved in the issue.

It was a silly position to take, considering the proposal was so terribly unpopular across the state, and considering the fact that our opposition had so misread the issue. After much internal maneuvering and no little argument we were able to present a public position of political sanity, which is another way of saying we came out against the proposal. The issue actually became critical to the success of our campaign.

Then there were disputes between Lilla and myself over selection of an advertising agency. Before I came on board as campaign manager she had caused the senator to drop his longtime television adviser, Robert Heller of Houston. In his place Bobby Goodman of Washington had been selected. Goodman was, and probably still is, an excellent producer of campaign television commercials. But he lived in and operated out of an environment that was not Texas. I wanted to supplement his work with someone or some agency in Texas who would be on the scene and capable of fast reaction to campaign developments. Also, Goodman was almost exclusively oriented toward television. I wanted someone who had capabilities in other media as well, particularly print. I had scoured the agency waterfront and come up with a recommendation that we select a firm called Ed Yardang and Associates in San Antonio. Two principals in that firm, Lionel Sosa and Bev Coiner, had talents I thought would be particularly valuable to us.

Lilla objected. We had "discussions" on the matter. She took the position that no Texas firm was up to the task, that premier talent in the advertising industry could be found only on the East Coast or the West Coast.

Finally, I asked her just what objections she had, fundamentally, to the selection of a Texas firm.

She was not hesitant in her reply. With her voice rising at each phrase, she all but shouted: "Because all Texas men are slow talking . . . and slow walking . . . and *slow witted.*"

I didn't know whether to laugh or cry. I didn't know if she was talking about me or her husband.

I never told Tower of the exchange. No need to add to the poor man's troubles.

In the end Tower became convinced it would be wise to go the route we had suggested. After all, Lilla would still have the final say in what the advertising agency produced. I discussed the matter with the firm, telling them we might have certain problems with the arrangement but that we wanted them designated as the campaign's principal agency. Their response was that they had dealt with difficult clients before. They thought they could handle it.

I doubt they had ever run up against anything quite so difficult.

One small illustration: At that time, during the presidency of Jimmy Carter, inflation and interest rates were skyrocketing. A terrible economic squeeze was afflicting the American middle class, that segment of the population where we found most of our support. We sought to solidify our support in that part of the populace.

We produced what I thought would be an effective, telling ad designed to run in the state's newspapers. Under the heading "I know how you feel," the ad made the point that the senator understood and sympathized with those caught in that intolerable financial situation. The ad was sent to Washington for approval.

Lilla objected.

She saw sexual overtones in the phrase "I know how you feel."

I was astounded. Try as I might, I could see no sexual overtones in a statement dealing with inflation and high interest rates. Nevertheless, the argument consumed days. In the end I ordered it run. It was an effective ad, but the delay had the effect of disrupting our ad schedule.

So it went, until finally I decided the situation was intolerable. I intercepted the senator in Corpus Christi, during a campaign swing, and told him if we could not change matters I would bow out. In fact, I said I no longer wanted her in my office except under one condition. That condition being that she could attend the usual Sunday morning staff conferences, at which reports were made on the week's activities and plans made for the ensuing week, and at those meetings she could put her thoughts on the table like everyone else's, where they would be weighed along with everyone else's. But when decisions were arrived at, everyone, including her, would abide by the decisions. The practice of her whispering in his ear on Monday night, changing decisions arrived at on Sunday morning, must cease.

I know it was a terrible dilemma to force upon a friend, but I saw the alternative as his certain defeat. We were faced with an opponent, or an opponent's managers, who had embarked upon the "new politics," where usual campaign rules of common decency did not apply, where viciousness had replaced civility, where the guiding rule was no rule.

I did not think we could survive by his spending so much of his time in Washington, attending to the votes, acting the role of a "statesman" while his opponent crisscrossed the state, beating his brains out at every stop, unless we had an effective, focused campaign in the state. And we could not have that focused, effective campaign if we had no ability to maintain a desired course on the one hand and respond quickly to opposition charges on the other.

I don't know how he worked it out, but she stopped coming to the staff conferences, and she never again set foot in my office. I do not remember ever speaking to her again. In fact, her trips to Texas during the campaign became less frequent. We were able to restore a sense of order and stability in a campaign sorely needing both.

Quite frankly, I could not understand the relationship between the senator and his new wife. Not, that is, until one day later in the campaign.

We had issued a press statement relating to some matter long gone from my memory. It intrigued a reporter for the *Dallas Times-Herald*, who called the Austin office for elaboration. Tower happened to be in the office at the time. The receptionist relayed the call to my office, where Tower was. He asked what I thought. Should he take the call?

My advice was that he should. If he didn't, we might get a brief mention concerning the press statement, but if he talked to the reporter and answered his questions we would probably fare much better. He took the call.

Unfortunately, while he was on the phone to the reporter, Lilla called him from Washington. The receptionist, unaware of the strictures Lilla had laid upon the senator, informed her that Tower could not come to the phone at the moment, that he was talking to a reporter. Lilla was furious. She hung on the phone until Tower's conversation with the reporter was finished, at which point the call was relayed.

Tower picked up the phone and was immediately met with a barrage of shouted criticism from his wife. The voice over the phone was so loud it was clearly audible to me, sitting a few feet away.

What did he mean talking to a reporter without her clearance?

He tried to defend himself by saying it was a small matter, he was merely elaborating on a press statement. She would not be mollified.

As the conversation continued I got up, embarrassed for the senator, and walked into the adjoining room of my secretary, Wini Chapoton. The wall separating her office from mine, a thin structure of plyboard, served only to muffle one end of the conversation. When it ended I returned to my office to find a shaken Tower, white as a ghost, with his head down.

I sat silent, thinking he would finally relay something of what happened. For a moment he, too, sat silent. Then he spoke.

"I've got to fire Carolyn Bacon."

I couldn't believe what I had heard. Carolyn was then his administrative assistant in Washington, running his staff operation there and having supervision of his office staff in Texas as well. She had been a longtime, faithful member of his staff, completely loyal to a man who had always said he valued loyalty above all else. It just didn't make sense.

"Senator, you can't do that."

"I've got to do it. Lilla says she will divorce me if I don't."

More silence.

"Well," I said, "this campaign can't stand another divorce. It would kill us."

"I know that," he said, his voice cracking.

"Let's move Carolyn down here," I urged. "We need her and we can use her here. She's too valuable to lose."

"I can't do that," he said. "She [Lilla] says she can't have any connection with either the office or the campaign. Or she'll divorce me."

More silence as we sat.

Finally I said, "Senator, I really don't understand what you see in that woman."

It was something I had been wanting to say since I met her. It was also something one man does not say to another man concerning his wife.

He looked up, his eyes focused on nothing in particular, and said, in a most pathetic tone, "Ken, you haven't seen me take a drink in seventeen months, have you?"

My first thought, left unsaid, was "What has that got to do with anything?" Then the thought, "How is it possible for any person to remember to the month the last time he had a drink?"

Truthfully, I had not seen him take a drink in the past seventeen months, or the past many years, for that matter, because I hadn't been around him for any length of time, other than the campaign then under way, since leaving his office in 1969.

He went on to say Lilla was responsible for this state of affairs. The picture began to come in focus.

Hoping to restore at least a portion of his self-esteem, I said, "Well, Senator, that may be true, but if that is the case surely you deserve part of the credit."

Again he looked down.

"No," he said, "it's all her doing. It's all her doing. Without her I would . . ." and here his voice trailed off as he sat in silence, looking at the top of the desk, to me a most tragic figure.

Finally, I had the explanation. Or at least an explanation. I had assumed her hold over him could only be explained by his consuming love for her, by his admiration of her intellect, her beauty, or something. To me he seemed her total captive, her total prisoner because of these things. Now it appeared he was captive of something else. A prisoner to his own fears that without her he would be lost. She had convinced him, or he had convinced himself, that he could not stand alone in this one arena.

At that moment my sorrow for him knew no bounds. What a terrible burden for a man, any man, to carry. In the midst of a campaign. Fighting for his political life. Fighting for his own self-respect. And having so much of both hanging by the thread of his own wife's vanity and drive for power.

The campaign ran its course. Tower, finally bestirred into forceful campaigning by incessant personal attacks upon him and his family, began to regain some of his old form and scored political points. The end approached. We had gone through the celebrated "no handshake" incident in Houston, where Tower was pictured as declining to shake the hand of his opponent, Democrat Robert Krueger. I had written a statement for him in which he was to point out that he had been raised to believe a handshake was a mark of respect, not a matter for political show. After some reluctance, he had delivered the statement, with embellishments. He then had to defend himself to a higher authority.

We urged exploitation of the issue, otherwise our response would be lost in the welter of last-minute campaigning. Tower was again reluctant. John Connally called. He, too, urged that we exploit the issue to the fullest. That recommendation was relayed to Tower. It helped mightily, for Tower had a high regard for Connally's political acumen. With guidance from John Knaggs, the campaign's press consultant, a last-minute television program was put together by the Yardang group in San Antonio focusing on the handshake incident. It was delivered by a Tower at his best, which was very good indeed.

The presentation had the desired effect. Our tracking polls began to show us making a recovery, but the election still hung in the balance. So much so that some on our own staff, primarily the young and inexperienced, began to lose heart. The days were difficult indeed.

A day or two before the vote a phone call came through from Ronald Reagan in California. The receptionist relayed the call. I picked up the phone, thinking I would have to go through the usual "hold the line please" while she made the connection. Instead the voice was that of Reagan.

"Ken, how are things going?" he asked.

I told him I thought it was going to be very close, but that we would probably win. Our tracking polls showed us closing well, and if things kept on track, if we could keep our wits about us, we would win.

We talked some more and he ended by saying, "Tell John I'm praying for him."

I did, the next day.

Tower looked incredulous. "Did he say that?" he asked.

"He said that, word for word."

Tower did not respond. He sat silent, thinking.

He had blistered Reagan unmercifully, and I thought unnecessarily, during the 1976 campaign during which Reagan challenged Ford for the nomination, which Ford won only to go on and lose to Jimmy Carter. Needless to say, Reagan and Tower had not been close after that incident.

Now came the phone call, and the "Tell John I'm praying for him."

From that day forward I never heard an unkind word from John Tower regarding Ronald Reagan. Strange, what a few kind words can do.

Until then there had seemed to be an element of personal, and perhaps professional, jealousy toward Reagan on Tower's part. Once, in the period leading up to the Nixon campaign in 1968, a member of Reagan's staff from California, Tom Reed, came to our Washington office and asked to visit with Tower. The senator refused to see him, telling me to see him instead. On that occasion he told me, "Oh, Ron's all right. It's just those people he has around him."

I never inquired of Tower the reasons for his seeming reluctance to be more supportive of Reagan's efforts during those years. One would think that since both were so supportive of Barry Goldwater during the 1964 race for the presidency, since both were so close philosophically, they would have been closer than they were, politically, during the ensuing years. But while politics has a way of putting strange people in bed together, it also has a way of keeping political soulmates from going to bed together. There is, after all, the matter of competing for adoration within the same power base.

And there is still another reason that may have entered the picture. Tower had always placed great stock in being part of the "club" of political party insiders. Reagan was considered very much a part of the "outsiders" club, relying for his support on the conservative, and populist, anti-Washington sentiment in the countryside. There is, among politicians, a sort of distrust between the two camps.

In the end we won the race. It would prove to be Tower's last political race, but hardly his last political hurrah.

It would prove, as well, to be my last political race with John Tower.

History books will record that his last race was won by the narrowest of margins. History will probably not record what might have been.

In my view, had his campaign not been forced to deal with the Lilla distraction, he would have won by a much bigger margin. Given that distraction I believe our opposition would have won the race had they not committed so many grievous blunders, had they not embarked upon a campaign so lacking in civility that they ended up losing many who should have been their natural allies.

Six years later, Tower would choose not to run again. His stated reasons, to me, for bowing out were that the Senate was no longer the kind of place it was when he first went there, that service there was no longer personally satisfying, that it had become a body bent upon partisan and personal advantage rather than a deliberative body devoted to the country's good.

I have no doubt he was being honest in his assessment of the matter, as far as it went. And perhaps that was the sum and substance of it. But I have always felt there was another reason.

Only a few months prior to his surprise announcement that he would not stand for reelection, he passed the word to some of us, for instance, that he intended to run again. Plans got under way to gather support for that race. Then Lilla resigned from her position as head of the Institute of Museum Services, an appointment arranged for her by Lyn Nofziger at Tower's urging. Press accounts of the resignation indicated she intended to devote her time to her husband's reelection.

A few days later, I encountered former governor Allan Shivers, a longtime Tower supporter.

"Ken," he said, "you know a shudder ran through the ranks with that news."

Shivers spoke the truth, of course, and my own feeling is that a shudder was felt elsewhere as well. I do not think Tower relished the idea of a campaign where Lilla would be a dominant, if not the dominant, force. By then he was getting the message.

At any rate he gave up his place in a body he loved for many years and embarked upon a career in the world of private citizens. He and Lilla eventually went their separate ways in the midst of much bitterness on her part (a bitterness that finally played itself out when she helped deny her former husband the one governmental position he wanted, in my view, above all others, the office of secretary of defense). From where I sat their divorce signaled he had finally come to grips with his situation and had decided he could stand on his own. Or, perhaps more to the point, he had decided he could never stand on his own unless his present situation was altered. His career in the private world flourished, which must have been a source of deep satisfaction to him. Too, he began to feel comfortable again with old friends and associates.

He never lost interest in government or politics. In the summer of 1987 he seriously considered entering the Texas governor's race but decided against it, telling me he had decided it was finally important to him that he become financially secure and that he was then in position for that to happen. There are politicians, of course, who would have seen it the other way around. They would have run for the governor's chair in order to become financially secure.

When George Bush was elected president he nominated Tower to be secretary of defense, a nomination finally rejected on a near party-line vote in the Senate. That vote, as far as I was concerned, was marked with both irony and hypocrisy. Ironic because Tower had always been so supportive of the Senate as an institution, so apologetic of its shortcomings and protective of its members regardless of their political leanings. Hypocritical because of the people involved. The case of one Daniel Patrick Moynihan is illustrative.

Many years before the vote, while I was deputy director for policy and plans at USIA, an occasion arose where I had to fly, almost at a moment's notice, to Australia for a quiet meeting with some British, Australian, and New Zealand officials. The Vietnam War was going on, and Moynihan was then serving as President Nixon's ambassador to India. Before that, Moynihan had served in the Nixon White House. The war, of course, was essentially an American and Vietnamese operation. The other Western powers were publicly maintaining a modified "arm's-length" stance, but were being helpful in other areas having to do with the conflict. They wanted to meet and discuss some of those problems, as well as some potential problems they saw in the region.

Gene Kopp was scheduled to make the trip, but a day or so before time to leave he came down with a case of flu, accompanied by high fever. I took his place.

The route was from Washington to New York, to London, to

New Delhi and on to Australia. That route was necessary in order that the entire flight could be paid for with "funny money" on deposit in India. That money was part of the buildup of American foreign aid money poured into India over the years and then building up at a rate even the Indians couldn't spend fast enough. This was one way to finance government travel in that part of the world. It was one way to get back a fraction of the money handed out to the sanctimonious government of India and which was supposed to be used to buy American goods and services. The problem, of course, was that there was too much money handed out in the way of "loans" and too little coming back in the way of purchases. (Eventually the entire debt would be "forgiven.")

People on "official business" in that part of the world were routed through New Delhi, where they were required to spend twenty-four hours, thus triggering the provision that made such expenditures from the foreign aid surplus legitimate, or at least theoretically legitimate.

I put down in New Delhi in an extremely exhausted state. The flight from Washington to India had been essentially nonstop, interrupted only by a brief stopover in London caused by "equipment malfunction." (Actually, in our approach to London, something fell off the new 747, which caused us to limp into the airport only to be met with lines of fire trucks and ambulances. We got down safely and had to wait for a different plane.) I wanted only to get some rest before continuing the flight.

But the ambassador heard I was coming to New Delhi and sent word he would appreciate a visit. I asked our staff if they thought it was just a courtesy deal, or if they thought I really ought to go. The reply was that the ambassador sounded as though it was important. So I went.

It was late. We had arrived in New Delhi shortly before dark, and now it was past time for the evening meal.

The ambassador and I visited alone in what I presumed to be his study. He had just returned from the dentist and was trying to reduce the pain with Scotch. I joined him with bourbon. He paced a great deal, holding his jaw and alleviating the pain with Scotch. By the time I left his company he was no longer complaining of the pain.

He was well aware of my association with Tower over the years. He was also aware I had run Nixon's campaign in Texas and that based upon that I had been brought into the administration.

The subject of the meeting was evidently to let me know that he and John Tower were great friends. He had attended the London School of Economics, as had Tower. They were on some sort of committee to raise funds for their old school. He had an extremely high regard for Tower. He wanted me to relay his warmest greetings to his old friend.

We talked as well about politics in Washington, particularly politics in the White House. And we talked a good bit about things going on in India at the time. I, quite frankly, was surprised by some of the rhetoric concerning what the Soviet Union was doing in India, which I knew about but which sounded somewhat strange coming from him. I would not have been surprised if I had heard the same comments at a precinct meeting of "right-wing, anti-Communist Republicans" back in Texas.

I left the meeting with the feeling that the primary purpose of the visit was that I should relay his "warmest" greetings to his good friend, John Tower, and that I spread the word in certain circles of the White House that he was doing a great job as ambassador to India.

I took my leave of the ambassador, and after a night's rest continued the journey.

The meeting in Canberra lasted only a couple of days. We got our ducks in a row, decided who was going to do what, where, and when, and I returned to Washington, where I relayed the ambassador's greetings to Tower.

He was most pleased.

A few years later, after the Reagan years and at the beginning of the Bush presidency, I watched on C-SPAN as the Senate voted on Tower's confirmation to the post of secretary of defense.

The clerk called the roll.

"Senator Moynihan?"

"Senator Moynihan votes *no*."

That may have been a very difficult vote for the New York senator, turning down his "good friend." But I doubt it.

Actually the vote came out about the way Tower expected. He had told me, a few days earlier, that he expected essentially "a straight, party-line vote" on the matter.

I had gone to Washington for a late February meeting of the Corporation for Public Broadcasting's board of directors, of which I was then serving as chairman. Customarily, I stayed at the Jefferson Hotel during those meetings, since it was within walking distance of our headquarters at 1111 16th Street NW, next door to the Soviet Embassy, which, much to the Soviet's discomfort, was across the street from a labor union headquarters where a huge banner hung proclaiming solidarity with the workers of Poland. It must have been a terrible eyesore for the Soviets.

Press reports indicated Tower was also staying at the Jefferson during the Senate battle over his nomination. I asked the desk clerk if Tower was "in residence," not really expecting that he would be. There were still a few days left before the vote, and I anticipated he would be out beating the bushes for support. The clerk said he was registered, but he wasn't sure if he was in. I left a message, telling the senator I was registered and would be happy to visit if it fit his schedule and mine.

I did not expect an answer. There had been very little contact between us since the 1978 campaign, during which Lilla and I had our problems. But now he and Lilla were divorced and she was actively seeking his downfall. I was surprised when, a few moments later, I received a call from him inviting me to come downstairs for a visit and dinner.

It was a most cordial affair, somewhat reminiscent of older, better days. The irritant, or at least the biggest irritant, was no longer around. I had a bourbon or two. He had about half a glass of wine. He introduced me to his companion, Mrs. Dorothy Heyser, who soon took her leave and our visit continued. He assured me quickly that they had separate quarters in the hotel, a fact I was unconcerned with.

I asked Tower if there was anything I could do to be helpful in the confirmation process. He thought not. The matter, he said, was all but over. It would be a straight party-line vote and he would lose.

He faced heavy odds. The determination of Senate Democrats to instruct a new president on where Washington political power actually resided, plus the determination of Tower's vengeful former wife Lilla that he be denied that which he sought above all else, were formidable obstacles indeed. A goodly portion of the Washington press corps had little sympathy for Tower's ambition to head the nation's defense establishment, and Lilla was a ready and willing source for damaging information in this regard.

I was puzzled by his reading of the potential vote. Surely he would get the votes of a few Senate Democrats, some of whom he had stood with on a variety of critical votes. There might be a couple, he thought, but only if their votes were not really needed by the opposition.

I asked where the government of Israel stood in the matter. He had no problem there, he thought.

"I talked to Peres [Shimon Peres, who has served in various ministerial positions in the Israeli government and as of this writing is that state's foreign minister] last week and he assured me they have no problems with me."

That was good news, for if it were otherwise the vote would have been even more lopsided than it finally was.

It may seem strange to some that Tower would have contacted an official of a foreign government while trying to assess his prospects for a favorable vote in the Senate of the United States to become secretary of defense. But those who understand the working of the U.S. Senate will not find it strange at all. On issues that might have even a peripheral bearing on their national defense the government of Israel, through its lobby in this country, is capable of exercising enormous influence on the American Congress.

Neither of us pursued the Israeli factor further. We both knew the background, and the reasons for my question. We both understood the rationale for his having called Peres.

Tower had chaired the president's Special Review Board inquiring into the Iran–Contra affair. The panel, named by President Ronald Reagan and which also included former Senator (and former Secretary of State) Ed Muskie, as well as former National Security Adviser Brent Scocroft, quickly ran into the "Israeli connection," until then a fairly well-guarded secret.

Robert "Bud" McFarlane, onetime NSC adviser to President Reagan, put the investigators on the Israeli trail in the early days of their probe. They learned, for instance, that the government of Israel was on the ground floor of the operation, going back to contacts as early as 1985, and that Peres, then the prime minister of Israel, was involved in the discussions. But from there the investigators ran into a stonewall, as far as the Israelis were concerned. Cooperation, Tower wrote in his book *Consequences*, was simply not forthcoming. That attitude, Tower wrote, "created a major obstacle for the investigation, but in the end we succeeded in spite of the Israeli effort to obscure its role in the Iran–Contra affair."

In pursuing the Israeli connection so diligently, and in publicly revealing that fact in their final report, members of the review board doubtless made few friends within the Israeli government. Accordingly, Tower had sufficient reasons to be concerned enough to contact Peres.

In fact, Tower had never been a particular favorite of the Israeli lobby. On more than one occasion he had voiced his exasperation, in private, concerning not only that lobby's tactics relative to government in America but its tactics in silencing any critic of its policies within the American Jewish community. He had seen some of his own Jewish supporters essentially ostracized within their community for taking positions opposed to official Israeli positions. He had made his thoughts known in private conversation, but private conversations by public officials have a way of circulating among interested groups.

The result was that Tower was targeted for "sensitizing" early in his Senate career. The first session in this regard, or at least the first that involved me, took place in 1965. We were visited by a delegation concerned, they said, that Tower might be showing signs of anti-Semitism. At that time I was the senator's administrative assistant and received the delegation in his absence. I was stunned by their comments, and asked on what they based their fears.

They had a ready answer. A member of our staff had taken part in a Washington conference put together by people who, they thought, probably had an anti-Israeli bias. I asked for details. They gave me their side of the matter.

According to members of the delegation, one of our staff members, a young attorney named Tom Cole from Houston then serving as the senator's legislative assistant, had appeared before a newly formed group called Liberty Lobby, if memory serves, to advise them concerning the manner by which legislative proposals become law. The group was ostensibly being put together to lobby against what they saw as excessive government spending, which in their view could lead only to higher taxes. No problem. But one of the directors of that organization had said something many months before, of which they had made note, and which they construed as being anti-Semitic. I asked what that comment was.

The comment, duly recorded in the annals of the Israeli lobby, had to do with foreign aid. One director had questioned the value of foreign aid in general, which, by extension, raised questions about foreign aid to Israel, as they saw it. Cole, by appearing at the function, was in their view lending the weight of the senator's office, again by extension, to comments by others that might prove detrimental to Israel. That amounted to his giving aid and comfort to anti-Semitism. They hoped this was merely an oversight on the part of the senator, that he really did not have anti-Semitic tendencies. They wanted me to relay the message that they were concerned and would be watching.

When I did so, the senator was furious. To him this smacked of "McCarthyism." Cole had done nothing wrong. He had done nothing out of the ordinary. One function of his job, as legislative assistant, was to explain to interested constituents the seemingly arcane ways of legislative maneuvering on Capitol Hill. He had done that in this instance, as he had done before and as he would do again. The irony of the matter was that Cole was probably the most "constituent sensitive" member of the staff, going out of his way to please. He was, by my own lights, the most liberal member of the staff, somewhat embarrassed by the right-wing proclivities of others, including myself, on the staff. And Tower, to my knowledge at least, had never indicated by word or deed that he had any anti-Semitic tendencies.

The episode rankled. So much so that he told me shortly after, in a morose fit, he did not want a Jew on his staff. If they wanted to lay an anti-Semitic guilt trip on him simply because a staff member had tried to help people who were trying to find out how things operated in Washington, he wanted nothing to do with them.

In time he cooled off and the matter passed. He did, in fact, have many Jews on his staff over the years, all of whom served well and honorably. He supported many Jewish candidates for office. But he never joined that chorus of senators the Israeli ambassador could count on for an automatic vote, no matter what the interests of the United States happened to be.

His votes relative to Mideast matters were weighed, in his own mind at least, as to their effect on the long-range security of the United States, not Israel. Usually he saw those interests as coinciding, but not always. It was this fact that caused him to believe he might be suspect in the eyes of the Israeli government, with all the attending political fallout. And it was this concern, in my view, that caused him to check with Peres when he started counting votes in the Senate.

Now assured by Peres that the government of Israel had no problems with his confirmation, his fate lay entirely in the field of domestic politics. And there he was going to lose.

I left our dinner meeting in the Jefferson lounge terribly saddened. I had thought the floor vote would be close, but that in the end he would have enough support to become secretary of defense. I realized, after our visit, that I was wrong, and certainly events proved he was right.

I was saddened not only for his sake. I felt he would make a good secretary of defense. He had served his state and his nation well and honorably, in my view, and I saw no reason he could not, or would not, have done the same in the area of defense.

Considering the tenacity with which Tower had waged the battle up to that point, he appeared remarkably relaxed and cheerful, both at the beginning of our conversation and at the end. He had given it his best shot and that was all he could do. In some respects it was typical Tower. He was perfectly capable of generating passion in the heat of battle, but once the battle was over he was also capable of accepting, somewhat stoically, whatever fate had handed out. I suppose that is why I was somewhat startled by the tone in that part of his own memoirs dealing with the Senate confirmation battle. There was an element of bitterness, of revenge-seeking, it seemed to me, toward those who had led the fight against his nomination. That was entirely understandable, given the manner in which he was treated by his former colleagues, but nevertheless it was not what I expected. It was not the Tower I knew, a man who could take his lumps and not look back. I put most of it down to the urging of his publishers.

At any rate, the battle over Tower's nomination was not the Senate's finest hour. The ludicrous spectacle of Democratic senators publicly exhibiting shock and disapproval over allegations of excessive drinking or "womanizing" by one of their peers did little, in my view, to elevate them in public esteem. Nor should it have made their sleep any sounder.

It is true, of course, that the coin of intellectual honesty is not highly valued in politics. Within political peer groups it is to be used sparingly, more admired than spent. In my own view the Senate spent very little of that particular coin during the debate over John Tower.

I would not have quarreled with the Senate's decision had it been based on honest differences with Tower over how the Department of Defense should be run, or might be run if he became secretary. Over the years I had my own differences with him, sometimes over strategy or tactics, sometimes over fundamental issues. But Tower was a man of considerable courage and honesty, as well as intellectual capacity. And he was, surely, a man with the nation's interests at heart. To obscure their real reasons for voting against him with allegations of unfitness based on the fact that at one period in his life he drank too much, or that he enjoyed too much the company of women, was hypocrisy run rampant.

If the hearings, and the vote, were not the Senate's finest hour, neither was reporting thereon the finest hour of the Washington press.

We have seen, in recent years, a full flowering of wolf pack reporting. This is particularly true in reporting out of Washington. A great deal of this, in my view, is simply caused by too many "journalists" crawling over each other looking for ways to prove primarily their presence and only incidentally their usefulness. But there is another aspect of it that I believe to be far more damaging, far more dangerous to the search for truth. That is the propensity to "kick 'em while they're down." The psychology of pack reporting only enhances this problem.

I first ran into that attitude many years ago in conversation with a friend and fellow reporter, Jim Mathis. Jim went on to become publisher of a paper at Edinburg in the Rio Grande Valley, but at that time was on the Capitol Bureau for the *Houston Post*. It was he who had called from Houston with the news I had won the Pulitzer Prize. Later we both found ourselves in Austin, where we lived a few blocks apart in the low-rent district not far from Zilker Elementary.

On this particular occasion, we were visiting about various aspects of our profession, and I told him of my seeming inability to simply relax and enjoy the work and the scenery around the work. One of the things that troubled me, I said, was the appearance of all of us "kicking" people when they were down, which was entirely opposite of what I was brought up to believe. As an illustration I recounted a time when Bascom Giles, then under investigation for his part in the veterans land scandals, was hauled before the DeWitt County grand jury.

I had gone over to the courthouse, hoping to intercept Giles before, or after, his grand jury appearance. I took along our old 4x5 Speed Graphic camera, then the standard for country newspapers. Giles had already entered the jury room, but his lawyer, an Austin attorney named Clint Small, was in the hallway. He assured me his client would have nothing to say, and he assured me further that he wouldn't be with the jurors very long. Giles had been told, Small said, to say nothing.

But Giles stayed and stayed. Small paced and paced, worrying aloud at one point that his client "must be in there spilling his guts." I sat on the floor of the hallway and waited. It was hot and there was no air conditioning.

Finally, Giles emerged. He closed the door behind him and stood for a moment, wiping the sweat from his brow, a look of utter defeat in his eyes, obviously unsure what to do next. Just above his head, in big, bold letters, the sign read "Grand Jury Room."

It would have been a beautiful picture, and I should have taken it. Any good reporter would have. Any good photographer would have. But suddenly my heart went out to him. I had, in some measure, been responsible for his arriving at this point. To do more, I told Mathis, would have been to "kick him when he was down." Besides, it would have added nothing to public understanding of the story.

Jim's response was quick and unexpected. "Ken, you're crazy. That's the best time to kick politicians, 'cause when they're down they can't kick back."

Jim and I were friends and remained friends throughout his lifetime, despite our differences concerning politics. He was as liberal as I was conservative, but that posed no problem concerning our friendship. He was, in my view, a better reporter than I, but we didn't see eye to eye, obviously.

I realize that reporters cannot back off a story merely because a politician (or a financier, or a general, or a publisher) gets in trouble and falls from grace. They not only can't, they shouldn't. Neither, in my mind, should they fawn over them, protect them, make little tin gods of them when they are on top.

The danger of wolf pack reporting is not only that truth often gets crushed in the rush; the danger is also that an unwanted, damaging impression is left at the doorstep of the press. Namely, that the wrong is not in the wrong, the wrong is in not being skillful enough to keep it hidden. Too often the stature of the politician is determined in the press not by his ideas or his honesty or courage, but by his "slickness," his ability to dodge bullets and come out on top.

TWENTY-TWO

Adventures in Public Broadcasting

In the spring of 1979 Lyn Nofziger, an old political warrior and friend from former days, came to Texas and asked if I would agree to come on board the Reagan campaign effort.

Too late. I had already committed to help, or rather try to help, the presidential aspirations of former Governor John Connally, who had, by then, served in the Nixon cabinet and announced his conversion to the Republican Party.

In a political sense it was probably one of the sillier decisions I had made up to that point. I honestly thought Connally would make a good president, if he could get elected. I never thought he would have made a good legislator, given as he was to an imperial style that runs counter to legislative accomplishment. But he did have a decisive quality about him that I thought would be beneficial to the presidency following Watergate. Too, I had no quarrel with what I regarded as his fundamental understanding of the American economy, or of America's potential role in world affairs. I never thought his chances were all that good, but I did think his candidacy could affect the way issues might be addressed during the campaign.

My problem, I suppose, was that I had never worked with Connally and knew little or nothing about the manner he went about making decisions. Had I known, I probably would have declined his offer, and his blandishments. (As his campaign developed it became apparent he was not prone to taking advice and counsel from those around him. Or, if he was, I was never able to determine who those advisers were. Once, for instance, he showed up for a campaign meeting in Houston and startled the assembled crew with the announcement that he was going to support statehood for Puerto Rico, which I thought was not only ill-conceived but politically disastrous for anyone running for president in a Republican primary.)

As it was, I agreed to come into the operation, primarily to help get the state organized. We never got to test whether we had done a reasonable job in that regard. The entire campaign faded and folded before it ever got to Texas.

But all that was in the future.

In fact, my entire involvement in the 1980 presidential race was marked by oddities. I had assumed I would be approached by the Reagan camp in due course. That was where my natural philosophical instincts lay, and it was where most of my political allies were. The first move, however, did not come from the Reagan camp, or the Connally camp, but from George Bush.

Bush called not long after he had announced his intention to run for the presidency and asked if I would join his campaign operation. That was after he had announced that Jim Baker would be in overall charge of his effort and after he had named one or two other top people in the operation. I agreed to do so, provided we could agree where I would fit in the effort and what I would be doing. I had no desire merely to go along for the ride. Bush said he would talk to Baker and that he (Baker) would be in touch to work out the details.

That never happened. Much later I took a call from Bush, who asked, "What happened? I thought we had an agreement."

I told him I also thought we had an agreement, but that I was still waiting for the call from Baker.

"You mean he hasn't called you yet?" he asked.

Assured that he hadn't, Bush said, "I'm going to see him in St. Louis this weekend. You can expect a call after that."

Baker and I had never been political classmates, but I did expect he would react positively to a suggestion from Bush, even if it was to say there would be no room.

The call never came. I have no way of knowing whether Bush forgot to bring up the subject with Baker again, or if Baker simply decided against it. In point of fact, I have never thoroughly understood the relationship between the two men.

In the meantime we went about our own business. Following the Tower campaign in 1978, we had organized a consulting firm to help elect conservative Republican candidates in Texas. At that moment in Texas history this was not a particularly well paying endeavor, since we tried to be selective in who we supported or who we helped. It proved mostly a labor of love. Our hearts tended to influence our heads, which is not wise in business. Enough money came in, on occasion, to pay the hired help, but beyond that there was not much.

That was no great surprise, for I had long since learned that many politicians, whether Democratic or Republican, are given to the idea that their own destiny is what is important, that the duty of others is to see that they are able to fulfill their destiny. The surprising thing is that so many others have such deep feelings about the fate of their country that they will agree, despite the track record, to be helpful in such endeavors. And it is good that they do. Otherwise government would be even less responsive than it is.

At the moment we were pushing the fortunes of some prospective House members in addition to a couple of state senators, and our fortunes did not exactly depend upon involvement in a presidential campaign. The candidate we were probably most heavily involved with was a young Gulf Coast district attorney named "Buster" Brown, running against an incumbent liberal Democratic senator, A. R. "Babe" Schwartz of Galveston. We figured it was an exceedingly long shot, but Schwartz needed beating for the sake of liberty, good government, and the people of Texas. In the end that's how it turned out, and Schwartz, who had made a career of running against the "big" guys and special interests, quickly became a lobbyist, surprising very few in the process.

When I heard no more from the Bush camp, and in the absence of any contact with the Reagan campaign, I joined the Connally effort. Since my activity on Connally's behalf was to be confined to the Texas scene, I felt we could continue our efforts on behalf of those candidates we were already committed to helping. That was the situation that prevailed when Nofziger showed up to ask that we come on board the Reagan campaign.

Lyn was understanding, but he didn't think the Connally effort would last the course. He had no doubt that Reagan would be the ultimate winner. He asked for a commitment that when the Connally campaign folded, I would join the Reagan effort as deputy press secretary and campaign press spokesman. He got it. After Connally abandoned the race and the nomination went to Reagan, I fulfilled my commitment to Lyn. My wife, Louise, joined our operation as office manager and I went off to Washington. John Knaggs took over responsibility for those state races we were involved with and did a fine job.

My own experience is that titles don't mean much in major campaigns. The function is what is important, and function does not always coincide with title. Where one stands in relation to the candidate may be important in some campaigns, but who does what and who reports to whom is important in all campaigns.

The Reagan campaign was fortunate in several respects. First and foremost, of course, there was the candidate. He was the best thing the campaign had going. I felt many times during the course of that campaign that were it not for the evolvement of American politics along the lines it has evolved, we would have been better off simply to abandon everything but the candidate and his immediate support units. Many candidates are essentially carried along by their campaign organization, by the various special interest groups, by the "ethnic" interests, by the political parties. All of that made precious little difference in the Reagan campaign. It was Reagan's persona and Reagan's thoughts that made the difference and ultimately carried the day.

The campaign was also fortunate in that it had Jimmy Carter as an opponent. Carter's campaign against Gerald Ford four years earlier pitted two incompetent campaigners, during which Ford proved himself the more inept. But four years in the White House did little more than confuse Carter, and that confusion showed up in spades during the Reagan–Carter contest. It even caused Carter to admit, on national television, that he had sought advice from his ten-year-old daughter, Amy, concerning the nation's most pressing problems. Her response, which evidently impressed him mightily, was "nuclear proliferation." Not even an adoring national media could overcome what was so obvious to the people.

I do not mean that the Reagan campaign did not benefit from the organization itself. It did. But the driving force of that campaign, as I saw it, was the rapport Reagan had with the unorganized people of the countryside, not with the leadership of special interest groups. The campaign's principal function was merely to play to the strengths of the candidate, not to mold or shape the candidate into something he was not.

A case in point: Reagan was invited, along with Carter, to address a gathering of the National Maritime Union. The union's leadership had already endorsed Carter. That endorsement had been carried in the organization's newspaper, along with a picture of the president. There was debate within the Reagan camp as to whether the candidate should even show up at the convention, since an endorsement had already been made.

Carter chose not to attend. He had the endorsement. Why waste the time? What was there to gain?

Reagan went. What was there to lose?

He made one of his speeches. The delegates liked what they heard. In the heat of the moment, one stood up and made the motion that the leadership's endorsement of Carter be reversed, and that they endorse Reagan. The motion carried, much to everyone's surprise. He was that kind of candidate.

The campaign was also fortunate, in my view, in that it had Bill Casey in the role of manager. I do not know that he was particularly astute in a political sense, but he was a marvel at certain aspects of campaign management. He was autocratic, hard-nosed, not given to wasting time with "show and tell" presentations at our early morning staff conferences. His usual response when a staffer arose to brag about his accomplishments during the preceding day was to silence him with a wave of the hand and a single mumbled sentence: "It's not important." It had the effect of making our staff meetings very short and to the point.

There were those, however, to whom Casey did listen. He usually gave an attentive ear to comments by Jim Baker and Ed Meese, when either of them happened to be present. And he paid attention to the reports of the campaign's pollster. Beyond that, there was little time wasted in speculative conversation. As one who had run campaigns, I found it most refreshing.

My own position in the campaign was probably one of the least enviable of all, with the possible exception of Nofziger's. Lyn was in charge of the overall campaign communications effort. It was he who flew with the candidate and, with the help of Rose Marie Monk, looked after the needs of the traveling press. That had to be a most difficult, thankless task. My job was to man the operation on the ground, to field the countless queries that came from members of the press who were not part of the traveling troupe, and to initiate or clear those statements coming from various segments of the national campaign operation. My day usually began at 7:30 in the morning and ended around 11:00 at night. It was not at all unusual to be one of the last to leave the building at night, and it was not at all unusual to ride down the elevator with Bill Casey.

I reported only to Casey and Nofziger, and primarily to Casey, since Lyn's days and hours were consumed with details of the candidate's presentation on the campaign trail. Only once during the course of the campaign did I have any direct contact with the candidate, and that was not relative to any matter of substance. Still, it was instructive.

A few days of rest and rehabilitation had been decreed for Reagan at his rented quarters near Middleburg, Virginia, a country home which had been a present to the wife of newly elected President John Kennedy. At the time of our visit it was owned by Texas Governor Bill Clements. Someone had come up with the bright idea that we should have a sort of Sunday picnic outing, during which staff members could rub shoulders with the candidate and top campaign officials. It turned out to be a delightful affair, despite the poor planning involved. (They ran out of fried chicken and other goodies.) For some reason, Reagan and I found ourselves walking back to the house together. He asked about Tower and the political situation in Texas. We were discussing that when I noticed a couple of horses on a hillside a hundred yards or so away. I asked if they belonged to him. Yes, he said, the one in front was Nancy's and the other his.

Then he stopped and gazed intently at the two animals.

"Well, now. Wait. I'm not sure. I think Nancy's is in front, but I'm not sure. To tell the truth I don't have my glasses and I can't be sure. I don't want to mislead you."

To tell the truth, I didn't care which horse belonged to whom. What difference did it make? But for some reason he thought it important not to mislead. That sounded exceedingly strange coming from a politician, any politician, and it was somewhat reassuring.

It became apparent, as the campaign neared its end, that we would win barring any last-minute blunder on our part. A good bit of energy was wasted worrying about an anticipated "October surprise" from the Carter camp, along with a good bit of time spent scurrying about, trying to find out what that surprise might be, but other than that it became merely a matter of time. The press, sensing Reagan's impending victory, began to worry about who would fill which positions in the new administration. During the final week of the campaign the bulk of press calls coming to my desk dealt with that subject.

Most of the calls concerning possible future positions centered on the secretary of state and the attorney general. I had no idea who might end up in either spot, or any other place for that matter, and said so to anyone who called. But the press, to its credit, can be most persistent. And there are techniques that can be used, and are used, to ferret out the desired information. It is not unusual for this to involve "speculative" stories quoting "informed sources." This amounts to trial balloons that can be shot down the next day by another "informed source." Finally, the field is narrowed.

In this case the questions centered on the possibility, indeed the probability, of Casey becoming secretary of state and Jim Baker or Ed Meese becoming attorney general. A reporter for *The New York Times* in particular had the idea that Casey was due to be secretary of state. She had a difficult time accepting my argument that this was not likely to happen. Indeed, I had no information that he would not go to State. Nor did I have any that he would go.

Why then, the reporter argued, did I think her "informant" was wrong in saying that was where Casey would end up?

Simply because Casey would not fit the job description. He did not suffer fools lightly, which would create havoc at State. He tended to be brusque and dogmatic, which would only compound that problem. True, he mumbled when he spoke, which could help, but it was not because of a tendency toward intellectual waffling. He was not the best of listeners. There was little about him, as far as I could see, that would make him comfortable at State or make State comfortable with him.

Trying to steer the reporter away from a story I thought would not hold up, I suggested that if I were in her shoes and merely doing a thumb-sucking story on who might go where, I would raise the possibility that Casey might go to the CIA.

"Why?" she asked.

He would be better suited for that than State, I thought, and he would probably enjoy it more. Besides, all the reasons — or at least most of the reasons — that would make him uncomfortable at State should make him comfortable at CIA. On top of all that his background included an early stint in activities not unrelated to that of CIA.

She wrote the story, which appeared the following day, and was probably as surprised as I when Casey was named to head the CIA a few weeks later. Or, she may have figured I knew what I was talking about, which I didn't.

While all this was going on, Jim Baker stopped by my office for no reason in particular. He was walking down the hall from his office (perhaps thirty or forty feet away, going toward the next door office of Charles Wick, a fundraiser for the Reagan campaign primarily among Jewish contributors). He was dressed in the most casual of attire, wearing jeans and an open-necked shirt, as if he were prepared to head for the ranch, or, in the alternative, as if he had just come from the ranch. The campaign had essentially run its course, and within two or three days it would be history. I told him of the calls we were getting concerning future assignments in what was likely to be the new administration, and asked his help. I didn't want to necessarily steer reporters toward any particular conclusion, but I did think we should be helpful, where possible, in steering them away from wrong conclusions. If he could be helpful I would appreciate it.

I asked if he was going to Justice as attorney general.

No, he said, that would go to French Smith, if Smith wanted it, and he did.

"Well, what about you? Where are you going?"

"I don't know," he said in a sort of resigned shrug. "Ken, you know, I've fought those people all my life. I don't know what they're going to do with me."

In all honesty I would have to say I was startled. In my ignorance I did not know there was a division between "those people" and the rest of us, whoever the rest of us were. I had assumed we were all in the battle together, that we were all "us" and there were no "them" or "those people."

It was true, of course, that I had generally placed Baker among those Texas Republicans who worried mightily, during the earlier days, that the party might be taken over by the more militant conservatives. The prospect of the party being unduly influenced by anti-Communist "John Birchers" was enough to cause consternation within the ranks of the leadership, concerned as they were with building a party that would be "socially acceptable" to those who shaped public opinion in the state. But I had also assumed those days and those worries were long since past.

While I was still trying to digest the meaning of his comments, Jim asked what I wanted in the new administration.

I told him "nothing." I came to Washington to try to help Reagan get elected because I thought it would help arrest and perhaps reverse the government's drift toward the left, toward a welfare state. I had served my time and wanted to get back to Texas. The only thing I really wanted in Washington was to head the USIA, but it was my understanding that position was going to Charlie Wick. In the absence of that post I had no desire to return to Washington for another tour of duty.

"Yes," said Baker, USIA was going to Wick, "if he wants it." And it was his understanding Wick wanted it.

A day or so after Reagan was elected it was announced that Jim Baker would be the new chief of the White House staff. I was probably the most puzzled person in Washington with the announcement.

Perhaps I should not have been. Some three or four weeks prior to the election Casey passed a short memorandum to the senior staff. He told us, in that memo, that in his absence we should turn to Jim Baker if we had any questions concerning policy or operations.

I was somewhat surprised, for I thought the memo would have indicated Ed Meese as the one to whom we should turn. Meese was closest to Reagan. He was clearly the one who understood and agreed with Reagan's philosophy. But perhaps Casey saw in Meese what many of us saw. Meese was highly intelligent and dedicated, but he was not the most organized person in the world. His desk, piled high with unanswered messages, was generally referred to as "the black hole."

Baker, on the other hand, was a model of proper organization. During the early morning staff conferences his comments, when he chose to make comments, were lucid. His thoughts were organized and presented in an organized fashion. It was he who "negotiated" with the Carter people concerning the presidential debates, aiming for a time and format acceptable to the Reagan campaign. The results coincided exactly with the plans. I suppose, in retrospect, it was natural for Casey to ask us to turn to Baker.

But the White House staff?

Going over to the White House to become chief of staff among "those people"? People he had "fought" all his life? Did Casey have anything to do with that? I don't know. Perhaps someday when Baker writes his own story he will tell us.

When the campaign ended I returned to Texas and tried to pick up the threads of normal existence. But the past kept intruding on the present. A flurry of press excitement arose during the "transition" over the possibility that John Tower was to be named secretary of defense by Reagan. From afar it had the appearance, at first, of being a trial balloon. But it wouldn't go away. Obviously, there were forces at work that wanted it to happen.

In early December I received a call from Lyn Nofziger in Washington, who was to join the White House staff as a sort of director of political affairs, or some such title. He was, in my view, concerned that the Reagan "revolution" have troops in place to carry on the fight. Lyn and his wife, Bonnie, were to head back to California for Christmas and he wanted to come through Texas to visit. Any visit with Nofziger was always a most delightful affair, and we welcomed the prospect.

But Lyn had something on his mind other than just reminiscing about the campaign. Among other things he wanted to know where all the rumors were being generated concerning Tower going to Defense.

I told him I supposed it came from someone in the new administration. Not so, he said, it didn't come from them.

In that case the only other place it could have come from, I speculated, was from Tower supporters who had to be reflecting the senator's wishes.

In any case, he said, it wasn't going to happen.

"I'll tell you who it's going to be," he said. "It's going to be Cap [Caspar] Weinberger. The decision is already made."

Then he recounted how he knew.

Immediately after Reagan was elected he returned to his home in California for a few days of rest. The first political visitors he received just happened to be from Texas, John Connally and Bill Clements, then the governor of Texas. I can't remember who Lyn said showed up first, but they came on separate days.

There was much speculation among the Reagan staff as to what the two wanted to discuss. At any rate they made sure that a staff member was present for both occasions, and on both occasions that staffer happened to be Lyn.

"We were always having this problem," he said, "of people meeting privately with Reagan and then going out and saying 'the governor told me,' and then Reagan reading it in the paper and saying 'I don't remember it that way,' so we decided to always have a staff member on hand."

All Connally talked about, according to Nofziger, was the Middle East, and how important it was that the newly elected president pursue even-handed policies in that region. That advice evidently fell on deaf ears, for Reagan was a thoroughgoing defender of Israel. But that's another story.

And all Clements wanted to talk about was the Department of Defense. The Texas governor had previously served as a deputy secretary at Defense and evidently still had an interest in how the department was run. He leaned on Reagan to appoint Cap Weinberger to the post. In fact, according to Lyn, Clements leaned rather heavily. After all, Clements is not the most diplomatic person in the world, not the kind of man any president would name to be ambassador to France. The old Soviet Union, perhaps. Or Israel, perhaps, where America could well benefit from a strong ambassador. But it is doubtful that he would feel comfortable with the protocols of Paris.

When Clements left, Reagan turned to Nofziger and said, in effect, "What about that."

Reagan went on to tell Lyn that he had lain awake most of the night, unable to sleep. The fact that he had been elected president of the United States was finally beginning to soak in and he had turned his thinking to "What am I going to do with all these people who have supported me over the years?"

He knew what he wanted to do at Defense. He wanted to rejuvenate America's armed forces. He knew that would cost money, and he wanted someone there who was good with budgets and with getting the most results with the least amount of money. His thinking turned to Weinberger, whose skill with budgets had earned him the nickname "Cap the Knife." Sometime around 2:00 in the morning he had settled on Weinberger.

Reagan didn't tell Clements he had already decided on Weinberger. No one else knew, since the decision had been made only hours earlier. He let it ride, telling Clements only that he agreed Weinberger was qualified for a cabinet position. In the end, of course, it worked that way. Weinberger did indeed become secretary of defense.

All of which is interesting, but in my own mind it raised an intriguing question: Why would Clements, the governor of Texas, be in California advocating the appointment of Caspar Weinberger as secretary of defense when he was bound to have known that John Tower also wanted the post?

I didn't have the answers then and I don't have them now.

The Reagan team wasted little time in staffing the new administration. It came in with a mission and quickly set about the task of placing people in position to carry out that mission. It was perhaps a mixed bag with mixed results, but at least it had a sense of direction, particularly during the early years. I was offered two "assistant secretary" positions, one in the Department of Energy, the other in the Department of Labor. Both were turned down. I had no real desire to go back to Washington. I did go over to the Energy Department for an interview with the new secretary, but that only served to reinforce the decision not to go back. Nothing about the place appealed to me. The prospect of again fighting the Washington traffic, of again being caught up in the never ending politics of the city, of again postponing reentry into private life, was not for me.

I thought that would end the matter. But then I got a call from White House personnel office asking if I would consider an appointment to the Corporation for Public Broadcasting. My response at first was noncommittal.

"I'm not even sure I like the way that operation is being run," I told the caller.

"Maybe that's why we want you there," was the reply.

That sounded interesting. Besides, it was supposed to be a nongovernment job, as well as a nonpaying job. The board only met once every two months, I was told, and would probably require only a couple of days away from home. I would be able, they argued, to continue doing whatever I was doing. The bad part about it, as I thought it through, would be getting back on airplanes. The good part about it was that the Corporation would pay for the tickets.

I knew absolutely nothing about the internal workings of the public broadcasting industry, much less about the working of the Corporation itself. I had no financial interest, nor had I ever had any financial interest, in any phase of broadcasting, public or commercial. My principal interest in broadcasting was its tremendous potential in the field of learning. Without doubt, television is the most effective propaganda vehicle on the scene today for mass audiences, which is another way of saying it also has tremendous potential for influencing thought. All I knew about public broadcasting was what I saw on the screen. There some of the programs were very good, and some were very bad. Some were balanced and objective in the presentation of issues, notably the MacNeil–Lehrer news programs, some were outstanding in fields of science and letters, and some were sheer propaganda for politically correct social agendas. Perhaps a place on the board would afford an opportunity to increase the number of good programs and decrease the number of bad.

With a certain amount of trepidation, I accepted the offer.

My first few months on the board involved a good bit of learning. I had assumed, wrongly, that since it was billed as a private corporation it would be run like a private corporation, that decisions made by the board would have impact upon what the viewer at home saw on his television screen. To a degree that turned out to be true, but only to a degree, and a very limited degree.

Indeed, as I soon learned, members of the board were expected to offer no criticism about what the system produced, either on radio or television. Public praise was always welcome, indeed expected, but public criticism was not. Board members were expected to have some background in the field of communications, or education, or related disciplines. But any such experience must be translated into broad "policy" matters, which, in time, and through circuitous routes, might or might not have implications upon the product paid for by American taxpayers.

Any criticism of what was produced and shown by the system was looked upon as "interference." That would have a "chilling effect" (a favorite phrase) upon creativity. The board was expected, rather, to afford a "heat shield" for criticism from any quarter, unless, of course, it came from those congressmen having control over the purse strings. And the board was also expected, naturally, to seek as much money from the national treasury as the traffic would bear.

The Corporation's board was then in a catch 22 situation. It was charged with upholding the law as written by Congress but was prevented by the same Congress from enforcing that law, and by rules and procedures it had enacted to mollify Congress and the "system." For instance, the law under which we operated said, in plain English, that programs or series of programs of a controversial nature should be balanced and objective. But any attempt to obey the law as written, any attempt to even inquire into whether we were in fact following the law, was met by cries of outrage in the Congress, in the "system," in the press, and by a majority of board members themselves.

Those who took this position, both in the Congress and within the public broadcasting system, knew exactly what they were doing and why. They knew they had a political bird nest on the ground, courtesy of the American taxpayer, and were determined to protect it at all costs. Over the years the system had evolved from its earlier days as "educational television" into an "alternative" to commercial

---

　　　　　　　　　　　　　　THE CHOW DIPPER

broadcasting with its attendant moral mindset. The dominant delusion within the system was that public broadcasting was pure of heart and noble of spirit, unlike those greedy capitalists in charge of commercial broadcasting. It then follows, as the night follows day, that those in Congress who supported public broadcasting were also pure of heart and noble of spirit, and therefore worthy of being supported in turn.

And what better vehicle to get that message across to the people than public television itself? It is only natural that a vehicle of expression, whether spoken or visual, become an extension of one's own personality. It is also natural that the first order of business for any living organism, whether individual or corporate, private or public, is survival. In this regard public broadcasting is no exception. The political message conveyed represented the dominant political thinking, however subtle, of those concerned with self-survival.

Unfortunately, there is not much difference in human nature, no matter the station in life. It did not take many months on the board to realize that people in public broadcasting were every bit as concerned with increasing their revenue as were those in commercial broadcasting. They were just not quite as honest about it as their brethren in commercial television, or commercial radio, who frankly admit they are in business for the purpose of generating as much revenue as possible. They merely sought their revenue from a different source, or different sources. They sought it from the Congress, which was generally liberal in its outlook, and which had a history of being most generous in funding those programs it felt would redound to the benefit of liberalism.

While Mark Twain may have been right when he said, essentially, that the principal difference between man and dog is that the dog will not bite the hand that feeds, my own observation is that the difference is not all that pronounced. Man may indeed bite the hand that feeds, but it doesn't happen very often. It was the men (and women) in Congress who helped feed the men (and women) who ran public broadcasting. In return, Congress seldom got bitten.

They also sought funding from private corporations and private foundations. Generally, the private corporations who underwrote public television productions were those who felt a need to be seen as supporting aspects of public life their critics also supported. In other words, they hoped to gain commercially by first gaining politically. And, one would have to admit, it was, and is, generally a good ploy on their part.

That was the situation that prevailed when I went on the board in the spring of 1981. The appointment, subject to Senate confirmation, was supposed to run for five years. At the end of six months I determined I had been there long enough. To me it appeared that service on the board was an exercise in futility, a waste of valuable time that could better be spent elsewhere, like making a living.

I suppose it didn't help that I had already gotten a taste of politics surrounding the board, if not too much on the board itself. Shortly after my appointment to the board I received a call from Senator Charles Percy of Illinois. With Reagan's election the Senate also went Republican, for a brief period, and Percy, as ranking Republican on the Senate Foreign Relations Committee, had been elevated to chairman.

At the moment I was in what I thought was an important meeting. Our firm had been retained as consultants by a candidate for lieutenant governor and we were in a strategy huddle I did not want to leave. But the receptionist said the senator felt his call was very important. As it turned out, the call was indeed very important to him.

The conversation started off with one of those "Ken, ole buddy, it's been years" routines, which I recognized as such. The senator and I seldom discussed matters of import when I was with Tower. But now he needed a favor.

His daughter, Sharon Rockefeller, then the wife of the Democratic West Virginia Governor Jay Rockefeller, was a member of the Corporation for Public Broadcasting's board of directors under appointment from the previous president. She had served one term and desired reappointment to a new five-year term. The senator was determined he would deliver the appointment for her.

But he had a problem. The White House was not responsive. In fact, the senator said, he couldn't even get them to set up a meeting where he could discuss the matter. They wouldn't return his calls. He blamed Ed Meese.

I could understand his frustration, as well as the White House's reluctance to meet with him. Percy was not noted as a Reaganite. They didn't figure they owed him a great deal at that stage of the game. Percy felt I could get through to Meese, where he couldn't. I tried to beg off, saying surely if Meese wouldn't talk to him about the subject, it was unlikely he would discuss it with me. But he thought otherwise. I had been part of the team that helped elect Reagan, he argued. Surely they would listen to me.

And he went further. What had started out as a friendly chat turned a good bit more specific and much more emphatic. He was going to be the chairman of the Foreign Relations Committee, he reminded me, and the administration was going to need him. Potential ambassadors would come before his committee for approval. Foreign policy matters would arise on which the administration would need his support. I should convey this thought to Meese, he said. He had not, he said, asked for anything else, nor was it likely he would ask for anything else. But on this one thing he was adamant. If Sharon did not get reappointed the new administration was going to have trouble with him.

It became clear to me that the father had a high regard for the daughter. At one point he made note of the fact that she was perfectly capable of running the General Motors Corporation better than it was being run, a comment the stockholders of General Motors could hardly have quarreled with at the time. It was a very long conversation.

I called Meese's office and asked that he call when he had the opportunity. The call was not quickly returned. Given my own experience with Ed's usual attention to small details, I figured that was not unusual. So I called Jim Baker's office, relaying the problem and the gist of the senator's comments, as well as his implied threats. It would be good, I said, if they would at least meet with him. My argument was that it would be far more harmful to have an unhappy senator as chairman of Foreign Relations than to have his daughter a director for the Corporation for Public Broadcasting.

They were aware of the problem. They just were not happy with the prospect of Sharon's reappointment, where, they felt, the Democratic wife of a Democratic governor could end up as chairman of the board in the first years of a Republican administration. My argument was that given the makeup of the board she was the best we were likely to get at the moment. When the makeup of the board changed, that could change as well. (It did, but not without a great deal of public fanfare.)

A few nights later I was rousted from deep sleep at the historic old Lamplighter Inn in Floydada, Texas, where I had gone to negotiate the purchase of the *Floyd County Hesperian* and *Lockney Beacon* newspapers, with a message delivered by Dorothy Hotchkiss, who with her husband Johnny ran the inn. Baker's office was calling. The message was short and simple: "The deed is done."

Sharon was reappointed. When it came time to select the next chairman, I urged her election. The vote was unanimous.

Thereafter we were occasionally on the same side of issues coming before the board. When we differed, she usually won. At that time she had the votes.

In a perverse sort of way the entire episode may well have cut short Percy's career in the Senate. He did, in fact, support the administration on some critical matters which I am not at all certain he would have done otherwise. As chairman of the Foreign Relations Committee, for instance, he supported the administration on the highly controversial decision to sell early warning aircraft (AWACs) to Saudi Arabia in the face of determined opposition from the Israeli government and the Israeli lobby in the United States. That lobby got its revenge when he ran for reelection to the Senate. Percy was defeated by Paul Simon, and a very clear message was sent to other senators.

The board then was an unwieldy group of fifteen people, many of whom, it seemed, were there to represent vested interests having to do with every phase of broadcasting except the viewing public. Given the fact that the board was generally proscribed from doing anything that might influence the content of programs produced by either television or radio, I suppose it was only natural that the only thing left to argue about was how this or that policy would affect this or that vested interest.

The result was that our board meetings were often fractious, prolonged affairs wherein we were frequently treated to lengthy monologues on the part of Kathleen Nolan, a Democratic party activist from Los Angeles, who was always worrying about how our policies would be viewed by those unions having to do with program productions, or Jose Rivera of New York, a voluble civil rights lawyer concerned about those things civil rights lawyers are (publicly) concerned about.

For one coming out of an arena where decisions were usually made and acted on with dispatch, my first impression of service on the board was exceedingly negative. It did not help, I suppose, that activist liberal Democrats held sway on a fifteen-member board that could count only five or six nominal Republicans and about that many nominal conservatives among both Republicans and Democrats.

One of those comparative conservatives among the Democrats was Paul Friedlander of Seattle, Washington. We had formed an early friendship on the board, and it was he I turned to when I made the decision to leave. Paul owed his membership on the board to friendship with Senator "Scoop" Jackson, the somewhat hawkish Democrat from Washington. (Without being disrespectful it might also have helped that his wife was a daughter of one of the co-founders of Sears–Roebuck, which meant he had enough money to be noticed in the political world.)

We had lunch. I told him of my frustrations and my decision. He urged me to reconsider. Things would get better, he argued, and there would be no chance to change things if one were not at the table. In the meantime I should simply wait and learn. Someday we would have enough help to make changes.

In the end I took his advice and settled in for the long haul. It was indeed a long haul.

My early frustrations with service on the board could be laid primarily, if not exclusively, to the fundamentally flawed and fundamentally duplicitous nature of the structure itself. Congress, of course, has the power to declare what is legal and what is not legal, what is lawful and what is not. But like so much of what Congress creates, what we see is not what we get.

When Congress, for instance, created the Corporation for Public Broadcasting to oversee (in theory) public broadcasting in America, it was to be a private corporation. One of the ostensible reasons for this figment was to create an entity that could provide a "heat shield" against political influence from any quarter. To buttress the corporation's heat shield capabilities, board members were given five-year terms subject to Senate confirmation, on the assumption that once confirmed members would be free to make independent judgments on what was best for development of public broadcasting.

But Congress also decreed that activities of the Corporation be circumscribed and subject to varying levels of public funding, which means, in practical terms, to the varying moods of Congress. They even decreed a "cap" on what the Corporation could pay its employees, with that cap corresponding to the pay scale of comparative federal employees. They maintained their right of review of the Corporation's activities, including the way it spent its funds.

What the American people saw when the Corporation for Public Broadcasting was created during Lyndon Johnson's presidency was a private corporation charged with the responsibility of independently overseeing development of an expanded public broadcasting system. What they got was a quasi-private, quasi-public operation that was neither fish nor fowl, or rather both fish and fowl, being forced to feed and breathe in one environment and swim in another.

All this may be eminently desirable. Any expenditure of public funds should be subject to review by those public bodies that dole out the funds. But why try to insist that the Corporation is in fact a private organization going about its business as one would expect of a private corporation?

To the average citizen this may seem a matter of little consequence. But to me it went to the heart of the problems plaguing public broadcasting at that time. It placed conscientious board members in the impossible position of trying to do what they thought was right for public broadcasting while at the same time trying to second guess the reaction of some politically biased congressional staff adviser to some powerful and politically biased subcommittee chairman bent upon a personal social or political agenda. Unhappy senators and congressmen could have a deleterious effect upon appropriations for the Corporation, which in turn would have a corresponding effect upon the entire public broadcasting system. That situation was to be avoided if at all possible.

It also created a situation where people in the industry could conduct end runs to their favorite senator or congressman with complaints about policies under consideration by the board. Quite naturally, this placed representatives of the larger television stations, those in metropolitan communities, in a much more politically advantageous position than their brethren from the smaller communities. In the world of practical politics, a station manager in a metropolitan community has much more to offer a sitting politician than does an honest board member who is proscribed from trying to influence program content along lines of balance and objectivity, and who may be trying to balance the interests of all stations, large and small.

All of which is to say the system had not evolved in the way its early champions had hoped. It evolved in the way many had feared, the way it could be expected to evolve given the manner it was constructed and circumscribed. About all the board could do then, or can do now, is try to make the best of a less than best situation. The wonder is that it has been able to do as well as it has.

At any rate, Friedlander was right. Things did get better. The

---

board was reduced from fifteen to ten, which reduced the wordiness and increased the focus of the board's endeavors. Some able people, along with some not so able, were appointed to the board. After going through a succession of corporation presidents, we finally found, in Donald Ledwig, a person who had management capabilities and enough backbone to exercise those capabilities. The internal power struggles were finally reduced from waves to mere ripples. The board did not, and could not, correct the basic internal weakness of the public broadcasting system, but we were able, over time, to influence the priorities by which appropriated monies were spent. And we were able, I believe, to inject a degree of internal discipline into operations of both the Corporation and the system.

One example: Soon after going on the board I was assigned to the Corporation's Audit Committee, where we were met with the unwelcome news that National Public Radio, which received substantial funding from the Corporation, was essentially bankrupt. Years of freewheeling, free spending irresponsibility with a bloated staff had resulted in NPR running up debts of some $9 million that could not be paid. So slip-shod was their accounting system, by accident or design, that the money trail could not even be traced with any degree of certainty. Money that the Corporation had forwarded to NPR for various productions was merely put in a pot, from which all sorts of expenditures were made.

Unable to pay their bills, NPR was faced with only two alternatives: to shut down or to have someone else pick up the tab. Quite naturally they preferred the latter, and the Corporation for Public Broadcasting was the only likely source for those funds.

I was prepared to see them go under. If we were in fact a "private corporation," and if National Public Radio was essentially an independent organization as it insisted it was, with its own board of directors responsible for oversight, then in my view they should be left to stew in their own juice. I did not see why we should take money away from the rest of the public broadcasting system to bail out an irresponsible operation.

My own views did not prevail. Many members of Congress, reacting in a predictable manner to entreaties from NPR reporters assigned to cover Capitol Hill, made their wishes known to those of us on the board. It was the same board that Congress had set up years before ostensibly to provide a "heat shield" against exactly this type pressure. The irony of it, and the hypocrisy of it, was that so-called "leaders" in the public broadcasting system, who often (and loudly) lectured the board concerning its heat shield responsibilities, thought nothing of running to Congress in an effort to bring heat upon CPB's board.

In the end the problem was worked out. The president of NPR, a former Kennedy aide, left and subsequently went to work for one of Washington's premier lobbying firms. A new president came on board. The corporation (CPB) "loaned" the money to NPR under condition that a system of accountability be put in place and that the money be repaid within a specified time. Both conditions were met, with much complaining. Many at NPR took the position that they were doing the Lord's work and that money didn't really matter, as long as it was someone else's money.

The battles within the system then were between those of us who wanted to see tax dollars spent on education, on children's programming, and on reflecting the history of America, and others who wanted the money spent on social agendas, on reshaping the thinking of America along politically "correct" lines. It was also between those who wanted a more powerful center and those of us concerned about protecting the independence and viability of smaller stations. The Corporation, quite naturally, got caught up in those battles. I suspect the battles are still along those lines.

During my ten years on the board I came to the firm conclusion that the entire issue of public broadcasting in America ought to be revisited by the Congress. I am still of that opinion. Not just with the thought that some tinkering ought to be undertaken by the Congress. The subject ought to be addressed in its fundamentals.

Is there still a need for a public, tax-funded system, given the development of commercial broadcasting in America since 1968?

When the present system came into being with the 1968 public broadcasting act, there was no cable system. There was no C-SPAN. There were no independent "learning" channels, no A&E, no CNN, no "super stations" bouncing signals off satellites. The broadcasting industry then was essentially ruled by an oligarchy of three money hungry networks determining what the people saw and what they didn't see. The networks then chafed under charges that they catered to the lowest common intellectual denominator, a charge that was valid then and even more valid now. The commercial networks were happy to support development of a publicly funded public broadcasting system, feeling this would get the monkey off their own backs.

They could slough off the responsibility of presenting decent programs and go their merry, money making ways.

But now there are alternatives to both the networks and to public broadcasting. Should a system, any system, put in place to solve one problem continue after the original problem no longer prevails?

It may very well be that a thorough examination of public broadcasting's place in the scheme of things would determine that indeed it should continue, and that it should be continued in exactly the structure and with the same funding mechanism now provided. But that question ought to be explored in depth and answered carefully, along with an equally important question: Why?

The "why" ought to be determined, in my view, because it goes to the heart of who should pay.

Broadcasters, particularly television broadcasters, enjoy a unique and lucrative position in American communications. A government-granted license to operate is a government-granted opportunity, indeed a government-protected opportunity, to reap vast fortunes. It is also a government-granted opportunity to shape political and social agendas in America. In my view they ought to pay for that privilege.

If a public broadcasting system is necessary because commercial broadcasters refuse to use public airways in a responsible manner, then commercial broadcasters should pick up the tab for that system. People ought not be taxed to fill the void left by their failure.

I am under no illusions that Congress will rush to reexamine the issue of public broadcasting. It is the nature of politicians to let sleeping dogs lie, under the theory that there is always the possibility the dog may bite when disturbed. And in the field of broadcasting there are many dogs who can indeed bite, first and foremost those in commercial television.

My years on Capitol Hill with John Tower taught me that few lobbies possess the power of that exercised by commercial television. It is not a matter of their contributing funds to a reelection campaign. It is simply that they have the power to grant or withhold that one thing a politician needs to stay in office: favorable public exposure. A politician would be stupid to make enemies of those who can grant such favors, and there are few stupid politicians on Capitol Hill. Dumb, maybe. But not stupid. Anyone who thinks otherwise hasn't spent much time there.

Commercial television would not be the only interested party dragging its feet in any reexamination of public broadcasting. Very few within the public broadcasting system think they now have the most desirable situation possible, but fewer still would willingly risk opening the subject to critical review. There would always be the risk that lucrative financial arrangements now comfortably in place might be placed in jeopardy.

Still, the project ought to be undertaken. I have no real concerns that public broadcasting would suffer in the process. In fact, I believe it would likely benefit. A better, more stable system for funding might result. The hypocrisy of blatant paid advertising under the guise of benevolent "underwriting" might become a thing of the past. Time and energy now spent in local fund solicitations could be devoted to better use.

I have no real problem with the manner in which members of the Corporation for Public Broadcasting are now chosen. Politics, in one form or another, will enter the process. That is a given, even if board members were selected by a group of supposedly nonpolitical academicians. In any event they will be selected by someone, and the president of the United States is as likely to select capable people to serve as will anyone else. The Senate, in its wisdom or lack of wisdom, is empowered to advise and consent. The opportunities are there, as far as ensuring service by capable people is concerned. The problem is not the people. It is, in my opinion, the system under which they must operate. It is a system that invites political tinkering by those lawmakers who are sensitive to such things, and conversely invites benign neglect from those who are not.

Neither the Reagan nor Bush White House showed any great interest in involving themselves in the general management of affairs in public broadcasting, but the same cannot be said about many members of Congress. The Reagan team, as opposed to the Bush team, showed an acute awareness early on of what was at stake in public broadcasting, as it did in all fields of communications. That awareness had a bearing on who they nominated for membership on the CPB board of directors. But once Reagan's appointees were in place, they were left to their own devices. There were no calls, of which I am aware, urging any particular vote or any particular direction. It was not unusual to get programming complaints from members of Congress, but I do not know of one from the White House.

The Bush administration, or more specifically the president's personnel office under Chase Untermeyer, seemed uninterested or unwilling to indicate, by the identifiable philosophical orientation of its appointees, any preference of direction. Membership on the board, a much sought after position, was used on more than one occasion to alleviate political pressure from real or imagined sources. (That happened only once during the Reagan years, the Charles Percy affair mentioned earlier, but then the political considerations were very real and very significant.) The results during the Bush administration were sometimes strange, even bizarre. It was not unusual for the appointment of a strong supporter of the president to be balanced by the appointment of someone backed by a strong critic of the president. That may be laudable in polite, nonpolitical circles, but it can do little to instill an overall sense of direction, or a feeling of support from those committed to carry out the perceived wishes of a president, any president. And there is no evidence that Bush ever reaped any extraneous political benefits from the misdirected machinations of his personnel office. Senators Lloyd Bentsen or Jay Rockefeller never became any less critical of the president after he appointed their choices to the board, despite what Untermeyer might have anticipated when he recommended them.

This is not to say that those appointed were any less dedicated to the welfare of public broadcasting than would have been the case had their Senate benefactors been supporters of the president. It is, rather, a reflection on the political acumen of the president's personnel office, a critical element in the success of any administration.

I finally served on the board for ten years, including two terms as chairman. I left with mixed emotions, feeling I had perhaps contributed in some small measure but also feeling there was so much to be done, that the system was capable of so much more than it was delivering in the areas I was concerned about. I went on the board feeling that much more could be done in the general field of learning, of American history, literacy, geography, and in such simple things as teaching youngsters where they were in the world. I left feeling we had moved forward slightly in these areas but that so much more could have been done and still ought to be done.

We were never able to provide any mechanism by which balance and objectivity could be assured in the presentation of controversial programs or series of programs, as was required by the laws under which we operated. Opposition throughout the system, and indeed throughout the liberal community, was simply too great. But we were able to raise the issue, keep it alive and ultimately cause Congress to address the matter, even if it did so halfheartedly.

We were never able to overcome the inherent structural weaknesses of the system, but we were able to make some progress in establishing a degree of accountability that seemed sorely lacking when I went on the board. And we put some teeth in the process of accountability. Whether those teeth will be used depends, as it does in all cases, upon the willingness to use them.

Service on the board ended up requiring much more time and attention than I had anticipated. In terms of personal finances it was very costly. It took time that should have been spent, and could have been spent, in looking after our own affairs. What was supposed to be a part-time, nonpaying position ended up being little short of a consuming, nonpaying obsession.

Upon reflection I suppose it could be said that anyone dumb enough to take an assignment like that isn't smart enough to handle the job anyway. Still, it was finally a rewarding experience, one I hope contributed in some small measure to the public good.

At any rate, service on the board ended my official involvement with government on the federal level. It did not end an interest in the affairs of government.

I took no part in the subsequent reelection campaign of President Bush, other than to give a small amount of money and advice. The money was accepted; the advice was not. That was probably just as well. In point of fact, his campaign may have been plagued by too much advice from too many advisers, few of whom had ever read Rudyard Kipling's *Tomlinson.* Or, if they read it, they did not take it to heart.

Kipling may have been of another age, but his message in *Tomlinson* is for all ages: A man is accepted nowhere unless he identifies himself positively somewhere.

Bush's campaign, indeed the last year of his administration, did not, as far as I could see, march to the cadence of a single drummer. It seemed too long led, to the extent it was led, by a variety of trombones, clarinets, flutes and piccolos, all played by tone-deaf musicians. When the maestro finally took charge, it was too late. The fat lady was ready to sing.

It was all very sad. Bush was and is a personally courageous individual. When duty called he did not run and hide. As president there was a calmness about him that served the nation well in difficult times. In my view, he was a kind and decent man, so much so that he seemed unable or unwilling to accept the fact, publicly at least, that his political enemies were actually determined to do him in.

The nation, I believe, chose wisely when it chose Bush over Dukakis. I do not believe it chose wisely when it chose Clinton over Bush. In Clinton there is, as I see it, an element of character flaw that is bound to influence the manner in which he conducts the affairs of state, and one I believe will not serve the nation well in the long haul. (This is being written shortly after he took the oath of office, and I hope time will prove me wrong. If it does, it won't be the first time.)

I am certainly no judge of who benefited the most, or who was damaged the most, by my own limited association with politics, the press, or government at various levels. In terms of impact, there is no question. Involvement with the government, if we include war as a governmental activity, certainly made a bigger impact on me than I on it—despite, I might add, my very best efforts.

I have the uneasy feeling that the same is true of all else.

Being the eternal optimist, I remain convinced that those who come later will do a better job, if, that is, they keep up the struggle.

Epilogue

"Go to the end and quit," the King said to the White Rabbit.
The end is not yet, but the time for summation is.

In some respects we have come full circle. To borrow a few lines from Rudyard Kipling's "The Return":

> Peace is declared, an' I return
> To 'Ackneystadt, but not the same,
> Things 'ave transpired which made me learn
> The size and meanin' of the game.
> I did no more than others did,
> I don't know where the change began.
> I started as a average kid,
> I finished as a thinkin' man.

During that final day in Shenyang's Hoten Prison Camp #1, in September 1945, there was much scurrying about. The appropriate Red Army authorities passed word we could leave China for home. Former prisoners, in a state of general confusion, were making ready to depart. Some were packing little mementos they hoped to keep; others were discarding everything but the clothes on their back.

One, whose name has long since escaped me, wanted to salvage his mess kit, or some such item. He thought in time it might mean something to someone. He was challenged by a friend who made clear that he wanted no such keepsake. When he left the walls, he said, he never wanted to think of prison again, as long as he lived. And he wanted nothing, or no one, around him that would remind him of the experience.

Nearby was an older prisoner, nay, former prisoner, who went by the name "Pops." He was, in fact, one of the few among the older enlisted men who made it through. He was an ancient sergeant, perhaps fifty years old, and the last years had not been kind to him. He was so old he had become a grandfather while in prison, a fact revealed to him when we broke open the warehouse containing letters from home.

For reasons of his own, "Pops" thrust himself into the conversation. Addressing no one in particular, he observed that there would be times when all of us looked back on the prison years as the best years of our lives.

He did not say the easiest years or the happiest years. He said the best years.

Nevertheless, he was disputed quite vigorously by everyone in hearing range, including myself. Some told him he was crazy as a loon. Others used stronger language. He merely smiled.

I have now lived long enough to realize he wasn't completely wrong.

I do not mean he was completely and totally right in all respects. I do not know many who would say those were indeed the best years of their life. But I have lived long enough to understand the message he was, I now believe, probably trying to convey. We had, to that point, endured the struggle and survived. He was old enough to understand this was important, and that it would be increasingly important as the years went by — especially to those much younger than he.

Too, he may have surmised, though merely a "dumb sergeant," that a few had learned something of their own nature and the nature of other humans. Unfortunately, however, the lessons learned in that regard seem to have a way of going to the grave with the learners. There is no real indication, so far as I have been able to observe, that humanity really learns much from war or the effects of war. The individuals who engage in war may, but the lessons they learn do not seem to rub off on many beyond their own circles. Perhaps the reason for this is that while wars may be plotted in the councils of government with logic and machination, they are fought on the field of battle by men of passion.

Those who plot wars seldom fight them. Those who fight wars seldom plot them.

Still, I do not know what other course there is when the concept of human liberty is challenged. At that point the alternatives are plain, and, in my own opinion, the race is fortunate that some will rise to its defense. There will always be those who run and hide, thinking themselves too important to undertake the battlefield risks of defending human liberty, saving themselves for what they see as greater glory, greater usefulness to themselves, if no other. And who, once the battle is won, seek to lead the victory parade. But for every one of those there are many more Francis Tuermans, and Alabama Freemans and George Williamses and Roy Creecys. Therein lies the hope of mankind.

My own view is that any endeavor, any undertaking, any situation that calls forth the best in men also affords the opportunity for the worst in men to surface. War, and the battlefields of war, are unique in this regard only by virtue of the vastness of the arena afforded and the ultimate risks at stake. But that arena, fortunately, is not always at hand for most men. What is at hand is the arena of everyday life. Acts of personal courage (or of personal cowardice) are as apt to be played out in this arena as any other. The form may be different. The shape may be different. But the substance remains.

The years have not provided any great clarity of thought on my part concerning the catholic affairs of men. I still see through the glass darkly, as I did many years ago. The only constant seems to be that which was, is, and will be. There is a God, as I understand God. He will remain. Some will believe; others will not. The struggle will go on.

Nor have the years provided complete clarity of thought relative to my own personal involvement in the affairs of men. But in terms of politics and government, I have been at peace with myself for many years. That was not always the case. There was a time, when we were much younger and the war and prison years were very much upon us, that it was readily apparent the world was a screwed-up place, run by old, uncaring men bent upon nothing but holding power. It would be a better world, I thought, if we could simply shoot the Pope, burn down existing institutions, and start over. Then we would create the ideal world, free from all the mistakes of the past. But gradually, after much reflection on human nature and no small amount of soul searching, that changed.

As I honestly (I believe honestly) sought to test my own wisdom against the wisdom of the ages, the wisdom of the ages seemed always to prevail. And since the collective wisdom of the ages is no more than the accumulated wisdom of countless individuals, it strikes me that freedom and liberty of the individual is what is of paramount importance. The individual is capable of progress, capable of accepting responsibility for his or her acts, capable of learning from his or her mistakes. Groups are not. The individual is capable of transmitting wisdom, however limited. Groups are not. Individuals are capable of leadership. Groups are not. Groups may be led by individuals, but those individuals are usually influenced by the group's lowest common denominator. And, like roving bands of city dogs, the group is inclined to get involved in all sorts of mischief its members would find unthinkable if left to their own individual consciences. Lenin knew this. Stalin knew this. Hitler knew this. So did Mao. All autocratic leaders know this.

It is that thought, I suppose, that has led me to oppose, as best I can, authoritarian government in all its forms. And in this age it has been, I believe, the "dictatorship of the proletariat" that has emerged, in one form or another, as the biggest enemy of individual liberty and freedom, the biggest promoter and biggest beneficiary of "politically correct" thinking.

The growing acceptance of group rights in a country founded on and dedicated to the concept of individual rights is difficult for me to comprehend, much less explain with any degree of certainty. One possible explanation is the rapidly changing demographics of the nation as a whole. This change, and the rapidity of this change, has provided fertile ground for power seekers in and out of public office.

Identity is important to people. And race, religion, ethnicity are important parts of that identity. Indeed, for some it is the only identity. How else could insignificant people rise to great heights in American politics, with no message save that their own group be recognized and treated to special favors?

In the absence of common bonds of culture, in the absence of common bonds regarding an appreciation of individual liberty, the identity of race, or of religion, or of ethnicity looms very large indeed.

Another possible explanation could be the growth of still another group or class, the political class, also convinced it has a "right" to public sinecure. The conscience of the politician, the true politician, is determined by numbers. There is where power lies. And accordingly, there, to the political class, is where truth lies. In the world of politics a group is easier to lead, to be convinced it has been wronged, and therefore deserving of redress, than is the individual. And groups, so convinced, deliver more votes.

At any rate, rightly or wrongly, that is my principal worry about my own country when I try to look down the road, still seeing through the glass darkly. There was a time, when as a prisoner of war I walked through the teeming, poverty-stricken multitudes of China a half century ago, that I was concerned lest the image before me then also be the image of my own country some 200 years distant. My fear was that we, too, would become a nation bursting at the seams with over-population and diminished resources, torn apart, as China was then, over the division of those resources.

The image I see now is somewhat different, and much closer at hand. Our danger, now that our principal military threat has collapsed, is that commitment to ideas concerning individual rights, and individual responsibilities, will also collapse, and that we turn ourselves into a Balkanized America, at odds with each other over class, gender, race, ethnicity, religion. And that our political forums be turned into fighting cockpits where each group has its own rooster determined to win at any price, without regard to individual rights and without any element of mercy.

When that happens the only solution will be an autocratic central government run by a career political class raised up from the dust by virtue of their own vices, capable of imposing order and a sort of restive peace in a nation, and among a people, that once lived in relative harmony. And we will have done it to ourselves.

We are not quite there yet. But we will be, unless we come to our senses.

I doubt that many lives have ever worked out exactly as planned or anticipated, even in the broadest of terms. This has been one of those lives that did not work out exactly as planned or even as anticipated. It has been a life in which some prayers were answered in ways I hoped, for which we give thanks, and in which some were not, for which we also give thanks. We have walked where we never thought to walk. To borrow, and paraphrase slightly, a line from "Blues in the Night," we have "been in some big places, and heard some big talk," but in the end we are still more comfortable among those who work for a living, among those who scratch their living from the soil, among those who rally for the country's defense—than among politicians, pharisees, and publicans. One difference the years have brought is the ability to walk, with a little more ease, in stations previously unknown to us and among those with whom we differ.

When I went to Washington many years ago, the plan was to

work for a few years, come back home, and return to the world of newspaper reporting. But that few years turned into many years. Many years "out of the loop." That should pose no problem, I thought. Some good newspaper would jump at the chance of having a reporter or editorial writer on staff who could pick up the phone and talk, on a first-name basis, to any number of knowledgeable people in Washington or in embassies around the world. Wrong.

I had overlooked a few things. A few critical things. Things like age, the passage of time, the changing nature of journalism with its growing emphasis on adversarial and politically correct, or "group-think," reporting, and the changing nature of the business itself, with its trend toward consolidation and corporate ownership.

For whatever reason, I soon found there was no room at the inn, or, at least, in those inns where I had thought to lodge. Unable to go where I wanted to go, and unwilling to go where I did not, we did what we thought was the next best thing, but which turned out to be the best thing. Using a goodly portion of our life's savings, we made the down payment on a couple of small weekly newspapers on the South Plains of West Texas, the *Floyd County Hesperian* and the *Lockney Beacon*, to which we have since added the *Crosby County News-Chronicle*. I have never regretted it. We are again involved in those things that matter most to people close to the soil: their births, their deaths, their children, their politics, their thoughts, and all those little things that happen to them along the way. It is a good life, made all the better by the fact that the operation is now run by our daughter, Alice, who seems to share our fundamental beliefs in politics as well as newspapering.

When this narrative began I determined that I should use the early years, the family years, the Corregidor years, the prison years, as a sort of predicate for the years of journalism, government, and politics that followed. Perhaps if family and friends could better understand the former years they could also understand, and make excuses for, the experience and thinking of the latter. In that sense, one could argue that the effort has been a self-serving enterprise. But I hope it is more. I hope it serves, in some small way, others as well.

The book's title evolved as the work went on, simply because it seemed to fit. The working title was "The Emperor's Guest," with the intention that it finally bear the title "Prisoner of the Sun-God." The "Emperor" bit was a natural, since our captors often referred to us in that fashion, as "guests of the emperor." "Prisoner of the Sun-

God" was more to my liking, for try as I might I have never been able to escape, completely, the fact that I was indeed a prisoner and in many respects remain so. In fact, it seems we are all prisoners in one way or another. It just becomes very important to us what we are prisoners of.

The "Chow Dipper" title just seemed to emerge as the narrative progressed. It was a title I felt comfortable with.

In my own case, it has been a mixed bag. I have never tried to escape my role as the "chow dipper," with all that experience entailed. In fact, I have tried to hold it tightly, repairing to it time after time in the course of life. After all, what small creature can ask for more than that he be afforded a modicum of recognition for fairness under conditions that prevailed among starving men? Or, for that matter, under conditions that prevail among humans generally, war or not, prison camp or not? I know, as well as anyone, that I have not always achieved that degree of perfection we all ought to expect of ourselves. Still, the role of the chow dipper, even the idea of the chow dipper, has been my own private touchstone.

But I have tried mightily to escape one other consequence of prison, mostly without success. Rightly or wrongly, I have tended to judge people, both men and women, by how I think they would have acted and reacted had they been in those camps or on those prison ships. Those I now call friend, those I most admire, are those I think would have served well and honorably. Perhaps they would not have made it through, had they been there. Most didn't. Still, while they had life, they would have been honest in their dealings with others.

Conversely, those I most despise are those I think would have been despised by men of honor on Corregidor, or on the prison ships or in the camps. A man of honor at Chappaquiddick bridge, had there been one, would likely have been a man of honor in the camps, or on the battlefield. Or so my reasoning has gone.

That judgmental quality on my part has no doubt been wrong in many cases. Not, I believe, in those who were judged fitting, but in probably making the wrong judgment concerning some who were judged unfit. After all, people have a way of surprising when put to the test.

There is bound to be a touch of vanity in the thought that one should, however sketchily, sum up one's life in a book, especially when great riches are not in store. But in this instance there is also a touch of hope—a hope that other small creatures may come to know they are not so small after all and that the struggle, in the end, is well worthwhile.

After all, Buckley was right, I believe, when he asked, "If we don't strike a blow for liberty when we have the chance, what will we tell our grandchildren?"

On my first trip home on leave from the hospital after the war, an elderly matron, a friend of the family, broke into tears. I was very thin. The diagnosis, among many other things, was tuberculosis. She had children about my own age, and perhaps that had a bearing on her thoughts. Through her tears she kept repeating, "Oh, you poor boy, you poor dear boy."

Strange.

I felt I was the luckiest person in all the world.

I still feel that way.

Index

Gee, Tom, 164
General Land Office, 147, 149, 150,
    151, 166, 167
Giddens, Kenneth, 294, 302
Giles, Bascom, 147, 148, 149, 150–
    152, 153, 154–156, 158, 161–162,
    166, 169, 171, 174, 175–176,
    378–379
"Ginger," 74–75, 76
Gobi Desert, 3
Goldwater, Barry, 198, 199, 206–211,
    216, 221, 222–229, 238, 256, 277,
    279, 368
Gonzales, Rev. Antonio, 248–249, 250
Goodman, Bobby, 362–363
Governor's Mansion, 59
"Greater East Asia Co-Prosperity
    Sphere," 93
Great Society, 246, 262, 303
Griffith, H. C., 12
Guevara, Che, 347

H
Haerle, Nola Smith, 359
    Paul, 356
Hafrey, Dan, 302
Hagan, C. O. "Booster," 144, 159,
    161, 163–165
Haley, Judge Harold J., 307
Hall, Gus, 160
Halsema, James, 346, 349–351
Hankins, Major, 98, 104
Hannah, Alvis, 126, 130–131, 190
Harbin, China, 82
Hardesty, Bob, 355
Hardin, John Wesley, 134–135
Harmon, Frank, 302
Headliners Club, 266
Heller, Robert, 362
Herbst, Dr., 73
Herschensohn, Bruce, 294, 302
Heyser, Dorothy, 373
Hiller, Pershing, 143
Hispanic voters, 236–237, 247–251,
    283
Hitler, Adolf, 4, 57, 410
Hoffman, Art, 302
Holly Sugar Beet company, 60
Homma, Gen. Masaharu, 37–38, 40
Horner, Captain, 98, 99
Hotchkiss, Dorothy, 395

Johnny, 395
Hoten Prison Camp #1, 69, 70–83,
    113, 148, 407–408
House Bill 4, 180
Houston Chronicle, 179
Houston Post, 179
Houston, Texas, 280–281
Howerton, Jack, 134, 135, 136, 137–
    138, 140–142, 146–147, 154, 168,
    172, 174–176, 177, 178, 188, 190,
    197
    Polly, 136, 154
Humphrey, Hubert, 275, 280, 282–
    283, 286, 287, 288, 291–292
Hurd, John, 283

I
Iba, 15
IBM Corporation, 225
Ickes, Harold, 212
Infantry Point, 31
Ingram, ———, 14
Institute of Museum Services, 369
integration, 185
International News Service, 179
Iran-Contra affair, 374
Ishikawa, Captain, 77, 86
Israeli government, 373–376, 396

J
Jackson, George, 307
    Jonathon, 307
    "Scoop," 397
Jacobs, John, 324–325
Jacobsen, Jake, 193–194, 261–262
James Ravine, 10, 21
Japan, postwar, 330–335
Javitts, Jacob, 232
Jawbone, 8, 37
Jefferson House, 198
Jenkins, Kempton, 310–311
Jewett, Texas, 59
Jim Wells County, Texas, 165
Johnson, B. K., 267, 269
    Lyndon, 163, 164, 179, 182, 183–
    184, 185–188, 193, 195, 197, 200,
    205, 207, 211–216, 222–223, 229,
    233, 236, 244, 246–247, 259,
    260–263, 264, 283, 288, 292,
    303–304, 356, 397
    Marcelle, 98